ECONOMIC FOUNDATIONS OF LAW AND ORGANIZATION

This book serves as a compact introduction to the economic analysis of law and organization. At the same time, it covers a broad spectrum of issues. It is aimed at undergraduate economic majors who are interested in law and organization, law students who want to know the economic basis for the law, and students in business and public policy schools who want to understand the economic approach to law and organization. The book covers such diverse topics as bankruptcy rules, corporate law, sports rules, the organization of Congress, federalism, intellectual property, crime, accident law, and insurance. Unlike other texts on the economic analysis of law, this text is not organized by legal categories such as property, torts, contracts, and so on, but by economic theory. The purpose of the book is to develop economic intuition and theory to a sufficient degree so that one can apply the ideas to a variety of areas in law and organization.

Donald Wittman is Professor of Economics at the University of California, Santa Cruz. He previously taught at the University of Chicago. Professor Wittman's book *The Myth of Democratic Failure* (1995) won the American Political Science Association award for the best book in political economy in the years 1994–1996. He is coeditor of the forthcoming *Oxford Handbook of Political Economy*. Professor Wittman's research has appeared in such journals as the *American Economic Review, Journal of Political Economy, American Political Science Review, Journal of Economic Theory, Journal of Legal Studies, Journal of Law and Economics,* and *Journal of Public Economics.* His research has been supported by various National Science Foundation programs.

D1362164

ECONOMIC FOUNDATIONS OF LAW AND ORGANIZATION

DONALD WITTMAN

University of California, Santa Cruz

CAMBRIDGE UNIVERSITY PRESS
Cambridge, New York, Melbourne, Madrid, Cape Town, Singapore, São Paulo

Cambridge University Press
32 Avenue of the Americas, New York, NY 10013-2473, USA

www.cambridge.org
Information on this title: www.cambridge.org/9780521859172

First published 2006

Printed in the United States of America

A catalog record for this publication is available from the British Library.

Library of Congress Cataloging in Publication Data

Wittman, Donald A.
Economic foundations of law and organization / Donald Wittman.
    p.   cm.
Includes bibliographical references and index.
ISBN 0-521-85917-4 (hardcover) – ISBN 0-521-68524-9 (pbk.)
1. Law and economics.   I. Title.
HB73.W58   2006
343′.07 – dc22   2006009907

ISBN-13   978-0-521-85917-2 hardback
ISBN-10   0-521-85917-4 hardback

ISBN-13   978-0-521-68524-5 paperback
ISBN-10   0-521-68524-9 paperback

For Martha

Contents

Preface   *page* ix

1. Introduction   1

PART ONE. ECONOMIC FUNDAMENTALS — RATIONALITY
AND EFFICIENCY

2. Rational Behavior, Preferences, and Prices   7

3. Pareto Optimality Versus Utilitarianism   13

4. Cost-Benefit Analysis   21

PART TWO. TRANSACTION COSTS AND THE COASEAN REVOLUTION

5. Transaction Costs   33

6. Fencing In and Fencing Out   41

7. Coase versus Pigou   49

PART THREE. COST-BENEFIT ANALYSIS AND THE LAW — DEVELOPING
ECONOMIC INTUITION

8. How to Think Like an Economist: Drunk Drivers, Hawks, and Baseballs   59

9. Smoking Regulations: Market Solutions to High-Transaction-Cost
   Situations   69

10. Rules of Thumb: Sports and Driving Rules   75

PART FOUR. RIGHTS

11. The Protection of Entitlements: Why One Method Is Chosen
    Over Another   91

12. Property Rights or Communal Rights in Knowledge?   103

13. Liability for Harm or Restitution for Benefit?   113

14. The Takings Clause: Should There Be Compensation for Regulation?   121

PART FIVE. TORTS AND CRIMES: LIABILITY RULES
AND PUNISHMENTS

15. Cost Minimization and Liability Rules   131

16. Negligence Rules 141

17. Crime and Criminal Law 153

PART SIX. THE ROLE OF SEQUENCE

18. Mitigation of Damages and Last Clear Chance 167

19. The Good Samaritan Rule 175

20. The Role of Being First in Allocating Rights: Coming to the Nuisance 181

PART SEVEN. CONTRACTS AND BREACH OF CONTRACT

21. Default Rules and Breach of Contract 193

22. When Is a Handshake a Contract and When Is a "Contract" Not a Contract? 207

23. Marriage as Contract: Family Law 217

PART EIGHT. HARMS ARISING BETWEEN CONTRACTING PARTIES

24. Exploding Coca-Cola Bottles 231

25. The Role of Asymmetric Information 239

26. Consumers and Producers Cause Damage: Lawnmowers 247

PART NINE. INSURANCE AND THE LAW

27. The Market for Insurance 257

28. Royalties for Artists and Insurance for Investors 269

29. Automobile Insurance 277

30. Bankruptcy 283

31. Deposit Insurance and Banking Crises 295

PART TEN. GOVERNANCE AND ORGANIZATION

32. The Governance of Organization 305

33. Corporate Law and Agency Problems 313

34. Insider Trading 323

35. Organizational Response to Opportunism: McDonald's, the Mafia, and Mutual of Omaha 331

36. The Organization of Legislatures 341

37. Federalism 349

38. The Internal Organization of the Family 357

PART ELEVEN. BARGAINING IN THE SHADOW OF A TRIAL

39. Settlement or Trial? 367

Index of Authors 379

Index 381

Case Index 390

Preface

Economic Foundations of Law and Organization, as the name suggests, provides an economic explanation for law and organization and thus is appropriate for any course dealing with these topics. It is meant as an introductory text, but the book contains many ideas that are new and of interest even to those who are experts in the field. Unlike other texts on the economic analysis of law, this text is not organized by legal categories (property, torts, contracts, etc.) but by economic theory. The purpose of the book is to develop economic intuition and theory to a sufficient degree so that one can apply the ideas to a variety of areas in law and organization. Just as when learning supply and demand one applies these curves to the market for oranges, beef, illegal drugs, and marriage, rather than studying each of these markets in particular, the ideas learned here cut across the standard legal categories. As a consequence, this book does not give a complete picture of the law in any one area; indeed, it does not cover everything that economists have said about any particular topic in the law. However, it does provide a strong and cohesive explication of various economic ideas in the context of interesting legal topics. As a result, this book could be called *Microeconomics Made Interesting* and be used as a complement to standard texts in intermediate microeconomic theory.

The pedagogical intent is to focus most chapters on a particular theoretical approach so that the reader truly understands the underlying logic. The book employs both formal logic and intuition so that the reader will find the argument compelling. I want the reader to walk away with a clear understanding of the material, not just a vague idea regarding the results. For example, I want the reader to have more than a vague idea that negligence rules are good. I want readers to be able to demonstrate on their own that the equilibrium outcome under a negligence rule is efficient. This is the key to how I have written much of the book. For each chapter, the reader should be able to reproduce the underlying logic of the chapter and apply it elsewhere. I do this by focusing on a particular model of the world rather than bringing in lots of ideas at once. I make the chapters short and to the point. When chapters are too long, students tend to read the material quickly as if they are reading a novel rather than read carefully so that they can reproduce the logic. When chapters cover too many ideas or too many alternative models, students either conflate the models or just get a sense of the results rather than a deeper understanding. Instead, I concentrate on the economic model that yields the most insight into the legal issue.

Speaking of students, I would like to thank all of my students who suffered through earlier versions of this book. It was their questions in class and mistakes on exams that led me to simplify and clarify. I would also like to thank Judy Walsh who, as a teaching assistant, gave me invaluable advice about writing when I first started on this adventure.

Finally, if you want to discuss any issues raised in this book, I am at wittman@ucsc.edu.

1 Introduction

A. Economics Provides the Analytic Framework 2

B. Organization of This Book 2

SUGGESTIONS FOR FURTHER READING 3

REVIEW QUESTIONS 3

REFERENCES 3

Should a surrogate mother be allowed to keep the fetus? Should the hospital, the donor, the Red Cross, or the patient be liable for the harm if a patient contracts hepatitis from a blood transfusion? Should there be regulations against smoking in airplanes? Should plea-bargaining be allowed? Should hostile corporate takeovers be encouraged? Should a bystander be found liable for not rescuing a drowning person if the rescue could have been accomplished with little risk to the potential rescuer? Should homeowners be allowed to force a cattle feedlot to move without compensation by the homeowners if the cattle feedlot was there before the homes were built? Why are nuclear power plants subject to strict liability? Why are there few consumer cooperatives? When should a firm vertically integrate? How should congressional committees be structured? What should be the creditor priority in bankruptcy?

A. ECONOMICS PROVIDES THE ANALYTIC FRAMEWORK

The answers to these questions are found in economic theory. In this book, we use economic analysis to explain various areas of the law, including criminal, corporate, contract, accident, bankruptcy, and environmental law. Along the way, we explain why relationships are organized in a certain way. For example, why McDonald's is a franchise, while Ace Hardware Stores are independently owned and Safeway stores are a single corporation. As another example, we explain why stockholders have limited liability. Hence, the title of this book – *Economic Foundations of Law and Organization*.

The connection between law, organization, and economics is very close. Economics is the study of what, how, and for whom. Standard textbooks in economics define the field as the study of resource allocation in the presence of scarcity. Laws affect resource allocation and help to determine what, how, and for whom. For example, a law that finds trucking companies liable for accidental harm will create incentives for more careful driving by truckers. A well-ordered society will tend to choose laws that promote economic efficiency. Laws create a public ordering; that is, they organize society in a certain way. Private entities are also organized in a certain way. For example, in corporations, stockholders supply capital and managers of the firm make day-to-day decisions. Economics provides the key to understanding why firms and society are organized in particular ways.

Economics also provides insight into many ethical issues. Why is theft wrong? If there are three starving men are in a lifeboat, is it ethical to kill one of them for food, and if so, how should this be decided? And returning to some of the questions posed at the beginning of this chapter (because legal and ethical issues are often entwined), when does being first deserve extra consideration and what duties are owed to strangers? Thus the title of the book could also have been *Economic Foundations of Law, Organization, and Ethics*.

B. ORGANIZATION OF THIS BOOK

This book is organized into sections. The sections need not be read in order, the major exception being Part II on the Coase theorem, which should be read first if the reader is not well acquainted with Coasean analysis.

Part I explains the concepts of rationality and efficiency and provides the underlying rationale for cost-benefit analysis. Part II introduces the concept of transaction costs and argues that this concept is critical to understanding law and organization. Part III develops the underlying intuition needed to grasp the economic implications of the law. Part IV discusses when and why property rights, liability rules, communal rights, restitution, or regulation is chosen instead of the other methods of protecting entitlements. Along the way, blackmail, patents, and the takings clause are considered. Part V derives optimal liability rules (including the optimal level of punishment for criminals). Among other things, why liability rules differ for falling trees, automobile accidents, and dangerous pets is explained. Part VI considers how sequential inputs changes the analysis provided in Part V. Topics such as coming to the nuisance, the Good Samaritan rule, and mitigation of damages are covered. Part VII considers the role of the courts in contract law, including marriage contracts. Part VIII focuses on explicit and implied warranties for exploding soda bottles, lawnmower accidents, and air conditioner failures. Part IX is concerned with the allocation of risk and the role of insurance in the law. This topic goes far beyond the narrow confines of what people ordinarily think of as insurance. For example, royalties for artists can be viewed as insurance for investors. Problems arising from over-regulating the insurance industry and under-regulating insured savings deposits are discussed. Part X, the longest section, is devoted to governance and organization and answers such questions as, why are investor-owned firms common, but worker-owned firms rare? Why do we have franchises? And how is Congress organized? Part XI is devoted to bargaining in the shadow of the law.

SUGGESTIONS FOR FURTHER READING

Three useful reference texts are the *New Palgrave Dictionary of Economics and the Law*, the *Encyclopedia of Law and Economics*, and the *Handbook of Law and Economics*.

REVIEW QUESTIONS

1. What does economics have to do with the law? Is it about how much we pay for lawyers and prisons? (3) Note that points in parentheses refer to the number of points the answer is worth and suggest approximately how many sentences should be used in answering the question.

REFERENCES

Bouckaert, Boudewijn, and Gerrit De Geest. (2000). *Encyclopedia of Law & Economics*. Cheltenham: Edward Elgar Publishing Limited. http://users.ugent.be/~gdegeest/

Newman, Peter (ed.). (1998). *The New Palgrave Dictionary of Economics and the Law*. London: Macmillan Reference Limited.

Polinsky, A. Mitchell, and Steven Shavell (eds.). (2006). *Handbook of Law and Economics*. Amsterdam: North Holland.

I ECONOMIC FUNDAMENTALS – RATIONALITY AND EFFICIENCY

In Part 1, we consider two fundamental building blocks of economics – rationality and efficiency.[1]

Almost all of economics assumes rational behavior by individuals in their roles as consumers, workers, or business owners. Rationality typically focuses on how individuals respond to prices. Rational consumers have downward-sloping demand curves and rational business owners have upward-sloping supply curves. Much of the legal system also assumes that individuals respond rationally to prices. If individuals are rational, then, other things being equal, larger fines for speeding will reduce the number of speeders. Suppose that individuals were irrational in this regard. Then the legal system would reduce fines for speeding to reduce the number of speeders, unless the legal system, itself, was irrational, in which case it would do the opposite. As this last thought experiment suggests, assuming irrationality leads to some unrealistic predictions about human behavior and legal rules.

Chapter 2 is devoted to a deeper discussion of rationality. We first show that the economist notion of rationality is nowhere near the cartoon caricature of rationality presented by the critics of rational behavior. Next, we show that when people are rational, the price reflects the benefit of the last item purchased. That is, if a person is rational, then paying $10 for an item means that the person valued the item for at least $10. This rather trivial insight allows us to undertake cost-benefit analysis, the subject of Chapter 4.

The theme of this book is that laws can be evaluated according to whether they are economically efficient and that many laws (particularly, judge-made laws) do, indeed, promote economic efficiency. But what does it mean to be economically efficient and why is that criterion chosen instead of another? This is the subject of Chapter 3. Economic efficiency (Pareto optimality) is a noncontroversial method of assessing welfare. It does not mean that individuals work without taking lunch or that pollution is ignored. Instead it just means that no one individual's welfare can be increased without reducing another individual's welfare. In Chapter 3, the concept of economic efficiency will be discussed in-depth because it is hard to understand from a mere definition. We also discuss why other approaches such as the utilitarian approach and various distributive approaches are not very helpful in evaluating legal rules.

In Chapter 4, we consider cost-benefit analysis. Cost-benefit analysis uses prices to measure welfare. As previously indicated, this is justified by the argument presented in Chapter 2 that rational individuals are willing to pay $X for an item only if the item is worth $X to them. We show how cost-benefit analysis is related to economic efficiency and why as a practical matter it is used rather than the Pareto criterion. Thus the theme of the book can be restated as follows: legal rules and organizational structure are often chosen on the basis of their costs and benefits.

Part I can be seen as the underlying argument for the use of cost-benefit analysis (to the exclusion of other criteria) in evaluating the law. For those who are already comfortable with the concept and don't desire a deeper understanding of cost-benefit analysis and don't need to be convinced that rationality is a plausible starting place for analyzing human behavior, Part I (and in particular chapters 2 and 4) can be skipped. For the rest, Part I provides the justification for the economic approach to law and organization.

---

[1]   In Chapter 15, we will consider the notion of equilibrium, another fundamental concept in economics.

2 Rational Behavior, Preferences, and Prices

A. Rational Behavior 8

B. Advertising # 9

C. Preferences and Utility Functions 10

D. Prices 11

E. Concluding Remarks 12

SUGGESTIONS FOR FURTHER READING 12

REVIEW QUESTIONS 12

REFERENCE 12

The basic premise of this book is that individuals generally act rationally. Because there is often confusion regarding what is meant by rationality and a great deal flows from assuming rationality, it is useful to start with a definition.

A. RATIONAL BEHAVIOR

The following is how economists define rationality. If a person can rank order her preferences (e.g., Tom prefers (A) to travel around the world and eat caviar every night over (B) working forty hours a week and eating burritos every night over (C) playing video games all day, living with his parents, and eating steak and potatoes) and the person chooses his most preferred *feasible* alternative, then the person is rational.[1] Rationality is a plausible assumption regarding human behavior. Isn't it a better theory of human behavior that people do what they prefer to do rather than that people behave randomly (they are arational) or that they consistently act against their own preferences (they are irrational)?[2]

For the most part, this book is devoted to explaining *aggregate* or market behavior rather than a particular individual's behavior. While one might argue that a particular person is either irrational or uninformed, it is much harder to claim this to be the case for the market.[3] Thus, for example, one might argue that a manager of a particular firm is paid more money than she is worth, but it is much harder to argue that managers in general tend to be paid more than they are worth. Because we are interested in aggregates, our predictions are not undermined if some people do not act rationally.

Note that there is no need to assume that individuals are perfectly informed. Rational people can be misinformed and make mistakes. For example, they may carry a raincoat on a day when it does not rain. However, people will not persist in their mistakes if the evidence is to the contrary. They will not carry a raincoat in Santa Cruz in July once they learn that it does not rain there in the summer. Of course, carrying a raincoat when it is does not rain is not very costly. If mistakes were very costly, rational individuals would gain more information ahead of time. For example, first-time strawberry farmers in Santa Cruz County will install irrigation systems to grow their crops in the summer rather than rely on rainfall.

Although people make mistakes, it is unlikely that people are consistently prone to misjudgments in a particular direction. I am skeptical of arguments that assume that people tend to underestimate or overestimate the dangers of some activity (for

---

[1] More formally: To act rationally an individual must have a complete set of ordered preferences over the set of outcomes and these preference rankings must be both transitive and reflexive. Transitivity implies that if you prefer chocolate to vanilla and vanilla to strawberry ice cream, then you prefer chocolate to strawberry ice cream. Reflexive means that a person does not strictly prefer something to itself. Hence, a person is indifferent when choosing between a bowl of chocolate ice cream and a bowl of identical chocolate ice cream.

[2] Presumably, individuals at different times are characterized by one of the three (rationality, irrationality, and arationality). The problem is that unless we can predict which characterization is operative (which would be the case if we could detect which part of the brain is being used or how much alcohol was consumed, for example), we can only determine ex post which one holds. Under such circumstances, to predict rather than merely define behavior, we need to go with the characterization that works the best. The argument here is that rationality works best.

[3] This holds when the information is available contemporaneously. Obviously, in the nineteenth century doctors did not know that penicillin killed bacteria.

example, underestimating the dangers of taking prescription drugs) when such information is public. Here, the basic premise is that some people may overestimate and others may underestimate the probability of a bad outcome, but over all issues, the average person's beliefs do not systematically differ from the experts' beliefs in a certain direction.

Note that being rational does not mean that the person is selfish. Rational people may be altruistic; but being rational, they will try to achieve their ends in the best way possible. A surgeon trying to save someone's life will use sterilized equipment when possible and will not purchase more expensive equipment if it is not better.

When it comes to producers, there is very strong pressure for rational profit maximizing behavior because large deviations from profit maximization are likely to result in the firm going out of business. Consider a farmer in North Dakota where the winters are cold and there is not much rain. If the farmer prays for rain but does not install an irrigation system or plants bananas instead of wheat, he will not survive for very long. Of course, if the farm is otherwise very profitable, there is room for some behavior that modestly deviates from profit maximization (for further discussion, see Chapter 33 on agency costs in corporations).

In this book, we sometimes use mathematics, including calculus, to explain people's behavior and at other times the arguments are counterintuitive. A common criticism is to assert that people do not have the cognitive skills to make such judgments. But we are not assuming that individuals actually use calculus in their decisions. Rather that calculus is a useful way to characterize their behavior. Perhaps, the easiest way to understand the logic behind my argument is to consider maple trees. The leaves on maple trees are not stacked in a row one right behind the other; instead they are arranged in a way to maximize the amount of light falling on all of the leaves. Advanced mathematics is needed to solve this maximization problem, but, as far as I know, no maple tree has ever gone to college. If trees can act rationally, it should not be unreasonable to assume that people act rationally as well.

So for the remainder of the book, we will assume that, on average, producers and consumers are rational and do not have biased expectations.

B. ADVERTISING # [4]

Now it is conceivable that people are manipulated by advertising and therefore they do not make rational choices. One could argue that without television advertising, fewer brand names would be sold. However, it would be much harder to argue that without television advertising, people would drink milk instead of smoke cigarettes, eat raw vegetables instead of fast food, buy bicycles instead of muscle cars, live in teepees instead of houses, and wear clothes until they fell apart instead of until they became unfashionable.

Of course, firms that advertise are not doing it for our pleasure. They are doing it to gain sales. Sales are gained in the following ways: (1) Some advertising is directly informative. When Nissan advertises the Titan truck, not surprisingly, it is advertising that it now provides large trucks. (2) Some advertising is just a reminder that the brand

---

[4] The pound symbol (#) indicates that the subsection can be skipped.

exists and serves as an implicit statement that the firm stands behind its product. A brand name is likely to be of higher quality than its unadvertised counterpart. Advertising content is irrelevant in such cases.[5]

Now it is possible that advertising tricks people. For example, the beautiful female in the passenger seat of a Corvette advertisement might convince someone to buy the Corvette in hopes of attracting similarly beautiful women. But if manipulation were that easy, then Prius would engage in a similar tactic and possibly sellers of hamburgers, milk, and bicycles would do the same; in which case, this manipulation would no longer determine what the susceptible person would buy.

Part of our enjoyment of life is aesthetic. Minimum daily food requirements can be met by spending less than $3.00 a day, but who wants to eat like that if they can afford to spend more? No one argues that it is advertising that drives us to eat more than the minimal cost diet. Yet when a person chooses a muscle car (such as a Corvette), others argue that the person is irrational (it does not maximize fuel economy) or that the person is susceptible to advertising. But advertising is geared to the person's aesthetic sensibilities and brand choice allows others to infer preferences of the purchaser. All of us employ different mental images of the typical Corvette owner in comparison to the typical Prius owner. Advertisers know that our minds are not a empty tablet; Prius does not engage in direct-mail campaigns to Corvette owners.

Of course, at the margin, advertising does have an effect. Advertising tries to capture the otherwise indifferent consumer of a competing brand. But the effect of advertising is limited. Burger King can advertise day and night that the Whopper is better than the Big Mac, but the demand will decrease dramatically if the price of the Whopper is doubled.

C. PREFERENCES AND UTILITY FUNCTIONS

The fundamental building block of rationality is that each individual can rank order their preferences and then choose the highest-feasible alternative. But writing down preference rankings is a time-consuming matter. As a result, *economists tend to formulate their discussion of preferences in terms of utility functions, which are a more concise method of characterizing preference relationships.*

To illustrate, we will consider a very simple preference ranking. Suppose that a person prefers more apples to fewer apples and more bananas to fewer bananas, but the person is indifferent between having two more bananas or one more apple. The person's preference rankings from most desired to least desired are then

{2 apples} or {4 bananas}
{1 apple and 1 banana} or {3 bananas}
{1 apple} or {2 bananas}
{1 banana}
{no fruit at all}

---

[5]   The main effect of banning cigarette advertising on television has been to make it more difficult to create new brands. There has been a secular decrease in cigarette smoking independent of the ban.

This ranking does not include the possibility of half an apple or ten apples. So such lists can be very long.

Fortunately, this preference ordering can be represented by a simple utility function: $U = 2A + B$. We can easily establish that this utility function represents the preference ordering above. For example, one apple and one banana provide the same utility (2 times 1 plus 1 times 1) as three bananas (2 times 0 plus 1 times 3). If individuals are rational, then they maximize their utility given the feasible set. For example, if a person has $2.00 to spend and apples and bananas cost $1 each, then the person will buy two apples.

Notice that the same preferences can also be characterized by the following utility function: $U = 100 + 20A + 10B$, as, once again, one apple is worth two bananas, and more apples or more bananas means more utility. In choosing between apples and bananas, it is not the absolute size of the utility that counts, but the relative size. This means that utility is an *ordinal* concept – we can say that the individual gets *greater* pleasure from eating two bananas than from eating one. We cannot say that the individual gets twice as much pleasure from eating two bananas than from eating one. The latter is known as a *cardinal* measure. Because we cannot measure happiness as we measure weight (a cardinal measure), it important that we treat utility as an ordinal relationship. And of course that is just what a ranking is – ordinal.

D. PRICES

If people are rational, we can translate their preferences at the margin into prices. If you spent $10 to buy a bottle of Kendall-Jackson Zinfandel, this is because you preferred doing that than spending your $10.00 elsewhere (e.g., spending $10 on Charles Krug Zinfandel). And being rational, you would not change your mind and buy Charles Krug if the price of Charles Krug increased from $10.00 to $11.00 or more and everything else remained the same. So we can say that Charles Krug was not worth more than $10 and that Kendall-Jackson was not worth less than $10 to you when you buy Kendall-Jackson but not Charles Krug. Indeed, whenever you make one choice over another, even if money is not involved, we can translate the choice into money by saying that you would have paid more for what was chosen than for what was not.

The advantage of prices is that they are observable and allow for easy comparison. If people are rational (and both goods are being purchased and are infinitely divisible), then the marginal utility from the last dollar spent on one good (say, apples) should equal the marginal utility from the last dollar spent on another item (say, pears). Suppose, to the contrary, that they would have gotten more pleasure from consuming an additional dollar's worth more of apples than from consuming that last dollar's worth of pears. Then they would have reduced their purchases of pears by a dollar and increased their purchases of apples by a dollar. This logic repeats itself until we do have equal marginal utility per dollar. If apples cost $1.00 each, we can say that the last apple you purchased was worth a dollar. In a nutshell, price reflects *marginal* value. Without water, we would die; but the price of water is very low, reflecting, the low value of that *last* gallon of water.

E. CONCLUDING REMARKS

The concept of rationality is rather trivial. Nobody had to read this chapter to discover that people generally choose what they prefer. However, as we will show in the remainder of the book, rationality in combination with other simple ideas produces nonobvious and deep insights into law and organization.

SUGGESTIONS FOR FURTHER READING

Experimental evidence suggests that people often have a basic notion of fairness rather than being purely self-regarding (selfish). There is also some evidence that individuals do not always act rationally. These experimental results have been incorporated into what is now known as behavioral law and economics (see, for example, Sunstein, 2000). This is an interesting area of investigation, but at present, the results are not sufficiently compelling to overturn the analysis based on rational actors.

REVIEW QUESTIONS

1. What is meant by economic rationality? (3)
2. If people are rational, why are there stupid ads on TV that do not discuss the merit of the product? Aren't consumers just being persuaded to irrationally purchase goods? (6)
3. What is the relationship between preferences and utility functions? (2)
4. If people are rational, what is the relationship between preferences and prices? Explain. (6)

REFERENCE

Sunstein, Cass R. (ed.). (2000). *Behavioral Law and Economics.* Cambridge: Cambridge University Press.

3 Pareto Optimality Versus Utilitarianism

A. Maximizing the Sum of Utilities 14

B. Pareto Optimality 16

C. What about Distribution? 18

D. Concluding Remarks 19

REVIEW QUESTIONS 19

Economics is used as both a descriptive and a prescriptive theory of human behavior and the law. A descriptive theory describes how things are, while a prescriptive theory explains how things should be. In the last chapter, we argued that rationality was a descriptive theory of human behavior. It is easy to see how it could also be used as prescriptive theory. If you want to maximize your happiness, choose your most preferred feasible alternative. Of course, in general, prescriptions and descriptions need not be the same. If you want to do well in a class, you *should* have studied for the exam, but instead you watched *Terminator 3*. Economic analysis of law also has descriptive and prescriptive elements. It is argued throughout the book that many laws obey a certain economic logic and furthermore that they should do so. But what is the desired objective of the law? The answer is that the law should promote efficient outcomes. In this chapter, we will introduce the concept of Pareto optimality, a term that economists often use to mean efficiency. In the next chapter, we will discuss the role of cost-benefit analysis.

Before delving into the particulars, it is useful to reflect on the more general problem of collective preference and choice when the basic component of analysis is individual preferences. As already mentioned, when there is only one person and we want to maximize the person's welfare, we instruct the person to choose his or her most preferred feasible position. Now suppose that there are three people X, Y, and Z, and their individual rankings of policies, A, B, C, and D, are as follows:

X	Y	Z
A.	C	B
B.	A	C
C.	D	A
D.	B	D

What is the group's most preferred policy? Should it make any difference in the group's preference ordering if X greatly prefers B to C? Should it make any difference in the group's choice if policy D is not available? Unfortunately, in this example, majority rule does not provide an answer as a majority (X and Y) prefer A to B, a majority (X and Z) prefer B to C, but a majority (Y and Z) prefer C to A; that is, majority rule is intransitive.

Every society must solve the problem of collective choice, but of course, not all do it with welfare or justice in mind. Collectively, the prescriptive and the descriptive are often at odds. Dictators may maximize their own utility, but the utility of others counts for very little, if at all. In this context, the search for a prescriptive theory of social welfare may seem quaint. Nevertheless, such musings have occupied philosophers for thousands of years. We will now show how the ideas regarding welfare have progressed overtime and why the prescriptive goal of efficiency is held in such high regard by economists. In later chapters, we will argue that the law tends to promote efficiency.

A. MAXIMIZING THE SUM OF UTILITIES

Jeremy Bentham (1748–1832) is considered the father of utilitarianism and sometimes the father of the economic analysis of law.[1] It was his view that that society should create the greatest amount of happiness for the greatest number of people. This prescription can

---

[1] Bentham was reading while he was still a toddler and was studying Latin by the time he was 3. He has been preserved and can be seen at University College, London, sitting on a chair.

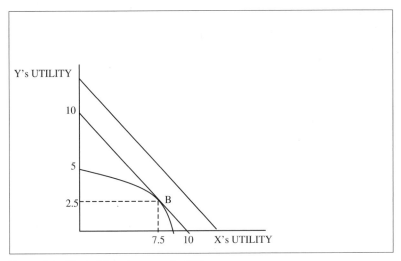

Figure 3.1. Maximizing the sum of utilities.

be translated into the following formula – society should maximize the sum of utilities. More formally, a society of N individuals should maximize $U_1 + U_2 + U_3 \cdots U_N$, where U_i is the utility of the ith individual. It is convenient to show this relationship in a diagram (Figure 3.1). The axes represent X's and Y's utility in "utiles." The downward sloping 45-degree lines are society's indifference curves. Society is indifferent between {X having 10 utiles and Y having 0 utiles} and {Y having 10 utiles and X having 0 utiles} or anything on the line in-between (such as both having 5 utiles), as in all these cases, the sum of utilities equals 10. The higher 45-degree line represents a higher society indifference curve as the sum of utiles is higher. Using the language of preference ranking, society prefers any point on the higher line to any point on the lower line, but society is indifferent between any two points on a particular downward sloping 45-degree line. The curved line and all the points below is the utility possibility set or feasible set. It corresponds to the production possibility set, but everything is translated into utiles. A simple example is to assume that X and Y are dividing pear sorbet. X likes pear sorbet and if X gets all of the sorbet, he will receive approximately 9 utiles in pleasure. In contrast, Y only gains about 5 utiles if she gets all of the sorbet. Society chooses that feasible point, B (for Bentham), which is on the highest society indifference curve. In this example, maximizing the sum of utilities results in X being happier than Y.

As we can see, maximization of utilities does provide an answer. It also has certain nice qualities. In particular, it treats different people the same – everyone's utility is weighted equally. However, there is a serious problem with Bentham's prescription. It requires cardinal *interpersonal comparisons* of utility. That is, it not only requires us to measure a person's utility as one would measure a person's weight, it also requires us to compare one person's happiness to another. But neither is possible. So economists have generally avoided the maximization of utilities approach. This is somewhat ironic because people typically associate economics with utilitarianism and of course utility functions are a basic part of economic methodology.[2] But as was shown in Chapter 2, utility is an ordinal concept, not a cardinal one.

---

[2] In a broader sense, economics is utilitarian in that policy prescriptions are based on individual preferences rather than on some other abstract notion of justice.

B. PARETO OPTIMALITY

It was Vilfredo Pareto (1848–1923) who made the above argument against utilitarianism and who provided an alternative ordinal measure that required no interpersonal comparisons of utility.[3] The essential idea is that if we can undertake a policy that will make one or more people better off (because they prefer the new policy) without making anybody worse off, we should undertake the policy. Such a move is known as a *Pareto improvement*. When we have a situation where no Pareto improvements can be made, we say that the outcome is *Pareto optimal* or *efficient*. More formally the definition for Pareto optimality is as follows:

> **DEFINITION:** To have a Pareto optimal allocation means that no one can be made better off without making someone else worse off. To not have a Pareto optimal allocation means that it is possible to make someone happier without making someone less happy.

The concept is an extremely useful one. In this world, people have different religions, values, and tastes. Some prefer rock music while others prefer classical music; some people like to drink alcohol while others think that it is immoral to do so; and some people believe that the Bible is the source of truth, while others believe that the Koran is. Even if there is broad agreement on certain values, most of these values are contingent. Is it "thou shall not kill" or thou should not kill unless it is in warfare, or perhaps not even in warfare unless it is also in self-defense? There is very little that we can agree on. The one concept where almost everyone can agree on is that if in going from situation A to situation B, we make some people better off (in terms of their own preferences and values) and nobody worse off (in terms of their preferences and values), then B should be should be chosen over A.

Because Pareto optimality has a double negative in its definition, the definition is often confusing to the reader. It is therefore useful to consider some simple examples to illustrate the concept. Suppose first that we have two pears and one apple to distribute costlessly between Xavier and Yvonne (X and Y, for short). We will assume selfishness because it is easier to illustrate. Of course, one could think of more complex examples (building more cars or buses and more farmland or more forest) with altruistic people but that would create too much confusion.

	Xavier	Yvonne
1.	2 pears, 1 apple	2 pears, 1 apple
2.	2 pears	1 pear, 1 apple
3.	1 pear, 1 apple	1 apple
4.	1 pear	2 pears
5.	1 apple	1 pear
6.	nothing	nothing

The list rankorders each person's preference from 1 to 6. From this list we can see that both Xavier and Yvonne would like all of the fruit for himself or herself. If this is

---

[3] Pareto was a great mathematical social scientist who developed various ideas that are now named after other people. What is known as the Edgeworth-Bowley box in economics was developed by Pareto and spread by his student Bowley. What is known as Zipf's law in sociology was discovered decades earlier by Pareto and is known by people outside of sociology as the Paretian distribution. Pareto can also be said to be a founding father of cognitive dissonance in psychology.

not possible, Xavier would then like to have two pears, while Yvonne would most like to have one pear and one apple if she could not have three pieces of fruit. As can be seen, Xavier prefers pears to apples, and Yvonne prefers apples to pears.

Because there are at most two pears and one apple to allocate, both Xavier and Yvonne cannot get their most preferred alternative. If Xavier gets, his most preferred alternative (two pears and an apple), then Yvonne must get nothing and the allocation is {X1, Y6}. If Xavier gets his second most preferred alternative (two pears), then Yvonne gets either nothing or her third most preferred alternative (one apple). The feasible sets are thus {X1, Y6}, {X2, Y3}, {X2, Y6}, {X3, Y5}, {X3, Y6}, {X4, Y2}, {X4, Y3}, {X4, Y5}, {X4, Y6}, {X5, Y4}, {X5, Y5}, {X5, Y6}, {X6, Y1}, {X6, Y2}, {X6, Y3}, {X6, Y4}, {X6, Y5}, and {X6, Y6}.

Because both Xavier and Yvonne prefer more to less (and reallocation is costless), any allocation that does not allocate all of the fruit is not Pareto optimal. An example is {X5, Y6}, where Xavier gets one apple and Yvonne gets nothing. The set {X5, Y5} is a Pareto improvement over {X5, X6} because one person (in this case Yvonne) is made better off while the other person is not made worse off. But {X5, Y5} is still not Pareto optimal.

More interesting is the case where the fruit goes to the wrong person. Consider {X5, Y4} where Xavier gets an apple and Yvonne gets two pears. Both would be better off if Xavier got the two pears and Yvonne got the apple {X2, Y3}. So {X2, Y3} is a Pareto improvement over {X5, Y4}. Another way of saying this is that {X2, Y3} is *Pareto superior* to {X5, Y4}.

More important {X2, Y3} is Pareto optimal. The only way to make Xavier better off is by giving him everything, in which case Yvonne gets nothing, Y6, which makes her worse off. The only way to make Yvonne better off is to make Xavier worse off. If we give Yvonne one pear, then Xavier will be worse off even if he gets an apple in exchange. At {X2, Y3}, there is no way to make X better off without making Y worse off and there is no way to make Y better off without making X worse off. Hence {X2, Y3} is Pareto optimal.

One good thing about the concept of Pareto optimality is that if we value people's individual happiness, then we can agree that {X2, Y3} is to be preferred over {X5, Y4}. Pareto optimality has two other characteristics that are very desirable for practical applications in the real world. (1) The concept deals with preference orderings, not happiness levels (cardinality). Xavier prefers X1 over X2. Nowhere do we say that Xavier is twice (or thrice) as happy with X1 than with X2. (2) Furthermore, Pareto optimality does not require any interpersonal comparison of happiness or utility. We do not compare Xavier's happiness with Yvonne's happiness and say that Xavier is happier.

Unfortunately, these desirable characteristics of Pareto optimality also have negative implications. In particular, there may be many Pareto optimal outcomes and Pareto optimality provides no guide to choose among them. For example, Xavier getting all of the fruit and Yvonne nothing {X1, Y6}, Yvonne getting all of the fruit and Xavier nothing {X6, Y1}, Xavier getting two pears and Yvonne getting one apple {X2, Y3}, and {X4, Y2} are all Pareto optimal.[4] Indeed, although Xavier getting one apple and Yvonne getting one pear {X5, Y5} is not Pareto optimal, while Xavier getting all the fruit

---

[4] Warning. The following two errors are commonly made: (1) If a change makes one person worse off, the new position is not Pareto optimal; and (2) Pareto optimality favors the status quo. These are wrong. In going from {X1, Y6} to {X6, Y1}, we are going from one Pareto outcome to another. Neither has dominance over the other.

and Yvonne getting nothing {X1, Y6} is Pareto optimal, we cannot say that {X1, Y6} is Pareto superior to {X5, Y5} because Yvonne would be worse off when she has one less pear. Hence, Pareto optimality is in general quite useless for making distributional judgments.

To make sure that the concept of Pareto optimality is understood, we will consider the case of three people, X, Y, and Z, dividing up a cake. Again, everyone is selfish, and there is a possibility that some of the cake is wasted. Consider the following chart where the numbers refer to the fraction of the cake allocated to each person, and A-F are the allocations:

	X	Y	Z
A	1/3	1/3	1/3
B	1/2	1/2	0
C	0	1/2	1/2
D	1/3	1/3	1/4
E	1/8	1/4	1/8
F	0	1/2	1/8

Allocations, A, B, and C are all Pareto optimal. There is no way to redistribute more to one of the three people without redistributing less to one or both of the other two. Allocations D, E, and F are not Pareto optimal. Allocation A is Pareto superior to allocation D as Z is better off under allocation A than under allocation D, while X and Y are indifferent between the two allocations. Allocation D is Pareto superior to E, while C is Pareto superior to F. Note, however, that Pareto optimal allocation A is not Pareto superior to the nonoptimal (inefficient) allocation F because Y would be worse off. Similarly, neither B nor C is Pareto superior to D or E.

C. WHAT ABOUT DISTRIBUTION?

We have spent a lot of time discussing efficiency in its various guises and no time discussing just theories of distribution (for example, which Pareto optimal outcome is best). In this book (and in the economic analysis of law, more generally) distributional questions are largely ignored for the following reasons. (1) The prescriptive theory of distribution is undeveloped with little consensus on what is just and with unclear application to the law. (2) Some notions of justice interfere with Pareto optimality. For example, equality might suggest that X, Y and Z each getting one-quarter of a pie is to be preferred over the less equal distribution where X gets one-half and Y and Z get one quarter. (3) As will be demonstrated in later chapters, in many cases, the law is incapable of affecting wealth distribution. (4) In other cases, the law is an extremely poor vehicle for doing so. For example, we could choose to make poor drunk drivers not liable when they smash into the cars of the wealthy, but this would be a bizarre method of redistributing from the rich to the poor. It makes much more sense to use the income tax and subsidy system to shift wealth from the rich to the poor if that is what we desire. And (5) certain explanations for just distribution (based on "natural law" or religious texts, for example) are in fact economic efficiency arguments in disguise. For example, theft is proscribed in the Bible on moral grounds. As we will see, the prohibition against theft has an economic efficiency explanation.

D. CONCLUDING REMARKS

Non-economists have often caricatured economic efficiency as the evil business owner squeezing the most production out of his or her workers even if their work time is made miserable. This is definitely not what economists mean by efficiency (Pareto optimality) because the basic unit of analysis is the welfare of each individual in the society. Similarly, focusing on economic efficiency does not mean that pollution is ignored because, other things being equal, individuals prefer less pollution to more pollution and efficiency is based on individual preferences.

REVIEW QUESTIONS

1. What is the difference between a prescriptive and a descriptive theory? (1)
2. Explain Bentham's maximization of utilities approach. (4) What desirable quality does it have? (2) What are the problems with it? (4)
3. Define precisely: Pareto optimality. (2) Pareto improving move. (2)
4. How can there be many Pareto optimal distributions? Provide an example. (3)
5. Show that if an allocation maximizes the sum of utilities, then it is Pareto optimal. (4)
6. Consider three different distributions (1, 2 and 3) of at most $100 to 3 selfish people (X, Y and Z), such that: Distribution 1 and distribution 2 are both Pareto optimal, but neither is Pareto superior to the other. Distribution 1 is Pareto superior to distribution 3, but distribution 2 is not Pareto superior to distribution 3. Write out the distributions. (6)

4 Cost-Benefit Analysis

A. Kaldor-Hicks Compensation Test 22

B. The Kaldor-Hicks Compensation Test May Be Inconsistent # 23

C. Wealth Maximization # 24

D. Quasi-Linear Utility Functions # 25

E. Cost-Benefit Analysis 26

F. Downward-Sloping Demand Curves and Quasi-Linear
    Utility # 27

G. Concluding Remarks 29

REVIEW QUESTIONS 30

REFERENCES 30

In the last chapter, we introduced the concept of Pareto-improving outcomes (where at least one person is made better off without making someone worse off). It is a powerful analytic tool, but it is not very practical. Once we get to a large society, it is difficult to make Pareto-improving changes because it is impossible to identify and compensate all the losers. To illustrate, consider the situation where a polluting brick factory is forced to reduce its output.[1] Those who like clean air will benefit from the restriction on the factory's output, while those who intended to build brick patios will be harmed because with fewer bricks available they will either have smaller brick patios or need to reduce their purchases of other items when the price of bricks increases.[2]

Let us play god for the moment and assume that we know everyone's preferences and that we can find a way for those who benefit from the cleaner air to give up some items (say, cans of food or dollar bills) and transfer those items to those who are hurt so that after the transfer everyone is better off than when the factory was polluting. This is a Pareto-improving move.

There are two practical problems with such a plan. First, collecting all those items and then redistributing them might cost more than the net benefit of having the factory reduce pollution. In which case, the move to clean air would not be a Pareto improvement. Furthermore, we are not God. It is costly, if not impossible, to discover people's true preferences. While we may have an idea about the average benefit (or harm) and even some idea about the distribution of benefits and harms, it would be very hard to assign the exact benefit or harm to particular individuals. Because a Pareto improvement requires that we tax those who benefit (and possibly tax more those who benefit more) to raise sufficient amounts to compensate the losers, we are unlikely to end up with a Pareto improvement because mistakes in measuring individual benefits and costs will be made even if we are correct on average. So we cannot use the Pareto criterion because the Pareto criterion never balances one person's gains against another person's losses; rather the Pareto criterion only compares cases where some gain and no one loses.

If we were all clones of each other with identical tastes and abilities, then we could ask any one person whether he or she preferred more clean air and fewer bricks or more bricks and less clean air. Equivalently, we could ask whether the person would pay more for cleaner air or for additional bricks. If the person answered cleaner air, then the value of the cleaner air would compensate this person and all the clones for the loss in value from having fewer bricks. But we are not clones (at least not yet). So we will need to search for other alternatives that allow us to generalize our notion of compensating benefit.

A. KALDOR-HICKS COMPENSATION TEST

In 1939 Nicolas Kaldor and John Hicks devised the following compensation test: Policy 2 (e.g., restricting pollution) is preferred to policy 1 (e.g., not restricting pollution) if those who gain from policy 2 could *hypothetically* compensate those who lose in going

---

[1]   Like many examples in this book, this example is derivative of a real case. See *Hadacheck v. Sebastian*, 239 U.S. 394 (1915), where a brick factory was forced to shut down.

[2]   Usually we think that it is the owner of the brick factory and the workers who are hurt by such a restriction, but the analysis is easier if we think of the final consumers of brick as being the ones who are hurt. Perhaps after the restriction is imposed the brick prices are higher and the new way of producing bricks requires just as much labor for fewer bricks.

from policy 1 to 2 so that everyone would be made (weakly) better off by moving from policy 1 to policy 2.[3] In a nutshell, policy 2 is preferred to policy 1 if it is potentially a Pareto improvement. The losers need not actually be compensated. This is now known as the Kaldor-Hicks compensation test.

It is helpful to consider a simple example. Suppose that you and your friend are deciding which movie to see together. If you want to go see *Terminator 14* and your friend wants to see *Matrix Reloaded Again* and he is willing to pay you $7.00 to see *Matrix* instead of *Terminator* and you prefer to have $7.00 in your pocket and watch *Matrix* over watching *Terminator* without that $7.00, then both of you should see *Matrix*, even if you are not compensated. If both of you went to see *Matrix* and your friend did pay you $7.00 to do so, then that would be a Pareto-improving move over both of you seeing *Terminator*, with no transfer of money between you and your friend. The Kaldor-Hicks compensation test says that you should see *Matrix* instead of *Terminator*, even if you are not paid to see *Matrix*, because in principle it is a Pareto-improving choice.

This test is not without its problems.

First, when there is no compensation, people may lie about their preferences. You say: "I wouldn't see *Matrix* if you gave me one million dollars." And your friend replies: "I wouldn't see *Terminator* if you gave me two million dollars." Below, we will discuss ways of getting around this problem (we uses prices and choices rather than statements).[4]

Second, we have moved away from the Pareto criterion. Using the Kaldor-Hicks compensation test, one could recommend policy 2 over policy 1 even though it made someone worse off. Indeed, the Kaldor-Hicks compensation test would recommend policy 2 over policy 1 even though this meant that a poor man was made a $1,000 poorer if a rich man was made $1,100 richer. Economists have two justifications. First they hope that if we employ the Kaldor-Hicks compensation principle in enough places and certain people are not consistently on the wrong side of the stick, eventually everyone will gain, even if in particular applications some people will lose. Second, economists think that issues of income distribution can be treated separately. If society is concerned that some people are poor, society should redistribute income directly to them. Society should not use other policies (e.g., pollution control) as a vehicle for income distribution; for example, not engaging in pollution control because some poor people will lose their jobs is a stupid way of redistributing income to the poor.

The third problem with the Kaldor-Hicks compensation test is that it may be internally inconsistent (unless there are certain restrictions on preferences). We discuss this problem of inconsistency and its resolution in the following three sections.

B. THE KALDOR-HICKS COMPENSATION TEST MAY BE INCONSISTENT

To illustrate the problem with the Kaldor-Hicks compensation test, let us look at Figure 4.1.

The diagram is of necessity cardinal (because distance is cardinal), but we will only be concerned with ordinal relationships. Policy 1 is represented by the steeper downward-sloping line; given policy 1, the line represents the maximum feasible utility combinations. Suppose that policy 1 results in position S (where X gets S utility and Y gets

---

[3] The term "weakly" allows for some people to be indifferent between the two policies. The hypothetical assumes away the cost of finding and distributing funds to those who need compensation.

[4] Even with prices there may be strategic maneuvering. However, cost-benefit analysis usually looks at prices established in competitive markets where such strategic maneuvering is minimized.

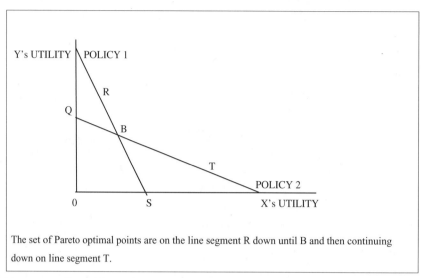

The set of Pareto optimal points are on the line segment R down until B and then continuing down on line segment T.

Figure 4.1. The Kaldor-Hicks criterion may be inconsistent.

0 utility), and that policy 2 results in position Q (where X gets 0 utility and Y gets Q utility). According to the Kaldor-Hicks compensation test, policy 2 is preferred to policy 1 because with policy 2 society could be at T instead of Q, and both X and Y prefer T to S. That is, Q is preferred to S because Y could compensate X by moving to T where both would be better off than if they were at S. Remember that this compensation need not take place.

The only problem with this argument is that a parallel argument shows that policy 1 and distribution S is preferred to policy 2 and distribution Q! According to Kaldor-Hicks, S is better than Q because X could compensate Y by going to position R. At position R, both X and Y are better off than they are at position Q. So policy 1 is preferred to policy 2. We have a complete contradiction. The Kaldor-Hicks criterion and its mirror opposite (known as the Skitovsky test) cannot choose between R and T either.

C. WEALTH MAXIMIZATION

This contradiction does not arise when the utility trade-off frontier of one policy is never to the left of the other policy. In Figure 4.2, policy 2 is always to the right of policy 1. In this case, all of the points on the utility possibility frontier of policy 2 are Pareto optimal (assuming that there are only these two policy possibilities); while none of the points on the utility frontier of policy 1 are. Under such circumstances, we can say that society under policy 2 is unambiguously *wealthier* than it would be under policy 1. We can also say that outcome Q is unambiguously preferred to outcome S according to the Kaldor-Hicks compensation criterion (as T is preferred to S but not vice versa). However, once you establish that one policy creates greater wealth than another, there is no need to do a separate investigation regarding compensation because a wealthier society always satisfies the Kaldor-Hicks compensation criterion without contradiction (and vice versa).[5]

---

[5] Note that wealth maximization is not equivalent to maximization of gross domestic product (GDP) if certain costs are not measured (such as pollution) or people are forced to produce. This is easily illustrated by considering a one-person Robinson Crusoe economy. By being forced to work eighteen hours a day, Robinson Crusoe would

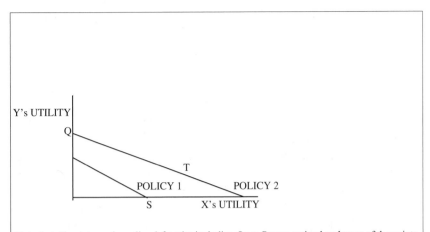

Note that all points on the policy 2 frontier including Q are Pareto optimal and none of the points on the policy 1 frontier are Pareto optimal. Nevertheless, Q is not Pareto superior to S as X is worse off. With quasi-linear utility functions, Kaldor-Hicks, wealth maximization, and cost-benefit analysis all generate Pareto optimal outcomes but not necessarily Pareto superior moves.

Figure 4.2. The measure of wealth is unambiguous and the Kaldor-Hicks test is consistent.

We are now left with only one practical problem. We have measured everything in terms of preference or ordinal utility. It would be easier to measure everything in dollars. Measuring wealth in terms of money also makes more intuitive sense. We will now turn to this issue.

If people valued only manna from heaven, then the more manna, regardless of how it was distributed, would be preferred to less manna (as long as people only cared about the amount of manna they received). The society with more manna would be wealthier. That is, we would have an unambiguous measure of wealth and Figure 4.2 rather than Figure 4.1 would characterize the choice between different policies. Society would choose the policy that maximized wealth (in this case policy 2).

But what if preferences were more complex? Can wealth be defined unambiguously? The answer is found in the following section.

D. QUASI-LINEAR UTILITY FUNCTIONS

We have an unambiguous measure of wealth and the Kaldor-Hicks compensation test is internally consistent when individual preferences can be characterized by a *quasi-linear utility function*. When individuals have quasi-linear utility functions, a redistribution of wealth does not change aggregate consumption and one good, money or manna, can be used as an ordinal measure of welfare. As noted in the previous section, if people only valued manna, then a society with more manna could in principle be made Pareto superior to a society with less manna if no one received less manna in the society with

produce more but he would be less happy and therefore less wealthy than if he were allowed to work and produce as much as he wanted and chose eight hours a day, instead. Furthermore, if some of this production yielded a lot of smoke and the cost to Crusoe of this smoke were greater than the benefit of what was being produced (and clean air was not being measured), then Robinson Crusoe would be worse off and therefore less wealthy than if he produced less with less smoke even though measured GDP were higher.

more manna available. With quasi-linear utility, even though people value many goods, manna can again be used as a consistent measure of ordinal welfare.

Quasi-linear utility is defined as follows: the utility of the ith person is $U_i = m + f^i(x_1, x_2, \ldots, x_n)$, where i stands for the ith person, x_j is the jth good or service, and m is numeraire good, money or manna. Person i's preference ordering over various combinations of n goods is represented by the function $f^i(x_1, x_2, \ldots, x_n)$. $f^i(x_1, x_2, \ldots, x_n)$ is quite general so that it can characterize a wide variety of preferences. For example, Xavier's utility for manna (m), wine (w), and caviar (c) might be $m + [wc]^{1/2}$, while Yvonne's utility function might be $m + \log(w) + c^{1/3}$. Notice that, in both cases, the person's utility for manna-money is a linear function of manna-money and is independent of how much wine and caviar the person consumes and the utility that a person gets from wine and caviar is independent of how much manna-money the person has. So this is the key to what is meant by a quasi-linear utility function – there is one good with constant marginal utility that does not depend on how much of the other goods are consumed.

It is not necessary to understand the formula for quasi linearity. What is important to know is the following: (1) demand for all goods, except manna-money does not depend on the person's wealth, only relative prices[6] and (2) money (manna) is a consistent measure of value that the person gets from a set of items. With quasi-linear preferences, redistribution of wealth does not alter any individual's consumption of items x_i, it only changes the amount of m that each person consumes – more m for one person is less m for another. Thus, when wealth is redistributed, aggregate demands do not change.[7] So prices do not change either. What this means is that we can convert everything into units of manna or money. And once again the more aggregate manna, the wealthier the society.

Going back to Figure 4.2, wealth maximization would recommend that policy 2 be chosen over policy 1, which could mean choosing Q (which allocates 0 to X and Q to Y) over S (which allocates S to X and 0 to Y) even though Q is not Pareto superior to S (as X is made worse off). Of course, wealth maximization and the Kaldor-Hicks compensation test do not say that losers are never compensated, only that compensation is not necessary.

E. COST-BENEFIT ANALYSIS

The Kaldor-Hicks compensation test is in terms of preferences and utility functions. But we rarely have direct knowledge about other people's preferences. Fortunately, if people are rational, we can infer preferences from prices. As discussed in Chapter 2, if a person pays $10 for that last liter of wine, it must be worth $10. If it were worth less, then the person would not have purchased it; if it were worth more, then the person would have purchased even more wine until the last unit of wine was worth $10 per liter (allowing for infinitesimal purchases).

---

[6] The consumer needs enough manna to be able to purchase the non-manna items.

[7] Here is a note for those who have a Ph.D. in economics. If individuals have Gorman-type preferences, then redistribution does not affect aggregate demand. Alternatively, if individuals have identical homothetic utility functions, aggregate demand will not be affected when there is a redistribution of income. So, quasi-linearity utility functions are not necessary to achieve this result.

Going back to the brick factory example, suppose that there will be a million fewer bricks produced each year if the factory is forced to reduce its output. Suppose further that the amount of particulants released into the air will be reduced by one hundred million per year. If the price of a brick is less than (or equal to) one hundred times the cost of a particulant, then the benefit of forcing the brick factory to reduce its output will exceed or equal the cost. Otherwise, the cost of forcing the brick factory to reduce its output will exceed the benefit.

So this is the basic idea behind cost-benefit analysis. If the benefit is greater than the cost, then one should undertake the activity. It is just a generalization of individual choice to the level of society. Furthermore, when benefits outweigh the costs, in principle, the winners could compensate the losers. Thus the Kaldor-Hicks criterion is also satisfied.

However, measuring benefits and costs is not a trivial exercise. We need to answer two questions. The first question is how do we establish a price for clean air (reducing particulants). After all, we do not see people purchasing clean air like they purchase cans of soda. The basic method of establishing the price of clean air is to use *hedonic pricing*. For example, observing how much more people pay for a house in a clean-air area over the identical house in an area with dirty air. The present value of clean air is reflected in the higher price for the house in the clean-air location.

The second question is how does one deal with changing prices? The more of a good, the lower the marginal benefit of the last unit is likely to be, and the lower the price consumers are willing to pay. That is, demand curves are generally downward sloping rather than being perfectly horizontal. So if there is more clean air, we can no longer talk about the price of clean air; instead, we have to consider the demand curve. We deal at length with this issue in the following section.

F. DOWNWARD-SLOPING DEMAND CURVES AND QUASI-LINEAR UTILITY

If people have quasi-linear utility functions, then the benefit that they receive from consuming a certain amount of a good is the *area* under the relevant portion of the demand curve. To illustrate, we start with a general demand curve (see Figure 4.3A). A demand curve is the amount demanded for a given price. To repeat what I said earlier, if a person will purchase one item when the price is $10, then that means that the person valued the first item at $10 and no more or no less. Because it is easier to illustrate with discrete units, let us switch over to Figure 4.3B, where the possible quantities are 1, 2, or 3. This demand curve shows that the person is willing to buy one unit when the price is $10 and that the person is willing to pay $8 each for two items. Now suppose that this is the demand curve of a person with a quasi-linear utility function. Quasi-linear utility allows us to make an addition inference – that the person would be willing to pay $8 for the second item even if the person paid $10 instead of $8 for the first because with quasi-linear utility, wealth has no effect on demand.. By paying $2 more for the first item, the person is less wealthy than if the person had paid $8 for the first item. But a change in wealth does not affect a person's demand (marginal valuation or benefit) for the second item when the person's utility is quasi-linear. Hence *with quasi-linear preferences, we can measure the area under the demand curve until Q^* as the individual's benefit* (in terms of dollars) from having Q^* instead of zero units (of clean air, for

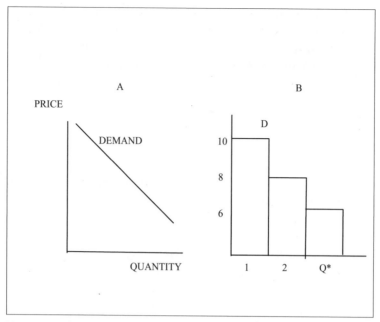

Figure 4.3. The area under the demand curve measures benefit when utility is quasi linear.

example). The argument has been made in terms of an individual demand, but market demand is just the sum of individual demands. So the same argument holds for market demand curves. When utility functions are quasi-linear, we can measure the benefit of a policy as the area under the relevant portion of the demand curve. The same holds for the supply or marginal cost curve, where total cost is the area under the relevant portion of the supply curve.

We have already shown (in Section D) that, with quasi-linear utility functions, prices will not change when the distribution of income changes. Hence, whether those who benefit compensate those who are harmed, the cost-benefit calculations (areas under the demand and supply curves) are the same.

Quasi-linearity means that cost-benefit calculations yield the same policy prescriptions as the Kaldor-Hicks compensation test and wealth maximization – all three are interchangeable. In the remainder of the book, we will stick to cost-benefit calculations because we observe prices rather than preferences and it is easier to make the cost-benefit calculations than to calculate total wealth. And getting back to Pareto optimality and efficiency, if we have maximized wealth (equivalently, we are at a point where there are no alternative policies such that the benefits of these alternative policies outweigh the costs), then we are at Pareto optimal point and the outcome is efficient.

What happens if preferences cannot be characterized by quasi-linear preferences? In the absence of quasi-linear utility, measuring the area under the demand curve provides an inaccurate measure of benefits. However, it may be a reasonable approximation.[8] Another way to justify the use of cost-benefit analysis in the absence of quasi-linear utility functions is that many decisions have insignificant effects on prices. For example, forcing a city brick factory to reduce output may have a negligible influence on brick

[8] For the argument, see Willig (1976).

prices if there are many brick factories located in many different areas so that most are not affected by the policy decision. Furthermore, even in the absence of quasi-linear utility, many policies have only minor second-order effects. When those who like clean air have to compensate those who like brick patios, the former are somewhat poorer and the latter are somewhat richer, but this change in wealth is unlikely to have any significant change in demand for any one good.[9]

To be more consistent with the economics of law literature, we will usually avoid the term "quasi-linearity utility." Instead, we will tend to use the following expression: "we will assume that a redistribution of wealth does not change the relevant consumer choices" except for manna-money. Of course, quasi-linearity implies the expression in quotes. And to reiterate what was said earlier, this assumption need not hold completely because we are mainly interested in the issue at hand. We really do not care all that much whether a farmer buys fewer clothes if he, rather than the neighboring rancher, has to pay for a fence; instead, we are interested in whether the fence will still be built if the farmer has to pay for the it.

G. CONCLUDING REMARKS

In general, we will use the word *efficient* as being interchangeable with Pareto optimality, wealth maximization, and maximizing benefits minus costs. The only time these words are not interchangeable is when wealth is not well defined (as might arise when preferences are not characterized by quasi-linearity utility), in which case we will explicitly deal with Pareto optimality.

Recall the following chart first presented in the last chapter. A, B, and C are all Pareto optimal allocations, while D, E, and F are not Pareto optimal. Note that Pareto optimal allocation B is not Pareto superior to D. Consequently, the Pareto criterion could make no recommendation in choosing between B and D. However, cost-benefit analysis does. It says that B is superior to D because the benefit to X and Y is greater than the cost to Z in moving from D to B, and in principle, Z could be compensated by X and Y so that all three were better off. The same logic holds in going from E or F to A, B, or C.

	X	Y	Z
A	1/3	1/3	1/3
B	1/2	1/2	0
C	0	1/2	1/2
D	1/3	1/3	1/4
E	1/8	1/4	1/8
F	0	1/2	1/8

In this chapter, we have undertaken a detailed argument justifying cost-benefit analysis. For the remainder of the book, cost-benefit analysis will be the underlying rationale for determining the appropriateness of legal rules.

---

[9] Our discussion has been in terms of *general equilibrium* (all markets are considered simultaneously), but both cost-benefit calculations and supply and demand curve analysis are typically done within a *partial equilibrium* framework, where at most one and only one good is being considered at a time and at most one price is changing.

REVIEW QUESTIONS

1. Why is a Pareto improvement not a good guide for actual policy prescription? (4)
2. What is the Kaldor-Hicks compensation test? (4)
3. What is meant by wealth maximization? (4)
4. What is cost-benefit analysis? (4)
5. How does one measure the value of clean air? (2)
6. How is Kaldor-Hicks compensation test employed in cost-benefit analysis? (2)

REFERENCES

Hicks, John R. (1939). The Foundations of Welfare Economics. 49 *Economic Journal* 696.

Kaldor, Nicholas. (1939). Welfare Propositions in Economics and Interpersonal Comparisons of Utility. 49 *Economic Journal* 549.

Willig, Robert D. (1976). Consumer's Surplus without Apology. 66 *American Economic Review* 589.

II TRANSACTION COSTS AND THE COASEAN REVOLUTION

The concept of transaction costs is critical for our understanding of law and organization. Consider the following seemingly unrelated questions: When do we have franchising instead of independent firms? What is the effect of contract law? Does making the owner of a neighboring property liable for damage from his trees falling on your property reduce the damage in comparison to the situation where you are liable? The answers to these and many of the other questions raised and answered in this book all depend on the level and nature of the transaction cost.

So what are transaction costs and why do they make a difference? In Chapter 5, we define transaction costs. In a nutshell, they are the cost of coming to an agreement and enforcing the agreement. Chapter 5 details the circumstances under which transaction costs tend to be high or low. When market transaction costs are high, the choice of legal regime (e.g., which party is liable for damage) is very important, as the parties will not be able to transact around the initial allocation of entitlements. An example is automobile accidents where the legal regime is critical (a negligence rule will result in different levels of care undertaken by drivers than a strict liability rule).

When transaction costs are low, the choice of legal regime is irrelevant regarding the level of care undertaken by the parties. This result is known as the Coase theorem. The logic is covered in Chapter 6.

In Chapter 7, we consider the Coasean analysis in greater detail. One of Coase's important ideas was to see the essential symmetry between the party that harms (e.g., the polluter) and the party that is being harmed (e.g., the pollutee). Both are inputs into the production of the harm and thus the burden of the solution need not fall on one party – the optimal method of reducing damage from pollution might be for the victim–pollutee to move away rather than for the polluter to install smoke filters.

So what about the questions raised at the beginning? Not all of them will be answered in Part II. As already suggested, transaction cost analysis lies at the very heart of this book. Part II provides the necessary framework. Still we can provide a quick summary to the questions posed. Firms try to economize on transaction costs. Under certain circumstances, the franchise arrangement reduces transaction costs over other forms of organization, such as single ownership of all of the outlets or independent ownership of the outlets (see Chapter 36). In general, contracts involve low transaction costs; so court rulings have little effect on the nature of the contract (see Chapter 22). A parallel example to the falling tree example is found in Chapter 6.

Part II is called the Coasean revolution because Ronald Coase is responsible for most of the insights. He is the person who emphasized the role of transaction costs in explaining the theory of the firm – firms and markets are organized to economize on transaction costs. He is also responsible for the Coase theorem and its opposite (when transaction costs are high, the choice of legal regime is very important). And as already noted he emphasized the symmetry between the parties. This is why he won a Nobel Prize in economics, and why I label Part II "the Coasean revolution."

5 Transaction Costs

A. **Transaction Costs** 34

    1. Negotiation Costs 35

    2. Monitoring, Enforcement, and Avoidance Costs 37

B. **An Intuitive Example** 37

C. **Some Subtleties** 38

D. **Concluding Remarks** 39

SUGGESTIONS FOR FURTHER READING 40

REVIEW QUESTIONS 40

REFERENCES 40

A rancher's cows stray onto the neighboring farmer's land where the cows trample the farmer's corn. If the rancher is liable for the damage to the farmer, will there be less damage to the farmer's corn than if the rancher is not liable?

This question was raised and answered in Ronald Coase's Nobel Prize–winning article, "The Problem of Social Cost," *Journal of Law and Economics* (1960). The article is so fundamental that we will take three chapters to explain fully. Although the economic analysis of law has roots as far back as the late eighteenth century, this article introduced many of the fundamental building blocks of analysis, including what has now become known as the *Coase theorem*.

COASE THEOREM: If there are zero transaction costs and mutually beneficial trades are always made when transaction costs are low, then, whatever the *initial* assignment of entitlements (a) the outcome will be efficient and (b) the outcome will be the same when changes in the distribution of wealth do not affect consumption patterns.[1]

The Coase theorem is quite a mouthful and difficult to digest in one sitting. Indeed, when Coase first presented his theory to a group of economists (including two future Nobel Prize winners) at the University of Chicago, it took him two hours before the group accepted his argument. So do not feel bad if you either do not understand or agree with the statement of the theorem on an initial reading.

A. TRANSACTION COSTS

Before trying to make sense of the theorem, it is important that we first understand what is meant by transaction costs.

Transaction costs are the costs of making and enforcing the transaction or exchange of entitlements. Haggling, waiting in line, carrying out threats (such as strikes and fire bombing), having the issue arbitrated, inspection of goods being traded to ensure that the seller has been honest, all have *economic* costs to society as a whole because scarce resources are being used up for the transaction. These scarce resources could be used in some other activity – this is the notion of opportunity cost. Note that purchasing an item for X dollars does not involve a cost to society of X dollars as the X dollars are merely transferred from one person to another. Only the time involved in actually exchanging the money (along with the other costs in coming to an agreement) is a transaction cost. For example, when you purchase a loaf of bread from a grocery store, the time cost of waiting in the checkout line and the salary for the cashier is the transaction cost.

What conditions foster high-market transaction costs? (1) Negotiation costs arising from the combination of *bilateral monopoly* with *many participants* on both sides. (2) The cost of monitoring and enforcing the agreement, as well as the cost incurred when one or both parties try to renege on the agreement.

---

[1] This statement of the theorem is somewhat different from the standard. The standard statement of the "theorem" is not a theorem, but a conjecture – that low transaction costs will lead to efficient bargains. The way for the standard statement to not be a conjecture is to assume that there are high transaction costs whenever one side does not know what the other side will accept in the bargain. This assumption is fine, but I find it more convenient to deal with my version of the theorem.

Initial means that the entitlement is assigned before (or independent of) behavior. If one obtained the entitlement by behavior (e.g., by building a house one obtained the right to have no shadows cast on the land), then the assignment of entitlements would affect the outcome. For a more in-depth discussion of how changes in wealth might or might not affect consumption patterns, see the sections on quasi-linear utility in Chapter 4.

1. Negotiation Costs

To illustrate negotiation costs, assume that I have the Hope diamond and you have Leonardo da Vinci's *The Last Supper*. I really want *The Last Supper* (LS) and would be willing to exchange my Hope diamond (HD) and $1 million for it. You really want the 45.52-carat Hope diamond and would be willing to give up *The Last Supper* for it. This is a bilateral monopoly. Each has what the other wants, but there are no terms of trade to establish what the exchange rate should be. Is it LS for HD or LS for HD + $1 million. Clearly, I prefer the former and you prefer the latter. We may bargain for somewhere in between. It may take several years of intermittent negotiations to come to an agreement. Other examples of bilateral monopoly are management and *unionized* workers, and Israel and Palestine control over their common border, wherever that may be.

Compare bilateral monopoly to a case of perfect competition. I have a bushel of wheat and you have two bushels of rice. Assume that wheat sells for twice the price of rice on the open market. If I want more than two bushels of rice for my bushel of wheat, you will purchase your wheat elsewhere; if you want more than a bushel of wheat for your two bushels of rice, I will purchase my rice elsewhere. There is no haggling because neither can get better terms of trade since the market price is uniquely defined by the presence of so many perfect substitutes. But the painting *Next to The Last Supper* by Donald Wittman is not a very good substitute for da Vinci's *The Last Supper*, nor is the "Hopeless zirconium" a good substitute for the Hope diamond.

Another way to characterize the difference between bilateral monopoly and perfect competition is in terms of the information that each side has about the other. When there is a well-established price for both goods, which would be the case when both goods are competitively supplied, then each side knows what price the other side will accept in the exchange. So there is no need to bargain. But when the price that the other side will accept is unknown, which would be the case when there is bilateral monopoly, there may be more haggling as each side tries to get the best deal possible and sometimes Pareto-improving trades will not take place.[2]

If more than two people are involved and a unanimous agreement is required, then bargaining costs increase dramatically and the likelihood of a successful agreement falls toward zero. To illustrate, consider the case where the state wants to build a freeway from the town of Los Gatos to the city of Mountain View. To make the analysis as easy as possible, suppose that the state is willing to pay up to a total of $300 million for the one hundred parcels of land that the freeway will cross. Assume further that each property owner would ordinarily be willing to sell the property for $1 million. Thus the surplus value of this project is $200,000,000(300 − 100 ∗ 1 = 200). If the state has to purchase these parcels on the open market, then each of the one hundred owners will try to extract the *full* surplus for herself. Each parcel owner is a monopolist. Without her consent, the freeway cannot be built – the freeway cannot dead-end at one parcel and start anew two parcels down. So each landowner will try to extort the surplus of $200 million (in addition to the $1 million it is worth to the landowner). It pays each landowner to be more intransigent than the rest, hoping that the other landowners will give in to a lower share of the surplus. For example, landowner 1 might say to the

---

[2] This problem of asymmetric information will be discussed in greater detail in later chapters (see, for example, Chapter 27 on insurance and Chapter 39 on bargaining in the shadow of the law).

other landowners: "I will accept nothing less than $200 million. You, the remaining ninety-nine landowners can share $100 million, which will make each of you better off than if the freeway is not built. Therefore, you should acquiesce to my selfish demands because if you don't, there will be no freeway and you will be worse off." Of course, the temptation is for all of the landowners to try to extract more than their fair share, so the total demanded by the landowners could well exceed the amount the state is willing to pay. Indeed the amount demanded could go as high as $20 billion ($100 \times 200,000,000$). Compare this to the situation where one person owned all the parcels – so we have a single monopolist. Knowing that the state was willing to pay at most $300 million, the person would not try to bargain for anything more. So an agreement would be much more likely.

Because a market failure is so likely in this case, governments (including capitalist governments) do not rely on the market when acquiring land for streets and highways. Instead, they force the landowners to sell by the rule of *eminent domain* and then compensate the landowners for "fair market value." Needless to say, fair market value is not determined by the landowners; instead, a third party (e.g., a judge) decides what is a fair price.[3] In contrast, if the government wants to build a post office, it does not use eminent domain; instead, the government buys the land like any other purchaser because the multiple monopoly holdout problem does not exist in this situation.

The *monopoly holdout* problem arises whenever unanimous agreement is needed. To hammer home the idea, I will consider one more example. Suppose that homeowners have the right to not have pollution, but they can sell this right to a factory that would like to engage in a highly profitable but pollution-intensive activity. Suppose further that the benefit to the factory owner is greater than the true cost to all of the homeowners. If unanimous agreement by the homeowners is needed for any agreement, then each homeowner will be in a monopoly position; if one homeowner does not agree, then no agreement can be made. Again, each owner will try to be a *monopoly holdout* and try to extract the surplus for herself. So the total amount demanded will be far greater than the benefit of engaging in the pollution-producing activity, which we have assumed is greater than the total cost to the homeowners. And so the high transaction costs of bargaining in this case will likely prevent a Pareto-improving outcome. Indeed, the likelihood of a sale of this property right to no pollution is so low that it generally is not saleable in the first place.[4]

The mirror image of the monopoly holdout problem is the *free rider* problem. Suppose that a factory is located near a housing development and that each homeowner prefers that the factory close down. Suppose that the benefit to each of the one thousand homeowners from closing the factory is $750 so that the total benefit to the homeowners from the factory closure is $750,000. Suppose further that the cost to the factory owners from closing the factory is $500,000. If the factory has the right to be there, then even if in principle the homeowners could buy the right from the factory owners, under a system of voluntary transactions, they probably will not. Each homeowner would be better off by paying $600 and having the factory shut down, but each homeowner would

---

[3] Note that there are some court transaction costs involved in determining the fair market price, but in this case, they are small in comparison to market transaction costs. Note also that eminent domain may be applied in situations where the argument is not as compelling as it is for building highways.

[4] For similar reasons, collective decisions rarely require unanimity and instead rely on majority or two-thirds majority rule.

be still better off if her neighbors paid enough to bribe the factory to shut down and she did not. In this way, she would have a free ride. Since most (if not all) homeowners are likely to think this way, an inadequate number of homeowners would voluntarily contribute to the closure of the factory.

The problem of free riding explains why economic markets are not used in many circumstances, even within capitalist systems. For example, almost all of the citizens benefit from national defense. So if the money for defense were raised through cookie sales and collection boxes, there would be a temptation to free ride on others' contributions. The amount collected would be insufficient – everyone would be better off if they were forced to pay for defense than relying on voluntary contributions.

2. Monitoring, Enforcement, and Avoidance Costs

In the typical economics textbook, a market exchange is a simple transaction (e.g., a farmer sells a bushel of wheat for $2.00). However, many exchange relationships are much more complex (e.g., employment contracts, defense contracts, or the settlement of the dispute between Israel and the Palestinians). Not only are the negotiations involved in establishing such contracts quite complex and time consuming (read: high in negotiation transaction costs) but also there are costs of *monitoring and enforcing* the contracts. That is, costs are involved in making sure that the exchange has taken place according to the agreement. These transaction costs clearly vary according to the complexity of the item being exchanged. Purchasing #2 Durum wheat requires less monitoring than buying a Star Wars weapon system from a defense contractor or verifying that an arms-control agreement has been honored by the other side. The level of the monitoring costs can also be affected by which particular entitlements are exchanged. Thus putting a door-to-door salesman on commission instead of paying hourly wages clearly reduces the need to monitor the amount of time a salesman puts into his job. Under a pure commission system, the salesman does not sell his entitlement to establishing his own work time because the cost of his employer monitoring the agreement if he did so would be too high. However, sales people in department stores are often supervised (monitored) to make sure that they do not take excessive lunch breaks and that they come to work in the first place.

Monitoring is needed because people may try to avoid fulfilling their end of the bargain. The owner of a car may claim that it is has never been driven, and the purchaser may check the speedometer. But if the seller has run the car in reverse while the car is raised off the ground, the seller may be able get away with claiming that a car with nine hundred miles has only been driven nine miles. In this example, the cost of the gas used in running the car in reverse is also a transaction cost. There are many interesting issues that arise because of such opportunistic behavior, and we will return to them later.

B. AN INTUITIVE EXAMPLE

It is easiest to understand the Coase theorem, if we first paraphrase it without the qualifiers, next illustrate it with a simple example, and finally consider the qualifications. So here is the imprecise but easier to grasp paraphrase: when transaction costs are low, the final allocation of entitlements is independent of the original allocation of entitlements. Now, for the simple, but easy to grasp, example:

Suppose that I have a ringside ticket to a boxing match, but I don't like boxing. Consider the following three scenarios: (1) I sell the ticket to Arnold, the highest bidder in my class. (2) I give the ticket to Arnold. (3) I give the ticket to Hillary. In the first scenario, Arnold was willing to pay the most for the ticket. I had the original entitlement, but he ended up with the ticket. In the second case, the ticket is allocated to Arnold. Under the circumstances, it seems extremely unlikely that a bargain could be struck whereby another student paid Arnold to give up the ticket. In the third scenario, Hillary is *likely* to sell the ticket to Arnold since we already know from the first scenario that Arnold is willing to outbid everyone else for the ticket.

In this example, whatever the original entitlement, Arnold ends up with the ticket. So this illustrates part B of the Coase theorem – when transaction costs are zero, the final allocation is the same regardless of the initial allocation. Furthermore, the final allocation is wealth maximizing – the item goes to the person who is willing to pay the most for it. So part A of the theorem holds as well – the outcome is Pareto optimal. Of course, Arnold prefers the second scenario in which he is given the ticket, rather than paying for it; and Hillary prefers the third scenario where Arnold pays her for the ticket.

C. SOME SUBTLETIES

The previous subsection provides the essence of the Coase theorem without the distracting conditional statements found in the formal statement of the theorem. It is this essence that needs to be mastered first. Nevertheless, there are some subtleties that need to be considered.

The first issue to consider is how the individuals involved change their spending patterns when their wealth changes due to a change in their entitlements (e.g., changing from scenario 2 where Arnold is given the ticket to scenario 3 where Arnold pays Hillary for the ticket). If changes in the distribution of wealth do not affect consumption patterns (in technical terms, individuals have quasi-linear utility functions), then, under the second scenario, Arnold will consume more manna and Hillary less (by an equivalent amount) than under the third scenario. All of their other purchases remain the same. Therefore, "the outcome is the same" regardless of the initial allocation of entitlements. A redistribution of wealth via a change in entitlements does not change the final outcome.

Now if, contrary to the assumption in part B of the theorem, consumption patterns change when wealth is redistributed, it is possible that Hillary will buy fewer bottles of wine and boxes of chocolate when she has less wealth (scenario 2 instead of scenario 3), and Arnold will buy more cigars and oysters when he has more wealth (scenario 2 instead of scenario 3). So some things might change when the entitlements change (so that there is a redistribution of wealth), but who ends up with the boxing tickets does not change. Focusing on the issue of who ends up with the tickets, the final outcome does not change in this case as well (even though we are speaking more loosely).

When people are wealthier, their spending patterns may change (if they do not have quasi-linear utility functions). When the ticket is given to Hillary (scenario 3), she is wealthier than under scenarios 1 and 2. It is conceivable that this increase in wealth means that she is willing to spend more on seeing a boxing match, possibly enough that she would no longer be willing to sell the ticket to Arnold at a price he was willing to pay. To illustrate, suppose that Hillary has $100 a month to spend on entertainment, and that she wants to spend $60 on the opera, leaving at most $40 to spend on a boxing match. Then Arnold, who is willing to spend $70, would not sell the ticket to Hillary in scenario 2 (nor would Hillary outbid Arnold in scenario 1). In scenario 3, Hillary gets the ticket for nothing; therefore, she can spend $100 on other entertainment and still see the boxing match. Hillary might prefer to spend $80 on a boxing match and $90 on other entertainment rather than spend all of the $170 on nonpugilistic entertainment. If Arnold offered her $70 for the ticket, she would not sell it to him because if she had $170, Hillary would then be willing to pay $80 for the boxing ticket.[5] In this example, a change in the initial distribution of entitlements does change the final distribution of entitlements. If Hillary is given the ticket, she will end up with the ticket; if Arnold is given the ticket, Arnold will end up with the ticket. The wealth-maximizing outcome is no longer well-defined because the outcome depends critically on the initial allocation of entitlements. However, all scenarios are still Pareto optimal, since there is no way to make one person better off without making another worse off. So part A of the Coase theorem still holds even though part B does not in this last example.

In most of the cases that we consider in this book, changing the initial ownership of the entitlement does not alter the demand for the entitlement, especially so when we are discussing the interaction of two firms where profits rather than tastes are the motivating force (as illustrated in the farmer-rancher example discussed in the next chapter). So, in most of the cases considered in this book, part B of the Coase theorem holds when part A does.

We next delve more deeply into the assumption that "mutually beneficial trades are always made when transaction costs are low." It is useful to consider the third scenario in more detail. I have argued that Arnold will end up buying the ticket from Hillary (if the tickets are worth more to Arnold). But such negotiations may be time consuming since Hillary wants to sell high and Arnold wants to sell low. There is an opportunity cost in such negotiations; perhaps Arnold and Hillary are spending less time studying. Furthermore, if both bargain too hard, the transaction may not take place. That is, our assumption that mutually benefiting trades *always* take place when there are low transaction costs may not hold (and, as a consequence, part A of the Coase theorem, that the outcome is always efficient, will not hold either). We will come back to this last point in a later chapter.

D. CONCLUDING REMARKS

We have shown that the transaction costs involved in negotiating and monitoring agreements need not be trivial and that when either a unanimous agreement is required or free riding is possible, market transaction costs are likely to be extremely high.

In this chapter, we have concentrated on market transaction costs. But, as will be seen in later chapters, there are also transaction costs within nonmarket settings. For example, a law limiting vehicular emissions includes the following transaction costs: lobbying by outside groups, bargaining within the legislature, enforcement by regulatory agencies, and the cost of going to court when the law or its application is in dispute.

---

[5] Another way of looking at this situation is to assume that I gave Hillary $70 before I auctioned off the tickets. She would then be willing to bid more than $70 for the tickets. Therefore, Hillary would outbid Arnold in scenario 1 and end up with the ticket in scenario 2.

HIGH TRANSACTION COST AND THE LAW

Suppose you are on the side of the road bleeding to death and a doctor comes along. You could bargain about the price of his services (if you were conscious), but by the time you came to an agreement, you might be dead. The law "cuts to the chase" by requiring the doctor to make his customary charge for such services. He cannot charge you more even if you agreed to it at the time. For similar reasons, admiralty law provides guidelines for salvaging a sinking ship. No use dickering while the water is up to your neck.

SUGGESTIONS FOR FURTHER READING

It is worthwhile to read Coase's original article on social cost. For an exhaustive coverage of the Coase theorem, see Medema and Zerbe (2000).

REVIEW QUESTIONS

1. Define transaction costs. (2)
   Under what circumstances are market transaction costs low? (2)
   Under what circumstances are market transaction costs high? Provide examples. (3)
2. When do monopoly holdouts occur? (2) Explain why monopoly holdouts create high market transaction costs. (3)
3. When do free riders arise? (2) Explain why free riders create high market transaction costs. (3)
4. Suppose that in bidding for a ticket, Arnold has the highest bid. Suppose instead that the ticket was given to Arnold. Explain why Hillary would be unlikely to buy the ticket from Arnold. (2) Suppose that the ticket was given to Hillary instead. Explain why it is *likely* that Arnold would buy the ticket from Hillary. (2) Explain why Hillary *might* not sell the ticket to Arnold in this last case. (4)

REFERENCES

Coase, Ronald H. (1960). The Problem of Social Cost. 3 *Journal of Law and Economics* 1.

Medema, Steven G., and Richard O. Zerbe, Jr. (2000). The Coase Theorem. In Boudewijn Bouckaert and Gerrit De Geest (eds.). *Encyclopedia of Law and Economics, V1.* Northampton, MA: Edward Elgar.

6 Fencing In and Fencing Out

A. A Formal Proof 42

B. Fencing In and Fencing Out 42

C. Do Pareto-Improving Exchanges Always Take Place
    When Transaction Costs Are Low? 44

D. The High Transaction Cost Case 45

E. Concluding Remarks 46

SUGGESTIONS FOR FURTHER READING 47

REVIEW QUESTIONS 47

REFERENCES 47

In the last chapter, we introduced the Coase theorem within the context of a simple example of exchange. In this chapter, we consider a more complex and less obvious example. At the same time, we demonstrate the insight that the theorem provides when its assumptions do not hold.

A. A FORMAL PROOF

Although the Coase theorem was introduced in the last chapter, it is useful to present it again, now that we have a better idea regarding its meaning.

Coase theorem: If there are zero transaction costs and mutually beneficial trades are always made when transaction costs are low, then, whatever the *initial* assignment of entitlements, the outcome (a) will be efficient and the outcome (b) will be the same when changes in the distribution of wealth do not affect consumption patterns.

The logic behind the Coase theorem is very simple. If there are no costs of exchange, then, by assumption, all mutually beneficial gains will be made and the outcome will be Pareto optimal. When it is also the case that a redistribution of wealth (due to a reallocation of entitlements) has no effect on (the relevant) consumption patterns, then consumption patterns and production will be the same regardless of the initial assignment of entitlements.

B. FENCING IN AND FENCING OUT

Stated this way, the theorem is obvious, but the application of the theorem need not be. To illustrate the counterintuitive nature of the theorem, let us consider the following example. Suppose that a rancher's cows trample a farmer's corn. Will the amount of damage be less if the farmer has the entitlement to not have his crops damaged than would be the case if the rancher has the entitlement to trample the farmer's corn? If transaction costs are low, Pareto-improving exchanges are made, and consumption patterns are not altered, then it makes no difference on the amount of damage made by cows if ranchers have the right to trample farmers' fields or farmers have the right to not have ranchers' cows trample the farmers' fields. We will demonstrate this by considering four different scenarios.

If the rancher has the right to damage the farmer's crops, but it is more efficient to not have cows trample the farmer's corn, then the farmer will pay (bribe) the rancher to keep his cows off the farmer's land. For example, suppose that it cost $30,000 a year to build and maintain a fence on the rancher's land, thereby reducing damage to the farmer's crops by $40,000 a year. The farmer would be willing to pay the rancher up to $40,000 to build a fence (if the cost of fencing was more expensive on the farmer's land). And the rancher would be willing to build the fence if he received at least $30,000. If the farmer pays the rancher $36,000 for the rancher to build a fence, then both the rancher and the farmer will be better off than if the fence had not been built.

If the farmer has the right to no damage and the costs and benefits are the same as in the preceding paragraph, then the outcome will be the same as well. The rancher cannot bribe the farmer to let the rancher's cows trample the farmer's field because the benefit to the rancher (not having to build a fence for $30,000) is outweighed by the cost to the farmer ($40,000). So again, the fence will be built, but, this time, it will be paid for by the rancher, who prefers to spend $30,000 on a fence rather than paying $40,000 in damages.

We next consider the possibility that the most efficient outcome is for the rancher's cows to trample the farmer's crops. For example, it might cost $50,000 a year to build and maintain a fence. If the rancher has the right to damage the farmer's property, then the farmer will not bribe the rancher to build a fence because the bribe would have to be at least $50,000, but the savings would only be $40,000. So the result will be that the rancher's cows trample the farmer's fields (no fence will be built).

If the farmer has the right to no damage and the costs and benefits are the same as in the preceding paragraph, then the outcome will be the same, as well. The rancher will pay the farmer somewhere between $40,000 and $50,000 per year for the right to inflict $40,000 worth of damage on the farmer's crops. In this way, the rancher's profits will be higher than if he built a fence for $50,000. Of course, the farmer (rancher) prefers the regime where he has the right to a regime where the rancher (farmer) has the right. When the farmer has the right, the rancher bribes the farmer for damage; when the rancher has the right, the farmer bribes the rancher for nondamage.

For illustrative purposes, I have used the example of a fence. But the analysis is far more general. For example, suppose that the profit from being in the cattle business were $38,000 a year (and again the cost of building a fence was $50,000, and the damage to the crops was $40,000). Then the rancher would go out of the cattle business and instead undertake some activity that did not harm the farmer's crops. If the farmer had the right to no damage, then the rancher would simply choose a different activity than cattle raising for his land. If the rancher had the right to damage the farmer's land, then the farmer would buy an easement on the rancher's property preventing its use for cattle ranching. In return, the farmer would pay $38,000–$40,000 a year for the agreement.

Furthermore, this analysis works on the margin. If one cow brings a profit of $10 to the rancher and creates $8 worth of damage to the farmer, then the rancher will buy the right to have one cow. If the agreed-upon price for this right is $9, then the rancher is better off than he would be if he had zero cows and zero profit because his profit will be $10 − $9 = $1. The farmer is also better off since he is being paid $9 for something that costs him only $8. If the second cow brings a profit of $9 but yields $11 worth of damage to the farmer, then the rancher cannot bribe the farmer for a second cow. If the rancher has the rights, the analysis is in reverse. The farmer will be able to bribe the rancher to not have the second cow by paying the rancher more than $9 but less than $11.

So far, we have not considered the possibility that a change in entitlements may change consumption patterns, which, in turn, may influence the behavior of the parties. For example, if the rule is changed so that farmers are entitled to no damages, then farmers are made richer and ranchers are made poorer, which, in turn, might lead to farmers eating more corn (especially so if they are vegetarians) and ranchers eating less beef (if utility is not quasi-linear). Then there will be more land devoted to corn. So where the fence is built might change, but the decision to build a fence will not change when the entitlement changes. Of course, even this example is farfetched as the effect on aggregate demand for corn and beef is likely to be negligible when the entitlement (to no damage) is given to farmers. Thus, in this example, we can safely ignore the effect of a change in wealth on aggregate consumption patterns.

When transaction costs are zero and the rancher and farmer always make mutually advantageous trades, it makes no difference whether the law makes the farmer or the rancher liable – the same efficient outcome will result. Of course, market transaction costs are not zero and mutually advantageous trades do not always take place. Thus the law should in general try initially to allocate entitlements to the party that is likely to end up with the entitlements if there were zero transaction cost of exchange. In this way, an unnecessary and costly transaction is likely to be avoided, and misallocation will not occur in those cases where transaction costs outweigh the returns to a better allocation. Thus, if the optimal decision were no damage by cows, we would want to give the right to no damage to farmers; if the optimal decision was to have no limits on cows, we would want to allow ranchers the right to damage cows.[1]

Although the rancher/farmer example may seem arcane, in fact it provides insight into the choice between fencing in (of cattle) and fencing out. In the first half of the nineteenth century, cattle were allowed to roam freely in most western states. If a farmer did not want cattle on her land, she had to fence them out. In the eastern United States, cattle usually had to be fenced in.[2] The economic explanation for the different treatments is transparent. Roaming cattle are more likely to do damage in residential and farming areas than in areas composed mainly of pasture. The cost of fencing in large tracts of ranch land to prevent potential damage to isolated farms is greater than the benefit. If it is worthwhile building a fence, it is probably best to put a fence around the farmer's land. In contrast, in those areas where ranching is rare, it is cheaper to build a fence around the isolated ranch than to have all the farmers build fences around their land. Even if only the adjacent farms built fences, it would in general be cheaper for the rancher to build one fence, then for his neighbors to build a series of fences around his land or to negotiate an agreement with the rancher to build a fence.

C. DO PARETO-IMPROVING EXCHANGES ALWAYS TAKE PLACE WHEN TRANSACTION COSTS ARE LOW?

The version of the Coase theorem that I have presented assumes that Pareto-improving exchanges will take place when the cost of negotiation is low. But is this assumption always warranted? The answer is no.

Suppose that I know that the value you place on my watch is somewhere between $50 and $100; and you know that the value I place on my watch is somewhere between $25 and $75. Even if I actually value my watch at $55 and you actually value my watch at $74, a trade may not take place. I may not be willing to accept less than $75 because my expected profit is lower. I prefer to make a final offer of $75 with a greater chance of the watch not being sold in return for a greater surplus when it is sold than offer $74. The mathematics is most readily understood if there is no dispute regarding how much I value the watch and the value you hold has a uniform distribution on $50–$100. If I demand $75, then there is a 50 percent chance that you will value the watch at $75 or above and buy the watch. I will then receive a surplus of $75 − $55 = $20. So my expected surplus is .50 × $20 = $10.00. If I price the watch at $74, then there is a 52 percent chance that you will accept the offer, but I will get a surplus of only $19. So

---

[1] Of course, sometimes the optimal might be somewhere in the middle.
[2] Today, a number of states, including Oregon and Arkansas, allow counties to choose whether the rule is fencing in or fencing out.

my expected surplus is $.52 \times \$19 = \$9.88$. So, I will not reduce the price below $75 (in fact, my optimal price will be $77.50). And a similar logic may hold for you as well (with two-sided imperfect information). You may prefer to offer a lower price because your expected consumer surplus is higher. The higher surplus that you receive when you buy the watch at a lower price more than makes up for the decreased likelihood of buying it. So a trade may not take place even if both sides would be better off by doing so. The same result will arise if both of us know each other's valuation but not on how hard a bargainer the other party is. Each may still hold out for a better bargain even at the risk of not making the bargain.[3]

Note that other bargaining strategies will not help. Suppose that I have a strategy that if you reject my price, I lower my price in the next round. Then it will always pay you to reject my first price and wait for a lower price. Because I know that you will respond in this way, I will not lower my price. There is no logical way out of the problem posed in the preceding paragraph. Thus bluffing and other rational bargaining strategies may lead to some Pareto optimal exchanges not taking place.

There is also experimental evidence that contradicts the Coase theorem assumption that beneficial trades will always be made when transaction costs are low. For example, in some experiments, one person (A) gets to divide a dollar and the other person (B) can either accept with both receiving their share or reject with neither getting anything. It has been observed that if A chooses a high share for herself, then B is likely to reject – a result that is not Pareto optimal since neither gets anything.

Does this experimental result along with the previous theoretical example seriously erode the applicability of the Coase theorem? My own view is that both are really examples of moderately high transaction costs. There is a bilateral monopoly (one buyer and one seller of the watch or only one partner at a time in the experiment). So one could plausibly argue that zero transaction costs do not hold. Furthermore, even in these cases, Pareto-improving exchanges typically take place.

D. THE HIGH TRANSACTION COST CASE

The mirror side of the Coase theorem is very useful for analyzing the law. Given high transaction costs, the initial allocation of entitlements will tend to be the final allocation of rights, and hence not all allocations will lead to wealth maximizing outcomes. Even when transactions are not very costly, they still should be economized on. Movement from one allocation of rights to the efficient allocation of rights involves transaction costs. Therefore, the initial allocation of entitlements should be the wealth-maximizing allocation to save on such costs.

Let us first consider a low transaction cost example. Should a landowner have the right to grow trees that cast shadows on his neighbor's land or should the neighbor have the right to prevent the landowner from planting trees that cast shadows on her land? For various reasons (including the likelihood that in many cases the neighbor might prefer the shade), one suspects that regardless of which side was assigned the right initially, most of the time the landowner would end up with the right to grow trees that cast shadows on neighboring land. Clearly, it would make sense to

---

[3] Note that some would consider this to be an example of high transaction costs because of lack of information about the other side's valuation and/or bargaining strategy.

grant the right to cast shadows in the first place – to grant the right to not have shadows would create unnecessary transaction costs and possibly would result in no agreement.

The allocation of rights is even more important in high transaction cost situations. Consider the case where landowners have the right to prevent trespassing, both on their land and the sky overhead (as was the case in Roman times), so that airlines would have to get permission from landowners to fly their airplanes. It would be virtually impossible for airlines to purchase this right even if they valued it more than the landowners. Every landowner along a flight path would try to extort all the value for himself by being the monopoly holdout since unanimous agreement is required. Hence, if landowners were given the property right to not have trespassing, there would be no flights.[4] On the other side, if airlines had the right to fly overhead (which they do if they do not fly too low), high transaction costs would prevent homeowners from purchasing the right from the airlines, even if homeowners valued airplane-free air more than airlines profited from having airplanes. There would be an intense *free rider* problem, each homeowner hoping that the other landowners would pay to not have plane flights.

Hence, it is very important to make the correct allocation of rights in the first place.

So what is the wealth-maximizing outcome? In this case, the answer comes easily. The value of the aesthetic loss (if any) from having airplanes flying 10,000 feet overhead is considerably less than the amount that airlines would be willing to pay for the privilege of having flights. Of course, not all questions in the law have such obvious answers. Consider, for example, such related questions as (1) Should airplanes be allowed to have more gradual flight paths so that airlines save fuel even though more houses are exposed to the greater noise from low flights? (2) Should airlines be allowed to take off or land after 11 p.m.? (3) Or should the supersonic Concorde (R.I.P.), which made more noise than subsonic jets, have been allowed to land in O'Hare Airport? Note that despite their complexity, all of these questions are answered with the same general cost-benefit methodology. We will come back to these issues in greater detail in the ensuing chapters.

E. CONCLUDING REMARKS

Transaction costs are key to understanding law and organization. When market transaction costs are low, the initial assignment of entitlements has no effect on the final assignment of entitlements, and one ownership structure can be transformed into another by simple bargaining and contract. When transaction costs are high, the initial assignment of entitlements is likely to be the final allocation. Therefore, society must be very careful in deciding how to allocate entitlements in the first place. Even when market transaction costs are not very high, the allocation of entitlements should not ignore such costs.

[4] Economic markets involve voluntary exchanges. In this airplane example, economic markets require unanimity. An alternative is to have a political market where there is majority rule. Majority rule gets rid of the hold-up problem but allows for other types of inefficiency, especially if the benefits or costs are not uniform across voters. See Chapter 36.

SUGGESTIONS FOR FURTHER READING

Ellickson (1991) looks at present-day customary rules in Shasta County, California, regarding who is liable for damage from stray cattle. Sanchez and Nugent (2000) look at voting data for Kansas in the 1870s, when counties were given the option to retain the traditional fence laws (requiring crops to be fenced in) or to adopt herd laws (requiring the restraining of animals by means of herding). They test various theories to explain why different counties voted differently. There is a large body of experimental work testing the Coase theorem. Hoffman and Spitzer (1982) find evidence to support the argument that the outcome will be efficient (part A). Knetch (1989) finds evidence of a status quo bias – that the initial allocation will influence the final allocation – thereby arguing against part B of the Coase theorem. In contrast, Plott and Zeiler (2005) argue that properly designed experiments show little status quo bias. In a theory paper, Myerson and Sattherwaite (1983) show that with two-sided asymmetric information, no mechanism can be designed such that efficient trades will always take place.

REVIEW QUESTIONS

1. State the Coase theorem. (2)
   Provide an intuitive explanation. (4)
   Illustrate using the rancher-farmer example provided by Coase. (4)
2. Provide an example demonstrating that the allocation of entitlements make a difference when there are high-transaction costs. (3)
3. Do people always trade to mutual advantage? (3)

REFERENCES

Ellickson, Robert C. (1991). *Order Without Law: How Neighbors Settle Disputes.* Cambridge, MA: Harvard University Press.

Hoffman, Elizabeth, and Matthew Spitzer. (1982). The Coase Theorem: Some Experimental Tests. *25 Journal of Law and Economics* 73.

Knetsch, J. L. (1989). The Endowment Effect and Evidence of Non-reversible Indifference Curves. *79 American Economic Review* 1277.

Myerson, Roger B., and Mark A. Sattherwaite. (1983). Efficient Mechanisms for Bilateral Trading. *28 Journal of Economic Theory* 265.

Plott, Charles R., and Kathryn Zeiler. (2005). The Willingness to Pay/Willingness to Accept Gap. *95 American Economic Review* 530.

Sanchez, Nicolas, and Jeffrey B. Nugent. (2000). Fence Laws vs. Herd Laws: A Nineteenth Century Kansas Paradox. *76 Land Economics* 518.

7 Coase versus Pigou

A. Zero Market Transaction Costs and the Marginal
    Cost Curve 51

B. Pigovian Taxes with High Market Transaction Costs 52

C. Symmetry 53

REVIEW QUESTIONS 54

REFERENCES 54

A speeding car careens off the street onto a sidewalk and smashes into a pedestrian. Who caused the harm to the pedestrian – the driver or the pedestrian? If pollution from a steel firm kills fish in a downstream reservoir, who caused the damage to the fish – the owner of the steel mill or the owner of the fishery? Should the steel firm be liable (either to the owner of the fishery or to the government) for the "externality"? Most people would answer that the driver of the speeding car caused the damage to the pedestrian and that the owner of steel firm caused the damage to the fish. With regard to the third question, most economic students would recommend producer liability so that the externality arising from steel production would be internalized by the owner of the steel mill. As will be shown, the standard answers to the first two questions are wrong, while the standard answer to the third question is often incorrect. Indeed, the question itself is misleading.

Let us pursue the second and third questions in more detail. Consider the standard beginning and intermediate textbook example of an externality problem, where firms are entitled to pollute. Let the horizontal axis be quantity of steel produced by a factory and the vertical axis be dollars (see Figure 7.1). The horizontal curve, XC, is the demand curve and represents the marginal value of steel to society.[1] The lower upward-sloping curve, VC, is the marginal "private" cost to the steel firm, including wages and payments for iron ore (for simplicity, there are no fixed costs). The marginal cost curve is upward sloping because the more steel that is produced, the more it costs to produce one more unit of steel. The steel firm also produces water pollution, which kills fish in a lake owned by a fish farmer. The marginal cost of the pollution to the owner of the fish farm is the vertical distance, W-V, between the two upward-sloping lines. This is the value of the fish killed for each unit of steel produced. The upper curve, WD, is the "social marginal cost" or "full marginal cost" of producing a unit of steel; it is equal to the sum of the marginal costs to the steel firm and to the fishery. The efficient outcome is at E, where the full marginal cost equals the marginal benefit. Beyond E, the extra cost of producing steel is greater than the extra benefit; until E, the extra benefit is greater than the extra cost. Note well that the *optimal* amount of pollution is not zero.

For perfectly competitive firms, the standard economic analysis argues that the steel firm's private marginal cost curve is the supply curve. The firm maximizes profit by producing until its private marginal cost equals marginal revenue (price). This is at quantity I (for inefficient), where revenue = price times quantity or X times I = the rectangle 0XCI, cost to the firm = the area under the private marginal cost curve = the quadrilateral 0VCI, and profit = revenue minus cost = triangle VXC. If the firm were to produce more steel, then the extra cost would be greater than the extra revenue and profits would be less: if the firm produced less steel, then the lost revenue would be greater than the cost savings and profits would again be less than at I. So, I is where the steel firm's profits are the greatest. But at I, the social marginal cost is greater than the marginal benefit. So, too much steel is produced.

The Pigovian solution is to have the steel firm pay a pollution (Pigovian) tax to the government for the "externality" – the marginal pollution tax is an amount equal to the horizontal distance between the two upward sloping lines, W-V. In this way, the firm's marginal cost is equated to the social marginal cost to society, and the firm's supply curve is now the upper line, WD. With this pollution tax, the firm will produce until

---

[1] To simplify the analysis, we assume that the demand curve is horizontal.

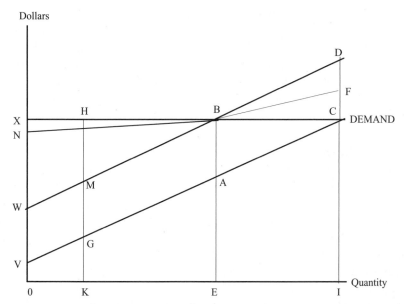

Figure 7.1. Steel production with pollution "externalities."

its marginal cost (now including the tax) equals marginal revenue, which is at point E. Before point E, the extra revenue is greater than the extra cost to the firm; and after point E, the extra revenue is less than the extra cost. So, the Pigovian tax solves the externality problem. This analysis was originally formulated by Alfred Pigou, although many of the mistakes made in analyzing Pigovian taxes are due to his followers rather than Pigou himself.

Coase demonstrated that this analysis is wrong. He made the following two points: (a) If there are zero market transaction costs, then the upper line, WD, is the steel firm's "implicit" marginal cost curve, even if the steel firm is given the right to pollute. There is no externality as the cost to the fishery is internalized by the steel firm. Consequently, there will be an efficient solution even without a tax. And (b) if transaction costs are very high, then the standard Pigovian analysis and tax remedy may be appropriate, but it is misleading since a symmetric problem is treated asymmetrically. Both the steel firm and the fishery are inputs into the damage.

A. ZERO MARKET TRANSACTION COSTS AND THE MARGINAL COST CURVE

We first consider the case where the steel firm has the entitlement to pollute. Suppose that the owner of the lake is on vacation when the steel firm makes it initial decision regarding production. By going beyond the efficient point (E), the extra profit to the steel firm is the triangle ABC – the difference between the additional revenue and the additional cost to the firm. At the same time, the additional cost to the pollutee (owner of the fishery) is the parallelogram ABDC.

When the lake owner comes back from vacation, she will want to negotiate with the steel firm. This is a low transaction costs situation – the pollutee (the owner of the lake) should be able to bribe the steel firm to move from the inefficient output to the efficient output. That is, the pollutee will implicitly buy off some of the rights to pollution from the steel firm. If the polluter produces at the efficient point (E) instead of I, the polluter might receive ABFC from the pollutee. The polluter is better off since ABFC is greater than the foregone production profits, ABC, in going from I to E. At the same time, the pollutee is better off because the cost of the bribe ABFC is less than the value of reduced pollution (ABDC). So the owner of the lake is ahead by BDF.[2] Thus, both sides are made better off.

The pollutee cannot bribe the polluter to produce less than the optimal amount of steel because the reduction in pollution cost to the fishery (ABMG when the output is K instead of E) is less than the reduction in profit (ABHG) to the steel firm.

We next consider the case where the owner of the lake has the entitlement to no pollution. If the pollutee has the entitlement to no pollution, we would not have a zero amount of steel produced with the steel firm making zero profits. Rather, the steel firm would buy off the right of the pollutee to have no pollution by paying her an amount VNBA to produce E. This would make the pollutee better off because the cost to the pollutee is only VWBA. At the same time, the polluter would be receiving additional profits VXBA, which would more than offset his additional costs in paying the pollutee, VNBA. Hence, the polluter's net profit would be XBN. This is greater than zero. So the polluter would be better off as well. Again, the exact amount of the bribe (the placement of N) is indeterminate as long as it is not less than W nor greater than X.

Hence, this is just a diagrammatic exposition of the Coase theorem (part B): when there are zero transaction costs, then the outcome will be the same whatever the initial distribution of entitlements.

B. PIGOVIAN TAXES WITH HIGH MARKET TRANSACTION COSTS

This may not be a low transaction cost situation. Indeed, this case is likely to involve high transaction costs because pollution often involves many pollutees and polluters (unlike our example, which involves only one polluter and one pollutee). This means that the participants cannot bargain and buy and sell entitlements. Giving polluters (factories) the entitlement to pollute will result in too much steel being produced (I) and too much pollution, while giving the pollutees (fisheries) the entitlement to be pollution-free will result in too little steel being produced (0) and too little pollution.

Hence, some other procedure is needed. For ease of analysis, let us consider just one factory. One possibility is to regulate the steel company and not allow it to produce more than E. Another method is to use a Pigovian tax equal to W-V per unit of steel produced. Because a bribe by the pollutee is not possible in this high-transaction cost case, curve WD will then be the polluter's marginal cost curve. Profit maximization will take place at quantity E where marginal revenue equals marginal cost (in this case, where WD intersects XC). This is also the socially optimal amount of steel production and pollution. Thus, the standard Pigovian solution in economics texts is OK if we assume high transaction costs.[3]

---

[2] F is somewhere between C and D. Its exact position is not determined by our analysis.
[3] For more on Pigovian taxes, see White and Wittman (1983) and Wittman (1985).

BUYING OUT A TOWN

According to the February 8, 2004, edition of the *New York Times*, sulfuric acid emissions from the massive coal-burning power plant in Cheshire, Ohio, caused sore throats, burning eyes, and blisters. Sometimes the smog was so thick that cars drove through the streets at noon with their headlights on. In a series of town meetings in the spring of 2002, lawyers presented an offer from American Electric Power to buy all of Cheshire for $20 million. The 200-odd residents would have to move, their houses would be razed, and their community would cease to exist – and in exchange, they would each receive about three times the assessed value of their property. Though a few dissenters stood up and said they would rather fight than leave, they could not sway their neighbors. In the end, everyone accepted the offer and waived their right to sue.

This example illustrates that the optimal outcome may be for the residents to move rather than for the polluter to reduce the pollution.

C. SYMMETRY

But even in the high transaction cost case, the graphical representation may be very misleading unless we truly understand the concept of cost. In ordinary economics, we talk about capital and labor as being two inputs into the output of some good. Here, too, we should realize that there are two inputs into the production of pollution damage. Both the pollutee and the polluter can have an effect on the amount of damage from pollution. The polluter can filter his output, reduce production, or move away; the pollutee can grow pollution resistant fish, filter the water, shunt it away from her lake, move elsewhere, and so on. The optimal mix of inputs depends on the technology at hand. Clearly, if it is very cheap (in relationship to the cost to the other side and also in relationship to the cost of the potential damage), for one side to eliminate the damage, then we want that side to do it.

Thus, the only difference between the neoclassical analysis of the firm and the analysis of efficient legal rules is that according to neoclassical economic theory, the owner of the firm has control over the inputs into the production process, while in the cases of interest in the law, different people have control over different inputs. The objective of the law should then be to design a system that encourages optimal behavior by these unrelated people.

The Pigovian tax diagram does not illustrate this symmetry. The diagram concentrates on the behavior of the polluter by showing his costs, benefits, and the costs that he imposes on the pollutee, but the optimal behavior of the pollutee is only implicitly assumed in the cost curve to the pollutee.[4] We have a very asymmetric diagram to illustrate a problem that is very symmetric.[5] Thus, the diagram tends to visually put the burden on the behavior of the polluter. Looking at the diagram; the way to reduce pollution damage is to reduce the production of steel. There is nothing in the diagram to suggest that the pollutee might be able to reduce pollution damage, as well. Until Coase,

---

[4] If the pollutee's cost curve is calculated correctly, the Pigovian diagram yields a correct answer.
[5] A more appropriate diagram is akin to the capital-labor isoquant diagram, except the axes represent pollution reduction inputs by the steel firm and the fishery, and the isoquant is the production of a bad rather than a good.

the accompanying discussion was almost always on how the behavior of the polluter could be changed and not on how the behavior of the pollutee might be changed.

In many ways, this concept of *symmetry* is the most important idea in Coase's remarkable paper. Until Coase, people talked about a driver causing harm to a pedestrian or factory smoke damaging laundry hung out to dry. After Coase's article, people realized that cause is an outmoded concept. Rather, the appropriate insight is to see that there are several inputs into the production of damage. In the automobile accident case, the care by the driver and choice by the pedestrian are both inputs into the accident. The question becomes, which combination of inputs is optimal? This, of course, depends on the marginal productivity of the input in reducing expected damage and the marginal cost of the input.

REVIEW QUESTIONS

1. Using a diagram like that used in the chapter, show why bargaining can lead to an efficient outcome even if the polluter is not liable for the damage to the pollutee. (10)
2. Using a diagram like that used in the chapter, show why bargaining can lead to an efficient outcome even if the pollutee has the entitlement to no pollution. (10)
3. If transaction costs are very high, the standard Pigovian tax is correct. Demonstrate. (3).

    However, it is misleading because it is asymmetric. Explain the important role of symmetry. (3)

    Provide three different examples of asymmetric characterization of a symmetric situation. (3)

REFERENCES

White, Michelle, and Donald Wittman. (1983). Pollution Taxes and Optimal Spatial Location. 49 *Economica* 297.

Wittman, Donald. (1985). Pigovian Taxes which Work in the Small Number Case. 12 *Journal of Environmental Economics and Management* 144.

III COST–BENEFIT ANALYSIS AND THE LAW — DEVELOPING ECONOMIC INTUITION

As was shown in Part II, when transaction costs are high, it does make a difference whether one side or the other is liable for the harm. So how does one decide the appropriate legal framework under such circumstances? Typically, economists would undertake a cost-benefit analysis to determine the optimal outcome and then determine which rule provides the appropriate incentive for achieving the efficient outcome. This sounds complicated and it certainly can be. But here in Part III, we develop the *economic intuition* without going into a more technical discussion.[1] We start with relatively easy cases where the costs and benefits can be readily determined.

Cost-benefit analysis treats the inputs into the production of damage symmetrically – both the injurer and the injured can reduce harm. The issue is which person can reduce the harm at the lowest cost and whether the cost of reducing harm is less than the benefit. In Chapter 8, we take this abstract concept of symmetry and show the reader how to think like an economist. The first step is to think of the set of possible actors that might influence the outcome; the second is to consider the various ways that the outcome could be altered; and the third step is to estimate the cost of the various methods. Because we choose somewhat simple examples, this exercise can be done without sophisticated econometric techniques. For example, we do not need a lot of detail to establish (1) that it is less costly for drivers to not drink than for pedestrians to wear cages around their bodies and (2) that making the driver liable for damage to the pedestrian will encourage this outcome more than the reverse (making the pedestrian liable for the damage to the pedestrian).

Chapter 8 also provides a number of thought exercises to help one establish the optimal allocation of resources. One method is to ask who would end up with the entitlement if transaction costs of exchanging the entitlement were low. In the driving example, the driver would in general not be able to buy the entitlement not to be hit by drunk drivers from the pedestrian. Or, to say the same thing, without the double negatives, the pedestrian would in general buy the entitlement to harm the pedestrian from the drunk driver.

Chapter 9 provides a way that economists can determine the optimal solution without engaging in their own cost-benefit analysis – look at the market solution. Presumably, the people involved (particularly, profit-maximizing firms) will have undertaken their own cost-benefit analyses. So this is another way of generating intuition for the efficient outcome – look to the market. The discussion is done within the context of smoking regulations. A topic often treated in an asymmetric manner but here shown to be symmetrical: the entitlement to smoke harms nonsmokers, while the entitlement to no smoke harms smokers.

Chapter 10 considers rules of the road and sports rules. Recall that one method of determining the efficient allocation of entitlements is to ask who would end up with the set of entitlements if the transaction cost of exchanging them were low. Here we show that the various rules are a low-cost method of implicitly making cost-benefit calculations. For example, consider the rule of the road that requires the lead car on a two-lane road to pull over to the side if there are five or more cars following it. If transaction costs were low (in particular, the free-rider problem were overcome), then

---

[1]   For a more formal presentation, see Chapter 15.

the people in the five cars would in general pay the driver in the first car to pull to the side – their benefit of going faster would on average outweigh the cost to the first driver of getting someplace slightly later. The purpose of the chapter is to make you, the reader, think intuitively about cost-benefit calculations, even when driving or playing sports.

8

How to Think Like an Economist: Drunk Drivers, Hawks, and Baseballs

A. Drunk Driving 61

B. Hawks and Power Lines 61

C. Who Owns Barry Bonds's Record-Making Baseball? 63

D. Concluding Remarks 66

SUGGESTIONS FOR FURTHER READING 66

REVIEW QUESTIONS 66

When judges think about the law, they think about precedents. When economists think about the law, they think about costs and benefits. Actually, when economists think about anything, they think about costs and benefits. If damages are involved, as would be the case in an automobile accident, a cost-benefit analysis would determine the cost of reducing either the probability of the accident (e.g., better tires) or the extent of the damage (rubber bumpers and seat belts) and then compare these costs to the benefit of reduced damage (fewer broken bones).[1] Interesting legal issues arise because different individuals may have control over different inputs into the production of damage.

A good way of getting insight into the relevant costs and benefits is to first ask which parties could influence the outcome and then determine how they could influence the outcome and at what cost. The final stage would be to ask how the law could be used to encourage the appropriate behavior.

There are several interrelated thought experiments that economists use as guides toward the correct answer. The first is to *ask what would have been done if there were a merger of all the relevant parties*. For example, in the last chapter, an economist would ask what would the steel firm do if it owned both the steel firm and the fishery. In this way, all of the costs and benefits fall on the owner of the steel firm. A second thought experiment is to ask *who would end up with which entitlements if the cost of making agreements were low* (in particular, there were no monopoly holdouts or free riders), although the costs of monitoring and enforcing the agreement might be high and thus still should be included. This type of exercise suggests that homeowners would decide whether they walked into their backyards, while airlines would decide whether they crossed the airspace 10,000 feet above, rather than vice versa. This approach is especially useful for analyzing contract law. A third thought experiment is more forward looking. It asks how individuals would respond to the law. *Does the law create incentives for efficient outcomes?* A fourth method is to *see how markets make allocations in similar circumstances* and then make rules for high-bargaining cost cases that approximate the market choice. This requires a more detailed discussion and will be covered in the next chapter.

Before dealing with individual cases, it is important to keep the following in mind. I have provided very short case summaries. Often these summaries are based on appellate court summaries of the original trial. At other times they are based on newspaper descriptions of the original trial. While I have tried to capture the salient issues, the summaries neither have all of the requisite information nor do they capture all of the issues raised. For example, in one of the cases discussed below, I mention that the cost of insulating electrical wires is likely to be prohibitive; but the appellate decision does not discuss the cost, and I do not know how expensive it would actually be. The purpose of presenting these cases is not to provide the definitive judgment for the case at hand, but to understand the general methodology. Furthermore, the actual court decision is based on the law, not necessarily on economic logic. While often the law displays an underlying economic logic even when the legal terminology differs from economics, sometimes the actual decision is made on totally different grounds.

---

[1] A more technical and advanced discussion is found in the chapter on cost minimization.

A. DRUNK DRIVING

To illustrate the economic methodology, we will consider three examples in depth. The first involves a drunk driver who drives onto a sidewalk and hits a pedestrian. Who should be liable?

The first question to ask is, which parties could have influenced the outcome? Everyone will mention the drunk driver; and those who remember the last chapter will mention the pedestrian. Two other possibilities come to mind (especially if you are the defense lawyer for the drunk driver): the city and the owner of property where the pedestrian was hurt.

The second question to ask is, how could these parties either prevent the accident or reduce the severity of damage? The drunk driver could have had apple juice instead of alcohol, taken a bus or taxi instead of driving a car, stayed at home, or driven a car with very large foam bumpers. The pedestrian could have driven instead of walked, stayed at home, or walked surrounded by a heavy cage to protect her in case of an accident. The city could have installed higher curbs or concrete barriers at the edge of the street to protect pedestrians, not allowed anyone to drive on the street, and so on. Finally, the owner of the property could have planted trees to protect pedestrians. A person with a good imagination could come up with many more possibilities.

The third step is to compare costs and benefits and decide on the efficient solution. Some of the suggestions in the previous paragraph are clearly impractical. That is, they are either very costly to implement or they provide little benefit. In general, the most efficacious solution is to have the drunk person not drive. However, the answer depends on the particular facts and the existing technology. If the sidewalk was next to the street, there was no curb, but there was plenty of traffic, then one might argue that the benefit of reduced harm to pedestrians from putting in curbs might outweigh the cost. Or if pedestrians could use a cheap and lightweight gadget that created a zone of protection around the pedestrian, we might want to make the pedestrian liable for not turning her gadget on.

The fourth step is to ask which rule promotes the efficient outcome. If the drunk driver is liable for the damage to the pedestrian, then the driver will have a greater incentive to take care (by not driving when drunk, for example) than if he is not liable. Thus, we want to make the driver liable for the damage to the pedestrian (because the gadget that protects pedestrians has not yet been invented).

B. HAWKS AND POWER LINES

If you excuse the pun, the drunk driving case was a rather pedestrian example. Let us now consider a more exotic one. Our second example is inspired by *Chase v. Washington Water Power* (111 P.2d 872). In that case two hawks were fighting. Their wings short-circuited a high-tension wire with a guy wire that touched a barbed-wire fence owned by Chase. The electrical charge went through the barbed-wire fence and set fire to Chase's barn, which was attached to the barbed-wire fence. To avoid the some of the technical details, I will describe a slightly different scenario. The wing tips of the hawks spanned the distance between two electrical lines. The resulting short circuit turned the hawks into a fireball that set the wooden (not barbed-wire) fence below on fire, as well as the barn connecting to it. The farmer who owned the fence sued the electric company for damages. Who should be liable for the damage?

As already noted, economics provides a methodology for answering such questions, by providing its own list of questions. The questions are derived from Coase's initial insight that there may be many inputs into the production of damage and that the law should encourage the most efficient use of resources.

Again, the first question to ask is, which parties could have influenced the outcome? In this case, the farmer, the power company, and the hawks are three obvious candidates. We will eliminate the hawks because neither they nor their children can be forced to pay for the fence. So taking them to court is useless (nevertheless, in the middle ages a number of animals were found guilty of criminal offenses and put to death). We note, however, that evolutionary forces will tend to eliminate hawks that engage in such activity. We further note that if someone owned the hawks, then we would want to include the hawk owner as one of the parties to the input.

The second question to ask is, what actions could each party undertake to prevent the damage? The electrical power company could have buried its wires underground, put on insulation, placed the wires farther apart, or not have the electrical lines going over the fence. The farmer could have built a steel fence, shot the birds, or built the fence elsewhere. Depending on one's imagination, one could come up with other solutions; for example, the farmer could have played Beethoven's Fifth Symphony to scare away the hawks (just as store owners sometimes play classical music to get rid of panhandlers and other undesirable elements from loitering around their store entrances).

The next step is to engage in a cost-benefit analysis. Such an analysis is often aided by asking what would one of the parties do if it owned both of the inputs. In this case, one might ask what would the power company do if it owned the electrical lines and the farmland below.

It seems that the likelihood of two fighting hawks spanning electric wires and causing serious fire damage is extremely small. Therefore, the optimal amount spent on preventing such an occurrence should also be very small, possibly zero. Thus insulating the lines or making them farther apart would be much more costly than the benefit derived. Obviously, the optimal distance between uninsulated wires is more than 4 inches – such a small distance is easily spanned by modestly sized birds, and the number of short circuits would be very high. But just as obviously, the optimal distance is less than the span of two hawks. The larger the span, the more costly it is to build electrical lines. Insulating lines is also very costly – the insulating material must defy weathering, and the supports must be stronger to carry the additional weight. Electrical wires get connected to buildings, so it is hard for power lines not to have fences below them.

It appears that the farmer could have prevented the damage at lowest cost by either building a fireproof fence or by scaring away the hawks. If the cost of prevention by the farmer were less than the expected damage, we would want to make the farmer liable to encourage the farmer to undertake preventive action. Realistically, it probably would not pay the farmer to undertake prevention either because the costs of prevention would likely outweigh the benefits. Hence, regardless of who was liable, neither party would undertake preventive measures. Thus, to reduce the costs of litigation, the farmer should be the party who is liable for the cost of his barn burning down.

Why doesn't the Coase theorem render the choice of liability irrelevant? After all, if the power company were liable, it could just pay the farmer to build a fireproof fence or, more simply, pay the farmer to accept liability. The answer is transaction costs. The costs of negotiating such a transfer of rights is not trivial. So to economize on transaction costs, the law should make the farmer liable as he would be the party who would end up with the liability. Furthermore, if the power company were liable and the negotiations failed or were not undertaken in the first place because of the rarity of the event, then farmers would sue the power company for damages whenever there was such an occurrence. Lawyers are expensive. By making the farmer liable, these court transaction costs are eliminated.

Of course, in this case, the farmer took the electrical power company to court. So transaction costs were not saved. But if the legal ruling were against the farmer, this would discourage people from taking similar cases to court in the future. Now another occurrence of two hawks creating a fireball is extremely unlikely. However, the law provides general principles. In this case, a ruling against the farmer would be saying don't bother suing a company when its cost of prevention greatly exceeds the resulting damage, which is unlikely in any event.

Depending on the costs and benefits, the court decision could change. California condors have a very large wingspan that can easily span the distance between electric wires. Because the California condor is an endangered species and because condors like to be on top of electricity poles, it is quite possible that the courts would insist on the electrical companies undertaking preventive action in those areas where condors are breeding.

We now go back to the original case. The jury found in favor of Chase, the plaintiff. The power company appealed the case. Appellate courts only make judgments of law, not fact (although, as we shall see here, the distinction is not always so clear). Three justices affirmed the case in favor of the plaintiff. Two of these judges stated that the jury made the decision on the facts of the case – to use my words, the jury made their own cost benefit-analysis and decided that the power company should have engaged in more preventive behavior – therefore, the appellant court had no basis to overrule the jury decision. The jury had determined that the power company had negligently allowed the guy wire to contact the barbed-wire fence. There were two dissenting opinions. The dissenters argued that it made no sense for the power company to engage in protective behavior from such a freak accident, and therefore, as a matter of law, the power company could not be considered negligent.

From the viewpoint of this course, the majority decision is an anomaly (but not as much of an anomaly as the derivative example that I have considered) because I argue that most court decisions are consistent with the promotion of economic efficiency. Nevertheless, I have included this case because of its quirky nature and the clarity of the analysis of the derivative example.

C. WHO OWNS BARRY BONDS'S RECORD-MAKING BASEBALL?

The third example is a more recent court case. When Barry Bonds hammered his record-breaking home run no. 73, the ball landed in the upper portion of the webbing of a softball glove worn by Alex Popov. He was thrown to the ground while still in the process of attempting to complete the catch. It is unclear whether he would have caught the ball even if he had not been knocked down. Patrick Hayashi was standing near Popov when the ball came into the stands. He, like Popov, was forced to the ground. Hayashi

SHOULD SAFETY SEATS BE REQUIRED FOR CHILDREN ON AIRPLANES?

Suppose that children under 2 years old are required to use child-restraint seats on planes instead of sitting on their parents' laps for free. How many children's deaths would that save? Surprisingly, the answer is that it would probably increase the number of deaths per year by 8. A 1995 analysis by the Federal Aviation Administration predicted that a child-restraint seat requirement would prevent as many as five child deaths per decade from plane crashes. But that report also predicted a net increase of eighty-two child deaths per decade because many parents would balk at buying a plane ticket for their child and opt to drive, which is much more dangerous than flying. For further discussion, see *Archives of Pediatrics and Adolescent Medicine,* October 2003.

CAR SMASHES INTO PEDESTRIANS: WHO SHOULD BE LIABLE?

In 2003, 87-year-old George Weller drove his speeding car into a weekly farmer's market held on a street in Santa Monica. Ten people were killed and sixty-three were injured. Some of the victims claimed that it was the city's fault because the city should have installed temporary concrete barriers. The city responded that such barriers would prevent emergency vehicles from entering the market. Of course it makes more sense to sue the city than the driver because the driver probably does not have that much money to spread among all those people. See http://www.insurancejournal.com/news/west/2004/12/09/48505.htm for more details.

CAN A MURDER INHERIT FROM THE PERSON WHOM HE HAS MURDERED?

Elmer Palmer poisoned his grandfather whose will left money to Elmer. Should the will be enforced or should Riggs, another relative of the grandfather, be allowed to inherit the property instead of Elmer? In *Riggs v. Palmer*, 22 N.E. 188 (1889), the court struggled with the issue of contract, but in the end ruled against Elmer.

The economic logic for this case is similar to the Bonds' baseball case. But the Coase theorem suggests that this court decision has had minor influence on inheritance. If the court had ruled in favor of Elmer, part of the boilerplate in wills would say that the inheritance was void if the person murdered the deceased. However, the court ruled against Elmer. It seems very unlikely that any wills say that the murder will still gain the inheritance. Because wills are not always written by lawyers and wills should not be unnecessarily long, the court made the right decision in ruling against Elmer.

committed no wrongful act. While on the ground he saw the loose ball and put it in his pocket. Who is entitled to the ball – Popov or Hayashi?[2]

The best economic insight into answering this question is to ask how the ruling would affect future behavior. If Popov did not get the ball, then, in the future, fans would be encouraged to shove the person likely to catch the ball. If Popov did get the ball, then

---

[2] We will not consider other alternatives such as Barry Bonds owning the ball.

CLINT EASTWOOD'S HOMETOWN

Carmel, California, is a quaint seaside town with uneven sidewalks down the main street and few sidewalks anywhere else. According to the November 14, 2004, *San Francisco Chronicle*, Carmel does not allow women to wear high heels to prevent lawsuits from women tripping over the sidewalks and the roots of heritage trees. It also does not allow street numbers or fast food, either. Evidently, you cannot sue the town for getting lost and/or hungry.

COST-BENEFIT ANALYSIS OF THE CLEAN AIR ACT

The Clean Air Act of 1970 required elimination of lead in gasoline, reduction of sulfur emitted from burning coal, and the reduction of other emissions such as nitrogen dioxide from cars and trucks. As a result, cars were equipped with catalytic converters and electrical-generating plants installed scrubbers and filters. In 1997, as required by law, the Environmental Protection Agency submitted "The Benefits and Costs of the Clean Air Act, 1970–1990" to Congress.

Undertaking such a cost-benefit analysis was not a trivial task. The authors of the report had to collect data on the cost of installing equipment to reduce emissions and to estimate the cost when the data were not available. Without lead, the cost of producing fuel that does not lead to engine knock increased. That too had to be factored in. The EPA estimated that the cost of compliance was approximately half a trillion dollars. The benefit side was even more complicated to estimate. Cleaner air means fewer respiratory problems such as asthma. But estimating the reduction in the number of asthmatic attacks is not easy and it is difficult to put a monetary value on not having an attack. People generally have an aesthetic preference for clean air (few people appreciate a yellow haze) and this too is difficult to price although we can observe how much more people will pay for property in a smog-free area. Cleaner air also resulted in less acid rain. Putting a dollar value on less acid rain is problematic, as well. Given all these difficulties, it is not surprising that the EPA's estimate of the benefit of the Clean Air Act over the ten-year period ranged by a factor of 10 – between $5.6 and $49.4 trillion. But even the lower value is significantly larger than the estimated cost. In the end it is nice to know that the benefits of the regulation clearly outweighed the costs and that so many economists were hired to undertake the study.

fans would be less likely to shove the person reaching for the ball, and, therefore, if the person dropped the ball, there would be no dispute regarding the reason why. With television cameras focused on where the ball would land, it would be relatively easy to determine whether there was any shoving.

The judge in the case ruled:

As a matter of fundamental fairness, Mr. Popov should have had the opportunity to try to complete his catch unimpeded by unlawful activity. To hold otherwise would be to allow the result in this case to be dictated by violence. . . . An award of the ball to Mr. Popov would be unfair to Mr. Hayashi. It would be premised on the assumption that Mr. Popov would have caught the ball. That assumption is not supported by the facts. An award of the ball to Mr. Hayashi would unfairly penalize Mr. Popov. It would be based on the assumption that Mr. Popov would have dropped the ball. That conclusion is also unsupported by the facts.... The court therefore declares that both plaintiff and defendant have an equal and undivided interest in the ball. In order to effectuate this ruling, the ball must be sold and the proceeds divided equally between the parties.[3]

D. CONCLUDING REMARKS

In this chapter, we have introduced a methodology for thinking about legal issues that incorporate core ideas from economics, including cost and benefits and incentives.

SUGGESTIONS FOR FURTHER READING

For legal, economic, and philosophical perspectives on cost-benefit analysis, see the *Journal of Legal Studies*, June 2000 issue, which is devoted to these topics.

REVIEW QUESTIONS

1. What are the steps that one might take in undertaking a cost-benefit analysis? (6)

    APPLICATIONS
    In each case try to determine the optimal allocation of the resource (ignoring court costs). You should perform a cost-benefit analysis. Among other things, the optimal outcome depends on relative costs of preventing the damage and the amount of damage. Do not use the law to explain your answer. The law is to be explained by economic reasoning. Note that generally there is no correct answer because you have not been presented with all the costs and benefits. It is how you argue that counts.

2. Should there be a two-hour parking limit on residential streets near a college campus (to prevent students from parking there all day)? (10) Hint: Who would buy out whom if one side owned the right to charge for parking spaces?

3. A person sets up a rest home for people with nonviolent psychological problems in a residential area. The neighbors complain. Should the hospital be allowed to stay? Ignore the issue of who was there first. (10)

4. In *Cornucopia Gold Mines v. Locken* 150 F.2d. 75 (1945), a trespasser was killed when she inadvertently touched a fallen high-voltage line hidden in the shrubbery. The high-voltage line was connected to the gold mine, which was in use intermittently. The gold mine owned the power plant that produced the electricity for the mine and a nearby town. The location of the accident was about a half mile off the road. Should Cornucopia be liable to the estate for the woman's death? (10)

5. *Fontainebleau Hotel Corporation v. Forty-five Twenty-Five, Inc.* 114 So.2d 357 (1959) involved two adjacent hotels, the Fontainebleau and the Eden Roc (owned by Forty-Five Twenty-Five) in Miami Beach. The Fontainebleau Hotel wanted to build a fourteen-story tower twenty feet from the northern edge of the property. This would create a

---

[3] See http://sportsillustrated.cnn.com/baseball/news/2002/12/18/bonds_ball_ap/ for more on this case.

shadow on Eden Roc's swimming pool that had been built on the southern portion of the Eden Roc property. The owners of Eden Roc received a temporary injunction, which prevented Fontainebleau from building the tower. Using the analytic tools developed in this book, determine whether the injunction should be made permanent. That is, using economic analysis determine whether Fontainebleau has the right to build a tower that casts a shadow on Eden Roc's swimming pool. Ignore who was first. (8) If the injunction were granted, does that mean that the addition would not be built? (2).

9 Smoking Regulations: Market Solutions to High-Transaction-Cost Situations

A. The Exchange of Rights to Smoke Often Involves High Transaction Costs 70

B. Cost-Benefit Analysis and the Role of Comparative Statics 70

C. Markets Provide the Answer 71

SUGGESTIONS FOR FURTHER READING 73

REVIEW QUESTIONS 74

REFERENCE 74

Should smokers have the entitlement to pollute the air or should nonsmokers have the right to smoke-free air? Should smoking be allowed on airplanes (in the United States it is not), in the workplace, in government buildings, or in restaurants and bars?

From Coase, we know that both smokers and nonsmokers may undertake action to reduce the damage to nonsmokers from smoke. Thus, we are not allowed to use any asymmetric arguments such as causation (because both sides are inputs) or restriction on freedom (because one side's freedom is always impinged upon – the freedom to smoke or the freedom to have smoke-free air). Instead, our argument will be based on efficiency grounds.

A. THE EXCHANGE OF RIGHTS TO SMOKE OFTEN INVOLVES HIGH TRANSACTION COSTS

We first note that in many (but not in all) situations the exchange of the right to smoke involves high transaction costs. For example, suppose that smokers were entitled to smoke in elevators. Even if nonsmokers valued smoke-free elevators more than smokers valued smoking, such an exchange would be unlikely to take place. First, it would be impossible to exchange rights if smokers had already left the elevator, though their smoke remained. Second, even if a smoker and nonsmoker simultaneously shared the elevator, the determination of the market-clearing price (which would depend on the particular preferences of the people involved) might take a considerable amount of time. The ride would be long over before any price could be established. Finally, if there were several nonsmokers, the free rider problem would arise. All nonsmokers benefit from smoke free air or equivalently are harmed by smoke.[1] If the smoker has an entitlement to smoke, each nonsmoker would like other nonsmokers to buy the right from the smoker. In this way, an individual nonsmoker would benefit from smoke free air and free ride on other nonsmokers paying for the right. This is an example of a pure externality: it is impossible to exclude any subset of nonsmokers from consuming smoke free air. If the nonsmokers had the right to no smoke (but it was legal to sell off the right), then each nonsmoker would try to be a monopoly holdout and capture all of the consumer surplus from the smokers. Thus, we have a situation of high transaction costs. In turn, this implies that if smokers (nonsmokers) are entitled to smoke (smoke free air) the right will not be exchanged even if nonsmokers (smokers) value the entitlement more.[2]

B. COST-BENEFIT ANALYSIS AND THE ROLE OF COMPARATIVE STATICS

The determination of the efficient outcome depends on costs and benefits, which, in turn, are based on preferences and technology. We illustrate with some outlandish examples to make the point. If smokers could purchase for one penny a device that made cigarettes smoke disappear, then we would expect that nonsmokers would have

---

[1] A smoker cannot be a free rider for smoking because the nonsmokers can sell the right to smoke to individual smokers. In contrast, all nonsmokers benefit from a nonsmoking policy.

[2] Even when transaction costs are low (for example, there is only one nonsmoker and one smoker together for a long period of time) and smoking is legal, we are unlikely to see the nonsmoker actually paying off the smoker not to smoke. However, we may observe requests that the person not smoke.

the right to no smoke.[3] If instead nonsmokers could put a little unobtrusive device on their heads, which kept smoke from their faces, then smokers would have the right to smoke. In these extreme cases, where benefits clearly outweigh costs, or vice versa, we can readily establish which side should have the right. But in many situations, the answer is not so clear. So, how do we arrive at an answer? There are three methods: (1) undertake a cost-benefit analysis, (2) undertake a comparative statics analysis, and (3) observe the market solution. (This last method will be covered in the next section.)

Cost-benefit analyses can be done with various levels of sophistication. At the sophisticated end, one can try to estimate how much the smokers are willing to pay to smoke and nonsmokers are willing to pay for smoke-free air (the data might be obtained by surveys or by more subtle statistical techniques). These numbers are then multiplied by the number of smokers and nonsmokers, respectively, to arrive at the total cost and benefit for each group. At the other end of the spectrum, one might base the cost-benefit analysis on introspection and casual observation. As noted in the previous chapter, an insightful method of deciding the allocation of rights and implicitly doing a cost-benefit analysis is to ask the following question: if bargaining were costless, would smokers end up with the right to smoke or would nonsmokers end up with the right to smoke free-air in airplanes? That is, which side values the right more? In surveying my classes, students usually argue that nonsmokers would end up with the right to smoke-free airplanes both because there are fewer smokers and because smoke is harmful to both smokers and nonsmokers.

In general, economists make *comparative statics predictions* rather than predictions regarding *level*. For example, economic theory predicts that, other things being equal, a *reduction in the price* of rutabagas will *increase the quantity* of rutabagas demanded by consumers; economic theory does not predict the *level* of rutabagas demanded in the first place. With regard to smoking, economists are more likely to make comparative statics predictions than to make cost-benefit calculations. The following illustrates comparative statics predictions: There are *fewer* rules against smoking outdoors because the cost of smoke in the open air is *relatively slight*. Hospitals are *more* likely than bars to have restrictions against smoking because the cost to patients from smoke is likely to be *greater* than the cost to bar patrons. Restrictions on the entitlement to smoke have *increased* in response to *increasing* scientific evidence that smoke harms both smokers and nonsmokers. So comparative statics analysis tells us that, other things being equal, if the cost of smoking goes up or the benefits go down, then the restrictions on smoking will not decrease and that in all likelihood they will increase. Comparative statics analysis will predict that airlines are less likely to impose nonsmoking rules than hospitals because the harm from smoke to passengers is less than the harm to patients, but it will not tell us whether airlines will or should impose such rules.

C. MARKETS PROVIDE THE ANSWER

Educated guesses can provide answers to the more clear-cut cases and more refined cost-benefit studies can give us some answers for the more problematic areas. However, in the

---

[3] Chewing gum laced with nicotine could be considered a smokeless substitute, but evidently smokers do not consider it to be a very good substitute.

absence of extensive research, is there any other way of determining whether smokers or nonsmokers should have the rights in airplanes, bars, and government-owned sports arenas?

The answer is yes. The method is to observe the market solution. It is quite clear that smokers implicitly buy the rights from nonsmokers in bars. At present, except in California and New York City, where smoking is not allowed, the owner of a bar can either allow smoking or prohibit it. Allowing smoke means that the smokers' demand for the bar increases while the nonsmokers' demand decreases. Banning smoke means that the nonsmokers are willing to pay more for drinks and smokers less. In this way, the externality problem of smokers is internalized with respect to the bar owner's profits. To increase profits, bar owners may try to attract a certain type of clientele, including bikers, lesbians, country music fans, college students, and the like, but this long list never includes nonsmokers. Evidently, nonsmoking drinkers do not value smoke-free air very much. Otherwise we would observe nonsmoking bars where nonsmokers compensated bar owners for the loss of customers who prefer to smoke when they drink. It is worthwhile to emphasize this point. When there are no government regulations against smoking, each bar owners can choose whether the bar will be smoke-free. One might expect that a sizable minority of bars would be smoke-free, but, as far as I can tell (not having visited them all), the number of smoke-free bars is close to zero when there are no government regulations against smoking.

Banning smoke makes nonsmokers better off; allowing smoke makes smokers better off. The argument here is that with regard to bars, *in principle* smokers could compensate nonsmokers for the smoke. This implicitly happens when profit-maximizing bar owners allow smoking. In contrast, a nonsmoking ban is inefficient because the evidence suggests that nonsmokers could not bribe smokers not to smoke in bars (even if there were no monopoly holdouts or other high transaction costs).

Sitting in a classroom one could come up with all kinds of reasons why nonsmokers would bribe smokers not to smoke (after all, who wants to get cancer). Indeed, the answer to my question posed earlier in the chapter has almost always been that the nonsmokers would end up with the right. But the market tells us differently. Before federal and state regulations, airline companies did not offer nonsmoking flights.[4] Because the passengers' willingness to pay for smoking (or nonsmoking) is reflected in the airlines' profits, and airlines are very aggressive in pursuing profits, we can reasonably assume that the virtual absence of any airline offering a nonsmoking policy indicated that the value to nonsmokers of smoke-free air was less than the value to smokers of being able to smoke. One could argue that a firm might fail to maximize profits; it is much harder to argue that a whole industry has failed to do so.

Hence, even a classroom composed of very bright students and a professor of economics should not be so arrogant as to believe that they know more about what maximizes profits in the airline industry than those whose incomes directly depend on airline

---

[4] Northwest Airlines began offering smoke-free flights shortly before regulation. A short-lived airline serving Los Angeles and Las Vegas also had a nonsmoking policy.

WHO OWNS THE CLOUDS

Cloud seeding is sometimes used to increase rain and at other times to reduce hail. Some people benefit from cloud seeding, but others may be harmed. For example, increased rain in one place may reduce the rain elsewhere. There have been a number of cases surrounding the issue of cloud seeding. Here we consider one such case, *Southwest Weather Research v. Rounsaville*, 320 S.W.2d 211 (1958).

Southwest Weather Research seeded clouds above ranch land to prevent hail on farmland. The ranchers alleged that the cloud seeding decreased rainfall on their land. The judge granted a temporary injunction to preserve the status quo ante (that is, Southwest Weather was not allowed to seed clouds). Southwest Weather appealed to the Texas Court of Civil Appeals and then to the Texas Supreme Court, both of which affirmed the issuance of the temporary injunction.

The court stated the following: "We believe that the landowner is entitled ... to such rainfall as may come from clouds over his own property that Nature, in her caprice, may provide. It follows, therefore, that this enjoyment of the benefits of Nature should be protected by the courts if interfered with improperly and unlawfully.... We do not mean to say or imply ... that the landowner has a right to prevent or control weather modification over land not his own. We do not pass upon that point here, and we do not intend any implication to that effect."

At the time of this case, there were neither state nor federal statutes or regulations on cloud seeding.

profitability. Likewise, one should ask who has a comparative advantage, Congress or the airline companies, in deciding what airline passengers value the most (smoking or nonsmoking). The answer is the airlines.

Of course, even if a majority of airlines had chosen to have smoke-free flights, this does not mean that there should be a regulation requiring all flights to be smoke-free. It is inefficient to force people with different tastes to consume identical items when people are willing to pay for items with different characteristics. We do not regulate that all cars look alike, and we should not regulate that all airlines provide the same amenities like leather seats, in-flight movies, or smoking policies. Instead, the market solution should serve either as a legal default rule (the rule that holds unless there is an express statement to the contrary) or as a guide for policies in areas where transaction costs are high. For example, smoking policies in public playgrounds might use smoking policies in private amusement parks as a guide for the appropriate policy.

SUGGESTIONS FOR FURTHER READING

Tollison and Wagner (1992) take a very strong stand against smoking regulations. Here is as good a place as any to state that I do not always agree with arguments made in the suggested readings.

REVIEW QUESTIONS

1. Explain why freedom to smoke and freedom not to smoke are symmetric concepts (3)
2. When are transaction costs high regarding the right to smoke (not smoke). Why? (5) When are transaction costs low (internalized)? (3)
3. Explain how technology might alter the efficient allocation of the rights (to smokers or nonsmokers). (2)
4. Show how profit-maximizing firms implicitly give the right to smoke or not to that side which values it the most. (7)

REFERENCE

Tollison, Robert D., and Richard E. Wagner. (1992). *The Economics of Smoking.* Boston: Kluwer Academic Publishers.

10 | Rules of Thumb: Sports and Driving Rules

A. Theoretical Model 76

B. Highway Safety 77
   1. Four-Way Stop Signs 77
   2. Other Traffic Situations 79

C. Sports Activity 80
   1. Skill as an Allocator 80
   2. The Allocation of Rights to Play in Unorganized Play: Marginal
      Productivity and Majority Rule 84
   3. Degrees of Complexity 85

D. Concluding Remarks 87

SUGGESTIONS FOR FURTHER READING 87

REVIEW QUESTIONS 87

REFERENCES 87

Rules of thumb such as "first come, first served," "the person on the right has the right-of-way," and "majority rule" are used in our everyday lives and are often enforced by legal sanctions. Such rules are often used as substitutes for ordinary economic markets when the price system involves high transaction costs, and as initial allocators of rights to facilitate the exchange of rights when transaction costs are low. Presumably, those rules that survive are the efficient ones.

In this chapter, I consider a number of rules of thumb and show how changes in technology and objective determine the appropriate rule. Testable propositions are developed, mainly within the context of highway safety and sporting activity. These situations are examples of cases where rights are often not transferable and severely limited in time – sometimes labeled as communal rights. The basic concepts will be introduced within the context of highway safety rules, while the main part of the analysis will be devoted to the allocation of rights in sports.

A. THEORETICAL MODEL

If information and decision making were costless, then every decision would involve weighing all the costs and benefits, for example, the decision as to which car should have the right-of-way at an intersection would depend on which side valued the right more. Because information processing and decision making are not costless, we may rely on some method that economizes on these costs. In ordinary economic markets, a price system is very effective in eliciting information concerning relative value. Unfortunately, in many situations the transactions costs involved in instituting a price system outweigh the benefits of demand revelation. This will tend to be the case when the costs of allocating the rights to the wrong person are minor, and when the price system is less successful in demand revelation (for example, when there are public goods). This characterizes the types of situations discussed in this chapter. General rules tend to economize on decision-making costs. Thus, rules of thumb are a substitute for both a price system and a complete investigation of relative value in each particular situation.

The basic theoretical argument is that only the most efficient rules will be implemented. Like all of economics, the analysis is based on costs and benefits. Those rules that involve the least costs and provide the greatest benefits will be used. This straightforward application of economics provides answers to questions such as the following: Which rule of thumb is chosen? When will rules of thumb be more or less complex? Under what conditions will different groups of people use different rules of thumb?

Different rules of thumb have different properties, thereby encouraging different outcomes and having different cost configurations. Economic efficiency dictates that, other things being equal, the more costly a rule of thumb is to use, the less likely it will be used. Two types of costs are relevant: costs associated with monitoring the rule of thumb and inappropriate incentives created by the rule. A rule of thumb is by its very nature supposed to save on information costs. If the information costs are very high, the rule of thumb is no longer maintaining its proper function. Furthermore, the rule should not create incentives for costly allocative behavior. We do not want to encourage costly production of an activity whose sole end is allocation rather than an increase in present or future consumption. To illustrate, in restaurants without reservations, those who show up first get seated first (if there is a table of the appropriate size). This simple rule of thumb reflects preferences – those who want to eat earlier will show up earlier.

Suppose instead that the restaurant provided seating to those who were wearing the most clothes. This might be very costly to the patrons when the weather was hot and disputes about who was really wearing the most clothes might easily arise. It is not surprising that such a rule of thumb does not exist. In a nutshell, we want a system with low transaction costs. In turn, "costs" depend on the problem at hand. For example, when time is at a premium, which is often the case in highway safety, split-second rules of thumb are desirable.

The nature and the amount of benefits also determine the kind of rules chosen. Different objectives create different demands. A rule of thumb that encourages safety on the highway is unlikely to be the same rule of thumb that encourages thrills in sporting events. If the benefits are substantial, it pays to have more complex rules or more accurate, albeit more costly, methods.

B. HIGHWAY SAFETY

1. Four-Way Stop Signs

It is useful to consider the issues within a very clear-cut case – the appropriate allocation of entitlements at a street intersection with a four-way stop sign. The law states that the first car that comes to the intersection has the entitlement to proceed first; if both arrive at the same time, the car to the right has the right-of-way; and if the cars are facing each other, the car making a left turn does not have the right-of-way. Before explaining why this set of rules is the most efficient method of allocating rights, I will first show why other methods either have high transaction costs or do not allocate the right to the party that is likely to value it the most.

a. Price System.   In ordinary economic markets, the price system is a very effective method of determining relative economic value with minimal transaction costs. However, in traffic situations, the transaction costs of a price system outweigh by far any benefits of it correctly allocating the rights to individual parties. For example, we might have an auctioneer who gives the right-of-way to the person willing to pay the highest price. Clearly, the price system would have very high administrative costs. We cannot get rid of the auctioneer and have the participants bribe each other, as the rights have not been established in the first place. Even if they were, it would still involve high transaction costs.

A price system, in the absence of administrative costs, can achieve Pareto optimality because the one individual can buy off the other so that both are made better off; unfortunately, in this case, the transaction costs outweigh the benefits. However, the concept of a pricing system with zero negotiation costs is a useful fiction. Whenever negotiation costs are high, one should ask who would end up with the rights if the transaction costs were low.

b. Cost-Benefit Analysis.   An economist could account for number of passengers, wait time, opportunity cost, and the like and then estimate which carload of passengers would benefit most from being first. I like this approach because it would increase the demand for economists and presumably my own salary would increase as well. However, this is a costly method (economists are not free) and not as accurate in determining relative value as an auction.

c. Majority Rule.   Another method is majority rule. The car with the most passengers has the right-of-way. In the absence of other information, majority rule is a good estimate of greater value. We have no reason to believe that the individual people in the car with fewer passengers value the right-of-way more or less than the passengers in the car with more passengers. In consequence, we would expect the *total* value to be greater in the car with more passengers. That is, where negotiation costs are high and a pricing system is not feasible, granting rights to the majority is a good rule of thumb for determining efficient allocations. Other things being equal, we would expect the majority to bribe the minority and obtain the rights if negotiation costs were low. Because convertibles are not very popular, it is more time consuming to count people than to give the right to the first comer or the person on the right. So majority rule is also ruled out.[1]

d. Rank.   A forth method is rank. A Cadillac might have the right-of-way over a Chevrolet. Again this might be a reasonable rule of thumb for achieving Pareto optimality. If there were a price mechanism for buying and selling rights, even if the right were initially assigned to the Chevrolet, the Cadillac owner would probably purchase it. Rights (privileges) at intersections are likely to be normal goods; that is, higher income will result in a greater demand. Because Cadillac owners tend to be richer than Chevrolet owners, we would expect Cadillac owners to purchase the right. This rule has some drawbacks, however. It would encourage people to buy Cadillacs, which involves a social cost. A second problem is that it may take too much time to determine rank. The one ranking we do allow is priority for police cars and ambulances, which are readily identifiable (but not unmarked police cars). Again we would expect this to be an efficient allocation of rights.

e. Skill.   Another method, which is more common in sports, is a test of skill. In this case, better drivers would get the right-of-way. It is plausible to believe that people who are more skilled in an activity derive more pleasure from the activity. First, if they enjoy the activity, then they will undertake the activity more often and thereby gain greater skill through practice. Second, if a person is naturally more skilled in one area, he will be more productive at gaining utility in that area. For both these reasons, we tend to see individuals undertaking both consumption and production in areas where they are comparatively skilled. If the more skilled get greater utility from the activity than the less skilled, then rewarding the more skilled is likely to increase efficiency. Other things being equal, and in the absence of other information, this is a reasonable assumption, we would expect the more skilled to end up with the rights (even if the rights were initially assigned to the less skilled) when transaction costs are zero. Despite these arguments, a skill test at a four-way stop sign is impractical.

f. First Come, First Served.   In the context of a four-way stop sign, "first come, first served" is a very appropriate allocating device. In the first place, it is very easy to determine. It is also less costly in terms of time. Clearly, it would be silly for the first car to wait a minute or two for the next car to come to see whether it should go first or

---

[1]   There are places where a bus has priority over a car.

not, according to some other criterion. Even when the difference in time involves only a second or two, we would expect that, in a low transaction cost case, the first person would end up with the rights; the extra cost in terms of time of his going second is greater than the extra cost of the second person going second.

g. Random.   Another mechanism of property rights allocation is a random allocation – flip of the coin, toss of a racket, and so on. In this case, being on the right is a random allocation since in a circle (four-way stop sign) being to the right is not transitive (while being earlier in a first come, first served situation will ensure that you have prior rights over all cars that come later).

Of the many random allocators, being on the right is the most efficient because it involves much lower costs than other alternatives, such as flipping a coin. It is also preferable to giving the rights to the person on the left. If the person on the right has the right-of-way and goes straight, he blocks the person on the left when he crosses the first lane. If the person on the left has the right-of-way and he goes straight, he blocks the person on his right when he crosses the second lane. Thus, giving rights to the person on the left involves a more costly allocation. In England, where they drive on the other side of the road, the driver on the left has the right-of-way.

2. Other Traffic Situations

Prices; majority rule; rank; first come, first served; tests of skill; and random selection are some of the more common methods of allocating property rights. Different circumstances will result in different rules of thumb being more efficient. Let us now turn toward the issue of predicting which method will be the most appropriate.

First come, first served is a very common rule in highway regulation (for example, the driver proceeding ahead of you in your lane has rights to her space), but it is by no means the only one. Other rules exist when they are either cheaper to administer or better predictors of relative valuation.

a. Majority Rule Used When Monitoring Costs Are Low.   Majority rule is more likely to be used when it is relatively easy to ascertain. The use of two-way stop signs at a four-way intersection is an example of majority rule. The drivers on the more heavily traveled road generally have the right-of-way even if they are not first at the intersection. Traffic signals with a longer green light for traffic on one of the cross streets is a compromise between majority rule and first come, first served. As another example, a slow-moving vehicle must pull to the side if followed by five or more cars and it is unsafe to pass but safe to pull aside.[2] Under this circumstance, first come, first served accedes to the more efficient majority rule.

b. Other Rules Used When They Are Better Estimators of Relative Value.   Both majority rule and first come, first served are inefficient in the following situation: on a narrow road, the vehicle descending should yield the right-of-way to the vehicle ascending and if necessary back up. Why not first come, first served? First, it is probably impossible to establish. Should we put a special marker halfway down the road so we

---

[2] My referent is always the California traffic code.

can determine who was first? Second, an alternative rule provides a quick and better prediction of which party would buy the rights in a zero transaction cost situation. The person in the more dangerous position should be given any advantage. It is more difficult and dangerous to back up and go downhill at the same time than to back up and go up the hill because backing down creates the possibility of accelerating dangerously downhill (both gravity and motor are pushing downhill). Thus, the person going uphill has the right-of-way. This rule is a better estimator of relative value than either first come, first served or majority rule.

c. Skill as an Allocator of the Right to Drive.   The decision regarding who has the rights (a license) to drive is based on skill. Again, because of high transaction costs, the pricing system is not a very good rule of thumb. While the transfer of a right to the highest bidder is usually efficient, it is not the case when there are negative externalities. In this case, individual bad drivers might outbid individual good drivers for the right to drive. Collectively, the good drivers could bribe the bad drivers not to drive, but the organizational costs would be too high for this to ever take place.

C. SPORTS ACTIVITY

The methodology developed in Section B can be applied to a variety of other areas, including etiquette, sports rules, and parliamentary procedure. I will concentrate on sports rules for two reasons: (1) similar rules of thumb are used in both highway safety and sports (for example, first come, first served); yet, the objectives of these two activities are not closely related; and (2) meaningful statistical data can be collected (which may not be the case for other areas, such as etiquette).

I will show how technological aspects of each sport determine which rule is chosen for allocating rights. For each sport, the following questions can be asked: What mechanism is used in establishing who has the entitlement to play in organized and unorganized activity? At the start of play, what type of rule is used in granting advantageous rights to one team or another (for example, who gets to serve first)? After play has been initiated, what type of rule is used in granting advantageous rights to one team or another after a point has been scored? And in what circumstances will rules in unorganized play differ from rules in organized play? Both rules that have been codified and more casual rules of thumb will be considered.

1. Skill as an Allocator
a. The Right to Play.   *Skill will be an allocator of the right to play when skill is relatively easy to determine and skill has a greater payoff to the participants.* Thus, professional and organized play will tend to use skill more than nonprofessional and nonorganized play as a determiner of the rights to play. In the first place, spectators will pay more to see skilled playing than nonskilled playing. That is, skill is a derived demand. Hence, only the most skilled teams play in the Stanley Cup Playoff, World Series, or the Super Bowl.[3] Furthermore, in organized play, skill rankings for postseason playoffs (as in hockey) or in seeding for tournaments (as in tennis) are relatively easy to determine because the

---

[3] Granting rights to play to the more skilled encourages greater skill.

team (or players) have played against each other or against comparable players. Contrast this with three or four people vying to play at a city tennis court. Here skill would be a very costly method of allocating rights. Furthermore, skill would not be as good a determiner of relative value.

Skill is less likely to be used as an allocator of rights at the beginning of a game than during the game where skill is more readily determined. Furthermore, *if skill is used, a special skill task (whose sole purpose is to determine allocation of rights) is more likely to be used at the beginning of play than during the game.* Finally, *skill is more likely to be used at the beginning of a game for those games in which skill is readily determined (at the beginning) than for those games where skill is costly to ascertain.*

b. Allocation at the Beginning of the Game.   Starting with the last point first, in many games it is extremely difficult (i.e., costly) to determine skill before the start of the game. Therefore, a skill mechanism is not used. For example, in tennis how does one determine skill starting from a neutral position without actually playing the game? To determine who serves first, should we have one play where one person serves first? This clearly makes no sense. At one time it was common in casual play to hit the ball over the net three times before a point could be scored to determine who got to serve first. But, unfortunately, this gives an unfair advantage to the person who hits the ball over the third time. To determine who shoots first in billiards, each side tries to hit the ball closest to the opposite edge (cushion). The person getting the closest obtains the entitlement to shoot first. In billiards this is a low-cost procedure, but a comparable method in tennis would be impossible. For example, if both tried to see who could serve closest to the back line, it would be very difficult to determine as the ball keeps on moving and the players would be too far away to judge. Thus, a random mechanism (spinning the racket) is used instead of a skill device.[4] In contrast, skill is much easier to determine in basketball. In casual play, each side may shoot baskets from the foul line to determine who gets the ball first. In professional play, the ball is tossed up by a referee. Both sides then jump for the ball.

c. Allocation during the Game vis-à-vis the Beginning.   Information on skill is readily obtained throughout the game. Therefore, allocation according to skill is more likely during the game than at the beginning of the game where a test of skill is relatively more costly. Thus football, badminton, and squash use a random method to allocate rights at the beginning of play (for example, in football the winner of the toss receives the kickoff), but a skill mechanism to determine allocation thereafter (for example, in football the side that scored kicks off to the other side).

When there is a tie game and the tie must be broken, skill during the game no longer differentiates, and a random device is again likely to be used. In both American football and ultimate Frisbee, a coin (or Frisbee) is tossed at the end of a tie game to determine who gains possession of the ball or the Frisbee. A special skill test to determine the right to receive the ball or Frisbee would be redundant for the skill test itself could then be used as a tie breaker.

[4] Spinning rackets (in racket games) and tossing coins are inexpensive random allocation methods. However, many children's games such as hide-and-seek do not have rackets and small children rarely carry money; therefore, rhymes such as "eeny-meeny" are substituted. For small children, the end result of an eeny-meeny rhyme is not predictable and thus appears random.

d. Special Skill Device.   (i) During the game vis-à-vis the beginning: if a special skill device is used solely for allocating rights (for example, the tip-off in basketball), it is more likely to be used at the beginning of the game than during the middle of the game. The reason is again on economic efficiency grounds. During the game, skill measures are obtained costlessly as a by-product of play. Thus, if a skill measure is used after a point has been scored, it is unnecessary to devise a special method. The cost of a special allocation device becomes prohibitive if it must be used very often. The history of basketball is illustrative. In basketball, at the beginning of a game there is a tip-off (a ball is tossed up in the air by a referee and one player from each side tries to tip it off to another player on his side). Formerly, after a basket was made, another tip-off took place, but this rule was inefficient. A tip-off after a basket has been made is redundant because the making of the basket is already a skill indicator. Setting up the players for a tip-off is time consuming, and it emphasizes skills that are not perfectly correlated with skills needed in the rest of the game. This means that scarce resources will be used to succeed in this allocation mechanism that are not appropriate for the rest of the game (in particular, excessive height without other basketball skills). Over time, there was a great increase in the number of points scored in a basketball game, making what would ordinarily appear to be a minor cost into a major misallocation of resources.[5] Therefore, this rule was abolished.

Hockey is a useful comparison to basketball. A face-off (the analog to the tip-off) is still used after every point. But there are two essential differences: the skills needed in the face-off are the same as those in the rest of the game, and there are very few points scored in a hockey game (rarely more than ten) so that the costs of redundantly measuring skill are minor.[6]

(ii) Property rights versus communal rights: *a special skill device is also more likely to be used in determining the allocation of rights when the allocation involves an important property right rather than an unimportant communal right.* A communal right is the right to use and not to exclude, while a property right involves exclusion. Thus in horseshoes, golf, and figure skating, the sequence of players is a communal right (no matter how skilled the previous players, all others will still get their turn). A special skill task would be a waste of time for such a trivial right. In contrast, possession of the hockey puck is a valuable property right (it not only provides an opportunity for scoring but also it reduces the time available to the other team), and therefore a special skill allocation is more reasonable.

e. Rewarding Skilled or Unskilled?   In basketball, American football, and soccer, if a team scores a point, the other team obtains the advantageous rights (possession of the ball). In volleyball and badminton, if a team scores a point, it keeps the advantageous

---

[5] Because basketball is a recent sport, the tip-off during the middle of the game may be seen as an early experiment that did not survive. The following quote from *Illustrated Basketball Rules* is insightful. "The elimination of the center jump after a score in 1937–38 was probably the most significant change in the history of the rules. No other rule change has been more experimented with and researched over a longer period of time than this one."

[6] Face-offs during the game are still used in other low-scoring games such as field hockey and lacrosse. However, championship ringers (marbles), pool, English billiards, and carom billiards have a special skill allocator (closest to the line in marbles, closest to the cushion in the other games) only at the beginning of the game. Shooting for the closest ball to the cushion every time a ball was pocketed in pool would be exceedingly costly and unnecessary. It would also be inefficient to repeat a random allocation. Thus, in tennis one spins the racket to determine who serves first, and then there is an alternation of the service. One does not spin the racket after each game.

rights (the right to serve, which is a prerequisite for scoring). In high jump and pole vault, if a person has three consecutive failures, he loses the right to jump. When skill is used as an allocator during a game, it is sometimes used to reward skill positively and other times to reward skill negatively. What is the explanation for the differential treatment of skill? The answer to this question is more tentative than the results in the rest of this chapter as there are exceptions to the theoretical results. As a consequence, here more than elsewhere, I emphasize that the propositions are statistical in nature (if *x*, then *y* is more likely). Essentially, the answer depends upon the fact that *many rules are derived demands, the interests of spectators determining the allocation of rights.*

(i) *Objective Sports Reward Skill:* In those games where the teams or players compete in terms of some objective measure (shortest time, highest or longest distance) without interference from the other players or teams, spectators want to see a record broken. As a consequence, if skill is used to allocate rights, it will be used to reward skill positively. For example, if there are more than eight contestants in javelin, shotput, discus, or hammer throw, the normal six trials are divided into two parts. Only the eight contestants with the longest distance in the first set of three trials can participate in the second set. As another example, in high jump, pole vault, long jump, and triple jump, a contestant is eliminated after three consecutive failures.

(ii) *Offensive-Defensive Sports Reward Unskilled:* In sports where the teams work against each other and there is an offense and a defense (such as basketball, American football, and soccer), the spectator obtains relatively greater thrills from a close contest.[7] As a result, to make the game closer, scoring points will more likely result in a loss of an advantageous right.[8] This will be especially so when the sport has many spectators (i.e., the derived demand of the spectators is very important) and when the rights granted are more akin to property rights than communal rights. For example, baseball grants communal rights: when a skilled team scores (without an "out" being made), it gets the opportunity to score again. However, no matter how many runs have been scored by a team and how much time the team has taken at bat, the other team still gets its turn. In contrast, in basketball and football, possession of the ball (an advantageous right) by one team reduces the time available to the other team. If the property right of excludability were given to the team which scored, the game would be less close and less exciting for the spectators. The team that scored would tend to be very cautious about losing possession of its advantageous right. Scoring would tend to be more lopsided, resulting in uninteresting final quarters where one team would be so far ahead that the other team would not have a chance to win in the time remaining.

(iii) *Historical Evidence*: Persuasive evidence for the demand for closeness is found when there are rule changes over time or when the sport is organized along two or more different modes. In offense-defense games, changes over time will be in the direction of giving advantageous rights to the team that has not scored rather than to the team that did. The previously discussed basketball rule change (1937–38) is an example. When the tip-off was no longer used, the team *not* gaining the point was given the right. In

---

[7] Spectators also derive financial benefits from betting, which is facilitated by evenly matched teams (the point spread is one method of compensating for inequality).

[8] Bullfighting has a number of rules that promote the equality between the bull and the bullfighter. For example, the picador is allowed a second thrust if the bull has injured the horse and is still running forward; reserve picadors are allowed into the game if a picador is injured. Thus, increased skill of the bull gives more advantageous rights to the bullfighter, and vice versa.

hockey the following rule change was made during the 1956–57 season. A player serving a minor penalty was now allowed to return when the opposing team scored a goal.

(iv) *Differing Rules under Differing Modes of Organization*: Many sports have several modes of organization. Automobile racing is the largest spectator sport in the United States. For major events such as the Indianapolis 500, where a major speed record may be broken and the cars are closely matched, the fastest car in the preheat gets the pole position (an advantageous, nontransferable property right). In contrast, in local races the fastest car is often put in a disadvantageous position to make the competition more equal because the cars are not so evenly matched and a major speed record is unlikely.[9] Perhaps even more important, if the fastest car does not get the pole position, a crash is more likely.

In unorganized neighborhood basketball, the team making the basket sometimes loses the ball to the other side and sometimes keeps the ball. There are no spectators in this sport, so the demand for a close game is not the reason for the variation. But here the demands of the players themselves (including the winning team) are important. For example, the demand by the third team (waiting to play the winner) is for the game to be over as soon as possible (which is more likely if the scorer gains possession of the ball). This is to be contrasted with organized basketball where there are more spectators and a greater demand for a close game and as a consequence the scoring team always loses possession of the ball.

2. The Allocation of Rights to Play in Unorganized Play: Marginal Productivity and Majority Rule

Majority rule and first come, first served are commonly used measures of relative value when the administrative costs of a price system make an ordinary market inefficient. Other things being equal, more people would buy out the right from fewer people, and those who come earlier and wait longer would buy out the right to play first from those who come later. Other things are not equal, however, and as a result, we have a choice between two imperfect measures of relative value. *When marginal productivity of a player is strongly positive, majority rule will prevail over first come, first served as a method of allocating access to public sports facilities. When marginal productivity is negative, majority rule will be a poor measure of relative value and first come, first served will be the prevailing method of allocation.*

a. The Marginal Productivity of a Tennis Player.

On public tennis courts, singles generally have priority over a solitary player even if the person was there first; however, doubles do not have priority over singles (although doubles may sometimes be allowed to have the court for a longer period of time), and triples never have priority over doubles. This can be explained in terms of marginal productivity. One person does not gain very much from being on a tennis court alone. The cost to the solitary player in not being able to play on the court is small in comparison to the benefits to the pair of single players being on the court. Thus majority rule prevails over first come, first served.[10] It should be noted that with the advent of serving machines and ball

---

[9]   Horse racing and harness racing have handicap and nonhandicap racing. The choice between the two run somewhat along the same lines as automobile racing. For example, the major horse racing events in the United States (Kentucky, Preakness, and Belmont) are not handicapped.

[10]   Solitary players who arrive first could be given the rights. Players with partners who arrived later could bribe the solitary players for the right. However, this would be inefficient. A needless transaction would take place.

sweeps, the marginal productivity of a solitary player is increased. As a consequence, solitary players in private tennis clubs commonly have the right to the tennis court even when doubles are waiting. Doubles do not have priority over singles, however, even on public courts. First come, first served has priority and is used instead of majority rule. Why? While majority rule is an estimate of a Pareto optimal allocation, it is not a very good estimator in this case, for it is not clear that doubles would buy off a pair of singles. If doubles were given priority over singles, this would create inefficient incentives for people to play in doubles to obtain the rights even when they preferred to play singles. Because singles is played harder, the marginal productivity of additional time decreases faster for single play; and thus, there is often a shorter time period for singles.

b. The Technology of Basketball.   In comparing basketball and tennis, we find different technologies and different sets of rules for establishing rights. The technology of basketball allows for greatly varying size teams (from one to five) and varying quality of players. These two attributes often make merger an efficient solution. If four players arrive at a basketball court with only two players, the four players cannot usurp the two players' right to play, and often the two players cannot keep the court to themselves. Typically, all six players will play on three-player teams. Or, if the court has two baskets, one game can be played at each basket, since the character of the game is only slightly changed when the play is only on half court. In fact, half court is generally preferred when there are very small teams. This is not possible in tennis.

It is very hard to organize six, eight, or ten people to play; so pickup (where players discover other players to play with at the court) is more common in basketball than in tennis where the organization costs are lower. Typically, there are many people coming and going in basketball pickup games; it is thus very hard to remember who came first. If there are an odd number of people practicing and a game is then organized, first come, first served is not a good rule because it is difficult to determine, and majority rule is meaningless. Fortunately, there is an alternative – shooting baskets from the foul line (not being blocked by the other side). Consequently, we would expect skill to allocate the rights to play in unorganized play relatively more often in basketball than in tennis. This is, in fact, the case.

3. Degrees of Complexity

Other things being equal, when the costs of making a mistaken allocation are large, rules of thumb will tend to be more complex. Clearly, vehicle codes are more extensive and complex than pedestrian codes. The same holds true in sports. In both polo and yachting, there are very detailed rights of way. In polo the rider going closest to the line in which the ball was hit has the right-of-way. If they both are of equal closeness, the rider to the right has the right-of-way. If both riders are riding along the same line, but in opposite directions, the rider going in the same direction as the path of the ball has the right-of-way. Field hockey does not have these complex rules. The reason for the difference is that the maneuverability of a horse is less than the maneuverability of a person, and the cost of collision is much greater in polo than in field hockey.

Furthermore, many individuals would come to the tennis court solely to get the right, which they would then transfer for a fee. This would increase the inefficiency.

PEDESTRIANS, KNIGHTS, AND CARRIAGES

What determines whether pedestrians, knights, and carriages proceed on the right or on the left of the road? The answer depends to a large extent on the fact that most people are right-handed. If you are a knight, you have your sword or lance in your right hand and want your weapon to be within striking distance of your enemy who is coming from the opposite direction. When you have a lance, you hold your weapon in your right hand and move it left to knock off the opposing knight from his horse. Therefore, you ride your horse on the right side of the barrier. The same issue arises in designing castles. The circular staircases wind up in a clockwise direction. The attackers have their swords crunched against the center axis, while the defenders who are coming down the stairs have much more freedom of movement. Because, drivers of horse-drawn carriages typically used their right hand to whip the horse, it made sense that the driver was on the right (unless they were driving a stagecoach and were high above and in the middle). To not hit the carriage coming from the opposite direction, it was best that both drivers were close to the center of the road so that they could more accurately judge how close the two carriages were. This suggests that carriage traffic was on the left. Pedestrians generally carry things in their right arms. People are less likely to knock into each other if their free arm is in the center of pedestrian traffic; and this way, even if they do knock into each other, the packages are less likely to be knocked down. Therefore, pedestrians tend to walk on the right to avoid contact in contrast to knights with lances who proceed on the right to increase contact. So what about cars? The gearshift is in the middle. The first gearshifts were hard to use and it made sense that the driver would be on the left and the right hand would be used for shifting. Again to best avoid collisions with oncoming traffic, it makes sense that the driver is closest to the center of the road. The optimal solution is to drive on the right. So what is the explanation for the United Kingdom and most of its former colonies where driving is on the left? The best answer I can provide is that they maintained the same rules when switching from carriages to automobiles (it is also the law of the sea).

RULES FOR GIRLS' BASKETBALL WERE DIFFERENT

In the 1930s and 1940s and in some places until the early 1980s, rules for high school basketball were different for girls. The court was divided into thirds. Forwards were only allowed in the third nearest the offensive basket, the center in the middle, and the guards in the other third. This was to make sure that the players did not overexert themselves. Players were only allowed to dribble twice, but they could throw the ball up into the air and catch it. According to the 1955–56 *Official Basketball Guide*, play during menstrual period was subject to approval by the woman directly in charge.

Because of the great cost of an accident in yachting, there are even more rules regarding right-of-way. Yachting, like other sports where players compete in terms of some objective measure without interference from the other team, has rules to prevent interference. Most of the rules give the right-of-way to the yacht, which is less able to maneuver or has less visibility. The capsized boat has the right-of-way, and the yacht that is overtaking another must keep clear of the preceding yacht. Thus the "least cost avoider" is the one who is liable, while the other has the right-of-way.

D. CONCLUDING REMARKS

First come, first served; majority rule; skill; and random mechanisms are some of the rules used to allocate rights in traffic and sports. Despite the disparate nature of these activities, the choice of rules relies on the same economic principles. The rule of thumb chosen should neither have high monitoring costs nor create incentives for costly but undesired behavior. Depending on the situation, differing demands, marginal productivities, and monitoring costs will result in different rules of thumb being chosen.

SUGGESTIONS FOR FURTHER READING

See Wittman (1983) for more sport and traffic rules and Epstein (2002) for parking rules.

REVIEW QUESTIONS

1. On what basis, should we choose rules of thumb? Explain. (4)
2. Suggest some alternative methods of allocating rights to proceed first in a four-way intersection. Suggest when each is the most efficient method of allocation. (10)
3. What determines how we allocate the rights to play and the rights to have an advantageous position within a game? (10)
4. Why do knights with lances ride on the right and pedestrians walk on the right? (4)

REFERENCES

Epstein, Richard A. (2002). The Allocation of the Commons: Parking on Public Roads. 31 *Journal of Legal Studies* 515.

Wittman, Donald A. (1982). Efficient Rules of Thumb in Highway Safety and Sporting Activity. 72 *American Economic Review* 78.

IV RIGHTS

There are different possible allocations of entitlements (person X but not person Y may have the entitlement to draw water from a stream), and there are different ways of protecting entitlements. For example, X may have the right to draw water from the stream, the right to prevent anyone else from drawing water from the stream, and the right to sell his entitlement (this is known as a property right). Alternatively, X may have the right to draw water from the stream but not the right to prevent Y from also drawing water (this is known as a communal right). As a third alternative, X might not be able to prevent Y from drawing water from X's stream, but the courts might determine the amount of money that Y must pay X for drawing the water (in this case, X's entitlement is protected by a liability rule). As a fourth alternative, X might provide water to Y without Y's prior consent and then demand payment from Y (this is known as a restitution rule). In the absence of transaction costs, the various methods would result in identical outcomes. But transaction costs are not zero. Part IV provides a transaction cost explanation for choosing one method of protecting entitlements over another.

Chapter 11 provides the framework of analysis. Property rights, communal rights, liability rules, and regulation are discussed at some length. We first show why entitlements are protected. We then provide reasons for the choice of one method over the other. For example, communal rights are employed when the misallocation arising from individuals shifting the cost onto others is not sufficiently large to overcome the cost of enforcing property rights, where such shifting does not occur.

Chapter 12 discusses the choice between property rights and communal rights in information. A property right to knowledge allows the owner of information to sell the information at a price, thereby encouraging the gathering of information in the first place. However, communal rights in knowledge mean that the information is freely available and not artificially restricted by a price above the marginal cost of disseminating the information. In this context, we discuss patents, the duty to disclose, blackmail, as well as other topics.

Chapter 13 considers the choice between liability for harm and restitution for benefit. The legal system generally punishes for harms while the private sector typically rewards for benefits. We first show that the harm-benefit distinction is meaningless in the absence of transaction costs. We then show why in the presence of transaction costs, the choice between liability and restitution makes perfectly good sense.

As a general rule, governments are required to compensate the owner for appropriating the owner's land even if the amount taken by the government is very small. However, governments in general are not required to compensate landowners for diminution of value due to a regulation, even if the regulation severely harms the landowner (as would be the case if a factory was forced to stop production). In Chapter 14, we consider the takings clause of the U.S. Constitution. We explain why the entitlement is protected by a liability rule (compensation is made) when land is taken, but typically not when rights to use the land in a certain way are taken away.

11

The Protection of Entitlements: Why One Method Is Chosen Over Another

A. Property Rights 92

B. Liability Rules 94

C. Communal Rights 96

D. Regulation of the Inputs 97

E. Concluding Remarks 100

SUGGESTIONS FOR FURTHER READING 100

REVIEW QUESTIONS 101

REFERENCES 101

An entitlement is a set of rights. For example, the entitlement to a specific piece of land may give you the right to grow crops (but not poppies), keep others off your land (but not shoot them if they trespass), and sell it (but not the right to force others to buy it). In a nutshell, an entitlement is the freedom to use resources in a certain way and the freedom to prevent others from using those same resources in certain ways.

The rights are bundled with each other because in general the owner of one right is likely to be the person who values the other right most highly (this is just another application of Coase). A simple illustration is the entitlement to bodily integrity. In general, and certainly before recent advances in surgery, the person who values a person's kidneys, stomach, and heart the most is the person in whom these parts reside. It certainly would create unnecessary transaction costs if someone else owned your stomach. A more down-to-earth example involves the rights that go with ownership of farmland. The right to grow wheat includes the right to decide when to plant the seed and the right to till the soil.

In certain cases, split ownership of rights may be value maximizing. A farmer is unlikely to own the space one mile above the land, and it is possible that the farmer does not own the land 50 feet below. Indeed, property owners often sell off the right to the oil, coal, and other minerals under their land. And in many countries, private citizens do not own the rights to oil deposits in the first place. Another example is a permanent easement allowing your neighbor to use your private road to gain access to her property. Such easements allow coordination between activities that are likely to run beyond the lives of the two people who made the easement.[1]

In general, one is entitled to the fruits of one's labor.[2] If you raise a cow, grow apples, or shoot a deer, you get to consume it or sell it to someone else. If individuals were not entitled to the fruits of their labor, they would underinvest. Why spend time growing apples when your neighbors can come in and take them away. Thus theft is proscribed. Even ignoring the investment issue, theft should be discouraged because those who engage in this occupation are not spending their time producing value.[3] So the commandment against theft is just an efficiency-enhancing rule.

Entitlements are protected via the following methods: property rights, liability rules, communal rights, and regulations. In the rest of the Chapter, we will argue that a particular method is chosen when it is the most efficient.

A. PROPERTY RIGHTS

In a system of property rights, *all transfers of rights are voluntary*. No one may take your blood without your permission. If you own an apple tree, you can prevent others from

---

[1] When I sell my old sofa to someone else, I can make the buyer promise to never eat while sitting on the sofa. But I cannot make the person, who buys the sofa from the person I sold it to, to not eat while sitting on the sofa. This is known as *privity of contract*. Privity of contract makes sense for most transactions. Enforcing such an agreement would be extremely difficult. One would need a registry. The benefits would be swamped by the costs. If the sofa meant a lot to me, I probably would not have sold it in the first place. Hence, the rights to eat on the sofa are bundled with ownership of the sofa. In contrast, easements on land run with the land. If I get an easement to run a road through your property so that my property connects to the highway, I will want that easement whoever owns your property. There is also a land registry.

[2] Of course, governments may impose a tax that takes away some of these fruits.

[3] The transfer itself is generally inefficient. The price that the thief gets for the good on the black market is considerably less than the victim originally paid for the item; that is, in monetary terms, the value of the item is worth less to the thief than it was to the victim.

taking your apples. In general, property rights are *transferable*. Voluntary transfers of property rights encourage efficient use of resources. I may have an apple, but I prefer your pear, while you prefer my apple to your pear. Both of us can be made better off by a voluntary exchange. Economists generally are favorably inclined toward such exchanges, whether it is apples, pears, or body parts.

Although most property rights are transferable, there are exceptions. I cannot sell my right to marry or sell my right to vote (these are known as inalienable rights). I do not have the right to sell my left kidney, although I do have the right to donate it while I am still alive. Reasons for inalienability include paternalism and third-party effects. If a person agrees to sell his house while in a drunken stupor, the courts will not uphold the contract. A 9-year-old cannot borrow money from a bank. Economists have long recognized certain limits on the assumption of rational behavior. Paternalism for idiots and children may require such inalienability.[4]

A third party may be affected by a contract between two people. My contract with the university does not allow me to give students a higher grade in exchange for money or for other favors because this would corrupt the grading system and harm other students not making such bribes. Other third-party effects include moral externalities. Others may find it repugnant that a person sells off parts of his body. However, some may find it repugnant that a person does not share his body parts with others. To prevent such repugnant feelings, a law of inalienability may be promulgated. In general, we will avoid using moral externalities as an explanation of legal rulings because they are an appeal to tastes and may not get us anywhere beyond the statement that laws reflect tastes. To the extent that we deal with these moral externalities, we will not treat them as givens but rather as repugnance for economic inefficiency. We have already explained the proscription against theft in this way; later in this chapter, we will explain the prohibition against rape.

Of course, a system of property rights must be enforced, and this too involves costs. To protect your apple trees, you might have a guard dog or grow apples in a desolate area. The state might put thieves in jail or engage in moral education against theft. All of these involve costs and they do not always work.

If the cost of enforcing the property right is high and the benefit is low, we may not observe property rights. For an obvious example, individuals do not have property rights to city streets. Suppose that one person owned the streets and was able to charge people more during rush hour so that some traffic was reallocated toward less congested times. There would be some benefit, but the cost of enforcing such a rule (e.g., making sure that drivers had paid the higher price for rush hour) would be prohibitive,[5] unless the traffic crossed a choke point (such as a bridge). A more interesting example is the "fair use" doctrine in copyright. Ordinarily, one does not have the right to make copies of copyrighted material in magazines and journals. But individuals are allowed to make single copies for their own fair use. The ubiquity of copying machines makes it too costly to monitor what is being copied and who is doing the copying; and the transaction cost of paying the owner of the copyright would in general be too high. So the property right to copyright has been dulled.

---

[4] The Supreme Court ruled in *Dexter v. Hall* 82 U.S. 9 (1872) that contracts with a lunatic or a person *non compos mentis* are voidable.

[5] Transponders and other inventions may make such charges feasible in the future.

To summarize the basic argument in favor of transferable property rights: When the costs of voluntary exchange of property rights are low and the costs of protecting property rights from involuntary exchange are low and the benefits of a property rights system are high, property rights are efficient and desirable. Later we will discuss situations where these conditions do not hold and therefore property rights are neither efficient nor desirable.

B. LIABILITY RULES

A liability rule allows *involuntary* transfers of entitlements, but the person is *compensated* by an objectively determined criterion. A classic example of such a liability rule is the rule of eminent domain. If the state of California decides to build a highway through your property, the state has the right to force you to sell the necessary land. You are then compensated for market value. Generally, liability rules are associated with civil trials – an automobile driver is found negligent and must compensate you for your injuries.

In buying land for use as a highway, the market transaction costs of a property rights system are too high because of the monopoly hold-up problem. As shown in Chapter 5, each landowner along the way is in a monopoly position because the highway cannot skip over the land. If transfers could not be forced, each landowner would try to gain the surplus for herself by holding out for the highest price. Hence, we have eminent domain to eliminate this problem. However, if someone wants to buy your house, she cannot expropriate it and then go to court to determine the appropriate price. In this case, transaction costs are low and your entitlement to the house is protected by a property right.

If someone drives their car off the street and into your house, they are liable for the damage. Your entitlement is protected via a liability rule. Why is your entitlement not protected by a property right? To understand the logic, consider first a situation where a property right is possible. Suppose that a motion picture producer wants to use your land as a setting for a war film. This might involve extensive damage to your property. Nevertheless, for an adequate price and/or an agreement to compensate you for any damage, you may be willing to rent your land to the production company. Such an agreement is feasible; and, consequently, your land is protected via a property right. No one can force a movie to be produced on your property.

Now consider the parallel situation regarding driving. Under a property rights system, drivers would have to contact all potential victims of their driving and purchase the property right of no harm from them. Drivers would either pay their potential victims up front for the possibility of damaging their property or agree to pay them a certain amount when and if damage takes place. Clearly, this involves enormous transaction costs. And we haven't even considered the monopoly holdout problem that would arise along major thoroughfares (where permission would have to be granted by all of the homeowners). So protecting homeowners from straying automobiles with a property right would be totally impractical. Because the benefits of driving tend to outweigh the costs, we allow driving, but protect others with a liability rule.

The same type of reasoning explains the differential legal treatment of trespass by (adult) people and trespass by animals. The former is protected against by a property right, while the latter is protected against by a liability rule. If a person wants to go on your property, the person can negotiate with you. And, if in the absence of an agreement the person deliberately chooses to trespass on your property, you can protect your property right by getting an injunction to stop future trespass or suing the person in court even if the benefit of the person's trespass (say finding a place to sleep) appears to be greater than the cost to you. If animal trespass were protected against by a property right, then the owner of the animal would have to negotiate with *all* the neighboring landowners where the animal might trespass. Such negotiations are costly and subject to the monopoly holdout problem. Thus animal trespass is only protected by a liability rule.

In a nutshell, *when the transaction costs of a property rights system are too high, a liability rule system is preferable.*

Liability rules compensate the victim for harm, but the amount of compensation is only a rough approximation of the true loss. To illustrate, let us start with eminent domain. Typically, compensation in eminent domain cases is based on the "fair market value" of the property (including buildings). True market value depends on what the highest bidder (including the owner) is willing to pay for the property. But the property is not put up for sale; instead, experts appraise the value of the property by comparing it to similar properties sold in the recent past. These estimates may be above or below the true market value. However, in eminent domain cases, market value tends to underestimate the value to the owners (who in most cases would have been the highest bidders for the property). The fact that before the eminent domain proceeding the person did not sell the property at market price means either that the person did not want to incur market transaction costs or that the person valued the property at a higher price. But how much more did the person value the property over market price? There are incentives for the person to exaggerate the amount of sentimental value and other values attached to the property. The courts tend to ignore these immeasurables. Because, in some cases, these immeasurables are truly valued by the seller, the objective price may underestimate the true value.[6]

In comparison to a voluntary exchange of property rights, the courts (or some other agency) can only imperfectly estimate relative value. Hence, *in those cases where exchanges in property rights are a viable alternative (that is, market transaction costs are small), society should discourage using liability rules as substitutes for property rights.*

Consider the buying and selling of cars. A car is sold when the seller prefers the money over owning the car, and the buyer prefers the car over the money paid for the car. That is, the exchange is Pareto improving. Even if all thieves were caught, we would not allow them to steal cars and then have the court determine the price of a car. Such a liability rule is inferior to the property right solution because the court is at a *comparative disadvantage* in estimating relative value. Juries and judges may make mistakes even if on average they are correct. Furthermore, because taxpayers pay for judges and courtrooms, society wants to discourage the inefficient shifting of decision-making costs by the potential buyer and seller of the car onto the courts. Hence criminals are implicitly charged not only for the cost of the crime (e.g., rental costs if the car is returned), but they are also given an added punishment to dissuade them from using the liability system when the property rights system is more appropriate.[7] This is why rape

---

[6] There are methods of encouraging more honest revelation of preferences. For example, each property owner could state the price at which he would be willing to sell the property. To prevent exaggeration, property taxes could be based on the property owner's stated price.

[7] Thieves are also implicitly charged with the cost of catching them and self-protection against theft. See the chapter on crime.

is a crime and protection against unwanted sexual intercourse is protected by a property right rather than a liability rule. If a sexual relationship is wealth maximizing, then the aggressor would be able to induce the other person to voluntarily have sex. The courts are at a comparative disadvantage in estimating the value of personal relationships, and the transaction costs in the romantic/sexual market are relatively low. Therefore, courts discourage involuntary sexual relations.

Why doesn't the Coase theorem come to the rescue? That is, if the court has undervalued the harm to me from someone else commandeering my car, why can't I buy the right back by bribing the potential thief to not steal my car. The problem is that there are too many potential entrants into this industry, so that having bribed thief #1 to not steal my car, I would then have to bribe thief #2, and so no. The transaction costs would be extremely high, and more important, the *total* cost of the bribes would rapidly outweigh the benefit of my owning a car. So even if I valued my car more than any one else, I would not keep it if the courts underpriced its value.

At times the harm to any one individual may be small, but the collective harm may be very large, as might be the case when a factory pours smoke into the air. It would not make economic sense for an individual or his lawyer to sue for harm. Yet the collective benefits of reducing the smoke might be greater than the cost to the factory of doing so. For this reason, American law allows for *class action* suits, where the lawyers represent the set of people in the class, who have agreed to be represented by the lawyer. Even when the individual benefit is large, it may make sense to save on legal costs by combining similar cases. Thus we have seen class action suits against tobacco companies and asbestos manufacturers.

The difference between a liability rule and a property right is one of degree. You are not allowed to go to your neighbor's house and smash her car (unless your neighbor has willingly sold you the right to do so). If you threaten to do so, your neighbor may get a court *injunction* to prevent you from carrying out your threat; she may even have police surveillance. This is property right, and the state will try to enforce her right against involuntary transfer. But you may still be able to smash her car and cause an involuntary transfer. When you drive, your entitlement to a whole car is typically protected by a liability rule. You cannot prevent all other people from driving. Yet certain people who are likely to damage your car can be prevented from threatening (i.e., driving) in the first place. This includes drunk drivers and others who do not have licenses.

In this section, we have provided a transaction cost explanation for the choice between liability rules and property rights. It also explains the structure of the law, in particular, the boundary between property law (where as the name suggests, entitlements are protected by property rights) and tort law (where liability rules are used).

C. COMMUNAL RIGHTS

Communal rights are the right to use but not to exclude. Examples include hunting, fishing, grazing on the commons, driving on the streets, and so on. Note that many of these communal rights eventually involve property rights. Once I catch the fish, my entitlement to the fish is protected by a property right.

Communal rights are appropriate *where transaction costs associated with the exchange of property rights are relatively high compared with any possible misallocation of rights because there is no right of exclusion.* Drawing limited amounts of water from a river imposes little or no costs on other users. So, where water is plentiful, it makes little sense to charge for its use and communal rights to water are standard. As another example, one could allocate the use of an urban street by charging a high toll during peak hours. However, the cost of the toll keeper might be greater than the benefits (faster driving time) that accrue when drivers make decisions (such as carpooling) when they pay for the cost of congestion.[8] The same argument in favor of communal rights holds when there are individual fishermen catching relatively few fish in a well-stocked lake. Any misallocation of resources arising from the inability to exclude when there is a communal right is outweighed by the cost of enforcing a property right.

However, when there is overgrazing and hypercongestion, communal rights start to fail. With regard to fishing, the only way to get the property right is to catch the fish. Throwing fish back into the lake until they are the optimal size will not benefit the person catching the fish because he has no claims on them. Thus there will be overfishing and inefficient allocation of resources devoted to getting the fish first. Not surprisingly, communal rights to ocean fish have led to inefficient depletion of these resources.

Many of the regulatory attempts to reduce overfishing of the commons have been costly and ineffective. For example, some varieties of fish can only be caught during certain seasons of the year. Fishermen buy bigger and faster boats with bigger nets so that they can catch more fish during the shortened time period. This again leads to overfishing, so the season is shortened still further; the response is to build ever more sophisticated and expensive boats to fish more effectively in the shorter season.[9]

Compare this communal right solution to the case where one firm has a property right to all of the fish. The firm will not overfish because it reduces the value of the capital more than the present extra return from fishing. The owner at all times maximizes the present discounted value of the fish (as long as the property rights are secure).[10]

A partial solution is to sell yearly quotas. In this way, individuals have a property right to a certain number of fish. There is still a downside to the quota system. (1) It requires monitoring and (2) individuals do not bear all the long-run consequences on the fishery and therefore may undertake inefficient behavior such as dredging, which improves profitability in the short run but inefficiently reduces production in the long run.

While some argue that private property and capitalism is the source of the overfishing problem, the true reason for a failure is the lack of property rights in this area.

D. REGULATION OF THE INPUTS

So far we have focused on private enforcement of entitlements. For example, an individual sues another person in court for the harm arising out of an automobile accident.

---

[8] A partial implementation of such a mechanism is having higher bridge tolls during commuting hours.

[9] An important reason for restricting fishing to seasons is that it is relatively inexpensive to monitor. It is easy to catch a boat with a load of salmon in the off-season. Regulation of smaller-scale commons tends to be more effective. For example, Eggertsson (1990) has shown that mountain pastures in Iceland, which are held in common, have been successfully protected from overgrazing by imposing communal standards. Note that government or social regulation tends to be a necessary complement to communal rights.

[10] Of course, the owner will have to expend resources to protect his property right; for example, patrolling the water to prevent others from poaching.

The government also enforces entitlements. A person can be fined for speeding and put in jail for manslaughter (as might be the case if a drunk driver killed a pedestrian). In Chapter 7, we considered a tax on pollution. Such Pigovian taxes are an alternative to a class action – the owner of the steel factory pays the government for the damage rather than paying the victims of pollution. In this section, we consider regulation of the inputs.

Government regulations are often used in high transaction costs cases. As was seen in the previous section, regulations are used to prevent overuse or inappropriate use of the commons. But why are they used instead of or in addition to liability rules that are based on the output? For example, why do we have regulations against speeding in addition to finding people liable when there is an accident? Shouldn't paying for the damage when there is an accident be an optimal *deterrent* because the speeder is taking into account both the benefits to herself and the harm to others?[11]

An important reason for regulating the input (speeding) in addition to making the injurer liable for the output (harm) is that the injurer may be judgment proof, that is, she may not have enough wealth to pay for all of the harm and therefore the incentive effect of finding her liable is not fully effective.[12] Whether a person is potentially liable for $100,000 or $1 million is immaterial when the person only has $20,000 in assets. The incentive to take care is also blunted when the driver has liability insurance. Consequently, speed, an input into harm, is regulated.[13] In this way, the driver is encouraged to drive at the appropriate speed by paying fines and higher insurance rates when she does not.

If regulation of the inputs is so great, why don't we always use regulation instead of liability rules? It is again the issue of comparative advantage. First, speeding need not lead to an accident so that there may be considerable monitoring and enforcement (read: transaction) cost in the absence of harm. Second, and probably more important, *there are numerous inputs into the production of damage, but not all of these inputs can be measured by third parties.* There are no regulations against daydreaming while driving because there is no way to enforce this regulation (at least not yet), but daydreaming may very well lead to an accident. If the only sanction were regulation of the inputs, then there would be inadequate incentives for care in the areas not monitored (such as daydreaming). Making the driver liable for harm encourages the driver to take into account these unmeasured inputs. From another viewpoint, regulations determine the optimal allocation of inputs for the average driver but not for the individual driver. Only if the driver is liable for the harm can the latter be accomplished. With regulation, above average drivers are forced to undertake excessive care, while below average drivers do not take adequate precaution.

---

[11] This is a question that only an economist would ask. Those who are not indoctrinated with the concept of the invisible hand tend to prefer regulation.

[12] Regulation may help insurance companies provide the appropriate price for the insurance (insurance rates increase for drivers who have been arrested for speeding and are thought to be more likely to be in accident in the future) and may reduce the cost of the insurance company assessing risk (if all tires are required to have certain safety features, the insurance company need not adjust the cost of the policy, depending on the nature of the tires purchased).

[13] But why not have the speeder be liable to others for speeding? Clearly, nonspeeders suing other drivers for speeding would involve enormous court transaction costs. So the less costly method of government regulation is chosen instead. A more thorough analysis of speed regulation is found in Chapter 18 on mitigation of damages.

WHEN ENTITLEMENTS ARE NOT TRANSFERABLE

In California, the entitlement to water is typically not transferable. Indeed, in certain areas, the rule is "use it or lose it." The price of water to agriculture is often under $20 an acre-foot (an acre-foot is enough water to cover an acre 1 foot deep). This is likely to be less than the cost of pumping the water from the source of the supply, which may be hundreds of miles away. Because of this "cheap" water, water-intensive crops, such as rice, are grown in the desert. At the same time, urban dwellers often pay $50 to $200 an acre-foot, and a number of cities have installed desalinization plants that produce water at a cost of more that $2,000 per acre-foot. If their rights to water were transferable, then farmers would sell their rights to city dwellers (who use less than 15% of the water). In this way, the water would go to its highest use (as predicted by Coase). Instead, there is an incredible misallocation of water. In recent years, there has been some change in water law, but progress has been slow. Farmers are afraid of losing their entitlements and urban residents do not believe that farmers deserve the entitlement because taxes paid for most of the cost of the aqueducts and reservoirs. For a further discussion of water allocation, see the box at the end of the Chapter 20 on being first.

WHO OWNS YOUR SURGICALLY REMOVED CANCEROUS SPLEEN

John Moore was treated for cancer at the University of California Medical Center, where his spleen was removed. The T-lymphocytes (white blood cells) in Moore's spleen overproduced a protein, which made genetic identification much easier. These cells were harvested from his spleen and the cell lines were later sold to a biotech company for nearly $2 million. Moore later sued the university for unlawful conversion of his property. Who has the property rights to his cells? In *Moore v. Regents of the University California*, 793 P.2d 479 (1990), the court ruled that the cell lines and the patents derived from them did not belong to Moore.

As is true for most of the cases that I cover, the simple summaries do not capture all the issues in the case. The patient had been informed that his spleen would be used for research purposes but not that the research might lead to valuable patents. The court ruled that the doctor failed in his fiduciary duty to the patient by not informing the patient of this possibility.

We have been discussing automobile accidents where the judgment proof problem is particularly acute. So let us turn our attention to another area where this problem does not arise. Suppose that it was U.S. government policy to reduce gasoline consumption in order to reduce the political power of oil producing countries. The government could regulate that automobiles and SUVs satisfy fuel economy standards; in fact, it indirectly does so by taxing automobile companies for not satisfying certain mileage requirements. The government could also encourage the use of hybrid gas-electric cars by giving special tax breaks; this policy too has been implemented. These solutions regulate the input. The economists' solution is to raise gasoline taxes (price the output). In this way, individuals can decide whether to drive less often, buy more fuel efficient but more expensive cars, or spend less on other items if driving a gas hog is worth more than spending money elsewhere. When there is such a tax, individuals internalize both costs and benefits. Regulations are inefficient because they allocate resources in a different way than individuals do.

Of course, gasoline taxes have distributive consequences. For example, trucking companies will have lower profits when they pay more in gasoline taxes. But others will have lower taxes because gasoline taxes are higher and therefore other taxes can be reduced. Furthermore, in principle, trucking companies could be given a reduction in their corporate income tax rates, so that the *average* trucking company was not harmed by the increase in gasoline taxes. The same goes for poor people who are hurt by an increase in gas prices – poor people, on average, could be compensated by subsidies and the reduction of inefficient regulations. In terms of a cost-benefit analysis, taxes are preferred to regulation in this example.

The choice between liability for the harm (where there are insufficient incentives toward care when the injurer is judgment proof) and regulation of the inputs (where inability to measure all inputs distorts the injurers' choice from the optimal) thus depends on the relative costs and benefits, just as the choice between property rights and liability rules and between property rights and communal rights depend on the costs and benefits for the case at hand.

E. CONCLUDING REMARKS

Whether one chooses property rights, liability rules, communal rights, or regulation to protect entitlements depends, like so many other choices discussed in this book, on their relative costs and benefits. The key to understanding is to determine which are the relevant costs and benefits. When market transaction costs are low, property rights are preferred over liability rules because the latter are imperfect estimators of relative value; when market transaction costs are high, liability rules are preferred over property rights. When the cost of overuse is low or nonexistent, then communal rights are preferred over both liability rules and property rights that are costly to enforce. And when the cost of regulation (from failure to measure the appropriate inputs) is less than the cost of a liability for damage system (due to insufficient incentives when people are judgment proof), then the input will be regulated.

SUGGESTIONS FOR FURTHER READING

The classic paper on the enforcement of entitlements is "Property Rules, Liability Rules, and Inalienability: One View from the Cathedral" by Calabresi and Malamed. Since then, many papers have played off the theme and/or the title. See, for example, Kaplow and Shavell (1996), Levmore (1997), Krier and Schwab (1997), and Bebchuk (2001). Demsetz (1967) saw the choice between property rights and communal rights in historical perspective. The June 2002 edition of the *Journal of Legal Studies* is devoted to the evolution of property rights. For the choice between regulation and liability rules, see Wittman (1977), White and Wittman (1982), and Shavell (1983). For a discussion of a futures market in organs, see Cohen (1989). Finally, for a general coverage of the property rights literature, see Lueck and Micelli (2006).

REVIEW QUESTIONS

1. Define precisely: entitlement, property right, excludability, transferability, liability rule, communal rights. (12)
2. Briefly why do excludability and transferability encourage economics efficiency? (4) What is the economic explanation for outlawing theft? (4)
3. What is the difference between an entitlement protected via a liability rule and one protected via a property right? (2) When is it more appropriate to use one method over the other? Why? (8) Provide examples. (4)
4. When is property right preferred over a communal right? Provide an example. (4) When is a communal right preferred over a property right? Provide an example. (4)
5. Why are communal rights to fishing inefficient when there are large-scale harvesting methods? (2)
6. Why don't people "over-fish" if there are property rights to fishing? (2)
7. In Maine, lobsters are grown in privately owned lobster pots in the ocean. What are the costs and benefits of this method of harvesting lobsters? (4)
8. In *Edwards v. Sims* 24 S.W.2d 619 (1929), the entrance of the Onyx cave was on one person's property, but much of the cave was under other people's property. Do the surface owners own the cave underneath?
9. Ellickson (1993) has argued that domesticating barking dogs was an important innovation that helped to make private property feasible. Others have argued that the invention of barbed wire encouraged the privatization of public lands. Explain. (4)
10. In the United States, you can donate or sell blood and sperm and you can donate a kidney, but you cannot sell any organ. Under the National Organ Transplant Act of 1984, it is even illegal to offer to pay for hospital or funeral expenses in order to encourage the donation of an organ. Furthermore, you cannot buy an organ that has already been harvested. What would happen to the supply of organs if it were legal to sell them? (2) Would poor people tend to be the suppliers? (2) Is this necessarily bad? (2)
11. What is privity of contract? Provide an example. (4)
12. I can impose an easement on land that "runs with the land" even if the land is sold to third parties. However, I cannot impose a condition on the care of a puppy that I sell that runs with the dog. Explain why. (8)

REFERENCES

Bebchuk, Lucian A. (2001). Property Rights and Liability Rules: The Ex Ante View of the Cathedral. 100 *Michigan Law Review* 601.

Calabresi, Guido, and A. Douglas Malamed. (1972). Property Rules, Liability Rules. And Inalienability: One View of the Cathedral. 85 *Harvard Law Review* 1089.

Cohen, Lloyd R. (1989). Increasing the Supply of Transplant Organs: The Virtues of a Futures Market. 58 *George Washington Law Review* 1.

Demsetz, Harold. (1967). Toward a Theory of Property Rights. 57 *American Economic Review Papers and Proceedings* 347.

Kaplow, Louis, and Steven Shavell. (1996). Property Rules versus Liability Rules: An Economic Analysis. 109 *Harvard Law Review* 713.

Krier, James E., and Stewart J. Schwab. (1997). The Cathedral at Twenty Five: Citations and Impressions. 106 *Yale Law Journal* 2121.

Levmore, Saul. (1997). Unifying Remedies: Property Rules, Liability Rules, and Startling Rules. 106 *Yale Law Journal* 2149.

Lueck, Dean, and Thomas J. Miceli. (2006). Property Rights and Property Law. In Steven Shavell and A. Mitchel Polinsky (eds.). *Handbook of Law and Economics.* Amsterdam: North-Holland.

Shavell, Steven. (1984). Liability for Harm versus Regulation of Safety. 13 *Journal of Legal Studies.* 357.

White, Michelle, and Donald Wittman. (1983). A Comparison of Regulation and Liability Rules Under Imperfect Information. 12 *Journal of Legal Studies* 413.

Wittman, Donald. (1977). Prior Regulation vs. Post Liability: The Choice Between Input and Output Monitoring. 6 *Journal of Legal Studies* 193.

12 Property Rights or Communal Rights in Knowledge?

A. The Duty to Disclose 104

B. Patents 105

C. AIDS 106

D. Blackmail 106

E. Trademarks 107

F. Names Used in Advertising 107

G. Concluding Remarks 110

SUGGESTIONS FOR FURTHER READING 111

REVIEW QUESTIONS 111

REFERENCES 112

If the seller knows that her house has termites, should the seller be forced to divulge the information to prospective buyers? Should a buyer of a photograph be forced to divulge to the seller that the photograph was not taken by the seller's great uncle Weston but by the famous photographer Edward Weston? Why is blackmail illegal? In this chapter, we consider the optimal allocation of entitlements to knowledge. In the process, we discuss intellectual property, including patents, copyrights, and trademarks.[1]

Property rights in information encourage the gathering of information but may discourage the dissemination of information. Communal rights to information encourage the dissemination of information but may discourage the gathering of information. As we will see, the appropriate balance between the two depends on the incentive effects.

A. THE DUTY TO DISCLOSE

When do individuals in a buyer-seller relationship have a duty to disclose information, and when can they keep the information private? The economic answer is that in general the person has a property right to information when it is costly to gain such information, but the person does not have a property right and therefore cannot take advantage of his information when the information is obtained at very low cost. When a petroleum engineer purchases land, he does not have to tell the seller that the land has petroleum deposits underneath. See *Neill v. Shamburg*, 158 PA. 263 (1893), where the court ruled that it is the right of every man to keep his business to himself. If a person were forced to divulge such information, his incentive to gain the information in the first place would be greatly diminished, and we would have suboptimal exploration. Similarly, the collector does not have to divulge to the seller that the photograph is by Edward Weston. We want photographs to move to their highest use. Experts facilitate the movement from garage sales to art galleries. If experts are not rewarded for their services, there will be insufficient expertise, and too many valuable photographs will end up as collages for grade-school art projects. Giving the rights to the buyer in this case is not without costs, however, as the seller may be more cautious in selling an item than otherwise.

In contrast, in most states, the seller of a house is obligated to tell the future buyer about its latent defects. As the owner of the house, the seller is likely to know the latent defects as a by-product of ownership (that is, no extra cost is involved in obtaining the information). For example, the person may have seen the termite droppings or noticed that the heating system does not work. So forcing discloser in this case is unlikely to reduce the amount of information gathered by the seller. See *Obde v. Schlemeyer*, 56 Wash. 2d 449, 353 P.2d 672 (1960), where the court argued that the seller has a duty to speak up about the termites, even though the buyer did not ask any questions in this regard. In contrast, it would be costly for the buyer on her own to discover the defects before purchase. And if there were several potential buyers, such costs would be multiplied.

---

[1] Not all intellectual innovations are given property right protection. Although Einstein worked for the Swiss Patent Office, he never took a patent out on $E = MC^2$, nor did he get a copyright on the formula.

B. PATENTS

Patent protection (a monopoly property right) was first instituted in Venice during the fifteenth century. The U.S. Constitution (Article 1, Section 8) gives Congress the power to protect patents and copyright. At present, certain technological innovations are granted a patent (property right) for twenty years and then turned into a communal right (anyone can use the innovation).

The holder of the patent is granted a monopoly. A monopoly allows the patent holder to charge more than the competitive price. In turn, this means that supply of the patented item will be less than the optimal. This suggests that no patents should be granted. However, if technological inventions were not patentable, the incentive for innovation would be suboptimal as the inventor could not adequately capture the return on her invention. Why would a pharmaceutical firm expend hundreds of millions of dollars on research if other manufacturers could make copies without engaging in such costly investment? Even if the pharmaceutical company gained some modest advantage from undertaking the research, the benefits would be tempered and therefore the incentives to do research in the first place would also be tempered.

To gain a patent, the invention should not only be novel, but nonobvious as well (17 U.S.C. §103). If the invention is obvious, there is no need to encourage the new knowledge as it will arise without effort. Perpetual motion machines are never granted patents because they defy the laws of physics. Designs for plutonium bombs are not granted patents, either, because they obey the laws of physics too well, and if the inventor were to be granted a patent, the design would be available to others. Instead, governments sponsor weapons research or payoff independent inventors. The inventions are also supposed to be useful, but as our example of the "holewich" (see box page 111) suggests, utility is in the eyes of the beholder.

In the absence of patents, transaction costs would be excessively high. To illustrate, suppose that a person devised a new type of refrigerator. If she kept the invention secret, she would realize higher returns. But how could she sell her invention? To find a producer, she would have to require each potential producer to sign a binding contract that he would neither produce the refrigerator without her permission nor provide others with the information. It would be costly to disseminate the information to the appropriate parties and difficult to monitor the terms of the contract. Once the refrigerator was produced, each user would have to promise not to look at the internal workings or allow others access. Clearly, such a contract is not enforceable because cheating could take place without detection.

If patents extended indefinitely, the boundaries of patents would become harder to establish, and the monopoly profits from having a patent would be excessive. Other innovations (such as an organizational form) are not patentable, possibly because it is harder to define what is new and detect when it is being used.

An alternative to patents is for the government to subsidize research. In this way, the government provides the incentive for the creation of intellectual knowledge without granting monopoly rights for twenty years. In the United States, the National Science Foundation, the National Institutes of Health, and the Defense Department subsidize research. Another variant on this theme is for the government to subsidize the purchase of the product so that the consumer does not face monopoly prices, but at the same time, the firm obtains a reasonable rate of return on its research. George W. Bush has proposed government subsidies for AIDS programs in Africa and pharmaceutical purchases under Medicare. Although the appropriate amount of subsidization is difficult to determine, the decision to subsidize does make sense.

C. AIDS

While we are on the subject of AIDS, it is useful to review the laws regarding the transmission of the disease. The criminal HIV laws in most states have three elements: (1) a person must reasonably know that he is infected with AIDS; (2) the person has engaged in a specific type of behavior like spitting, donating blood, or having sexual intercourse; and (3) the person failed to inform the victim about his/her disease.

These laws have a perverse effect by creating an incentive not to get tested. By not knowing that you have AIDS, you cannot be held criminally liable. But if you know that you are HIV-positive, then there is an added responsibility not to put other people at risk. So these three elements encourage the spread of the information but reduce the likelihood that the information is obtained in the first place.

D. BLACKMAIL

Information about one's private life also has elements of both a property right and a communal right. In general, one has the right not to divulge information about one's personal life. Your neighbor cannot demand that you divulge information regarding your sex life and then have a court decision regarding the appropriate level of compensation. However, if your neighbor discovers secrets about you and you are a public figure, he or she is allowed to sell them to newspapers and television stations. (It is reported that Roseanne offered $1 million to Monica Lewinsky to appear on her talk show.) However, you are not allowed to buy the information back from the person – blackmail is illegal. But why is it illegal? Don't economists believe in contracts and aren't both parties better off if the blackmail is consummated? The person who is paying the blackmail prefers that the information remain private, and presumably the blackmailer is getting a better deal than going elsewhere.

Like much of economics, the answer lies in long-run incentive effects. If blackmail were legal, then people would engage in obtaining "blackmailable" information. Snooping and spying are costly, but this production is useless to the person who purchases it back. After all, the person being blackmailed knows what he (she) had been doing. So if blackmail were legal, people would engage in costly activities to transfer wealth to themselves. It would be digging up dirt just to bury it again. The net product would be negative.

There is another reason for outlawing blackmail. Because there is no property right to information, the full value of information cannot be captured by news organizations. As a consequence, the price such an organization is willing to pay is far less than the social marginal value. To illustrate, if the person were not able to obtain the information in any other way, the average person in the United States might have been willing to pay $1 to find out about the scandal between Monica Lewinsky and President Clinton. If the conditional statement held, then a news organization could gain about $300 million from the citizens in the United States. However, the conditional statement does not hold – the information can spread to those who have not paid for a newspaper subscription or cable news programming. The value to the news organization could easily be less than the value to President Clinton, even though the value to society in obtaining the information might be much greater. So preventing blackmail is a way to subsidize public information that would otherwise be buried by the person being blackmailed.

E. TRADEMARKS

Owners of trademarks have a property right that continues as long as the owner is making use of the trademark. It is easy to understand why we have trademarks. The owner gains value from the trademark and will maintain a certain level of quality. Without trademark protection, others will have an incentive to provide shoddier but cheaper to produce goods and then pretend that they are selling the trademarked items. If there are no trademarks, buyers will have to rely on more costly methods such as inspection of the item and/or establishment of long-term relationships with sellers. This is why liquor during Prohibition and street drugs today are less pure than their legal counterparts. "Marlboro Marijuana" would provide a consistent level of quality.

Trademarks are useful to the extent that they distinguish one company's products (or services) from another. You are not allowed to start a hamburger outlet called MacDonald's even if that is your name because it might be confused with McDonald's. However, you can own a hardware store called McDonald's Hardware if there is not another one located nearby. Few people will confuse McDonald's hardware with McDonald's hamburgers.

A trademark is useful because it allows one firm to distinguish itself from another. A trademark cannot be too encompassing because it would then make it too difficult to have other trademarks that easily identified the product. For example, "milk" cannot be trademarked. If it could, then other firms would have to call their product "liquid from a cow's udder." And if that awkward phrase could also be trademarked, then it would be really difficult to know what liquid was in another producer's carton.

F. NAMES USED IN ADVERTISING

Movie stars have a property right in photographs of themselves when the photographs are used in advertisements, but there is a communal right in using their photographs in news stories.[2] When Paul Newman has the property right to use photographs of himself or his name in advertising, he can sell that right to others for a price that maximizes the return on his human capital.[3] In this way, sales are value maximizing. However, such a property right system involves some exchange costs. Paul Newman must be contacted, and a price must be negotiated. These costs are not trivial; yet, they are unlikely to be

---

[2] The photographer, however, may own the photograph. Similarly, Walt Disney's cartoon characters cannot be used to advertise products without permission. As always, the controversial cases arise when the answers are not obvious. Should the law allow Mickey Mouse (registered trademark) to be used satirically in a salacious comic book parody without permission of Disney? Once? Often? Should rap groups be allowed to use whole songs from other groups without permission (and possibly without payment)? No. Should they be allowed to use parts of songs? Maybe.

[3] Many designers license their names to producers who put the designers' names on products even though these designers have nothing to do with the design or production of the product.

TRADE SECRETS

Sometimes intellectual property is protected by contract and/or by secret behavior. The formula for Coca-Cola is neither patented nor copyrighted. Instead, the formula has been kept a secret by maintaining the recipe in the hands of just a few people and by trade-secret law. Those who are privy to the making of the syrup must sign a contract that they will not divulge any information. Nowadays, contract is often used to protect intellectual property. When you buy software, you must promise not to make it available to other parties. In contrast, when you buy a book, there is nothing on the front cover that says that you cannot sell it to someone else. Can you come up with an explanation for the differential treatment?

TRADEMARK INFRINGEMENT

In *Brother Records Inc. v. Jardine*, 318 F.3d 900 (2003), the appellate court ruled that former Beach Boys singer Al Jardine cannot use the term "Beach Boys" in his touring band, Beach Boys Family and Friends. The court found that Jardine was infringing on the trademark of Brother Records Inc., which owns the rights to the Beach Boys works. Jardine, Mike Love, Brian Wilson, and the estate of Carl Wilson, the original founders of the 1960s group, jointly own Brother Records. Because Jardine and lead singer Love were unwilling to tour together after Carl Wilson's death, the band's remaining members agreed to let a new group formed by Love perform as the Beach Boys. As part of the agreement, the new band pays royalties to Brother Records. Jardine without the consent of the others set up The Beach Boys Family and Friends. With two bands touring as the Beach Boys or as a similar-sounding combination, organizers and fans were often confused about which group they were seeing.

very large because this is not a case of bilateral monopoly (as hard as it is to believe, there are substitutes for Paul Newman, perhaps Sean Penn). Furthermore, only a few people might be involved.

If there were a communal right to Paul Newman's name in advertising, then his name would be overused and used in such a way as to lower the value of his capital. The reasoning closely parallels the logic for trademarks. "Paul Newman Bail Bonds" might bring in increased profits to the bail bondsman but decrease the overall profits of products (salad dressing, popcorn, etc.) with his name. Turning this communal right into Paul Newman's property right would be extremely expensive. Every time he bought out one person, another person would arise to make use of his name or picture. So the right would remain a communal right, with overuse but no exchange costs. Even if Paul Newman could buy back the rights, the cost would be very high – he would have to buy the right from many to stop them from using his name (this should be compared with the case in which Paul Newman is given the right and then sells it to a few).

If the law gives Paul Newman the property right to his picture for advertising, even if the allocation is incorrect, it is easily remedied. If the law mistakenly provides a communal right to his picture, it cannot be remedied. Therefore, one should be very

IS IT VICTOR'S OR VICTORIA'S SECRET

Victoria's Secret is a large chain known for its sexy lingerie. Victor's Little Secret is a small-town shop that sells lingerie and pornographic items. Victoria's Secret claims that Victor's secret tarnishes its trademark. Should Victor have a name change if not a sex change? In a unanimous decision, the Supreme Court overturned a 6th Circuit ruling that "dilution" of a mark will occur if a mark is distinctive, even if no actual harm had been proved (*Moseley v. Victoria Secret Catalogue*, 123 S. Ct. 1115). According to the Supreme Court, the Federal Trademark Dilution Act requires proof that a junior mark has been used that is sufficiently similar to the famous mark to evoke in consumers a mental association of the two and that such confusion has caused actual economic harm to the owner of the famous mark by lessening its former selling power. The case was sent back to the lower courts to determine whether there was actual harm.

This is an important narrowing of the scope of a trademark. Firms such as McDonald's and Coca-Cola spend a lot of time threatening trademark infringement. Some of it is questionable. Do you think that consumers thought that they were going to McDonald's when they were purchasing fast food from McDharmas, a vegetarian restaurant, now known as Dharmas after receiving a threatening letter from McDonald's?

However, Coca-Cola needs to make sure that when you order rum and coke you get Coca-Cola. If they did not, Coke would no longer be a trademark but pass into the public domain like aspirin, zipper, Yo-Yo, and thermos bottle did (see *King-Seeley Thermos Co. v. Aladdin Industries, Incorporated*, 321 F.2d 577 (1963).

sure that the allocation under a communal right system is optimal if a property right system is a viable alternative.

Although the Paul Newman example may seem farfetched, it resembles a number of actual court cases. In *Bette Midler v. Ford Motor Co.*, 849 F.2d 460 (1988), an unidentified and unseen singer had mimicked Bette Midler's style in a television advertisement. It was natural for the television audience to think that Bette Midler was peddling the product. Although, previously, style could not be copyrighted, Midler won this case. This ruling makes sense because there was a natural intent to deceive the television viewer and use up Midler's human capital. In 1979, Johnny Carson, the precursor to Jay Leno on the *Tonight Show*, filed a $1.1 million lawsuit against Detroit entrepreneur Earl Braxton for marketing a portable toilet under the trade name "Here's Johnny!," which was Ed McMahon's famous introduction at the beginning of Carson's show. In *John W. Carson v. Here's Johnny Portable Toilets*, 698 F. 2d 831 (1983), the court held that the trade name was an intentional appropriation of Carson's identity for commercial exploitation and that it violated his right of publicity.

Newspaper stories do not like to print yesterday's news. Gaining permission to print photographs of movie stars in time would be exceedingly costly (unless they gained prior permission). Hence, a property rights system involves high transaction costs. So the initial allocation of rights is important. One, therefore, makes a decision about which allocation is more efficient by asking who would end up with the rights if the cost of bargaining were low. The cost to the movie star of the photograph is likely to be

BLACKMAIL?

The Palm Beach County State Attorney's Office began investigating Rush Limbaugh after his former maid told them she had been supplying him prescription painkillers for years. They discovered that Limbaugh received more than two thousand painkillers, prescribed by four doctors, at a pharmacy near his $24 million Palm Beach mansion.

Roy Black, Limbaugh's lawyer, alleged that Limbaugh's former maid, Wilma Cline, learned of his addiction and threatened to sell the story to the *National Enquirer*. Black said that she and her husband, David Cline, demanded millions and were "paid substantial amounts of money." Limbaugh allegedly withdrew cash thirty to forty times in amounts just under the $10,000 limit that requires a bank to report the transaction to the federal government. The action drew suspicion because it can be a federal crime to structure financial transactions below the $10,000 limit. Black said Limbaugh paid money to the Clines because they were blackmailing him – not because he was laundering money. The attorney for the Clines denied Black's allegation. West Palm Beach, Fla. (AP) December 23, 2003. Reported in the *New York Times*.

THE TERMINATOR

Arnold Schwarzenegger sued an Ohio car dealership for $20 million claiming that it unlawfully used his picture in a newspaper ad. In the middle of a full-page advertisement in the *Akron Beacon Journal* was a 1-inch photograph of Schwarzenegger as the "Terminator," accompanied with a bubble quotation that read, "Terminate early at Fred Martin." Schwarzenegger sued the dealer in Los Angeles federal court, claiming that the dealer used his photo to sell cars without his permission, that it was an invasion of his right to privacy, and that the use of his picture violated his self-imposed ban on appearing in commercials in the United States. In *Schwarzenegger v. Fred Martin Motor Co.*, 374 F.3d 797 (2004), the court ruled that he could not pursue the privacy issue in a California court. The litigants eventually settled out of court. The dealer issued a written apology to Schwarzenegger for the improper use of his image in addition to agreeing to pay an undisclosed sum of money to *All-Stars*, a charity founded in 1991 by Schwarzenegger.

substantially less for news stories than for advertisements; in all likelihood, the movie stars prefer the free publicity. Thus, we should not be surprised that they do not have the rights to their pictures. Of course, some movie stars would prefer not to have their names or pictures in print, but this misallocation cost is more than made up for by the reduced transaction cost of a communal right to information.

G. CONCLUDING REMARKS

In this chapter, we covered a host of seeming unrelated topics, including blackmail, duty to disclose, and patents. However, all these topics involve the conflict between generating and dispersing of information. When insufficient generation is the major problem, property rights to information is the solution. When insufficient dissemination is the major problem, communal rights to information is the solution.

PATENT

Clayton T. Holbrook has been granted patent No. 6,599,545 for a new way to make sandwiches. In his invention, a hole is drilled in a bun and the filling (meat, cheese, or chopped vegetables) is inserted, using a collar that can be slid out, leaving the filling encased. The patent includes more than two dozen pages of drawings and diagrams, among them drills and collars.

Should the food be called a holebrook or a holewich? By the way, the Earl of Sandwich (the alleged inventor of the eponymous food) never got a patent for his invention.

LATENT DEFECTS

If you are selling a haunted house, must you disclose this information to the buyer? Helen Ackley, the seller of the house, claimed that she had seen various apparitions. These claims were reported in *Reader's Digest* and the local press. But when she sold the house, she never told the buyer of these claims. When the buyer found out, he wanted the sale of the house to be rescinded. In *Stambovsky v. Ackley*, 169 A.D.2d 254 (1991), the court ruled that the seller had a duty to disclose and voided the sale.

Given our previous analysis, the court decision is sensible. When a house is reputed to be haunted, this can affect its resale value. Therefore, it was valuable to disclose such information to the buyer. Given all the publicity, the information was certainly not private.

SUGGESTIONS FOR FURTHER READING

Landes and Posner (2003) provide a comprehensive treatment of intellectual property law. See also Gordon (2003). Scotchmer (2003) provides historical background as well as models dealing with the breadth and depth of patents. For a different view of blackmail, see Gordon (1993).

REVIEW QUESTIONS

1. What are the benefits and costs to having a property right in information as opposed to a communal right? (6)
2. Why are buyers of antiques not required to tell the seller of the true value of the item? (4)
3. Why is the seller of a house required to notify the buyer of latent defects?
4. What are the cost and benefits of a patent system? (6)
5. Why are trademarks a property right? Why are trademarks for as long as the company is in business and not just for twenty years as patents are? (4)
6. Why does Paul Newman have the property right to his name? (6)
7. Should rap groups be allowed to include phrases from other singers' recordings without compensation? (10)

8. Should telephone directories be copyrighted or should one company be allowed to copy the phone directory of another company without charge? A publisher could include phony people and phone numbers to catch those who copy directly from its phone book. (10)

REFERENCES

Gordon, Wendy J. (2003). Intellectual Property Law. In Peter Cane and Mark Tushnet (eds.), *Oxford Handbook of Legal Studies*. Oxford: Oxford University Press.

Gordon, Wendy J. (1993). Truth and Consequences: The Force of Blackmail's Central Case. 141 *University of Pennsylvania Law Review* 1741.

Landes, William M., and Richard A. Posner. (2003). *The Economic Structure of Intellectual Property Law*. Cambridge, MA: Harvard University Press.

Scotchmer, Suzanne. (2004). *Innovation and Incentive*. Cambridge, MA: MIT Press.

13 Liability for Harm or Restitution for Benefit?

A. Negative Externalities 114

B. Long-Run Entry and Exit 115

C. Positive Externalities 116

D. Economic Markets 117

E. Concluding Remarks 118

SUGGESTIONS FOR FURTHER READING 118

REVIEW QUESTIONS 119

REFERENCES 119

Why do ordinary economic markets tend to rely on positive incentives (the carrot), while governments tend to rely on coercion (the stick)? Should a person who witnesses a crime be rewarded for reporting it or punished for not doing so? If an area becomes more urban, should the owner of a feedlot be compensated for moving or should the owner be held liable for the smell if the feedlot remains? If a mine owner, in the process of draining water from her mine, drains her neighbor's mine of water as well, should she be compensated for the benefit to the neighbor? If a mine owner floods her mine with water, which, at the same time, floods her neighbor's mine, should she be liable to her neighbor for the harm? Should a polluter be taxed for creating too much pollution or subsidized for undertaking pollution control?

In a world of zero transaction costs, the distinctions between harm and benefit and punishment and reward disappear, and these questions cannot be answered. For example, one could be rewarded $200 for reporting a crime; alternatively, one could be fined $200 for not reporting a crime. Not receiving a $200 reward when not reporting a crime can be viewed as a punishment, while not receiving a $200 fine when reporting a crime can be viewed as a reward. The marginals are the same because the person is $200 richer by reporting the crime under either scenario, and thus the behavior is the same under either scenario (as long as there are no wealth effects; for example, the utility functions are quasi-linear). As another example, consider the situation in which factory smoke irritates nearby residents. Reducing smoke emissions benefits the residents and harms the factory owner (under the assumption that smoke reduction is costly); increasing smoke emissions benefits the factory owner and harms the residents. Because, either way, one side is harmed and the other side is benefited, the harm-benefit distinction is useless as a guide to policy. If installing smoke scrubbers were the optimal solution, the factory could be subsidized for installing smoke scrubbers; equivalently, it could be made liable for the cost imposed on the residents if the scrubbers are not installed. If relocating the residences were the optimal solution, the factory owner might compensate the homeowners for the cost of relocation; alternatively, the homeowners might bear the cost of the smoke if they remained in the area. So ultimately, the issue is one of property rights and entitlements. Does the factory owner have the right to put smoke in the air, do the residents have the right to smoke-free air, or does the right fall somewhere in-between (for example, the factory owner has the right to put two tons of particulants in the air, but no more)? In a world without transaction costs, there are no answers because any allocation of entitlements will lead to an efficient result. And without a zero reference (entitlement) point, the extent of the relevant harm or benefit cannot be measured.

But, as we will now show, once transaction costs are considered and the efficient outcome is determined (not always an easy task), then the appropriate allocation of entitlements is obvious, the harm-benefit distinction becomes relevant, and the these questions can be answered.

A. NEGATIVE EXTERNALITIES

When negative externalities are involved, the efficient outcome is the baseline. Consider the situation of factories polluting the air, where the efficient solution is for each factory to install a smoke scrubber that removes some but not all of the pollution. If the efficient outcome were the baseline, then a factory would be liable for the harm to the residents only when the factory did not install the smoke scrubber. The harm to the residents is greater than the cost savings from not having a smoke scrubber (since we have assumed that installing the scrubber is the optimal outcome). Hence only rarely or perhaps not at all would a factory act inefficiently by not installing the scrubber and the residents take the factory to court.

Suppose we took any other baseline. If factories had the right to emit as many particles into the air as they wanted, then factory owners would have to be compensated for the benefit of installing scrubbers. This would involve a great number of court cases (and/or negotiated settlements) because the efficient outcome would require those who benefit to compensate the factories for the cost of the scrubbers. Suppose instead that the residents had the right to smoke-free air. Then factories would still choose to install scrubbers, but the owners of the factory would be liable for any particulants emitted despite the presence of the scrubber, even though by assumption it is efficient to not reduce the emissions still further. The homeowners would now sue the factory owners. Again, there would be a great number of court cases.

So, in this situation, any other baseline (set of entitlements) besides the efficient one involves extremely large court transaction costs. Once we choose efficiency as the baseline, harm and benefit, and punishment and reward become meaningful as they are measured from the efficient outcome.

So far the discussion has been in terms of liability rules, but a similar analysis holds for other incentive schemes as well. Consider the choice between pollution taxes and subsidies for installing scrubbers. The best choice is then to tax the firm only if its pollution level is above the optimal. Similarly, if regulation is used instead of nuisance law, regulations would require the firm to produce no more than the optimal level of smoke.

B. LONG-RUN ENTRY AND EXIT

In the short run, factories can install scrubbers and/or residents can install air-conditioners. In the long run, damage prevention can also be achieved by exit of factories or residents from the area or by one or the other not entering the area in the first place. Suppose that the courts can determine at relatively low cost whether the factory is optimally located. Then the baseline should be that the factory is not liable if it is appropriately located in the area and it has undertaken cost-effective short-run behavior such as installing a smoke scrubber. Under this scenario, there would be few court cases. Only if a mistake has been made – the firm mistakenly thought that it was optimally located and acting efficiently or the residents mistakenly thought that the firm was acting inefficiently – would a court case arise.

All other baselines involve *extremely* large transaction costs. Consider first, the case where residents have the right to clean air. Even with scrubbers, the factories still create some air pollution. We have already shown that in the short-run, all homeowners would have to be compensated under such an entitlement scheme. In the long run, developers who would have built homes in the absence of pollution but instead developed the land for other uses that were not sensitive to pollution would also have to be compensated for their reduced profits. Both the numbers of court cases and the requisite information needed would increase by an order of magnitude. Any attempt to limit compensation to only those uses that are harmed in the short run would lead to inappropriate long-run entry and exit decisions.

If instead factories were given the right to pollute the air, then long-run considerations would require compensation to landowners when they chose to develop nonpolluting uses for their land, even though profits would have been higher if they had built pollution-creating factories. Clearly, the information costs of such a scheme would be very large. The alternative of only compensating those firms that actually pollute would create inappropriate incentives to enter the pollution creating industry.

C. POSITIVE EXTERNALITIES

Positive externalities create more problems. Consider the situation where a firm needs to filter river water for its own use and this results in a benefit to the many downstream owners in comparison to a situation where there is no firm and no filtration. Assume further that a better filtration system (a scrubber) would be uneconomic for the firm to take up on its own but that the additional benefits of an improved system to the downstream owners would outweigh the costs to the firm. This characterization is thus symmetric to the air pollution example. Is the carrot or the stick more appropriate?

If one merely looked at the short run, the policy recommendation would be to require firms to install scrubbers without compensation. For example, firms might be liable for the harm to water quality where the water-quality benchmark was based on the scrubbers being in place. Installing the scrubbers would be less than the cost to the firms of not scrubbing so the firms would choose to do so, and there would be no need for a court transaction.

The problem arises in the long run. If the previously stated policy were implemented, then profits would be reduced and firms might shut down or not enter the industry (or area) in the first place. In a world without transaction costs, one could make firms (or people) liable for cleaning the water whether or not they were in the industry. Then firms would have the correct long-run incentives because they could not avoid liability by not entering the industry. But in the real world, the cost of determining who would have been in the industry if they had not been forced to install scrubber is extremely high. The realistic alternative is to only deal with the people in the industry. As already shown, not compensating them for the scrubbers reduces the number of firms in the industry below optimal. However, compensating them involves a transaction cost. So the major alternatives are as follows: (1) Treat a neutral effect on water quality as the baseline but not require restitution for benefits conferred. This situation has zero court transaction costs, but there is a cost due to the underprovision of water quality by existing firms and perhaps too few firms in the industry compared with the optimal number of firms. (2) Treat a neutral effect on water quality as the baseline, but allow the firm to collect for benefits conferred. This method has high court costs but the optimal amount of filtration is provided. (3) Treat the optimal amount of water-quality enhancement as the baseline and make the existing firm liable for any harm from lower quality. This method definitely has too few firms in the industry, but those that are in the industry provide the optimal amount of filtration.

Which solution is the best depends on the circumstances. However, a few general results can be stated. Because of transaction costs, the appropriate baseline is more difficult to determine when there are positive externalities than when there are negative externalities. Collecting for benefits conferred when there is a positive externality is less likely than paying for harms imposed when there is a negative externality. These theoretical conclusions are corroborated in the law – restitution for benefits is rare compared with liability for harm and the circumstances whereby one collects restitution is more difficult to predict on theoretical grounds.

It now becomes critical to show that positive and negative externalities are not plagued with the same symmetry inherent in the harm-benefit distinction. That is, we must show that a negative externality is not just a positive externality from another viewpoint. We reach this result by establishing the efficient outcome as the point of reference. Liability for harm and restitution for benefit will have different long-run effects. If liability is based on the short run, then there are positive externalities if any amount of liability results in too few firms in the industry; if restitution is based on the short run, then there are negative externalities if any amount of restitution results in too many firms in the long run.

D. ECONOMIC MARKETS

In ordinary economic markets the consumer pays the farmer for purchasing the farmer's apples. We do not observe the farmer's paying the consumer for the apples not purchased. Both ways the consumer "pays" for purchasing apples, either by paying the farmer ten cents for each apple consumed or by not receiving ten cents from the farmer for each apple consumed. Because we rarely see the latter and typically see the former method, our economic intuition tells us that there are persuasive economic arguments in favor of the former, and, in fact, there are. Once again transaction cost is the key.

Assume that the farmer had to pay consumers for the benefit he derives from their not consuming his apples. Even in the absence of a transfer of apples to the consumer, a transaction between the two would be necessary as the farmer would have to pay the consumer. In comparison to the normal situation where there is a transfer of money only when there is a transfer of apples, here there is a transfer of money when there is no transfer of apples. Clearly, the normal way of doing things involves lower transaction costs by several orders of magnitude. In the long run, the problem is even worse. If the farmer did not go into the apple-growing business, he would not be providing apples. Therefore, he would still owe the potential consumers money, which would clearly involve high information and transaction costs. If we tried to reduce these costs by charging the farmer only when he actually grew apples, this would create an incentive to not engage in apple production.

Similar problems would appear on the consumer side. Society would either have to determine a priori who would consume the apples in the first place (which involves high information costs) or have the farmer pay most of the people for not consuming when they were not going to consume his goods anyway. Instead of having five people buy from one farmer, we might have everyone transacting (getting money for purchasing less than the dollar amount owed by the farmer or paying money for purchasing more than the dollar amount of apples owed).

In this mirror world, there is no longer a natural baseline. If the seller is to pay the buyer for nonpurchase, how much money is to be paid for each nontransaction? Is it to be assumed that the buyer receives $100 because he has not taken one thousand apples at ten cents each or $15 because he has not taken one hundred apples at fifteen cents each? For this system to work, we must take into account all the goods that could have been traded but were not, where the status quo in the event of no trade is not uniquely defined. In the ordinary property rights situation, the baseline apart from transactions is, however, uniquely determined. The farmer keeps his apples and the consumer his money until they determine the suitable conditions for exchange. Using the efficient outcome as a baseline would require an extraordinary amount of information in comparison with tort situations, in which the government has already committed itself to a determination of the efficient level of precautions in setting the negligence standard. With sales transactions, the state of nature (no interaction) affords the best baseline point, as theories of justice generally require.

E. CONCLUDING REMARKS

When there are negative externalities, the tort system enables the victim of a harm to sue the injurer. But when there are positive externalities, only under very special circumstances is the benefactor allowed to sue the person who gained. Why are these symmetric situations treated so asymmetrically? The answer is that there are great asymmetries in administrative costs. Great asymmetries in administrative costs also explain why markets tend to use the carrot while governments tend to use the stick (when controlling for negative externalities) rather than the reverse. In both the negative externality case and in exchange markets, it is too costly to have a payment when the parties are not already transacting. Thus in ordinary markets, there is only payment between people who are otherwise exchanging goods and services. When there are negative externalities, there is no ongoing transaction between the parties – that is why it is considered an externality. Therefore, when there are negative externalities, to save on transaction costs people are not held liable if they are acting efficiently.

Most of the answers posed at the beginning of the chapter have been implicitly answered, except possibly the question whether a witness should be punished for not reporting a crime or rewarded for reporting one. It seems that the solution in this case is to reward witnesses. The reverse is very hard to establish because if a witness does not report a crime, it may be very difficult to know who the witness was. Furthermore, in reporting the crime, the witness is already transacting with the police so that the additional transaction cost of paying the witness is slight.

SUGGESTIONS FOR FURTHER READING

Much of the argument in this chapter relies on Wittman (1984). Restitution is a minor area of the law, but it has captured the interest of a number of academic writers. Epstein (1994) has a wide-ranging discussion that starts with Aristotle and covers numerous areas in the law. Levmore (1985) treats restitution as non-bargained-for benefits (e.g., a doctor should be compensated for treating an unconscious patient), while Dari-Mattiacci (2004) suggests that punishments are more versatile than rewards.

REVIEW QUESTIONS

1. When is the harm-benefit distinction meaningful? (4)
2. Why do economic markets tend to use carrots, while pollution and traffic safety use sticks? (8)
3. Why do long-run entry and exit decisions affect our choice regarding punishment and reward? (6)
4. Why do negative externalities create clear guidelines concerning punishment (you should be punished for deviating from efficiency), while positive externalities create less clear guidelines (it is not clear that you should be rewarded for acting efficiently)? (6)
5. In *Rylands v. Fletcher*, 3 HL 330 (1868), the defendants had dammed an area covering an old abandoned coal mine to create a water mill. The coal mine had not been completely blocked off, and consequently, the water drained into the abandoned mine and into adjacent mines directly connected to the old mine. The adjacent mines were still operating and the plaintiff sued for damages. Who should be liable? (10)
6. If your neighbor's house needed a paint job, why couldn't you collect from the neighbor if you decided to paint her house on your own? (2)

REFERENCES

Dari-Mattiacci, Giuseppi. (2004). Negative Liability. Paper given at the *American Law and Economic Association Annual Meeting*.

Epstein, Richard A. (1994). The Ubiquity of the Benefit Principle. 67 *Southern California Law Review* 1369.

· Levmore, Saul. (1985). Explaining Restitution. 71 *Virginia Law Review* 65.

Wittman, Donald. (1984). Liability for Harm of Restitution for Benefit. 13 *Journal of Legal Studies* 57.

14 The Takings Clause: Should There Be Compensation for Regulation?

Amendment 5: "... nor shall private property be taken for public use, without just compensation."

U.S. Constitution

A. Negative Externalities 122

B. Positive Externalities 124

C. Concluding Remarks 125

SUGGESTIONS FOR FURTHER READING 127

REVIEW QUESTIONS 127

REFERENCES 127

We know from previous chapters that governments compensate for the taking of land regardless of the amount or value of the land involved. But should the government compensate landowners when the value of their property is reduced because of regulation? And if so, under what circumstances should compensation take place? Consider the following situations: The government requires cedar trees to be cut down because pests deadly to apple trees, but causing no harm to cedar trees, reside in the cedar trees. Should the owners of the cedar trees be compensated? A city zoning regulation forces a quarry operation to shut down. Should the owner of the quarry be compensated? A building is designated a historical landmark and therefore the owner cannot make additions to the building that would make it more valuable. Should the owner of the building be compensated? A developer dredges a pond and creates a marina. The government requires free public access to the marina, which reduces the developer's profits. Should the government compensate the developer?

As we will see, many of the answers depend on the extent of administrative (transaction) costs associated with compensation and the long-run incentive effects.

A. NEGATIVE EXTERNALITIES

In *Miller v. Schoene*, 276 U.S. 272 (1958), the Supreme Court said that the state of Virginia did not have to compensate owners of cedar trees when a Virginia statute was enacted requiring destruction of cedar trees infested with a pest deadly to nearby apple orchards but harmless to the host cedars themselves. This Supreme Court ruling has caused apoplexy among conservatives and libertarians. Epstein (1985) argued that the owner of the land has the property right to grow anything on it as long as it does not physically invade others. The cedar trees did not invade other's property (as smoke does) and therefore Epstein believed that the owners should be compensated for the destruction of the trees.

What does economic theory tell us? Cedar trees and apple trees are inputs into the production of damaged apples. As a consequence, causality cannot provide an acceptable explanation for whether the owners of cedars should be compensated because both the cedars and the apple trees caused the damage. What difference does it make whether the trees release spores that harm neighboring apple trees (where Epstein would approve of no compensation) or the cedar trees are a primary vector for pests that harm apple trees (where Epstein desires compensation)?

Growing cedars harms apple growers and benefits owners of cedar trees; cutting cedars harms owners of cedar trees and benefits apple growers. In the absence of transaction costs, no one of the following can be privileged over the other: (1) the apple tree owners are compensated for the harm to them when there is no regulation against the growing of cedar trees; (2) the apple tree owners pay for the harm to the cedar tree growers when there is a regulation against the growing of cedar trees; (3) the cedar tree owners pay for the harm to apple growers when there is no regulation against the growing of cedar trees; (4) the cedar tree owners are compensated for the harm to them when there is a regulation against the growing of cedar trees; or (5) neither party is compensated or charged in the presence or absence of a regulation against the growing of cedar trees.[1]

---

[1]   In the absence of transaction costs, it makes sense to have pairs (2 and 4 or 1 and 3). In this way, the benefits are measured against the costs and the proper incentives are more likely to be in place. This could be done either by direct payments from winners to losers or indirectly through government taxes and expenditures.

There can be a taking only when an entitlement is taken, but how are entitlements determined in the first place? When there are negative externalities, efficiency determines entitlements; no one is compensated for a taking of their rights because no rights are taken. That is, the baseline for allocating rights is efficiency, not the inefficient world in the absence of a regulation.

Apples are an important agricultural crop in Virginia, while cedars are used mainly as windbreaks, fencing, and for ornamental purposes. Where the balance lies between the cost and benefit of cutting down cedar trees is clear.[2] But determining the actual cost to the many individual owners of cedar trees is quite costly. *Furthermore, because a regulation affects landowners who might have undertaken the activity (such as planting cedar trees) in the future if it were not proscribed by the regulation, the harm to these landowners would also have to be taken into account if there were a system of compensation for regulation.* So a system of compensation is totally impractical. Efficiency argues that the landowners should not have the right to grow cedars. Compensation would not create incentives for greater efficiency (the usual economic justification for compensation) because the regulation has already achieved that goal; but compensation would involve unnecessary court costs in order to transfer wealth from the taxpayers to the cedar tree owners. Therefore, cedar tree owners should not be compensated when their trees are cut down. The court implicitly accepted this argument.

In contrast, compensating for the physical taking of land involves much lower transaction costs. The particular properties taken are legally transferred to the state. So the additional transaction cost of paying for the transfer is relatively minor. The purchase of a property by the state mirrors citizens' purchases of property and services (see the previous chapter).

City zoning regulations often prevent activities that were previously allowed. This is especially the case when the city expands to encompass more rural areas and animal husbandry is no longer acceptable. It is also true for rock quarrying and other highly noxious activities. Generally, the government does not have to compensate for lost value to these firms if the regulation is efficient. See, for example, *Hadacheck v. Sebastian*, 239 U.S. 394 (1915) where a zoning ordinance forced a brickyard within recently expanded Los Angeles city limits to shutdown and *Consolidated Rock Products Co. v. The City of Los Angeles*, 370 P.2d 342 (1962) where a quarry was forced to shutdown. In neither case was compensation granted. When zoning regulations affect *many* properties, compensation would involve extremely high transaction costs. Therefore, the present efficient outcome is the baseline, not the previously efficient outcome.

All entitlements are contingent. The way to look at the quarry case is to say that the quarry had the right to be in operation as long as it was not within city limits. In this way, the quarry never had the right to operate in the city of Los Angeles and therefore did not have to be compensated for losing a right that it did not have.[3]

Not compensating the quarry has an additional beneficial effect. It encourages the owner to anticipate the growing urbanization and the increased likelihood of having to close operations. Because the owner's investment will not be compensated, the owner

---

[2] In those states and countries where cedar trees (or similar vectors) are important economically and apples are relatively unimportant, owners are not forced to remove their cedar trees. This illustrates the argument that the law should give the entitlement to the side that values the entitlement the most.

[3] For more on sequence, see Chapter 20 on the role of being first.

will allow the buildings and equipment to depreciate rather than engaging in an inefficient upgrading of the facilities.

B. POSITIVE EXTERNALITIES

In *Penn Central Transport Co. v. New York City*, 438 U.S. 104 (1978), New York City designated Grand Central Station as a historical landmark, thereby preventing Penn Central from building an office building on top of the station.[4] Penn Central claimed that it lost $6 million in potential profits, for which it demanded compensation under the takings clause of the U.S. Constitution. A majority of the United States Supreme Court rejected Penn Central's argument.

Ignoring temporarily the cost of administering compensation, the court majority was in error. Punishing Penn Central for owning a historical landmark encourages people to build nondistinguished buildings or, more important, to convert distinguished buildings into ordinary ones before they are designated historical landmarks. The net result is too few landmark buildings will be built or retained. The diametrically opposed rule from compensation is to extract payments from all those who did not maintain, or even construct, a landmark building. Obviously, this requires an inordinate amount of information and is totally infeasible. Burdening only those who own landmark buildings reduces court administrative and information costs but creates the wrong incentives because some will avoid having their buildings become landmarks in the first place.

Because a system of compensation does involve considerable administrative costs, one must weigh these costs against the long-run misallocation costs under a system of regulation without compensation. Without a serious empirical study, one cannot come up with a definitive answer regarding relative costs; however, the evidence appears to be in favor of compensation. Individual landmarks are designated in a case-by-case adjudication, thereby providing some inkling of the costs to the landmark owner. The contrast to wide-ranging antipollution regulation is clear. With landmark cases, the burdens are heavily concentrated; the costs of administering compensation are low, and the distortions from not compensating are obvious. However, there is one major problem with a compensation rule – those who owned landmark buildings would have an incentive to claim (even if it were not the case) that they wanted to make additions not allowed by the landmark status. If successful, these owners would be compensated for a loss that they did not really incur.

It is useful to compare the Penn Central case to that of *Maher v. City of New Orleans*, 516 F.2D 1051 (1975). The plaintiff wanted to replace a building in the Vieux Carré of New Orleans. This is an area of one hundred city blocks containing a whole community of buildings dating from before the Civil War and is a major tourist attraction. Most of the buildings in the district are not individually distinguished, rather the ambience of the district accounts for its special character. The value of Maher's land was much higher because of the general restriction against changing the character of the place. Thus the regulation did not hurt landowners in Vieux Carré. Of course, any one landowner (by being able to build a large hotel) would greatly benefit from being the exception to the general restriction, but her benefit would result in an even greater harm to her

---

[4] The city granted extra "air rights" for other buildings that Penn Central owned in exchange. The value of a landmark often accrues to others besides the owner of the landmark because such landmarks increase tourism.

neighbors. So, in this case, not granting compensation for the regulation is an easy call, even though preserving old buildings is a positive externality.

Finally, we turn to a case where the court ruled in favor of compensation for regulation. At great expense, the Kaiser Corporation deepened a shallow pond and then built a marina by connecting it to the ocean. Afterward, the Army Corps of Engineers demanded that the marina provide public access. Many states require public access to coastal land without triggering the takings clause. But, in this case, *Kaiser Aetna v. United States*, 444 U.S. 164 (1979), the court ruled that if the state wanted public access it would have to pay. The difference lies in the long-run incentive effects. If such government regulations could be imposed without compensation, then the incentive to create marinas and the like would be reduced. Furthermore, this regulation was very particularistic in that it was aimed at this one marina. Hence, the court transaction costs are smaller than if the regulation affected a great number of uses. Finally, if it were truly better for the marina to open up to the public, Kaiser could have captured the benefits by charging the users – this is not an externality case (the same holds for public access more generally).

This segues into the issue of why governments pay for goods. First, there is already a transaction; for example, the government is ordering a computer, so the extra transaction cost of paying for it is slight. Second, we have to worry about long-run incentive effects. If governments took computers without paying for them, then some firms might not be in the industry in the first place. To avoid these long-run disincentive effects, the government would have to identify who should be in the industry, an extremely costly and totally impractical undertaking. For the same reasons economic market use carrots instead of sticks, the government must use carrots rather than sticks when it wants to procure goods and services.[5]

C. CONCLUDING REMARKS

Government regulation is a substitute for civil law. For example, a brick factory might be shut down because it violates city zoning regulations or because residences ask for a permanent injunction against the factory and the courts find the brick factory to be a nuisance. Although the subject of the chapter is government regulation, the same analysis holds for its civil counterparts. If residences should not have to compensate a brick factory for shutting down (which is generally the case),[6] then the same logic holds for government – it should not have to compensate the brick factory for shutting down either. And if the government should not pay, then neither should the residences.

The analysis in this chapter has suggested that in general there should be no compensation for efficient regulation. But what if the government regulation is inefficient? In such cases, the party should be compensated. Consider for example *Averne Bay Construction Company v. Thatcher*, 15 N.E. 2d 587 (1938). The plaintiff wanted to build a gas station, but the city had zoned the property residential. The trial court established that there were no residences within a mile of the proposed gas station and for good reason. In the vicinity, the city operated an incinerator that "gave off offensive fumes which permeated the plaintiff's premises." Near the premises, "sanitary sewage emptied into an open creak resulting in nauseating odors which [also] permeated the ... property."

---

[5] The drafting of soldiers is an interesting counterexample.
[6] See Chapter 20.

EAGLE FEATHERS

The code of federal regulations states that bald eagles and golden eagles, live or dead, or their parts which were lawfully acquired before 1940 in the case of bald eagles and before 1962 in the case of golden eagles can be possessed and transported but cannot be imported, exported, purchased, sold, traded, or bartered (50 CFR §22.2(a) 1978). In *Andrus v. Allard*, 444 U.S. 51 (1979), Allard argued that the prohibition of such sales constituted a taking of his private property without just compensation as he acquired the eagle feathers when it was legal to do so. The Supreme Court ruled that this was not a taking. Part of the court's argument relied on the fact that it was difficult to determine whether feathers were old or recent. Therefore, feathers obtained from recently killed endangered eagles could be passed off as being obtained a long time ago. Once again we see how important technology is. If there were a low-cost way of detecting age, then the act might have been written differently in the first place. Similar issues surround the sale of ivory. Elephants are endangered in certain areas and in other areas they need to be culled. Selling ivory from the latter areas makes sense if the ivory can be distinguished.

IS A MORATORIUM A TAKING?

The Supreme Court in *Tahoe Sierra Preservation Council v. Tahoe Regional Planning Agency*, 535 U.S. 302 (2002), upheld the power of the Lake Tahoe Planning Commission to impose a rolling moratorium on new home construction in the Lake Tahoe basin. The case arose when the planning agency imposed a series of moratoriums on land in the Lake Tahoe basin to protect the lake's clarity from runoff. These moratoria allowed no exceptions and forbade any land use whatsoever.

Throughout this book, I have provided efficiency explanations for the law. Richard Epstein, who writes from a libertarian point of view, has a different take on the takings issue. He sees this decision as legalized theft. Here are his comments excerpted from the *National Law Journal* (May 6, 2002): "All the dislocations were created by the incumbent owners; yet none of the options before the planning board required the residents to cut back on their continued property use. Instead, the brunt of new restrictions all fell on nonresident property owners, who had caused no damage but who had only limited clout in the planning process. The politics of self-interest are all too apparent: The means of environmental control chosen did more than preserve the status quo on the lake. It conferred a huge windfall on current homeowners. Land densities and housing stock were both reduced. The two forces together drove up the price of built homes, which current owners can capture either by use or by sale. The unbuilt plots essentially are worth nothing."

The court found the zoning unsuitable given the conditions of the surrounding area and held that "an ordinance which permanently so restricts the property that it cannot be used for any reasonable purpose ... must be recognized as a taking of the property."

SUGGESTIONS FOR FURTHER READING

Buchanan (1974) threw an early salvo against the decision in *Miller v. Schoene*. See also Epstein (1985). For a complete historical account of the issues in this case, see Fischel (2004). As suggested in one of the boxed examples, Epstein has a more negative view of government behavior, in general, and the court decisions regarding the takings issue, in particular. Epstein (1985) expounds on these arguments. Fischel (1995) shows the importance of local politics in controlling excessive behavior by the government (a topic that we will discuss at length in the chapter on federalism). Blume and Rubinfeld (1984) consider the insurance role of takings and suggest that it should apply to regulatory takings as well. We will briefly cover the insurance issue in a boxed example on takings in Chapter 27.

REVIEW QUESTIONS

1. If the government takes your property, it must compensate you. But if through regulation it diminishes the value of your property by an equivalent amount, the government does not have to compensate you. Why? As always, only use economic arguments, not legal ones. (10)
2. Under what circumstances should the government compensate for regulation? Explain. (4)
3. Why are we more inclined to compensate for positive externalities than for negative externalities? (6)
4. Even when there are positive externalities, compensating for regulation is problematic. Explain. (6)

REFERENCES

Blume, Lawrence, and Daniel Rubinfeld. (1984). Compensation for Takings: An Economic Analysis. 72 *California Law Review* 569.

Buchanan, James M. (1972). Politics, Property, and the Law: An Alternative Interpretation of *Miller et al. V. Schoene*. 15 *Journal of Law and Economics* 439.

Epstein, Richard A. (1985). *Taking: Private Property and the Power of Eminent Domain.* Cambridge, MA: Harvard University Press.

Fischel, William A. (1995). *Regulatory Taking: Law, Economics, and Politics.* Cambridge, MA: Harvard University Press.

Fischel, William A. (2004). The Law and Economics of Cedar-Apple Rust: State Action and Just Compensation in *Miller v. Schoene. Dartmouth College Economics Department Working Paper.*

V TORTS AND CRIMES: LIABILITY RULES AND PUNISHMENTS

In Part V we consider torts and crimes. The word "torts" has the same root as torsion and means twist. In modern parlance, a tort is a harm, such as the harm to a pedestrian when a car crashes onto a sidewalk. So torts and crimes are two different kinds of harms litigated in two different courts (civil and criminal, respectively).[1] The legal system has a much more specific meaning for tort than harm (for example, harms that occur because of breach of contract are part of contract law not tort law); but here we will consider harm in a more abstract way so that the logic need not be restricted to any one area of the law.

The subheading of Part V is liability rules and punishments. In Part IV, we introduced the generic notion of a liability rule – a charge for an involuntary transfer. But liability rules come in many flavors. In Part V, we consider several variations, including strict liability, no liability, and negligence liability. All of this requires a more formal presentation than previously undertaken.

So in Chapter 15, we start off with a rigorous presentation of cost-benefit analysis and derive the *marginal* conditions for an *efficient* outcome. In words, optimality requires that the last dollar spent on damage prevention by the victim (Y) reduces expected damage by one dollar, and similarly that the last dollar spent on damage prevention by the injurer (X) reduces expected damage by one dollar. Letting Ω (omega) stand for optimal, the optimal amount of prevention undertaken by X is labeled x^{Ω} and the optimal amount of damage undertaken by Y is y^{Ω}.

The key is to find a liability rule, where the *equilibrium* levels of prevention undertaken by the injurer and the victim (x^e, y^e) coincide with the optimal levels, x^{Ω}, y^{Ω}. Along with efficiency and rationality, the notion of equilibrium is a fundamental concept in economics (it is also a fundamental concept in sciences such as physics and chemistry, but unfortunately the concept seems to be missing from much of social science research outside of economics). We therefore devote a significant part of Chapter 15 to explicating the concept of equilibrium.

In the remaining part of Chapter 15, we consider whether strict liability or no liability results in an efficient outcome. In general, neither does. In Chapter 16, we consider negligence rules. We demonstrate that appropriately designed negligence rules do lead to an efficient equilibrium. We note that while the analysis is concerned with the optimal structure of liability rules, the same logic holds for the optimal design of contracts.

In Chapter 17, we consider criminal law. We argue that criminals are rational and that they have downward sloping demand curves for crime just as ordinary citizens have downward sloping demand curves for other goods. We can thus use cost-benefit analysis in deriving the optimal punishment for crime. We then show why the civil justice system in general and the tort system in particular is inadequate in controlling crime as opposed to other harms, and thus there is a need for a separate criminal justice system.

---

[1] In Chapter 17, we will explain this differential treatment.

15

COST MINIMIZATION AND LIABILITY RULES

A. Society Minimizes the Total Cost of Damage
   and Damage Prevention 132

B. Cournot-Nash Equilibria 134

C. Equilibria Need Not Be Pareto Optimal # 134

D. Strict Liability by X 136

E. No Liability by X 137

F. Concluding Remarks 139

SUGGESTIONS FOR FURTHER READING 139

REVIEW QUESTIONS 139

REFERENCE 139

Until now, we have talked about liability rules in a generic sense – the victim is compensated for an involuntary transfer of her entitlement. We will now discuss the various liability rules and the reason for choosing one over another.

In this and the following three chapters, we ignore the cost of courts, the possibility of error, and risk aversion. The analysis is difficult enough without bringing these issues to bear. High transaction costs will be assumed. If there were zero transaction costs, then all liability rules would be equally good in producing an efficient outcome, as the individuals would transact around them and implicitly create an efficient liability rule if the original rule was not efficient (this is just an application of the Coase theorem). The primary example regards liability for automobile accidents, the classic case of high transaction costs. However, many of the insights apply to low transaction costs cases, as well.

Before we can get to liability rules, we first need to understand cost minimization. We have already discussed cost-benefit analysis in an intuitive way. It is now time to present the ideas more formally. For precision, some of the analysis uses mathematical equations. However, the basic idea is first presented in standard English so that the reader can gain an intuitive understanding even if the reader skims over the mathematics.

A. SOCIETY MINIMIZES THE TOTAL COST OF DAMAGE AND DAMAGE PREVENTION

Once again we undertake a cost-benefit analysis. Society minimizes the total cost of damage and damage prevention (e.g., expenditures on better tires) by the injurer and the victim. The injurer should increase his spending on damage prevention until the last dollar spent on damage prevention by the injurer reduces damages by a dollar. Until then, an extra dollar spent on damage reduction reduces damages by more than a dollar; after that an extra dollar spent on damage reduction reduces damages by less than a dollar. Similarly, the victim should increase her spending on damage prevention until the last dollar she spends on damage prevention reduces damages by a dollar. In this way, we determine the optimal amount of precaution (damage prevention) by the injurer and the victim. Notice that the optimal may require both sides to undertake precaution. For example, the driver of the car should have his lights adjusted and the pedestrian should wear light-colored clothes at night when there is no snow and walk on the sidewalk instead of the street.

We now proceed to the more formal presentation. As in most of economic thinking, we start our analysis with the objective function. Society minimizes the expected total cost, C^S, which is equal to the expected cost of the damage plus the cost of damage prevention by the victim and the injurer,

$$C^S = D(x, y) + x + y$$

Where x is the dollar amount that X, the injurer, spends on damage prevention, y is the dollar amount that Y, the injured, spends on damage prevention, and D is the expected level of damage to Y given x and y. If X is a driver, then x might be the dollar amount spent on safer tires and good brakes. If Y is a pedestrian, then y might be the dollar amount spent on light-reflecting clothes, a flashlight, and the time cost of walking on sidewalks instead of walking along the road. Note that $D(x, y)$ is expected damage to the victim Y.[1] We could have broken this term down into two parts: $D(x, y) = P(x, y)d(x, y)$, where P is the probability of an accident and $d(x, y)$ is the damage given that an accident has occurred. We have chosen the simpler term, $D(x, y)$, to reduce the amount of clutter.[2] Note also how symmetric the cost equation is – both x and y are inputs into the reduction of harm. This is in line with the argument made by Coase.

Society minimizes the total cost of damage to Y and damage prevention by X and Y rather than just minimizing the harm from accidents. If the latter were true, there would be policemen on every mile of freeway and the speed limit would be reduced to 30 miles an hour. As in other areas of economics, both benefits and costs must be considered. None of my students drives a tank to school even though it would be safer. $D(x, y)$ can also stand for the damage from pollution. As seen in our discussion of the Coase theorem, society's objective is not to minimize pollution damage; rather, society's objective is to minimize the sum of pollution damage and the cost of pollution prevention, $D(x, y) + x + y$.

Sometimes it is hard to understand the damage function in an abstract sense. To help in the intuition, we will illustrate with the following damage function: $D(x, y) = 100 - 4x^{1/2} - 16y^{1/2}$.

Let $D_x = \frac{\partial D}{\partial x}$ be the partial derivative of damage, $D(x, y)$, with respect to x. It is the effect of an increase of x, damage prevention by X, on the amount of the expected damage, holding everything else constant. If X spends more on damage prevention, then expected damage should decrease. That is, $D_x < 0$. Similarly, $D_y < 0$. That is, when Y spends more on damage prevention, expected damage will decrease, as well. In our example, $D_x = -2x^{-1/2}$ and $D_y = -8y^{-1/2} < 0$ for all positive values of x and y.

As in other areas of economics marginal productivity is decreasing. That is, additional dollars spent on damage prevention reduce (expected) damage at a decreasing rate. Simply put, if you spend a dollar on damage prevention, you will spend it where you get the biggest bang for your buck. As you spend more and more dollars, you still reduce damage, but the decrease in damage decreases. For example, the first dollar spent might reduce damage by $10; the second dollar spent might reduce damages by $9 for a total decrease of 19. More formally, $D_{xx} > 0$ and $D_{yy} > 0$. These second derivatives are positive because a decrease in the decrease is a double negative and therefore a positive. In our numerical example, $D_{xx} = x^{-3/2} > 0$ and $D_{yy} = 4y^{-3/2} > 0$.

We also assume that $D_{xy}D_{xy} < D_{xx}D_{yy}$. This implies that the inputs are substitutes. That is, when one input goes up, the marginal productivity of the other goes down and vice versa. For example, if there is a drunk driver who lives down the street, mothers will spend more time preventing their children from running in the street than they would otherwise. From the other direction, if a busy street is turned into a cul de sac, parents will exercise less precaution.

---

[1] To make the analysis easier, we assume that the driver-injurer is not hurt.
[2] 1/100 of a chance of $100,000 worth of damage is equivalent to a 100% chance of $1,000 damage. To reduce confusion, in the next two chapters we will often treat damage as being certain so that $D(x, y)$ stands for actual damage rather than expected damage. In this way, we can substitute "cost" to society rather than having to say "expected cost."

The first-order conditions for expected cost minimization are

$$C_x^s = 1 + D_x(x, y) = 1 - 2x^{-1/2} = 0,$$
$$C_y^s = 1 + D_y(x, y) = 1 - 8y^{-1/2} = 0.$$

That is, cost minimization requires that expenditures on damage prevention increase until the last dollar spent on damage prevention by X, the injurer (and Y, the victim) reduces expected damage by $1. Again, this is standard economics from a slightly different view. If a dollar's worth of damage prevention reduces expected damage by more than a dollar, you will spend the extra dollar. But you won't spend an additional dollar on damage prevention if it reduces expected damage by less than a dollar.

That x, y, which satisfy the first-order conditions, will be denoted by x^Ω, y^Ω. Omega $= \Omega$, which stands for optimal. That is, x^Ω, y^Ω is the optimal amount of damage prevention spent by X and Y, respectively. Clearly, if $y < y^\Omega$, then a marginal increase in y would decrease expected damages by more than a dollar, and if $y > y^\Omega$, then a decrease in y would result in an increase in expected damage by less than a dollar. In our example, $x^\Omega = 4$ and $y^\Omega = 64$.

Second-order conditions are

$$C_{xx}^s = D_{xx}(x, y) = x^{-3/2} > 0,$$
$$C_{yy}^s = D_{yy}(x, y) = 4y^{-3/2} > 0,$$
$$C_{xx}^s C_{yy}^s = x^{-3/2} 4y^{-3/2} > C_{xy}^s C_{xx}^s = 0.$$

These conditions ensure that we have a minimum rather than a maximum (or an inflection point).

B. COURNOT-NASH EQUILIBRIA

Society's problem is to create the correct incentive structure through a liability rule system so that two individuals X and Y each choose the correct allocation of inputs into damage reduction. This is not a trivial task. X and Y are individuals who may not even know of each other's existence; yet, society must create the appropriate incentives such that their equilibrium choices coincide with the optimal.

Before we can proceed, we need to have a precise understanding of equilibrium.

DEFINITION: An outcome, x^e, y^e is a Cournot-Nash equilibrium, if given y^e, that x, which maximizes X's utility is x^e; and given x^e, that y, which maximizes Y's utility is y^e.

That is, *we have an equilibrium, if given Y's choice, X does not want to change his choice, and given X's choice, Y does not want to change her choice.* In this way, neither will want to move given that the other person will not move. So we have an equilibrium.

C. EQUILIBRIA NEED NOT BE PARETO OPTIMAL

Equilibrium and Pareto optimality are the fundamental building blocks of economics, but they are sometimes conflated. The following game matrices should give a feeling for the concept of equilibrium and how it differs from the concept of Pareto optimality:

The first example is a zero-sum game where Column pays Row. We illustrate via a simple card game. Column can choose to put a red queen card (C_1) or a black queen card (C_2) face down on the table.

Row also has a choice between placing a red queen card (R_1) or a black queen card (R_2) face down on the table. After both have put their cards on the table, the cards are turned over. If both cards are red, then Column pays Row $100; if both cards are black, then Column pays Row $120. If Column's card is red and Row's card is black, then Column pays Row $50; if the reverse is the case, then Column pays Row $110. This information is conveniently put into the matrix form below:

	C_1 Red	C_2 Black
R_1 Red	100	110
R_2 Black	50	120

One might ask why Column would play such a game, where she is sure to lose. Perhaps, Column has no choice or perhaps Row pays Column $100 to play the game. For our purposes, we will ignore such considerations.

In a zero-sum game, all outcomes in the matrix are Pareto optimal – one person cannot be made better off without the other person being made worse off. For example, R_2, C_1 is Pareto optimal because any improvement in Row's welfare will lead to a decrease in Column's welfare.

R_1, C_1 is a Cournot-Nash equilibrium. Given R_1, the best Column can do is to choose C_1; given C_1, the best that Row can do is choose R_1. For example, suppose that Row had cheated and observed that Column had chosen red (C_1). Row would still choose red (R_1). Similarly, if Column had cheated and observed that Row had chosen red (R_1), then Column would still choose red (C_1).

It is easy to show that there are no other Cournot-Nash equilibria. For example, if C were to chose C_2, then R would chooses R_2, and then C would choose C_1, and then R would choose R_1.

The next game is the Prisoners' Dilemma. In this game, two robbery suspects are put into different cells and told that if they squeal on the other person, they will get fewer years in prison. The choices and the outcomes given those choices are detailed in the following game matrix. The numbers to the left of the comma are years in prison for Row; the numbers to the right of the comma are years in prison for Column. Here smaller numbers are preferred.

	Years in Prison for Row, Column Larger number is worse	
	C_1	C_2
	Squeal	Not Squeal
R_1 Squeal	10, 10	5, 20
R_2 Not Squeal	20, 5	7, 7

Whatever Column does, Row is better off by squealing. Whatever Row does, Column is better off by squealing. So R_1, C_1 is not only a Cournot-Nash equilibrium but a dominant strategy equilibrium, as well. However, from the viewpoint of the prisoners, the outcome is not Pareto optimal. R_2, C_2 is Pareto superior to R_1, C_1 as both prisoners serve fewer years if neither squeals. So R^e, C^e is not equal to R^Ω, C^Ω. Note that all the other possibilities are Pareto optimal.[3] This is not a hypothetical scenario; prosecutor often creates strong incentives for one party to squeal on the other. Furthermore, a similar matrix characterizes other activities such as overfishing and competition between duopolists.

We next consider the game of chicken. In the game of chicken, two cars drive toward each other. The driver who swerves is chicken. Each driver prefers that the other driver swerves. The worst outcome is that neither swerves. Note that here the numbers represent utility. So that the larger the number, the greater the utility.

	Utility for Row, Column Larger number is better	
	C_1 Swerve	C_2 Not Swerve
R_1 Swerve	10, 10	5, 20
R_2 Not Swerve	20, 5	1, 1

R_1, C_2 is a Cournot-Nash equilibrium. Given that Column does not swerve, the best that R can do is swerve; given that Row swerves, the best that Column can do is not swerve. For similar reasons, R_2, C_1 is also a Cournot-Nash equilibrium.

(R_1, C_2), (R_2, C_1), and (R_1, C_1) are all Pareto optimal. For example, the only way to increase Row's welfare from 5 is to decrease Column's welfare. Clearly R_2, C_2 is not Pareto optimal as both Row and Column prefer R_1, C_1.[4]

The way to win the game of chicken is throw out your steering wheel first so that you are unable to swerve.

Now that we have a good understanding of equilibrium and Pareto optimality, we are ready to consider the various liability rules.

D. STRICT LIABILITY BY X

We start with an analysis of strict liability, which means that the injurer, X, is strictly liable for all damage to the injured party, Y. Each party is responsible for his/her own prevention costs. Nuclear power plants are strictly liable for all damage (up to a $560 million limit – 42 U.S.C. §2210) from a nuclear explosion. When the injurer is liable for all damage, the victim has little incentive to undertake precaution. If optimality requires a positive level of precaution undertaken by the victim, then strict liability is inefficient. Let us now undertake a more formal analysis.

In mathematical terms, the cost to X and Y under strict liability is, respectively, $C^{X:SL}$ and $C^{Y:SL}$. These costs are characterized as follows:

---

[3] Unlike much of the book, we assume here that there can be no binding side agreements and that utility cannot be implicitly transferred.

[4] The game of chicken is in utility units, where utility is not transferable. However the same numbers could be used to represent a different situation where the payoff was in dollars. Because dollars are transferable, a cost benefit analysis would no longer treat 10, 10 as being efficient as the total income is less than 5, 20. In the latter case, income could be redistributed so that the final distribution was 10, 15.

$$C^{X:SL} = x + D(x, y)$$ X pays for damage prevention by X and is liable for any damage to Y.

$$C^{Y:SL} = y + D(x, y) - D(x, y) = y$$ Y only pays for damage prevention by Y. Y is not liable for damage to Y.

In words, under strict liability, X is liable to Y for the damage to Y. X must also pay for his own prevention costs (for example, building reactors that are unlikely to meltdown). Under strict liability, Y must pay for her own prevention costs, but X compensates Y for any damage to Y.

Y wants to minimize her costs, $C^{Y:SL} = y$. This expression is minimized at $y = 0$. The logic is straightforward. The only cost that Y faces is the cost of prevention. Under strict liability, Y is not liable for the harm. Y will therefore not undertake any cost of prevention.[5]

X will try to minimize his cost, given that Y has set y equal to 0. First-order conditions for X: $C_x^{X:SL} = 1 + D_x(x, 0) = 0$. That is, X will continue spending on damage prevention until the last dollar spent on damage prevention reduces damage by $1.

If the optimal amount of prevention by Y is greater than zero (that is, $y^{\Omega} > 0$), then the Cournot-Nash equilibrium under strict liability is not efficient since, under strict liability, Y will choose to spend nothing on prevention (that is, $y^e = 0$). Also if $y^{\Omega} > 0$, then $x^e > x^{\Omega}$ when $y = 0$. When Y chooses too little y, X's cost minimization response is to choose a larger x than otherwise (since x and y are substitutes).

So strict liability is efficient only when the optimal amount of damage prevention (y) by the injured person, Y, is zero. Damage from nuclear power plant explosions roughly approximates the situation where the victim can do little to prevent harm. The potential victim could walk around in a lead suit, but that is not cost-effective given the low likelihood of a nuclear mishap. Pregnant women and families with small children could move elsewhere because they are the most susceptible to being harmed by nuclear radiation, but again, given the low likelihood of a nuclear mishap, such preventative measures might not be cost effective. Although both parties are inputs into the production of damage, when it comes to damage from nuclear power, the optimal (cost-effective) amount of damage prevention by the victim is close to zero and therefore strict liability is appropriate. Another example is airplanes crashing into houses. One might build stronger roofs to withstand airplane crashes, but this hardly seems worth the cost. So strict liability would be optimal in this case, as well.

E. NO LIABILITY BY X

The mirror situation to strict liability by X is no liability by X. Under this rule the victim is liable for her damages and the "injurer" only incurs prevention costs. Under this rule, the injurer has little or no incentive to undertake precaution. No liability is very common. If you catch a cold or the flu from me, you cannot sue me for damages.[6] And

---

[5] We assume compensation for the damage, but clearly for severe injuries and death there is not full compensation. The analysis thus most closely mimics a situation where there is only property damage. When bodily injury is possible, under-compensation may lead to self-protection by the victim even under a regime of strict liability. But recall from our earlier discussion that the potential victim does not act as if her life were infinitely valuable for low probability events. Just about everyone is willing to go out for entertainment even though they may be killed in transit.

[6] One reason for not being able to sue someone for getting a cold or flu is because it is very difficult to determine the source. Influenza survives because the person is contagious before having symptoms. Therefore, the threat of being sued would not be very helpful in limiting the spread of the flu.

PECUNIARY EXTERNALITIES

When Wal-Mart comes to town, grocery store chains like Safeway lose profits. In addition, Safeway's unionized workers lose out to the lower-paid Wal-Mart workers. This is known as a pecuniary externality. Unlike nonpecuniary externalities, such as smoke pollution, a firm cannot be sued for pecuniary externalities. Why? Safeway's lost profits and workers lower wages are more than made up for by lower prices to consumers and increased profits to Wal-Mart. So the cost-benefit calculations are in Wal-Mart's favor.

Nevertheless, grocery stores and their workers try to circumvent the issue by passing local legislation aimed at Wal-Mart stores. Sometimes the regulations can be justified on other grounds – a large store might take away from the small-town ambience. But sometimes the regulation is more blatant. Consider the following regulation passed by the Alameda County supervisors (Alameda County is part of the greater San Francisco metropolitan area and encompasses the cities of Oakland and Berkeley): the ordinance prohibited stores with a sales area of more than 100,000 square feet from devoting more than 10% of the space to nontaxable merchandise such as groceries and prescription drugs. In January 2004, Wal-Mart filed a civil suit. The Board of Supervisors quickly reversed the ordinance.

if you get stabbing pains, you cannot sue me for putting pins into your voodoo doll. No liability (by X) is characterized by the following pair of cost functions:

$$C^{X:0L} = x$$

X only pays for X's prevention costs, x. X is not liable for $D(x, y)$.

$$C^{Y:0L} = y + D(x, y)$$

Y pays for both Y's prevention costs and damage to Y, $D(x, y)$. Y is liable for damages to Y.

Again we have a corner solution, but this time for X. X is not liable for damage to Y, and therefore X will choose to spend nothing ($x = 0$) on preventing damage to Y. Y's cost function will therefore be $C^{Y:0L} = y + D(0, y)$. Y will minimize this function. The first order conditions are: $C_y^{Y:0L} = 1 + D(0, y) = 0$. Y will spend money on damage prevention until the last dollar spent on damage prevention reduces damages by \$1.

If $x^\Omega = 0$, then the Cournot-Nash equilibrium under no liability will yield the efficient result. However, if the optimal amount of damage prevention is greater than zero (that is, $x^\Omega > 0$), then no liability produces an inefficient equilibrium. X will spend too little on damage prevention and Y will spend too much on damage prevention (because of substitutability). With regard to a cold, people may choose to go shopping even though they may put others at risk. Parents may choose to keep their healthy children at home when they go shopping, fearing that they may catch a cold. It would be more cost-effective if Y (the parents) spent less and X (the person with the cold) spent more on damage prevention. If Y could bribe X to spend more on preventing damage to Y (e.g., by having Y stay home), both sides would be better off.

F. CONCLUDING REMARKS

Economics science is based on equilibrium behavior. As was shown earlier in this chapter, equilibrium outcomes need not be Pareto optimal. With regard to the law, when transaction costs are high, the equilibrium outcome under strict liability – no care by the victim – is only efficient if it is indeed the case that the victim should not undertake any level of precaution. In general, however, both the victim and the injurer should undertake precaution, which means that the equilibrium outcome under either strict liability or no liability is in general inefficient.

SUGGESTIONS FOR FURTHER READING

For a detailed application of game theory to the law, see Baird et al. (1994).

REVIEW QUESTIONS

1. Define a Cournot-Nash Equilibrium. Define Pareto Optimality. (4)
2. Using game matrices, provide examples and explain a situation of a single Cournot-Nash equilibrium that is Pareto optimal; a Cournot-Nash equilibrium that is not optimal; a situation where there is more than one Cournot-Nash equilibrium. In each case, for all four possibilities in the matrix, indicate which outcomes are efficient and which are not. (9)
3. Derive the conditions for cost minimization when there are two inputs into the reduction of the damage. Discuss the signs of the first and second partial derivatives and derive the first-order conditions. Provide an intuitive understanding of all the relationships. (12)
4. What is the Cournot-Nash equilibrium when the rule is strict liability? Explain. Provide an example where strict liability is efficient. Provide an example where strict liability is inefficient. (8)
5. What is the Cournot-Nash equilibrium when the rule is no liability (by the injurer)? Explain. Provide an example where no liability is efficient. Provide an example where no liability is inefficient. (8)

REFERENCE

Baird, Douglas, Robert Gertner, and Randal Picker. (1994). *Game Theory and the Law.* Cambridge, MA: Harvard University Press.

16 Negligence Rules

A. Simple Negligence: An Intuitive Exposition 142

B. Simple Negligence: A More Formal Exposition # 142

C. Negligence with Contributory Negligence # 143

D. Comparative Negligence: An Intuitive Exposition 144

E. Comparative Negligence: A Formal Presentation # 145

F. Negligence versus Strict Liability 146

G. Acts of God 147

H. Jury Outcomes and Negligence Rules 147

I. Concluding Remarks 150

SUGGESTIONS FOR FURTHER READING 150

REVIEW QUESTIONS 151

REFERENCES 151

As was demonstrated in the previous chapter, strict liability and no liability are appropriate only for corner solutions where only one side, the injurer in the case of strict liability or the victim in the case of no liability, can effectively reduce damage. So what about all the middle cases where efficiency demands that both sides undertake precaution? It is the negligence family of rules that have been designed to take care of this possibility.

A. SIMPLE NEGLIGENCE: AN INTUITIVE EXPOSITION

Negligence is a legal concept. *Economists define negligence as spending less than the optimal on damage prevention. Thus* X *is negligent if* $x < x^\Omega$, *and* Y *is negligent if* $y < y^\Omega$. There are a number of negligence rules. We start with the simplest – negligence (by the injurer). An example of such a rule is medical malpractice.[1] Only if the doctor (or hospital) was negligent will the doctor be liable for the harm to the patient. Otherwise, the doctor is not liable for the harm to the patient.

Before going through a formal presentation, it is worthwhile to provide an intuitive explanation for equilibrium behavior under a simple negligence rule. Under a simple negligence rule, the injurer is liable for the damage to the victim only when the injurer spends less than the optimal on damage prevention. The injurer will not want to spend more than necessary (that is, more than the optimal) on damage prevention because this does not reduce the injurer's liability to the victim, as the injurer's liability is already zero. So let us consider the other possibility that the injurer is spending less than the optimal on damage prevention and is therefore liable to the victim. If the injurer spends an extra dollar on damage prevention, then the expected cost of damage will go down by more than a dollar as long as the injurer is spending less than the optimal. Because the injurer is liable for the damage, the injurer will keep on spending until the last dollar spent on damage reduction reduces expected damage by $1, which is at the optimal. And once at the optimal, the injurer gets an added benefit because the injurer is no longer liable.

Turning our attention to the victim, given that the injurer is choosing the optimal level of precaution and is not liable, the victim is liable for the damage to the victim. The victim will increase spending until the last dollar spent decreases expected damage by a dollar. This is the optimal level of precaution. So given that the injurer has chosen the optimal level of precaution, the victim will want to choose the optimal level of precaution; and given that the victim has chosen the optimal level of precaution, the injurer will want to choose the optimal level of precaution. Thus under a negligence rule, there is an equilibrium, where both sides act optimally.

B. SIMPLE NEGLIGENCE: A MORE FORMAL EXPOSITION

We now undertake a more formal presentation. A simple negligence rule is defined as follows:

If $x < x^\Omega$, that is, if X is negligent (equivalently, X is spending less than the optimal):

$C^{X:N} = x + D(x, y)$. X pays for the cost of damage prevention by X and any damage to Y.

---

[1]   Note that medical malpractice falls under contract. But, as we have argued all along, the economic analytics cuts across traditional legal domains. The underlying economic logic of the negligence rule was first elucidated by Judge Learned Hand in *United States v. Carroll Towing Co.*, 159 F.2d 169 (1947).

$C^{Y:N} = y + D(x, y) - D(x, y) = y$. Y pays for the cost of damage prevention by Y and is compensated by X for the damage to Y.

If $x \geq x^{\Omega}$, that is, if X is not negligent,

$C^{X:N} = x$. X only pays for the cost of damage prevention undertaken by X.
$C^{Y:N} = y + D(x, y)$. Y pays for Y's prevention costs and is not compensated for the damage to Y.

This rule creates incentives for efficient behavior; x^{Ω}, $y^{\Omega} = x^e$, y^e. That is, under a simple negligence rule, the efficient outcome is a Cournot-Nash equilibrium. The logic is as follows:

If Y has chosen her optimal amount of precaution, y^{Ω}, then X will choose his optimal amount of precaution, x^{Ω}. If X spends at least the optimal amount on damage prevention (that is, if $x \geq x^{\Omega}$), then X is not liable for the damage to Y; so X's cost function is $C^{X:N} = x$. Spending more than x^{Ω} on damage prevention imposes extra costs on X without any additional benefits to X because he is not liable for the damage to Y. Therefore, X will not spend more than x^{Ω}.

Now suppose that X has chosen less than the optimal amount of precaution; that is, $x < x^{\Omega}$. Then X is liable to Y for the harm to Y, and X's cost function is $C^{X:N} = x + D(x, y^{\Omega})$. By spending an additional dollar, damage will be reduced by more than a dollar and therefore it will be cost effective for X to increase his expenditures until $x = x^{\Omega}$, where the last dollar spent reduces damages by a dollar. At $x = x^{\Omega}$, X gets an additional bang for his buck because he is no longer liable for the damage. Therefore, given y^{Ω}, X will choose x^{Ω}.

Now given that X has chosen the optimal amount of precaution (that is, $x = x^{\Omega}$), Y is liable for the damage to Y and thus Y's cost function is $C^{Y:N} = y + D(x^{\Omega}, y)$. Y will increase y until the last dollar spent on damage prevention reduces damage by a dollar. But that is y^{Ω}. So indeed, x^{Ω}, y^{Ω} is a Cournot-Nash equilibrium.

Under the simple negligence rule, the victim is liable for the damage to the victim unless the injurer is negligent. There is a symmetric rule, *strict liability with contributory negligence*, where the injurer is liable for damage to the victim unless the victim is negligent. Once again, the liability rule encourages both parties to undertake optimal care, but in this case the injurer pays for the damage when neither is negligent. This rule is sometimes implicitly applied in product liability cases.

C. NEGLIGENCE WITH CONTRIBUTORY NEGLIGENCE

Until the mid-1970s, the rule of negligence with contributory negligence was the operative rule in the vast majority of states in the United States.[2] Negligence with contributory negligence means that the injurer compensates the victim only if the injurer is negligent and the victim is not negligent. Otherwise, the victim is liable for the harm. More formally:

If $x < x^{\Omega}$ and $y \geq y^{\Omega}$, that is, X is negligent and Y is not negligent:

$C^{X:NCN} = x + D(x, y)$. X pays for X's prevention costs and is liable for the damage to Y.

[2] Contributory negligence was introduced in *Butterfield v. Forrester*, 103 Eng. Rep 926 (1809), where the plaintiff who had been riding recklessly was barred from collecting from the defendant who had negligently placed an obstruction in the road.

$C^{Y:NCN} = y + D(x, y) - D(x, y) = y$. Y is compensated for damage but pays for prevention costs.

Otherwise:

$C^{X:NCN} = x$. X pays for x, the cost of prevention undertaken by X.
$C^{Y:NCN} = y + D(x, y)$. Y pays for prevention costs, y, and is liable for the damage to Y.

Negligence with contributory negligence produces an efficient equilibrium. Assume that $y = y^{\Omega}$. Then X's cost function is the same as it is under the simple negligence rule, and X will again choose $x = x^{\Omega}$. Similarly, given $x = x^{\Omega}$, Y's cost function is the same as it is under the simple negligence rule. So Y will again choose y^{Ω}. So x^{Ω}, y^{Ω} is indeed a Cournot-Nash equilibrium.

So both negligence liability and negligence with contributory negligence produce the same efficient outcome. The advantage of the negligence with contributory negligence rule is that fewer transfers are required. Only if the injurer was negligent and the victim was not will the injurer be liable. This appears to be the prime explanation for the much greater prevalence of negligence with contributory negligence than pure negligence in accident law.

D. COMPARATIVE NEGLIGENCE: AN INTUITIVE EXPOSITION

Suppose that both the injurer and the victim were driving 70 miles per hour (mph) in a 60 mph zone. Under negligence with contributory negligence, the victim would get nothing from the injurer; under a simple negligence rule, the victim would collect 100 percent of the damages from the injurer. These all-or-nothing-at-all compensation schemes seem unfair to many people. As a consequence, the rule of comparative negligence was devised. Under this rule, the greater the injurer's relative negligence compared with the victim's, the greater the percentage of the damage the injurer pays. In the above example, the injurer would be responsible for 50% of the damages.

Under a comparative-negligence rule, each party's performance is compared to the optimal performance. If one party is not negligent and the other party is, then the negligent party is liable for 100% of the damages to the victim. Thus, for example, if the negligent party is the victim, the victim will collect nothing from the injurer. A more complicated situation arises when both parties are negligent, but their degree of negligence differs. Suppose, for example, that the injurer was going 20 mph above the speed limit while the victim was going 10 mph above the speed limit. Then the injurer would be twice as negligent and would be liable for twice as much of the damages as the victim. That is, the injurer would be liable for two-thirds of the damage, while the victim would be liable for one-third. Another possibility is that neither is negligent, in which case the injurer is not liable and the victim must pay for the damages.

It is easy to demonstrate that under comparative negligence, the efficient outcome is a Cournot-Nash equilibrium. The logic is similar to the other negligence rules. Suppose that the injurer is acting efficiently. Then the victim is liable for all the damage. The victim will therefore undertake expenditures on damage prevention until the last dollar spent reduces damages by $1. But this is the efficient point. Next let us consider the injurer's behavior, given that the victim has chosen the efficient level of care. The injurer will not want to spend less than the optimal. Suppose to the contrary. If the injurer chooses less than the optimal, then the injurer is liable for all of the damage to the victim. The injurer will undertake expenditures on damage prevention until the last dollar spent reduces damages by $1. But this is the efficient point for the injurer, where he will then no longer be liable at all. The injurer will not want to spend more than the optimal on care because this is costly to the injurer but does not decrease his liability to the victim since it is already zero. So we do indeed have an efficient equilibrium under comparative negligence.

E. COMPARATIVE NEGLIGENCE: A FORMAL PRESENTATION

We now undertake a more formal presentation. To deal with comparative negligence, we first need a measure of the injurer's relative negligence, R^X.

(A) If $x \geq x^\Omega$, then $R^X = 0$.

That is, if X is not negligent, X's relative negligence is 0 and he is liable for none of the damage to Y.[3]

(B) If $x < x^\Omega$ and $y \geq y^\Omega$, then $R^X = 1$.

That is, if X is negligent and Y is not, then X's relative negligence is 1, and he is liable for all of the damages.

(C) If $x < x^\Omega$ and $y < y^\Omega$, then $R^X = \dfrac{x^\Omega - x}{x^\Omega - x + y^\Omega - y}$.

Thus if both sides are equally negligent, X's relative negligence (R^X) is 1/2. In the earlier speeding example, the injurer was 20 mph from the optimal and the victim was 10 mph from the optimal: $(20)/(20 + 10) = 2/3$.[4] So the injurer is liable for two-thirds of the damage. If the injurer was 10 mph above the optimal and the victim 20 mph above the optimal, then the injurer would be liable for one-third of the damage. Of course, it is not always easy to determine the exact percentages. For example if Y's brake lights were not working and X was driving with bald tires, the jury might have to deliberate for a long time before they decided on X's relative negligence.

The cost function under comparative negligence is as follows.

(a) When $x \geq x^\Omega$ (that is, when X is not negligent):

$$C^{X:CN} = x,$$
$$C^{Y:CN} = y + D(x, y).$$

(b) When $x < x^\Omega$ and $y \geq y^\Omega$ (that is, when X is negligent and Y is not negligent):

$$C^{X:CN} = x + D(x, y),$$
$$C^{Y:CN} = y.$$

(c) When $x < x^\Omega$ and $y < y^\Omega$ (that is, when both X and Y are negligent):

$$C^{X:CN} = x + R^X D(x, y) = x + \frac{x^\Omega - x}{x^\Omega - x + y^\Omega - y} D(x, y),$$

$$C^{Y:CN} = y + [1 - R^X] D(x, y) = y + \frac{y^\Omega - y}{x^\Omega - x + y^\Omega - y} D(x, y).$$

---

[3] There are several variants of the comparative negligence rule across the various jurisdictions.
[4] A person could also be held liable when she drove too slowly.

For example, if the damages to Y were a $100,000 and both sides were equally negligent, then X would pay Y $50,000. Note that the shares add up to one.

Once again, x^Ω, y^Ω is a Cournot-Nash equilibrium. Suppose that Y has chosen y^Ω. If X chooses $x < x^\Omega$, then $R^X = 1$ and X is 100 percent liable for the damage; if $x \geq x^\Omega$, then $R^X = 0$ and X is not at all liable for the damage. From X's point of view, this looks like a simple negligence rule, and consequently X will choose x^Ω. If $x = x^\Omega$, then Y is fully liable for any damage to Y. From Y's point of view, this too looks like the simple negligence rule, and, by the same logic, Y will choose y^Ω. Thus x^Ω, y^Ω is a Cournot-Nash equilibrium for all three negligence rules.

In comparison to negligence with contributory negligence, comparative negligence is "fairer." Damages are shared according to relative negligence rather than one person being liable for all or nothing at all. However, comparative negligence does involve many more transfers than negligence with contributory negligence.

F. NEGLIGENCE VERSUS STRICT LIABILITY

Typically, a negligence rule determines the optimal amount of inputs given that an activity takes place but not the optimal amount of the activity. Thus, in automobile accidents, the court determines whether the person was driving with the appropriate level of care; the court does not determine whether the person should have driven to the corner to get a newspaper in the first place. Optimal behavior might have meant walking instead. Thus, a negligence rule means that there will be too many drivers and too few pedestrian (if only pedestrians get hurt when cars smash into pedestrians), but both pedestrians and drivers act optimally given that they are driving or walking. In contrast, strict liability will result in too many pedestrians and too few drivers with pedestrians undertaking too little care and drivers undertaking excessive care.

Automobile accidents generally involve two drivers rather than a driver and a pedestrian. So the problem of a negligence rule creating an incentive for too many drivers is relatively minor because drivers face the potential of uncompensated harm under a negligence rule (when they are the victim rather than the injurer).

Strict liability is implemented when it is unclear whether the injurer should be undertaking the activity in the first place and prevention by the victim is not cost effective. As an example, urban owners of wild animals are strictly liable for damage when their animals escape even if the owner had been very careful and not at all negligent in trying to prevent an escape. It is not cost effective for neighbors and people just passing by to walk around under a portable cage or to carry a gun. At the same time, it is not at all clear that raising wild animals in the city is an appropriate activity. Making the owner of the wild animals strictly liable for the damage from escaped animals means that the owner will consider these costs when deciding to raise wild animals.

A negligence rule would achieve the same short-term incentives, but different long-term incentives for entry into the activity. Y would not undertake any costs of prevention because we have assumed that $y^\Omega = 0$ in this situation.[5] Under a negligence rule, the owner of the wild animal would be liable only if negligent; that is, the wild-animal owner would be liable for damage to Y only if $x < x^\Omega$. As we have shown before, X would

---

[5] Even here we would want to discourage neighbors from putting their hands in the cage. So negligence by the victim could come into play.

choose to be nonnegligent by spending x^{Ω}. Under a strict liability rule, the wild-animal owner would be strictly liable for damage regardless of the wild-animal owner's level of care. Since X is strictly liable, X faces $x + D(x, 0)$ and will spend until the last dollar of prevention reduces damages by one dollar, which is again x^{Ω}. So both rules would encourage the appropriate level of care (for example, cages with double locks).

However, under a negligence rule, the wild-animal owner does not pay for damage to Y when the wild-animal owner is not negligent. Therefore, under a negligence rule, in deciding whether to raise wild animals in the city, the wild-animal owner would not take into account the expected damage to Y (when X is nonnegligent). Since it is not clear whether we should have wild animals in the city, we impose a strict liability rule which forces the owners to consider all costs that they impose instead of only costs that they negligently impose.

For ultrahazardous activity, the activity might not be worthwhile to undertake even if X is careful (not negligent). Thus, strict liability holds for blasting operations and nuclear power plants, as well as for raising wild animals in the city. In contrast, where the presumption is that the activity is appropriate (such as driving), a negligence rule is invoked.

Unlike automobile accidents cases, nuisance cases typically consider the issue of long-run entry. Suppose that there is a polluting factory. The courts first determine whether the factory should be located in the area. Alternatively, zoning regulations exist to prevent factories from inappropriately locating in the wrong area, in the first place. If it is appropriate for the factory to be in the location, then the courts determine the optimal level of smoke abatement. The factory is considered a nuisance if it either is inappropriately located or it undertakes less than the optimal amount of abatement. So, nuisance laws consider both the activity level and the appropriate level of care given the activity level. In this way, there is no excessive entry under a nuisance standard as there is under a negligence standard in accident law.[6]

G. ACTS OF GOD

Suppose that your neighbor's healthy tree falls down during an unusually severe windstorm and destroys your garage. Who should be liable if the tree was healthy? Such occurrences might be labeled as acts of God, which is legalese for the optimal prevention costs by both sides being zero (that is, $x^{\Omega} = y^{\Omega} = 0$). It would not be cost effective for the garage to be built with steel girders or built elsewhere; nor would it be cost effective for the tree to be planted elsewhere or for a different tree to be planted in the first place. Whether, there was no liability, strict liability, or negligence liability, the same level of prevention would be undertaken by both sides. In general, the role of liability rules is to discourage suboptimal behavior, not to compensate for damage. Here, the behavior by all parties would be the same regardless of the liability rule. So, to save on court costs, the owner of the tree is not held liable for damage.

H. JURY OUTCOMES AND NEGLIGENCE RULES

In discussing liability rules, we distinguished between negligence with contributory negligence (NCN) and comparative negligence. Under negligence with contributory

---

[6] For more on the conflict between long-run and short-run incentives in nuisance law, see Chapter 20.

negligence, there are only two possibilities: (1) the defendant is liable to the plaintiff for all of the harm if the plaintiff was not negligent (and the defendant was negligent) or (2) the defendant is liable for none of the harm if the plaintiff was negligent (and/or the defendant was not negligent). In contrast, under comparative negligence, the plaintiff's negligence will reduce, but not eliminate, the award (if the defendant was at all negligent). Under comparative negligence, if both litigants were equally negligent, the defendant will be liable for half of the harm to the plaintiff (in contrast to NCN where the defendant would not be liable at all).

Because most states switched from NCN to comparative negligence in the 1970s and 1980s, we can test whether juries changed their behavior when the liability-rule regime switched. California (which has the best data) switched regime in November 1975. I therefore looked at 582 automobile accident trials during the 1974–1976 time period.[7]

As stated earlier, under NCN, plaintiff negligence will lead to a verdict in favor of the defendant. Under comparative negligence, plaintiff negligence does not increase the probability of a verdict in favor of the defendant; instead, the amount of the award is reduced. So the first test was to see whether the plaintiff's culpability had any effect on the *probability of the verdict being in favor of the defendant*. Culpability was a number assigned to the plaintiff (and defendant), according to what was said in the summary of the accident (1 if the litigant was not accused of wrongdoing; 2 if the litigant was accused of modest wrongdoing, say, going above the speed limit; and 3 if the litigant was accused of serious wrongdoing, say going 20 mph above the speed limit).[8]

The results showed that under negligence with contributory negligence, defendant culpability reduced the likelihood of a verdict in favor of the defendant, while plaintiff culpability increased the likelihood of a verdict in favor of the defendant, as one would expect. However, the effect of plaintiff culpability was significantly weaker than the effect of defendant culpability, suggesting that some juries implicitly employed a comparative-negligence standard (possibility on the fairness grounds mentioned earlier in Section D).

I then looked at cases decided under the comparative negligence regime. Under a regime of comparative negligence, plaintiff culpability should have no effect on whether the verdict is in favor of the defendant (only on the amount of the award given a verdict in favor of the plaintiff), and this was indeed the case.

Next, I looked *only* at cases where the verdict was in favor of the plaintiff. Under negligence with contributory negligence, the reward to the plaintiff should not depend on the relative negligence of the defendant, where the measure of relative negligence is

$$\frac{\text{defendant culpability}}{\text{defendant culpability} + \text{plaintiff culpability}}.$$

Under negligence with contributory negligence, the plaintiff should be completely compensated for the harm to the plaintiff (when the verdict is in favor of the plaintiff)

---

[7] The material in this subsection is based on Wittman (1986).
[8] The culpability score was made independently of the jury verdict decision regarding negligence.

DANGEROUS FURNITURE

A guest of the Ritz-Carlton hotel in San Francisco struck his right eye while attempting to open a faux door of an armoire in his room. The accident caused a detached retina. Victor D'Amore sued both the hotel and Drexel Heritage, the armoire manufacturer, claiming that the armoire was defectively designed. Drexel Heritage denied the design defect claim, noting that despite the presence of 303 such armoires in the hotel over 10 years, with more than 1 million users, this was the first reported accident of its kind. In May 2003, a California jury found for the defendants. *D'Amore v. Ritz Carlton*, No. 01CC16169 [Orange Co., Calif., Super. Ct.].

WILD ANIMALS

OCTOBER 2003 – Antoine Yates kept a tiger named Ming in his fifth-floor New York apartment since the tiger was a 6-week-old cub. Police discovered the existence of the tiger after Yates was mauled by the 400-pound, 20-month old cat. Yates said that Ming attacked him in an attempt to get at a pet kitten in the apartment. Yates faces a charge of reckless endangerment and two counts of possession of a wild animal. Conviction for reckless endangerment carries a sentence of up to seven years. Animal control officers also found a 5-foot-long alligator in his apartment. For photos, see: http://www.nydailynews.com/news/local/story/133611p-119125c.html

BARS AND BRAWLS

While at Banana Joe's Bar and Grill, Derrick Roy and his companions were attacked by another group. A bouncer made both groups leave the premises via the back exit, where Roy and his companions were again attacked. Another bouncer let them back into the bar, where they stayed for 15 minutes longer until closing time. Roy then asked whether he and his companions could leave by the front exit, rather than by the back exit where the attack took place. Banana Joe's staff refused and they were let outside through the back door, where they were attacked for a third time by the same group. Roy was hit in the face with a bottle and subsequently lost vision in one of his eyes. Roy sued Banana Joe's for negligent security. The bar contended that it was not responsible for the act of the assailant. The jury awarded $1.9 million to Roy. Minnesota Court of Appeals unpublished opinion (2004).

and obviously not at all compensated if the verdict is in favor of the defendant. That is, under NCN the relative culpability of the defendant should have no effect on the award, *given* that the verdict is in favor the plaintiff. In contrast, under comparative negligence, the plaintiff is compensated according to the defendant's relative negligence. The more reckless the defendant relative to the plaintiff, the more the plaintiff should be compensated.

Under NCN, juries did to some degree increase the award when the defendant's relative culpability was higher (given a plaintiff verdict), again suggesting that some juries implicitly used a standard of comparative negligence when the rule was NCN.

> ### COLLATERAL SOURCE RULE
>
> The possibility of compensation from the injurer encourages a victim to sue for damages. But automobile accident law is concerned more with incentives than with compensation for injuries. For example, when neither side is negligent, the victim does not collect from the injurer. A more compelling example is the collateral source rule. Suppose that you have a health insurance policy that pays for your medical care. Under this rule, the injurer's liability is not reduced when your medical insurance (the collateral source) pays for the doctor bills arising from an automobile accident. If this were the case, then the injurer would not have the appropriate incentive to take care.
>
> In principle, the insurance company could require the successful plaintiff to pay back the company for claims made by the insured, but this is rarely done as it is hard to determine the allocation of the award. How much of the award was for pain and suffering and how much was for medical bills paid by the insurance company? The appropriate determination might require another trial, which is expensive.

However, the effect of the defendant's relative culpability was about ten times as high under comparative negligence. This and the previous test suggest that juries did indeed respond to the change in the liability regime as predicted, but that some juries had implicitly applied comparative negligence when negligence with contributory negligence was the rule.

I. CONCLUDING REMARKS

Accidents can happen even when both parties take the optimal amount of care. Under negligence, NCN, and comparative negligence, the injurer is not liable unless negligent. So the victim may not be compensated, even if the victim had been acting optimally.

Over time, the common law has developed various versions of the negligence rule. As we have seen, some of these versions are quite complex; yet, all provide the correct incentives for optimal behavior. The question naturally arises whether juries actually implement these complicated liability rules. The evidence suggests that they do.

SUGGESTIONS FOR FURTHER READING

The classic paper on negligence rules is by Brown (1973). A more detailed treatment of tort law is found in Landes and Posner (1987). Shavell (1987) considers the situation where injurers can buy liability insurance. There are an incredible number of articles on liability rules. Some of these assume that the negligence standard is imperfectly known (see, for example, White, 1989), while others assume that litigation is costly (see, for example, Hylton, 1990). Wittman et al. (1997) and Zheng (2001) consider liability rules within a dynamic setting. They show that comparative negligence converges more rapidly to the efficient equilibrium than does negligence with contributory negligence.

REVIEW QUESTIONS

1. For each liability rule below state what the rule is (4), and explain the equilibrium behavior. Show when the rule is and when it is not appropriate (8):
    a. Strict liability for damages
    b. Negligence liability
    c. Negligence with contributory negligence
    d. Comparative negligence.
2. In *Guille v. Swan*, 19 Johns. 381 (1822), a balloonist crash-landed his hot-air balloon in the plaintiff's vegetable garden. The plaintiff sued the balloonist for the damage both from the landing and from the spectators who had originally come to see him ascend nearby. Who should be liable? (6)
3. Why are owners of wild animals held strictly liable rather than being held liable only if negligent? (4)
4. What is the economics interpretation of "acts of God?" (4)
5. What is the difference between negligence with contributory negligence and comparative negligence? (4) How can one test whether juries act according to one rule or the other? Explain. (10)

REFERENCES

Brown, John P. (1973). Toward an Economic Theory of Liability. 2 *Journal of Legal Studies* 323.

Hylton, Keith N. (1990). The Influence of Litigation Costs on Deterrence under Strict Liability and under Negligence. 10 *International Review of Law and Economics* 161.

Landes, William M., and Richard A. Posner. (1987). *Economic Structure of Tort Law.* Cambridge, MA: Harvard University Press.

Shavell, Steven. (1987). *Economic Analysis of Accident Law.* Cambridge, MA: Harvard University Press.

White, Michelle J. (1989). An Empirical Test of the Comparative and Contributory Negligence Rules in Accident Law. *20 Rand Journal of Economics* 308.

Wittman, Donald. (1986). The Price of Negligence. 29 *Journal of Law and Economics* 151.

Wittman, Donald, Daniel Friedman, Stephanie Crevier, and Aron Braskin. (1997). Learning Liability Rules. 26 *Journal of Legal Studies* 145.

Zheng, Mingli. (2001). Liability Rules and Evolutionary Dynamics. 157 *Journal of Institutional and Theoretical Economics* 520.

17 Crime and Criminal Law

A. Criminals Respond to Incentives 154

B. The Optimal Punishment 154

C. Why Do We Have Both a Tort System and a Criminal Justice System? 157

D. Do Increases in Probability Deter More Than Do Increases in the Severity of Punishment? 158

E. Intent 159

F. Imprisonment as Prevention 159

G. Other Ways to Reduce Crime 159

H. Concluding Remarks 160

SUGGESTIONS FOR FURTHER READING 161

REVIEW QUESTIONS 162

REFERENCES 163

Suppose that you could not be punished for speeding, selling marijuana, not filing your income taxes, or parking illegally. Would you be more likely to engage in any of these activities? If the fine for illegal parking increased from $20 to $60 or the probability of getting a $20 parking ticket increased from 1% to 40%, would you reduce the number of times that you park illegally? Perhaps you would not do any of these things even if the price were zero, just as some vegetarians would not eat meat even if the price were zero. But we are interested in aggregates, and surely the market response would be in the direction predicted by economic theory – the higher the expected price the lower the demand.

A. CRIMINALS RESPOND TO INCENTIVES

The expected price of a crime is the probability of punishment times the cost of the punishment. Economists believe that criminals are rational and have downward-sloping demand curves for crime just as noncriminals have a downward-sloping demand for rutabagas. There is no need for a special psychology of the criminal mind. Criminals may have a different set of preferences or a different opportunity set from noncriminals. Either way, criminals tend to respond to incentives like noncriminals do. When the price of a McDonald's hamburger goes up, criminals will tend to shift their purchases toward Burger King; when the price of crime goes up, criminals will tend to shift their focus to noncriminal activities. Of course, some people have a more inelastic demand. Even if the price of a hamburger triples, not everyone will shift to eating chicken; even when the price of a crime triples, not everyone will shift to noncriminal activity. There are endless debates concerning the marginal effect of capital punishment on the murder rate, but does anyone doubt that the number of murders would go up if the punishment for murder were only ninety days in jail?

While I have characterized the situation in terms of the demand for crime, most commentators have viewed criminals as supplying crime, and I will follow this convention from now on. Thus imprisonment is just another cost of supplying heroin. As the cost increases, the supply at any given price of heroin decreases.

B. THE OPTIMAL PUNISHMENT

Determining the optimal punishment for a crime is somewhat akin to determining the optimal level of liability for a tort, but there are additional costs to consider because there are real economic costs involved in detection and in imprisonment.

We first show that there is an inverse relationship between the probability of being caught and the level of punishment. To keep the logic as clear as possible, we initially make a number of simplifying assumptions; later we will drop these simplifications. Suppose that there are no detection costs or costs of punishment (the fine is a monetary one, which involves just a transfer, not a net social cost) and that courts can determine the harm to the victim costlessly (this latter assumption gets rid of the issue that we want to discourage a conversion of a property right into a liability rule). Also assume risk neutrality. As in our analysis of torts, society wants to charge the person for the harm (H). The important difference here is that the criminal is not always caught. Therefore, the expected punishment, probability of being punished (P) times the fine (F), is set equal to the harm from the crime. That is, PF = H. Thus the *lower the probability of being caught, the higher the level of punishment should be.*

To illustrate, suppose that you put bread in your shopping basket and Safeway "catches" you at the checkout stand and charges you $2.00. If they only caught you half the time, they could charge you $4.00 every time that they did "catch" you. And if they only caught you 1/100 times, then Safeway would charge you $200.00 for a loaf of bread when they did. In each case, the expected fine is $2.00. The same logic holds if you stole from people's homes or stole their cars.

This inverse relationship seems to explain some within-country differences over time, as well as some cross-country differences. Countries that do not have well-developed forensic capabilities may catch criminals less often, and therefore the punishment for minor crimes may be much more severe. Before London instituted a police force, many crimes were punishable by death; today, some countries with rudimentary detective capabilities still cut off hands for theft.

A risk neutral criminal is indifferent to whether she is punished with a $10,000 fine one-tenth of the time or a $20,000 fine one-twentieth of the time. But the social cost of the former is higher than the latter as it takes real resources to catch and prosecute a criminal. Because of this, cost minimization would recommend large punishments coupled with a low probability of punishment. This recommendation would be magnified if criminals are risk averse and mitigated if criminals are risk-preferring (see Section D for further explication).

The real world is more complicated than our example of taking bread from Safeway. As a result, the criminal is charged for additional costs:

1. Theft and many other criminal activities substitute a forced conversion for a market exchange. If X values someone's car more than Y does, then X can always offer to buy it from Y instead of stealing it from her. If the thief only paid for the "market price" of the car, this would allow the thief to convert a low transaction cost–property rights system into a higher transaction cost–liability rule system. The criminal-justice system discourages conversion of a property right into a liability right by charging the thief for this conversion in addition to any harm suffered by the victim.
2. The criminal should pay for the costs of his detection. Criminals try to avoid detection. As a result, police have to do investigative work. The criminal needs to pay for these detection costs again divided by the probability of being caught.

Thus, the logic of punishing for a crime is in many ways similar to the logic for having a liability rule for a tort. However, the potential for bankruptcy limits the effectiveness of monetary sanctions. In turn, this creates important differences between criminal and tort law.

The punishment for even "minor" crimes can be very high. To illustrate, consider the case where a person was robbed of $50 at gunpoint. The person who gave up her wallet to avoid being shot was not a volunteer to the transaction. To prevent the conversion of a property right into a liability rule, an additional fine should be imposed on the perpetrator beyond the payment for the actual harm, which itself may be very high (people do not like to be subjected to the threat of physical violence). But unlike breach of contract and many other types of torts, it is often hard to detect the perpetrator of a crime. So the criminal should pay for the cost of detection. This raises the price of the crime still higher for those who are actually caught. As already noted, if the criminal is not always caught, the price paid has to be multiplied by 1 over the probability of being punished. The final number can easily be in the tens of thousands of dollars. As a result, the criminal may not have enough wealth to pay the fine. The term for this is "judgment proof."

Judgment proof means that the person is not sufficiently deterred unless additional costs, such as imprisonment, are imposed on the person. But these additional costs (unlike fines that are merely a transfer) are costly to society. For example, prisons must be built and guards must be paid. Society wants to economize on such costs and may be willing to trade-off such costs for more crime.

To illustrate, consider vandalism such as spray-painting buildings, trashing schools, and the like. If the perpetrators had sufficient funds, then they would be charged for the harm that they caused (including the cost of detection), divided by the probability of being caught. If the perpetrators do not have the funds, society has to balance the cost of incarceration against the benefit of reduced vandalism. If prosecuting vandals and putting them in jail for a month costs $100,000 a year and this reduces the cost of vandalism by $200,000 a year, then such a policy makes sense (assuming that there are no other costs). But if putting the vandals in jail for two months costs an additional $80,000 a year and this only reduces the harm from vandalism by an additional $60,000, then a policy of two-month jail terms should not be undertaken.

When there are costs of punishment, society needs to account for the *elasticity of response* – the percent change in the crime over the percent change in the amount of punishment. The more inelastic the supply of vandals, the lower the punishment should be. Why put people in prison for longer terms if it has a negligible effect on the number of crimes?[1]

Whether those who are convicted of robbery should be in jail for 5, 10, or 20 years thus depends on the elasticity of response. This requires empirical estimation, not a priori thinking. In contrast, when the punishment is in terms of fines, there is no social cost. The fine is set equal to the harm done divided by the probability of getting caught without any reference to elasticities.

In designing an optimal system of punishments, society must consider the *marginal effect* of punishment. The death penalty for robbery may reduce robberies but increase the number of murders. By murdering the victim, the robber lowers his chance of being caught since a witness is eliminated. Also the marginal cost of murder is decreased since the robber will face the death penalty if he is convicted of robbery whether or not he has murdered the victim. Marginal effects also come into play in distinguishing attempts from successes. A person faces a lesser punishment for attempted murder than for murder itself. If a person shoots and misses, we want to discourage the person from trying again. The Catholic Church must also consider marginal deterrence. If a person is already going to hell for committing robbery, then going to hell will not deter the person from further criminal activity. The church solves this problem by granting absolution. The more severe the crime or number of crimes committed, the lower the probability of absolution and the higher the expected punishment.

---

[1]   If a person is truly crazy, they will not respond to incentives. So it makes no sense to punish such people for the crimes that they commit. However, they may need to be locked up to prevent further crimes.

Should there be the death penalty for murder? The answer depends to a great degree on the deterrent effect of capital punishment relative to life imprisonment. It seems implausible that a great many potential murderers would be deterred by the threat of capital punishment, but not by life imprisonment, the major exception being those who are already facing life imprisonment for another crime. Introspection is a useful starting point, but empirical evidence is much more convincing. Unfortunately, the evidence is not clear-cut. Even in the United States, very few murderers are put to death, and those who are may live ten or more years on death row. It is therefore hard to disentangle the effect of capital punishment from other influences on the murder rate such as the supply of weapons, demand for illegal drugs, advances in medical care (which makes guns less lethal), and so forth. Not surprisingly, the empirical studies are inconclusive although the weight of the evidence is somewhat in favor of the deterrent effect. Now some have argued that even if there is a significant deterrent effect (say two less murders for each executed murderer) that it is immoral to take another person's life. The problem with that argument is that either way lives are taken. Suppose that we have exhausted other ways of preventing murder (such as education) and that for every ten people executed, there are fifteen fewer murders. Furthermore, assume that one out of ten executed people is innocent. Capital punishment then means that there are fourteen fewer innocent people killed and nine more murderers executed. Banning capital punishment means nine fewer murderers executed and fourteen more innocent killed. If we weigh all lives equally, then capital punishment is the preferred policy. Even if the number of lives taken were the same either way, one might choose to distribute life to the innocent rather than to the murderer.

C. WHY DO WE HAVE BOTH A TORT SYSTEM AND A CRIMINAL JUSTICE SYSTEM?

The tort system deals with harms, so why do need a separate system for crimes? For example, why is assault a crime in addition to being a tort? The tort system is inadequate when criminals are judgment proof. If the criminal is judgment proof, then the victim of the crime will not have sufficient incentive to find the criminal and bring him to court, and the criminal will not be sufficiently deterred by the tort system (even if brought to court).[2] So the criminal needs a nonmonetary punishment such as a prison sentence to adequately deter and/or to physically restrain if deterrence is not sufficient.

Sometimes the cost of a person's actions falls on a large number of people, but the cost to any one individual might be minor. An example might be blocking a public highway. It would not be worthwhile for any individual to sue and the transaction costs of a class action suit (where the victims collectively sue) would outweigh the benefits of winning the suit. Here, too, something more than a civil remedy is needed.

It should be recognized that the judgment-proof and transaction cost explanations are not the whole story. Criminals may be jailed for petty crimes even when they are

---

[2] Because potential victims know that they will not be sufficiently compensated, they may undertake self-protection (hiring bodyguards, installing extra locks, etc.). So optimal punishment should also take into account these preventive costs that criminal activity engenders.

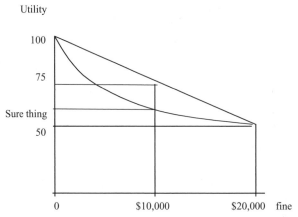

Figure 17.1.

wealthy, wealthy anti-trust defendants may be both prosecuted for their crimes and sued for their torts, and there are victimless crimes that are not torts.

D. DO INCREASES IN PROBABILITY DETER MORE THAN DO INCREASES IN THE SEVERITY OF PUNISHMENT?

Are criminals deterred more by increases in the probability or by increases in the severity of punishment? I do not have an answer to this question, but most people think they do. Let us try the following thought experiment. Suppose that society has the choice of either doubling the probability of being convicted (say, from 50% to 100%) or doubling the level of punishment if convicted (say, from $10,000 to $20,000). Which method will reduce the crime rate the most? Students almost always answer that increasing the probability of punishment will deter criminal activity more. If this answer is correct, then criminals prefer risk. In both cases, the expected punishment is the same –$10,000. But if the criminal dislikes the sure thing of losing $10,000 more than he dislikes the gamble with the same expected loss, then he will be more deterred by the sure thing than the gamble. If society wants to deter criminal activity, it should give the criminal what he does not want. When the criminal prefers gambles to the equivalent sure thing, society should give him the sure punishment.

If criminals prefer risk, this is equivalent to saying that their utility for money is convex. To illustrate, consider Figure 17.1.

The utility of the criminal is a convex function of the fine. The numbers on the right are utiles (remember that utility and utiles are just an easy way to characterize preferences). If the criminal is fined $0, then the criminal has 100 utiles; and if the criminal is fined $20,000, then the criminal has 50 utiles. If the criminal is always fined $10,000, then he will receive about 60 utiles (the sure thing). If the criminal receives a $0 fine half the time and a $20,000 fine half the time, the expected fine is $10,000 but the expected utility is .5 (100) +.5 (50) = 75 utiles. So the criminal prefers the gamble. The straight line is the criminal's expected utility. If the criminal were risk neutral, he would have the straight-line utility function. Typically, in economics, we assume that the person is risk averse (a concave function), and therefore the person would prefer the sure thing over the gamble. For such people, the gamble would deter more than the certain fine of $10,000.

E. INTENT

Criminal law is concerned with intentional harm or criminal intent. But intent is not an economic term. Therefore, we need to provide an economic underpinning for intent just as we provided an economic underpinning for the legal-term, negligence. The difference between a tortious harm and a criminal harm is that the first comes as a by-product of productive activity and is costly to the tortfeasor to prevent while in criminal cases it is costly to the criminal to do the harm. Each year, many pedestrians are killed by automobiles. In general, drivers are not found to be engaging in criminal activity when they drive; but if they purposely swerved into a group of pedestrians (when going straight involved no cost to the driver) that would be criminal intent (even if they missed) since they engaged in a costly activity whose sole purpose was to increase the likelihood of harm to others.

Premeditated murder is punished more severely than murder committed in a fit of passion. A partial explanation is that premeditated murder is done with advanced planning, which is likely to include plans for avoiding detection. As noted earlier a lower probability of being caught requires a higher punishment when caught in order to optimally deter.

F. IMPRISONMENT AS PREVENTION

Imprisonment reduces crime in two ways. The threat of imprisonment is a deterrent; while actual imprisonment may physically prevent a person from committing more crime.[3] The preventive role is of course more important for those who are likely to repeat their crimes.

Although some have claimed a rehabilitative role for imprisonment, there is little evidence for such claims, and it is not clear why training, psychotherapy, and other modes of rehabilitation would need to take place within prison if rehabilitation were the sole explanation.

G. OTHER WAYS TO REDUCE CRIME

Economists focus on prices because they are easier to measure and fluctuate more than other variables like religious values. With regard to crime, a legislature can easily change the minimum jail term for drugs or introduce a three-strikes law. Changing the attitudes of drug users is much harder. But this does not mean that price is the only variable that can affect the crime rate. As briefly mentioned in the opening paragraphs, the opportunity set can also affect a person's propensity for crime. When unemployment rates are high, selling drugs and stealing cars become more desirable at the margin.

---

[3] I use the word "may" since criminals may commit crime while in prison or direct others to commit crimes on the outside.

LAST MEAL

What would you order for your last meal before you were going to be executed? Real killers eat cheeseburgers, onion rings, and pizza. See www.deadmaneating.com.

TRAPPED BY A BOOBY TRAP

Can an owner protect personal property in an unoccupied boarded-up farmhouse against trespassers and thieves by a spring gun capable of inflicting death or serious injury? In *Katko v. Briney*, 183 N.W.2d 657 (1971), Briney, the defendant, had posted no trespassing signs, but the house had been broken into several times. So Briney secured a 20-gauge shotgun to an iron bed with the barrel pointed at the bedroom door. It was rigged with wire from the doorknob to the gun's trigger so it would fire when the door was opened. Katko, the plaintiff, entered the house to steal old bottles. The shotgun caused serious injury to Katko's leg. Katko sued Briney.

The jury returned a verdict for Katko and against the defendant for $20,000 actual and $10,000 punitive damages. The Iowa Supreme Court upheld the ruling.

SHOPLIFTING, INTERRUPTED

Winona Ryder was found guilty of shoplifting from Saks Fifth Avenue. After the trial, Saks Fifth Avenue suggested burning the evidence, including a $760 Marc Jacobs cashmere top, a $540 Natori purse, and other upscale items.

Ryder's attorney, Mark Geragos (who represented Michael Jackson for a short while and Scott Peterson, the man found guilty of killing his pregnant wife) replied: "Something's wrong when the county, which is in the middle of a budget crisis, is sponsoring a bonfire of thousands of dollars' worth of merchandise." The prosecutor responded that Ryder's suggestion of an auction for charity would undermine deterrence because the defendant would get a tax-deduction benefit, as well as a publicity advantage. Geragos countered that the prosecutor would not make much of a tax attorney if the prosecutor thinks his convicted client would be eligible for a write-off.

I think that Ryder did not take the case to a higher court because she was concerned about her movie career and was afraid that she would lose her Saks appeal. See the *National Law Journal*, April 14, 2003.

When people have few marketable skills, the returns to illegal activity may be relatively high, as well. So from an economic perspective, job training may be a way to reduce crime. Of course, any type of intervention is costly, and one must weigh the benefits against the costs.

H. CONCLUDING REMARKS

An interesting question is whether drugs such as alcohol, marijuana, Ecstasy, cocaine, and heroin should be illegal. When these are illegal, their price is higher and the demand is less. But making them illegal entails costs such as prison, corruption of law

YOU ARE NEVER TOO OLD

Until he died in 2004, J. L. Rountree was America's oldest bank robber. In 2003, the 91-year-old Texan walked into an Abilene bank and handed a teller an envelope with the word "ROBBERY" printed on it. Rountree fled with $2,000. But he was arrested 30 minutes later by the police who had been given his license-plate number. He was given a 12-year sentence. Rountree had been convicted on bank robbery charges twice before. In a 2001 interview, Rountree said that he disliked savings institutions ever since one in Texas "forced [him] into bankruptcy." He also said that he got a great thrill from robbing banks.

DEATH IN A LIFEBOAT

On July 5, 1884, Thomas Dudley and Edwin Stephens, along with a person named Brooks and a 17-year-old boy were cast away in a storm on the high seas 1,600 miles from the Cape of Good Hope. They were in a lifeboat that had no supply of water and no supply of food, except two 1-pound tins of turnips, and for three days they had nothing else to subsist on. On the fourth day they caught a small turtle. By the twelfth day the remains of the turtle were entirely consumed, and for the next eight days they had nothing to eat. On the eighteenth day, when they had been seven days without food and five without water, Dudley and Stephens suggested that someone should be sacrificed to save the rest, but Brooks dissented, and the boy, was not consulted. On the nineteenth day, Dudley proposed to Stephens and Brooks that lots should be cast to determine who should be put to death to save the rest, but Brooks refused to consent, and again the boy was not consulted. There was no drawing of lots. On the twentieth day, Dudley and Stephens decided to kill the boy, who was lying at the bottom of the boat, extremely weakened by famine and by drinking seawater, and unable to make any resistance. The three men fed on the body and blood of the boy for four days. On the twenty-fourth day, when a passing vessel rescued them, the occupants were barely alive.

The jury found Dudley and Stephens guilty of murder but asked for leniency. The judged sentenced them to death, but their sentences were commuted to 6 months' imprisonment. *Queen v. Dudley and Stephens*, 14 Q.B.D. 273 (1884).

enforcement agencies, deaths due to lack of quality control that comes with brand names, and theft to pay for the high price of the illegal drugs. Even if one believed that any consumption of these drugs was bad, one should still undertake a cost-benefit analysis to determine whether the costs of making these drugs illegal are greater than the benefits. Much of the answer will depend on the relevant elasticities.

SUGGESTIONS FOR FURTHER READING

Although Jeremy Bentham is viewed as the founding father of the economics of crime and punishment, Becker (1968) is the modern classic. Posner (1985) is an important paper on criminal law. Mitchell Polinsky and Steven Shavell have written many papers on optimal punishment. Much of their work is covered in Polinsky and Shavell (2000).

The boxed lifeboat case has been the source of much philosophical speculation. Review question number 8 suggests that contract theory might provide insight into its resolution. In Chapter 21, we will come back to some more subtle issues regarding the writing of such a contract. To ensure that lifeboat participants do not take a life in the absence of being in truly dire straights, one might want to insist on a severe punishment such as life imprisonment or taking away the murderers' lifetime earnings. But these punishments are costly (imprisonment requires guards and reduces productivity, while taking away all earnings reduces the incentive to work) and seem inappropriate if the murder and subsequent cannibalism was justified. For more on cannibalism and the law, see Simpson (1984).

I have generally refrained from discussing econometric work in this book because it is often very technical, and the data are almost always subject to limitations that cannot be summarized easily. Furthermore, no one piece of empirical work is definitive. Three researchers who have been in the center of considerable controversy are Steve Levitt, John Donohue and John Lott. Levitt and Donohue argue that unwanted children are more likely to commit crime. When abortion was made legal in the United States, the number of unwanted children decreased. Their data shows that the crime rate dropped eighteen years later when the unwanted and aborted children were not around to commit crimes (the crime rate dropping earlier for those states that made abortion legal earlier). This work is discussed in a nontechnical way in Levitt and Dubner (2005). For a critique of their work, see Joyce (2004). Lott (2000) argues that concealed handguns reduce crime because criminals never know whether the person that they are attempting to mug has a concealed weapon. This reduces the demand for mugging because the cost of doing so increases. Ayres and Donohue (2002) come to a different conclusion. For evidence demonstrating the deterrent effect of capital punishment see Dezhbakhsh et al. (2003); for a contrary view, see Donohue and Wolfers (2005). Expect to see more arguments and counterarguments on these topics in the future.

REVIEW QUESTIONS

1. How is the optimal price of a crime established if the punishment is in the form of a fine? Explain. (4)
2. Show how the answer to question 1 changes when it is costly to punish criminals? (5)
3. Why does society have to worry about marginal deterrence? (2)
4. Why do we have criminal law in addition to tort law? (8)
5. Using a well-labeled graph, show that risk-preferring criminals prefer a doubling of the punishment over a doubling of the probability of being punished. (10)
6. In 1985 Joe Simpson and Simon Yates were descending a mountain in Peru when Simpson broke his leg. Yates lowered Simpson down on a rope, but Simpson was hanging over a crevasse and Yates was about to be pulled down, himself. So Yates cut the rope. The story is told in the 2003 movie *Touching the Void*. Simpson survived. If he did not, should Yates have been tried for manslaughter?
7. Using economic analysis, what do you think is the correct decision in *Katko v. Briney*? (10)

8. Using the concepts developed in this book, Should Dudley and Stephens be punished for murder? (6) If before setting sail, all four had signed a contract allowing lots to be drawn under these circumstances, should they be punished for murder? (6)

REFERENCES

Ayres, Ian, and John J. Donohue III. (2002). Shooting Down the More Guns, Less Crime Hypothesis. *Stanford Law and Economics Working Paper No. 247*.

Becker, Gary S. (1968). Crime and Punishment: An Economic Approach. 76 *Journal of Political Economy* 169.

Bentham, Jeremy. (1789, 1990). *An Introduction to the Principles of Morals and Legislation*. J. H. Burns and H. L. A. Hart (eds.). Oxford: Clarendon Press.

Dezhbakhsh, Hashem, Paul H. Rubin and Joanna M. Shepherd. (2003). Does Capital Punishment Have a Deterrent Effect? New Evidence from Postmoratorium Panel Data. 5 *American Law and Economic Review* 344.

Donohue, John J. and Justin Wolfers. (2005). Uses and Abuses of Empirical Evidence in the Death Penalty Debate. 58 *Stanford Law Review* 791.

Joyce, Ted. (2004). Further Tests of Abortion and Crime. *National Bureau of Economic Research Working Paper No. 10564*.

Levitt, Steven D., and Stephen Dubner. (2005). *Freakeconomics: A Rogue Economist Explores the Hidden Side of Everything*. New York: HarperCollins Publishers.

Lott, John R. Jr. (2000). *More Guns, Less Crime*, 2nd ed. Chicago: University of Chicago Press.

Polinsky, A. Mitchell, and Steven Shavell. (2000). Public Enforcement of Law. *Encyclopedia of Law and Economics*. Vol. 5. Boudewijn Bouckaert and Gerritt De Geest (eds.). Northampton, MA: Edward Elgar.

Simpson, A. W. Brian. (1984). *Cannibalism and the Common Law: The Story of the Tragic Last Voyage of the Mignonette and the Strange Legal Proceedings to Which It Gave Rise*. Chicago: University of Chicago Press.

VI THE ROLE OF SEQUENCE

We have discussed at length the design of liability rules when the inputs are simultaneous in nature. But does the analysis change if the inputs are sequential? For example, does it make any difference who was there first – the polluting factory or the pollution sensitive fishery? As another example, does it make a difference that a donkey had been left standing in the middle of the road before a coach careened into it. The short answer is yes, sometimes. The more detailed answer is found in remainder of Part VI.

Once again, economic logic provides insight into various areas of the law. In Chapter 18, we consider last clear chance in accident law, mitigation of damages in contract law, and coming to the nuisance in nuisance law and show that the appropriate remedy relies on the same underlying economic thinking.

In Chapter 19, we consider the Good Samaritan rule. In England and in the United States, potential rescuers are not liable for the harm to someone they failed to rescue even if the victim could have been rescued at very low cost by the potential rescuer. Continental Europe has a contrary set of rules. The victim is liable for his/her rescue (that is, the victim must pay the rescuer for the rescue), but the potential rescuer is liable to the victim if the rescuer did not try to save the victim despite the low cost to the rescuer. We show why the Continental rule is superior.

In Chapter 20, we show how property rights are affected by who was first. The key economic intuition is that rights cannot invariably be given to the party who was there first because then there will be inappropriate incentives to be first.

18 Mitigation of Damages and Last Clear Chance

A. Applications 168

   1. Mitigation of Damages in Contract Law 168

   2. Last Clear Chance in Accident Law 169

   3. Avoidable Consequences and Coming to the Nuisance 172

B. Concluding Remarks 172

SUGGESTIONS FOR FURTHER READING 173

REVIEW QUESTIONS 173

REFERENCES 174

If a motorcycle is parked illegally in the middle of the road and a truck smashes into it, who should be liable for the damage to the motorcycle? When a sulfur factory emits fumes that kill a neighboring crop, what should be the extent of the factory owner's liability? In both of these examples, each party controls a different input into the production of the output; but, unlike many cases that we have considered, these inputs are characterized be a clearly defined sequence – the motorcycle is parked in the middle of the road and then a truck comes; the sulfur fumes are in the air and then the crop is planted.

As we have seen in an earlier chapter, when these inputs occur simultaneously, a variety of liability rules create the proper incentives for an efficient outcome. For example, under a rule of negligence with contributory negligence, the owner would be liable for all of the damage to her motorcycle. This would discourage owners of motorcycles from inefficiently parking their motorcycles in the middle of the road in the first place.

However, when the inputs occur *sequentially*, none of the *damage-based* liability rules create the optimal incentives both for long-run efficiency and for second-best outcomes when the long-run efficient choice is not made. For example, a comparative negligence rule cannot discourage truck drivers from smashing into motorcycles and simultaneously discourage motorcyclists from leaving their motorcycles in the middle of the road. If comparative negligence provides the correct incentives for truck drivers to swerve and avoid hitting parked motorcycles, then motorcyclists will have insufficient incentive to park their motorcycles in appropriate areas in the first place. If comparative negligence provides the correct incentives for motorcyclists to park appropriately, then they will rarely park in the middle of the road; but on those occasions when they do, there will be insufficient incentives for truck drivers to optimally avoid damaging motorcycles. In a nutshell, none of the standard liability rules can provide the right incentives for both equilibrium and out-of-equilibrium behavior.

The way out of this dilemma is to have a *marginal cost* liability rule. *The first party in the sequence is liable to the second party for any additional prevention cost that the second party should undertake in response to the first party's suboptimal behavior plus any damage (to either party) that would still occur if the second party responds optimally to the situation created by the first party. The second party is then liable for any damage and own prevention cost.* Because the second party is being compensated by the first, if the second party's response to the first party is optimal, then the net liability of the second party for damage and additional prevention will be zero. The logic will now be elucidated within the context of several examples.

A. APPLICATIONS

1. Mitigation of Damages in Contract Law

In contract law, marginal cost liability is known as the doctrine of *mitigation of damages*. The plaintiff in a breach-of-contract case cannot collect for losses (damages) that he could have avoided by reasonable effort without risk of substantial loss or injury. In economic terms, "reasonable effort" means best response. The plaintiff can collect, however, for the avoidance costs that he should undertake in response to the breach. His recovery against the defendant will be exactly the same regardless of whether he makes the effort to mitigate his loss.

A good illustration of the concept is in the first Restatement of Contracts (1932) §336 at 538. A sells to B a quantity of pork packed in barrels of brine with a warranty that the barrels will not leak. B finds that some of the barrels are leaky but does not repack the pork in good barrels. B can get judgment for only the cost of repacking in good barrels and the value of the pork spoiled before her discovery of the defects, not for the pork spoiled after her discovery. The victim is compensated for the additional prevention cost incurred by the victim and resulting damage when she mitigates optimally. Whether or not the victim did indeed act optimally. Of course, given this rule, the victim will have the appropriate incentive to act optimally because the cost of any inefficient response by the victim falls on the victim.

As another example, consider *Daley v. Irwin*, 205 P. 76 (1922). In this case, the plaintiff purchased defective seed but found out that the seed was defective before planting it. The court ruled that a buyer who plants defective seed, knowing of its defects and having an opportunity to avoid the loss of the crop, cannot recover damages for the losses on the doomed-to-fail crop. The buyer's recovery is limited to the difference in market value between the seed as warranted and the defective seed delivered.

The court decision makes sense in terms of our economic analysis. If the farmer knows that the seed is defective (that is, the farmer's decision comes second in the sequence), we want the farmer to undertake *cost-effective strategies to mitigate the damage*. In particular, the farmer should not go through the expense of planting seed that he knows to be defective; instead, he should purchase new seed that is not defective and plant it. So the court ruled that the farmer could only collect for the cost of purchasing good seed (whether he did so or not). In general, the farmer should only collect for the *additional* cost of prevention and any subsequent damage that would occur (perhaps the new seeds had to be sown a week later reducing the output) if the farmer were to *optimally* mitigate. The farmer cannot collect for damage that could have been prevented by the farmer. Of course, if the farmer did not know that the seed was defective (perhaps it was irradiated), then the farmer could also collect for the cost of planting the seed.

In situations where a breach of contract does not give the plaintiff a last clear chance to avoid damages (i.e., the inputs do not take place sequentially but are simultaneous), the plaintiff can collect for the full amount of damages. In *Parkersburg Rig and Reel Co. v. Freed Oil and Gas Co.*, 205 P. 1020 (1922), the court held that the plaintiff need not build dams in anticipation of breaks in oil tanks built by the defendant (a breach of contract) and therefore could recover for all damages. Another situation where the plaintiff does not have the last clear chance is when the defendant assures the plaintiff that the contract is not repudiated. In these cases, too, the defendant is liable for all damages.

Contracting involves relatively low transaction costs. The marginal cost liability rule reduces transaction costs still further because it is a reasonable starting point for any negotiation. That is, the rule provides a good estimate of the likely agreement if the breach were anticipated beforehand.

2. Last Clear Chance in Accident Law

The doctrine of *last clear chance* makes the last person who could have reasonably avoided an accident liable. This doctrine originated in 1842 in the case of *Davies v.*

Mann, 152 Eng. Rep, 588. The plaintiff negligently left his donkey tied up in the middle of the road somewhat below the crest of a hill. The defendant was driving his carriage at an excessive speed, and when the defendant came over the crest of the hill, he was going too fast to avoid hitting the donkey. The donkey subsequently died. Had the defendant swerved in time, the donkey would not have been killed. The court found the carriage driver liable as he had the last clear chance to avoid the accident.

Let us consider a modern version where a truck runs into a motorcycle parked in the middle of a road. The person (Y) who left her motorcycle on the road was the least-cost avoider; but *given* that the motorcycle was already there, the driver of the truck (X) should be encouraged not to smash into it. Making Y liable for the damage will, in the future, discourage people from parking their motorcycles in the middle of the road, but not *sufficiently* discourage others from smashing into them. Making X liable for the damage will create the proper incentives for X to avoid smashing into Y but will not sufficiently discourage people from parking their motorcycles in the middle of road.

Once again, the appropriate rule is to make Y liable for the marginal costs that she imposes on X whether there is an accident or not. In this case, the motorcyclist who parks in the middle of the road would pay for the *additional* cost (swerving, braking, etc.) that she imposes on other drivers, even in the absence of any damage from an accident. This payment would internalize the cost that the motorcyclist is imposing on others. Therefore, most motorcyclists would not park in the middle of the road in the first place and those that did would pay. The next step is to make the second party, X, liable for the marginal costs that he imposes on Y if he fails to respond properly to the dangerous situation. The truck driver is then liable for any costs that he imposes on the motorcyclist beyond those that would occur if he had acted optimally in response to the dangerous situation. Hence, the truck driver also has the incentive to swerve if this is the optimal thing to do (obviously, it would not be optimal for the truck driver to swerve into oncoming traffic).

The person (Y) who left her motorcycle in the middle of the road should pay (to the extent feasible) for the marginal costs she imposes on others. In this way, Y will make efficient choices. Clearly, a system of liability to all drivers who swerve or drive on another road in *order* to avoid hitting the motorcycle is totally impractical. The cost to individual drivers is minimal, but the sum total to all the drivers may be quite significant; therefore, we want the driver of the parked motorcycle to pay for the cost she shifts onto others. The appropriate solution is to charge Y a fine equal to the total marginal cost imposed on others (a Pigovian tax on the input). This fine will create the same incentives for Y as marginal cost civil liability. Whether Y pays to the state or to an individual, the incentive effect on Y is the same. If Y is not always caught parking illegally on the highway, the fine can be increased to compensate for the reduction in probability. For example, if Y is only caught half the time, the fine would be twice as large as it would be if she were caught all the time.

We now investigate the effect of this Pigovian tax solution on truck and car drivers. Under a marginal cost *liability* scheme, these drivers are compensated for the cost of preventive behavior, regardless of their taking preventive measures. Compensation does not affect their behavior because it is not based on any decision they make but rather on the decision Y makes. Consequently, if Y pays a fine to the state instead of being liable to drivers who swerved, her payment will have no effect on the *care level* of these drivers. In other words, *compensation* for marginal costs that should be incurred is not necessary for the system to work properly.

We want drivers to take into account the marginal costs that they impose. The doctrine of last clear chance, by making drivers liable for the damage when they are truly the second in the sequence, encourages them to make efficient decisions. Thus, a ticket for illegally parking the motorcycle in the middle of the road and liability for the damage on the driver of the moving truck (because he had the last clear chance) is a marginal cost liability rule applied in sequence.

This analysis also provides an important reason for fining people for inputs such as drunken or reckless driving instead of relying only on liability for the resulting damage. Other drivers may swerve out of the way to avoid an accident (and the legal system should encourage them to do so). To the extent that these other drivers are successful, reckless drivers will not pay for their behavior if liability depends only on actual damage. Reckless drivers are not *sufficiently* deterred if the costs of protection are shifted onto other drivers. In other words, if liability were only based on damages, reckless drivers would not pay for *some* of the negative externalities that they create. Therefore, we have fines to make these reckless drivers liable for the cost of damage prevention they shift onto others.

As demonstrated earlier, when there is a sequence of events, marginal cost liability should be applied regardless of whether there is damage or who is actually damaged. The law, in fact, reflects the symmetry of this analysis. A person is fined for illegal parking regardless of whether an accident occurred. Depending on which party had the last clear chance, the doctrine can be used against the defendant in favor of the plaintiff or against the plaintiff in favor of the defendant. Let us consider this latter possibility in greater detail.

Suppose that it was the truck that was parked illegally on the road and the motorcycle smashed into it, harming the motorcyclist but not the truck.[1] The truck would get a ticket for illegal parking. If the motorcyclist had the last clear chance, then the motorcyclist would be liable for the damage to the motorcyclist; if the motorcyclist did not have the last clear chance, then the truck would also be liable for the damage to the motorcyclist.

In accident law, *marginal cost civil* liability is rare, but in contract law, it is the rule. There are several reason for these two areas of law having different methods of determining liability: (1) In contract cases, the second party in the sequence (who can mitigate damages) always knows who created the initial wrong – the breacher of the contract. The same does not hold for accident cases. If a car swerved suddenly to avoid hitting another car driving in the other direction but on the wrong side of the road, it could be very difficult to discover afterward who the reckless driver was. (2) When a breach of contract occurs, cost-effective preventive action by the person who has the last clear chance may be very costly; for example, repacking those leaky pickle barrels. Therefore, it pays for the plaintiffs in breach-of-contract cases to sue even when there is "no damage" because sufficient marginal costs are involved in preventive action to make it worthwhile for the plaintiff to collect for these costs (which are also known as damages in the legal literature). In contrast, the amount of liability that any one driver could collect for swerving (and thereby avoiding an accident) would not be

---

[1] For parallel legal case, see *Topping v. Oshawa Street Railway*, 66 Ont. L. R. 618 (1931).

enough to compensate for the transaction cost of litigation. (3) It is much easier to determine sequence (who was first and who was last) in breach-of-contract than in accident cases. For all these reasons, we would expect the sequence of events to be much more important for breach of contract – where mitigation of damages is the rule – than for accidents where last clear chance is rarely applied. The differences in the two areas of civil law are thus due to the different costs of information and the benefits of litigation.

3. Avoidable Consequences and Coming to the Nuisance

In nuisance law, when "damages" are awarded, they are typically for the costs of reasonable preventive behavior by the plaintiff and any damage occurring (or that would have occurred) after preventive action had been taken. In other words, there is marginal cost liability. For example, in *United Verde Extension Mining v. Ralston*, 296 P. 262 (1931), the court held that the plaintiff need not plant a hopeless crop that would be swept by sulfur fumes and should not recover for the damage to the crop if he did. In this case, the plaintiff had the last clear chance and could have mitigated damages and prevented wasted seed and crop damage by not planting. However, the plaintiff recovered for profits forgone in not planting the crop. Thus, we have marginal cost liability or, in legal terminology, the doctrine of avoidable consequence. "This doctrine states that a party cannot recover damages flowing from consequences which the party could reasonably have avoided.... The doctrine has a necessary corollary – the person who reasonably attempts to minimize his damages can recover expenses incurred."

Marginal cost liability was also employed in *Spur Industries v. Del E. Webb Development Corporation*, 494 P. 2d 700 (1972). In this case, Del Webb built a retirement community next to an existing cattle-feeding operation, located in an agricultural area well outside the boundaries of any city. The retirement community asked the court to shut down the cattle-feeding operation. The court held that the developer was entitled to enjoin the cattle-feeding operation as a nuisance, but it was required to indemnify the cattle feeder for the reasonable cost of moving or shutting down. This novel solution by the court reflects the fact that there are three stages to this sequential game: the feedlot was there first; the developer should have built elsewhere and thus had the "last clear chance"; but given that the plaintiff had built next to it, the feedlot had the *last* "last clear chance" to mitigate the damage. The location of the feedlot faraway from any city imposes little marginal cost on potential developers as they could readily avoid the nuisance by building elsewhere. However, given that the developer had located near the feedlot, it was best to have the feedlot move. Because the developer imposed the marginal costs, he should pay for them.

B. CONCLUDING REMARKS

A legal system should provide the appropriate incentives for individuals to act optimally. But even under the best of circumstances, not everyone does. In such cases, the legal system needs to encourage the "second-best" solution without interfering with the incentives for the "first-best" solution. The marginal cost liability rules (mitigation of damages, avoidable consequences, etc.) have been designed to encourage the first-best outcome, and when there has been a failure in this regard, to encourage the best behavior in response.

The negligence rules that we encountered in an earlier chapter are not adequate to deal with sequential inputs. These negligence rules require the negligent party to pay for the *damage* from an accident. But when the first party to the sequence has acted inefficiently, we want the second party in the sequence to increase precaution. As a result of this increased precaution, there may be no accident and no damage, but there will be the increased precaution cost, which we want the first party to pay for. When it comes to traffic, this suboptimal behavior by the first party is usually paid to the state in the form of a traffic fine rather than being paid to the second party via a liability rule.

For economists, but not for normal folks, the puzzle is why we fine drivers for speeding and poor driving rather than just making such drivers liable for the damage from accidents. Earlier, we provided the judgment proof explanation; now we have a more compelling argument for regulating the input. If we don't charge poor drivers for bad driving, these drivers may shift the cost of accident avoidance onto other drivers.

The conflict between incentives for long-run optimal behavior and short-run solutions to suboptimal behavior arises in all kinds of situations. Consider bankruptcy. We want the cost of bankruptcy to fall as much as possible on the bankrupt party. In this way, the person will not undertake excessive (nonoptimal) risk because the costs as well as the benefits accrue to the individual. But given that a person is bankrupt, making the person pay back all debts may discourage the person from productive work (as might be the case if 80% of the person's salary were allocated to paying back creditors). More generally, people make better decisions when all the costs and benefits fall on them, but either by bad luck or bad judgment a person might be facing unusually high costs. Any attempt to mitigate those costs (say, by insurance) may encourage the bad outcome in the first place.

SUGGESTIONS FOR FURTHER READING

A more technical discussion can be found in Wittman (1981). For additional results, see Shavell (1983). Micelli et al. (2001) have an interesting application of mitigation of damages to landlord-tenant law. When the property is agricultural land and a tenant breaks the lease, the best solution is for the landlord to let the land lie fallow. When the property is an apartment, then the optimal solution is to find another tenant. In the latter case, the landlord has a duty to mitigate by finding a new tenant, but traditionally not in the first case, where the landlord had no such duty.

REVIEW QUESTIONS

1. Why do we have marginal cost liability in addition to ordinary negligence rules? (10).
2. What is the doctrine of last clear chance in accident law? Provide an example and a justification for its use. (8)
3. What is the doctrine of mitigation of damages in contract law? Provide an example and a justification for its use. (8)
4. What is the doctrine of avoidable consequences in nuisance law? Provide an example and a justification for its use. (8)

REFERENCES

Miceli, Thomas J., C. F. Sirmans, and Geoffrey K. Turnbull. (2001). The Duty to Mitigate Damages in Leases: Out with the Old Rule and in with the New. *Center for Real Estate Working Paper No. 307.* http://ssrn.com/abstract=304963.

Shavell, Steven. (1983). Torts in which Victim and Injurer Act Sequentially. 26 *Journal of Law and Economics* 589–612.

Wittman, Donald A. (1981). Optimal Pricing of Sequential Inputs: Last Clear Chance, Mitigation of Damages and Related Doctrines in the Law. 10 *Journal of Legal Studies* 65.

19 The Good Samaritan Rule

A. The Economic Logic Underlying the Continental Rule 176

B. The Anglo-American Rule 177

C. When the Cost of Rescue Is High 178

D. Concluding Remarks 178

SUGGESTIONS FOR FURTHER READING 179

REVIEW QUESTIONS 179

REFERENCES 179

A person is lying unconscious across a railroad track. Should a passerby be compensated for saving the unconscious person's life or be found liable for not saving his life? In general, Anglo-American courts require no affirmative duties of bystanders, and rarely is there a legal obligation to compensate the rescuer for the minor costs incurred in rescuing. In contrast, the Continental rule imposes Good Samaritan duties on mere bystanders when the cost of rescue is trivial and entitles the successful rescuer to a reward. Which system is better?

Before we get to the details of the economic argument, it is worthwhile to deal with some noneconomic answers to the puzzle. One might argue that there is a great difference between the sin of commission (pulling the unconscious person onto the tracks) and the sin of omission (not pulling the unconscious person off the tracks). And therefore, the former should be punished but not the latter. Economic reasoning shows such a distinction to be next to meaningless because there is only a very small cost difference between the commission and omission; and it is clearly cost effective for a bystander to rescue the unconscious person. Nor is it helpful to say that the bystander did not "cause" the death because the bystander's input would have prevented such an outcome.

A. THE ECONOMIC LOGIC UNDERLYING THE CONTINENTAL RULE

If a person can be rescued at low cost, it is clearly economically efficient to do so. The Continental rule encourages low-cost rescues in two ways. First, the rescuer is compensated for the small costs of rescue; second, if the potential rescuer's costs are somewhat higher than the average so that the reward does not fully cover all of the rescuer's costs, then the threat of being liable for damage to the potential rescuee will motivate the person to rescue.

The rule also provides the appropriate incentives for those who might need rescue. By charging for the average cost of the rescue, the rescuee takes the appropriate level of care. A higher price for rescue would result in the potential rescuee being overly cautious and needing too few rescues. For example, consider the possibility of a person deciding to swim at a beach. If the lifeguards charge $10,000 for a simple rescue, the person might not go swimming in the first place, or if the person does, the swimmer might buy some very expensive equipment to haul along so that the swimmer can perform a self-rescue. However, if the price paid to rescuers is lower than the costs that the rescuers incur in rescue, then either there will be too many people needing rescue and being rescued (if the low price does not affect the supply of potential rescuers) or there will be too few rescuers and, as a consequence, too few people putting themselves at risk. To understand the logic behind the latter case, suppose that tow truck operators were paid less than their cost of towing stalled cars off the freeway to an auto repair facility. Then there would be fewer tow trucks and fewer than the optimal number of cars on the road that were likely to need towing. A less prosaic example is the rescue of boat people who were fleeing Vietnam. Ships that rescued these boat people were not compensated for their rescue efforts. Consequently, many ships undertook circuitous routes to avoid areas where there were likely to be boat people in need of rescue. In turn, this meant that there were fewer boat people than optimal because the danger to them was unnecessarily high.

In a nutshell, for there to be the correct economic incentives, both liability by the rescuee for being rescued and liability by the rescuer for nonrescue must be in place. The Continental rule employs both. The Anglo-American rule employs neither.

B. THE ANGLO-AMERICAN RULE

If the Continental rule is so sensible, why have the Anglo-American courts generally ruled otherwise? There have been a number of attempts to find an economic explanation, but despite the cleverness of the ideas, none of the suggested answers are fully convincing. For example, it has been argued that people either are truly altruistic or desire to have a reputation for being altruistic and that a law that made people liable for nonrescue would interfere with this motivation – people could not claim that their behavior was altruistically motivated if the law punished them for not behaving in an "altruistic" way.[1] There are several problems with such an explanation. It is not clear why a law backing up desirable behavior diminishes it. Much desirable behavior is reinforced by legal sanctions and many religions use the threat of eternal damnation if the person does not act righteously. In the example at hand, the altruistic person could always give back the money for rescuing. And it is hard to conceive of the case where punishing for nonrescue would deter an altruistic person from rescuing. A counterargument is that people are altruistic when it is a choice of someone losing a life and their being slightly inconvenienced; once there is an imposed payment, the choice is between collecting or not collecting and not collecting means that the Samaritan is giving up something to benefit someone else by an equal amount. Therefore, the altruistic motive will no longer be operative, and the rescuer will want to collect on the reward. If most people are altruists when it comes to saving lives, then the effect of requiring an award will be a needless costly transaction. But there are also problems with this counterargument. If people do not have to pay for their rescue, people will take too many risks. Furthermore, once we allow altruism as a motivation for the rescuer's behavior, we may have to reconsider the motivation of the rescued person as well. For example, would something akin to altruism motivate the rescued person to reward the rescuer? Finally, do we want to argue that a system of rewards and punishments is not needed in English-speaking countries because they are more altruistic?

It has also been argued that the cost of tracking down nonrescuers could be so large (it may be hard to discover who was in the area or whether they witnessed the event) that the benefits of such a rule would be undermined. There are problems with such an argument. The person will be tracked down only if the cost of tracking is less than the liability, which is the cost of nonrescue. Because by hypothesis the cost of rescue was slight, even in the presence of search costs, it is efficient to make the nonrescuer liable. Another argument against making nonrescuers liable is that there might be multiple tortfeasors: if there were ten people watching someone drown, there is the question of how to allocate liability. But the problem of multiple tortfeasors can be handled by making them jointly and severally liable or by creating a more complicated scheme if the tortfeasors vary in their ability to rescue.

---

[1]   See Posner and Landes (1978) for this argument. More generally, a number of people have argued that putting a price on behavior commodifies it, thereby undermining the desire to undertake such behavior.

Rather than trying to justify the Anglo-American rule, it may be more insightful to see the many exceptions based on special relationships. A number of statutes require a driver who is involved in an accident to offer assistance to the accident victims regardless of fault. In most American jurisdictions, the captain (or ship owner) is liable if he fails to take reasonable measures to rescue passengers or crew who jump overboard. Passengers (crew) pay for these rescue services via higher ticket prices (lower wages). More important, "individuals in charge of a vessel shall render assistance to any individual found at sea in danger of being lost, so far as the . . . individual in charge can do so without serious danger to the . . . individual's vessel or individuals on board" (46 U.S.C. §2304; also see Canada Shipping Act, R.S.C. 1985 c. S-9, s. 451(1), and the U.K. Maritime Convention Act, 1911, 1 & 2 Geo. 5, c. 57, s. 6). Failure to do so may lead to a fine and/or imprisonment. As a final example, a physician who treats an unconscious person can collect her regular fee.

C. WHEN THE COST OF RESCUE IS HIGH

The cost of rescue is not always trivial, and because of that, people are sometimes prevented from undertaking certain risky action in the first place. Eagle Sarmount wanted to fly his hang glider (powered with a snowmobile engine) from New York to Paris. But when he got to Canada, the Royal Canadian Mounted Police would not let him fly over the Atlantic even though it was his life to lose (*Santa Cruz Sentinel*, July 23, 1980). The Canadians realized that if his plane did go down in the Atlantic, they would be responsible for saving him. They knew that Eagle did not have the wherewithal to pay for his rescue, and they knew that Eagle knew this also. Rather than allowing him to impose such a cost on others, they prevented him from flying any further.

There are other solutions besides regulation. In some mountain-climbing areas, climbers must post bond for their rescue. Poor swimmers can risk drowning in public swimming pools because the price of admission includes a lifeguard. On the open seas, ships are liable to their rescuers; if they were not, professional rescuers and salvage ships would not be available. There is no need for liability for nonrescue because the profit from rescue is sufficient to encourage rescue attempts when it is efficient to do so.

D. CONCLUDING REMARKS

We have investigated high transaction cost situations where the cost of rescue is trivial but the cost of nonrescue is great. A two-part rule, liability by the rescuee for being rescued and liability by the potential rescuer for nonrescue, creates the proper incentives for all actors. This two-part rule also puts breaks on the use of affirmative obligation. For example, Epstein (1973) argues that a natural extension of the Good Samaritan rule would require the rich to give charity to the poor. But a two-part liability rule does not involve redistribution – those that are saved must pay for their rescue.

Economic theory provides general concepts for understanding seemingly unrelated issues in the law. A clear illustration is the last two chapters. The Good Samaritan rule would appear to have little to do with last clear chance in accident law or mitigation of damages in contract law, but all three employ the same two-part liability rule. In the case of driving, a motorcycle that is parked in the middle of the road must pay for its rescue (not being hit) by paying a fine for illegally parking on the road; the truck that had the last clear chance to avoid hitting the motorcycle is liable for nonrescue – the damage to the motorcycle when the truck hits it.

SUGGESTIONS FOR FURTHER READING

The good Samaritan rule has generated much philosophical debate. See Ratcliff (1966), Epstein (1973), Posner and Landes (1978), Weinrib (1980), and Levmore (1986) for views different from those presented here.

REVIEW QUESTIONS

1. What is the Good Samaritan rule? How does it differ in the English-speaking countries versus continental Europe? Explain the benefits and costs of each system. (10)

REFERENCES

Epstein, Richard. (1973). A Theory of Strict Liability. 2 *Journal of Legal Studies* 151.

Landes, William, and Richard A. Posner. (1978). Salvors, Finders, Good Samaritans and Other Rescuers: An Economic Study of Law and Altruism. 7 *Journal of Legal Studies* 83.

Levmore, Saul. (1986). Waiting for Rescue: An Essay on the Evolution and Incentive Structure of the Law of Obligations. 72 *Virginia Law Review* 879.

Ratcliffe, James M. (ed.). (1966). *The Good Samaritan and the Law.* Garden City, NY: Anchor Books.

Weinrib, Ernest J. (1980). The Case for a Duty to Rescue. *90 Yale Law Journal* 247.

20

The Role of Being First in Allocating Rights: Coming to the Nuisance

If my neighbour makes a tan-yard, so as to annoy and render less salubrious the air of my house or gardens, the law will furnish me with a remedy; but if he is first in possession of the air, and I fix my habitation near him, the nuisance is of my own seeking, and must continue.

(Blackstone 1766: 402–403)

A. Character of the Area Predetermined 183

B. Character of the Place Determined by Its First Use 184

C. Character of the Place Determined by the Second Use 184

D. The Character of the Place Is Determined by the Second Use, but the Second Use Should Not Have Been There 186

E. Concluding Remarks 188

SUGGESTIONS FOR FURTHER READING 188

REVIEW QUESTIONS 188

REFERENCES 189

For Blackstone, the allocation of rights is determined by who was there first: when the nuisance is first, then the nuisance has the right to continue; when the plaintiff is first, then the plaintiff has the right to prevent the nuisance from locating nearby. This rule has the benefit of simplicity, but economic efficiency requires a more nuanced approach. Allocation on the basis of being first entails costs associated with getting "there" first and staying there. Giving free tickets to a rock concert to the first ten people in line on Monday morning may result in people camping out in line over the whole weekend. With regard to land use, premature investment in tanneries or homes may occur to establish prior rights. In a nutshell, giving rights to the first person creates high transaction costs.

However, intuition suggests that being first should count for something. So how do we resolve these conflicting views on being first? Fortunately, economic logic comes to the rescue by clarifying the contingencies when being first counts and the doctrine of coming to the nuisance should be invoked. The key to understanding is to view the problem as an issue of resource allocation over time. One should first determine which sequence is optimal and then design rules that promote the efficient outcome. Thus, the determination of which side should have the right depends on the costs and benefits of the entire income stream, not just on those costs and benefits after the second party came.

To make the logic as clear as possible, we will consider two time periods and two plots of adjacent land. We further assume that one plot of land can be used for residential housing or left vacant while the other plot of land can be used by the nuisance (say a cattle feedlot or smoking factory) or left vacant. We will also assume that it is economically efficient for either the residences or the nuisance (but not both) to be located in the area in the first period. We make these simplifying assumptions so that we can limit the set of possible combinations and sequences to a manageable number.

The efficient sequential allocation of resources will be one of the following scenarios: (1) the nuisance comes first and the residences never come to the area; (2) the nuisance comes first, the residences come second, and the nuisance leaves; (3) the nuisance comes first, the residences come second, and both remain with each mitigating the damage optimally given that the other is there; (4) the residences come first and the nuisance never comes; (5) the residences come first, the nuisance comes second, and the residences leave; and (6) the residences come first, and the nuisance comes second with each mitigating the damage optimally given that the other is there.

The optimal sequence depends on the particular set of circumstances. Some areas, even before either the nuisance or the houses are present, are clearly inappropriate for one or the other use. In such cases, the right goes to the appropriate use, regardless of who was there first. Other areas have no distinguishing characteristics, and it is the first use that creates the character of the area. In such cases, it is the first that gains the right. Finally, the optimal character of a place may change over time. In such cases, the moving costs of the party that was there first and should have been there first are considered in the calculations. This will become apparent when we get to the case studies.

After determining the optimal sequence, the next step is to determine the liability rule or property right allocation that promotes the efficient sequence. Strategic behavior by the participants trying to be first and thereby gaining extra consideration is avoided by granting extra consideration to the side that *should* have been first instead of to the side that was actually first. The extra consideration is the inclusion of moving costs by the side that should have been first into the cost-benefit calculations. As can be seen from the six possible efficient scenarios, moving costs of the second party are not part of the cost-benefit calculations because no efficient sequence would have the second party move in and then move out right away.

So far, the discussion has been at a highly abstract level. We will now illustrate the ideas within the context of particular situations and cases.

A. CHARACTER OF THE AREA PREDETERMINED

Sometimes an area is particularly appropriate for one use. Parties should anticipate what this use is, especially when the future is easy to see. In *Gau v. Ley*, 38 Ohio C.C. 235 (1916), the nuisance came to the residents. The court held that the plaintiff was not entitled to relief from the noise arising from the operation of the defendant's plant, which was built after the plaintiff constructed his home. Two railroads were operating on tracks nearby long before the plaintiff and others located their homes in the vicinity. "[I]t was not reasonable to presume that plaintiff in the presence of all these facts, could not *have foreseen* that in the large and growing city of Cincinnati, the march of business would sooner or later follow the line of these railroads and convert the adjacent strip of land into business uses." Even though the residential area was there first, the residents should have foreseen that the location was ideally suited for the nuisance. Consequently, the residents should not have been there first and their moving costs should not be included in weighing the costs and benefits of alternative land use. Of course, even if the cost of moving the homes were included, the balance would have been against the homeowners. In this case, it is more efficient that the homes were built elsewhere in the first place than having the appropriately located business mitigate the damage to the inappropriately located houses. Therefore, the burden of mitigation was left entirely to the homeowners.

The court's judgment in *Gau v. Ley* is neither unusual nor controversial. The logic is mirrored in *Bove v. Donner-Hanna Coke Corporation*, 258 N.Y.S. 229 (1932), where the court stated: "It is true that the appellant was a resident of this locality for several years before defendant came on the scene . . . and that when the plaintiff built her house, the land on which these coke ovens now stand was a hickory grove. This region was never fitted for a residential district [low land, river, seven railroads]."

Notice that in comparing the costs and benefits of the homeowner versus the factory owner it is inappropriate to consider the costs of the homeowner rebuilding because the homeowner should not have been there in the first place. Appellate court decisions serve as a precedent. The court ruling means that in the future residents will choose the appropriate location in the first place. We can also ask which party would end up with the right if transaction costs were zero. The trick here is to know when the question should be asked. It should be asked before the residents have built their homes (more generally, before either side has made an investment).

By symmetry, the logic can be applied equally well to a nuisance that inappropriately builds in an area most suitable for residential housing.

B. CHARACTER OF THE PLACE DETERMINED BY ITS FIRST USE

Swamps and railroad tracks are appropriate locations for heavy industry and inappropriate for housing; hilltop locations in urban areas are appropriate for housing and inappropriate for heavy industry. But sometimes, large expanses of land are featureless, and the first use of the land establishes its character.

This was the case in *Mahlstadt v. City of Indianola*, 100 N.W. 2d 189 (1959). Mahlstadt, a housing developer, had asked for a court injunction barring the operation of a city dump neighboring his property. The appellate court ruled in favor of the city. There was nothing peculiar to the location, making it particularly appropriate or inappropriate for housing or for a dump. Therefore, the first activity determined the character of the location. The court held that the dump's "prior operation at that place should be given substantial weight in determining the character of the locality and the reasonableness or unreasonableness of operating it there." City dumps need to be located near cities – the cost of transporting garbage is very high. The long-run stream of costs and benefits made it appropriate for the dump to be located there initially and to maintain operation as the area became more residential. However, if the residents were there first, it would have been inefficient to locate a dump next to them and the courts would have ruled in favor of the plaintiffs. In a nutshell, when the character of the place is determined by the first user, the doctrine of coming to the nuisance and its converse are invoked.

Suppose that developers could collect damages or force dumps to move. Would developers or homeowners be better off in the long run? Surprisingly, the answer is no. Consider the case where homeowners receive $10,000 per house for being next to a preexisting city dump. Then they would be willing to pay $10,000 more for their homes; the same holds for the developer. So, in this situation, a system of compensation does not make homeowners or developers better off. The only person that is affected by the rule is the original owner of the undeveloped property. And if this original owner owned the land on which the dump was built as well, such a transfer would go from the left pocket to the right.

C. CHARACTER OF THE PLACE DETERMINED BY THE SECOND USE

There are many situations where the first party should have been there first; yet, the second party creates the dominating character of the place. Cities often expand into rural areas. Rural areas are appropriate for animal husbandry, but cities and cattle feedlots do not mix very well. Of the three possibilities, cities leapfrog around cattle feedlots, urban housing and businesses border cattle feedlots, and feedlots relocate, the last is clearly the most efficient. And the law unambiguously reflects this economic logic.

In such situations, the law is unlikely to compensate for the costs of relocation, even though the party was there first and should have been there first. There are several reasons for such a policy. First, alternative land uses are likely to be more profitable, so that the feedlot owner would benefit from relocating. Second, over time, the owner of the property could have let the property depreciate rather than undertake repairs and upgrades. Third, a system of compensation would be costly because, in the absence of compensation, the outcome (shutting down the feedlot) is the same, and a court case is rarely needed. And fourth, a system of compensating feedlots for moving would encourage owners to hold onto their businesses to collect damages and more generally to not anticipate the future (the problems that arise in the absence of compensation, too few feedlots in period 1 or too much expansion of the urban area in period 2 are less likely except at the very margin). Often the rationale for compensation is to create the correct incentives for the person who is liable rather than to benefit the person who was harmed. In this case, compensation would, if anything, create the wrong incentives.

The taking away of a property right without compensation might appear to violate some basic notions of the inviolability of property. But this paradox is resolved if we realize that all property rights are contingent in space and time. For example, I have the right to dig holes on my land but not to throw dirt at people passing by. Similarly, people have the right to have cattle feedlots on their property but not if the area is urban. That is, when the city grows around the cattle feedlot and the feedlot is forced to move without compensation, the owner of the feedlot is not losing his property rights because the owner never had the right to have a feedlot within an urban area.[1]

Even though, the cost of relocating feedlots is factored in, it is easy to see that the efficient outcome is for the feedlots to move as the city expands. For other kinds of activity, where there are more substantial moving costs and smaller negative externalities, the stream of benefits may make it economically efficient to give rights to an activity when it should have been first, even if the activity would have been outlawed if it had not been first. Thus, there is "*nonconforming land use*" for those activities that should have been there first and should remain, while initiation of similar activities are prevented because the cost-benefit stream dictates that they should be undertaken elsewhere.

> There is a very marked distinction to be observed in reason and equity between the case of a business long established in a particular locality, which has become a nuisance from the growth of population and the erection of dwellings in proximity to it and that of a new erection or business threatened in such vicinity; and it requires a much clearer case to justify a court of equity in interfering by injunction to compel a person to remove an establishment in which he has invested his capital and been carrying on business for a long period of time than would be required to prevent the establishment of an objectionable business by one who comes into the neighborhood proposing to establish such a business for the first time and is met at the threshold of his enterprise by a remonstrance of the inhabitants. *Barth v. Christian Psychopathic Hospital Association*, 163 N.W. 62 (1917)

Once again, the doctrine of coming to the nuisance and its converse are invoked in a more modified form than used by Blackstone.

The role of sequence in allowing for nonconforming land use is very evident when there is severe damage to the nonconforming structure due to fire, earthquake, and so on. Then the prior use is no longer prior and cannot be reinstated. "With the improvement substantially destroyed, the land on which it is located will presumably have approximately as much value for use in conformity with the ordinance as otherwise and the public interest in conformity with the ordinance will be served if he is not permitted to continue the nonconforming land use" (*O'Mara v. Council of the City of Newark*, 91 CA3d 156 [1965]).

Sometimes the nonconforming land use is allowed a certain amortization period. Consistent with our economic analysis, such a scheme must be reasonable in character

---

[1] We made a similar argument when discussing takings in Chapter 14.

RIGHTS TO SURFACE WATER

The law regarding the use of surface water varies within and across countries. The eastern United States generally follows a system of water rights derived from English common law. Under this system, the entitlement to water is based on ownership of property that is adjacent to the stream. All riparian owners have an equal entitlement to the water. This is a communal rights system. A major problem with the common law riparian system is that it restricts the use of water to riparian owners and requires that water be used only on riparian land. The water may be more useful if it is used elsewhere.

Many western United States (particularly those that have little rainfall) use the prior appropriation system. This system originated because gold miners used large quantities of water for their mining operations. A mining operation would be of little use if the water needed for mining could be expropriated by later users. For both water and gold, the miners used "first in time, first in right." Individuals who first appropriate water by diverting it have superior rights to those who appropriate the water later.* During water shortages, earlier users are entitled to their full allocation, while later users can be cut off completely. This is basically a property rights system, but advantageous property rights are gained by being first. Furthermore, a person will often continue to draw the appropriated amount, even if it is more than necessary, to maintain the entitlement.

Another system for controlling water use is regulation. A government agency grants permits to use water depending on the amount of water available and the need for water by the particular landowner. Under this system, the regulatory agency takes a central role in water allocation and dispute resolution.

*To reduce the acquisition of rights by wasting water, the *beneficial use* doctrine was implemented. Under this doctrine, an individual's water entitlement is limited to the quantity that is actually used for beneficial purposes.

and commensurate with the investment involved. The relevant factors include remaining useful life, the harm to the public if the structure remains standing beyond the prescribed amortization period, and cost of moving. See *United Business Com. v. City of San Diego*, 91 CA3d 156 (1979) and *City of Los Angeles v. Gage*, 127 Cal. App. 2d 442 (1954).

Note that the logic of the argument does not depend on whether it is a government regulation or a private suit in a court of law. The optimal sequence is the optimal sequence whether it is enforced by private suit or government regulation.

D. THE CHARACTER OF THE PLACE IS DETERMINED BY THE SECOND USE, BUT THE SECOND USE SHOULD NOT HAVE BEEN THERE

We now come to the most complicated situation, which is also the most enlightening. It is possible that the second use creates the character of the area; yet, the second use should not have been there in the first place.

In *Spur Industries v. Del E. Webb Development Co.*, 494 P. 2d 700 (1972), Spur Industries had a cattle feedlot in an agricultural area well outside the boundaries of any city. Subsequently, Del Webb, a real estate developer purchased land nearby and began to

WHO SHOULD OWN THE GOLD FROM A 150-YEAR-OLD SHIPWRECK?

The SS *Central America* sank on September 12, 1857. The precise whereabouts of the wreck remained unknown until 1988, when the Columbus-America Discovery Group located it 8,000 feet below sea level. The company then salvaged gold from the shipwreck. Insurers who had originally underwritten the gold for its ocean voyage argued that they owned the gold. Other claimants included inventors of a computer-ized "treasure map" to locate the gold. The trial court found for Columbus-America on all issues. The underwriters appealed. In *Columbus-America v. Atlantic Mutual Insurance Co.*, 974 F.2d 450 (1992), the appellate court sent the case back to the district court for further action. In 1998, the federal district court divided the treasure in the following way: 92% to the Columbus-America Discovery Group and 8% to the insurers.

If the wreck had occurred in 1978, who should own the gold? Insight is gained by first realizing that the choice is between the insurance company having a property right and the discovery groups having a communal right – in the latter situation, whichever discovery group finds the gold first, gains the right. A communal right will result in too much investment in being first, as this is the only way to gain the entitlement. And just as there is overfishing for fish when there are communal rights, there will be overfishing for the ship. This means that too many people will engage in the search, resulting in a higher than necessary total cost of search and a lower probability of being the first to discover the wreck. In contrast, if the insurance company owns the right, then the insurance company can have the discovery groups bid for the right to search. Presumably, the discovery group that allows the highest percentage to the insurance company will get the contract. Note that such bidding is relatively costless and that the total investment is smaller than if the insurance company gave the right to the group that found the wreck first. Under a property rights system, the insurance company will end up with a larger share. Of course, this is not the only possible contract that the insurance company might devise. I switched the date because I did not want to deal with issues arising from the great length of time between the wreck and its discovery.

build a large retirement community. The court held that the developer was entitled to enjoin the cattle-feeding operation as a nuisance but was required to *indemnify* the cattle feedlot owner for the reasonable cost of moving or shutting down. The novel solution in this case reflects the fact that the cattle feedlot owner could not have reasonably foreseen the development of a retirement community nearby and therefore should be compensated for all costs associated with moving his business.

If the court had not questioned whether the developer should have been there in the first place, the court would have ruled for the feedlot to move without compensation, as it was cheaper to move the feedlot than to move the residents. But without compensation an inefficient precedent would have been established. Developers would choose areas inappropriate from a social cost-benefit analysis because the developers would not incur the costs to the adjacent nuisance of moving away. In future situations, even if it were cheaper for the builder to develop elsewhere than to make the feedlot move, the developer might move near the feedlot (if the developer did not have to compensate the feedlot owner). Thus courts are encouraging individuals to make efficient decisions by anticipating the future and considering the *whole* stream of costs and benefits and not just those costs and benefits that arise after both parties are located in the area.

E. CONCLUDING REMARKS

The law has developed an intricate, but economically sensible, set of rules to encourage the optimal sequence of investments by conflicting land uses. By granting the entitlement to the party who *should have been* first, rather than merely to the party who was first, the law avoids encouraging premature and costly investment to be first. Furthermore, given that the law is in place, it will generally be the case that the party who is first should have been first, as well.

Giving entitlement to the person who was merely first results in overinvestment in being first. This problem arises in other areas besides land use and waiting in line for "free" tickets. Patents are given to the party who first came up with the invention (United States) or to the party who first applied for the patent (Europe). Either way creates patent races. The hunt for shipwrecks and lost treasure may also involve a race to be first. In our boxed example, we show how rights can be allocated so that this problem is avoided.

SUGGESTIONS FOR FURTHER READING

As noted at both the beginning of this chapter and its conclusion, when rights are granted to the first person, people will undertake costly action to be first. This problem arises in all kinds of contexts, and a number of solutions have been provided. See Scotchmer (2004) for an analysis of patent races and Barzel (1997) for a discussion of allocating water rights. Lueck (1995) covers the law of first possession regarding the ownership of wild game. Ellickson (1989) looks at whaling rules – depending on the species of whale and the dangers involved, the rights of first possession differ.

REVIEW QUESTIONS

1. What problems arise if rights are given to the first person or entity? (4) What problems arise if we ignore who was first? (2) How do we avoid strategic behavior by the participants? (2)
2. When should being first be considered? (2) When should moving costs be weighed in the cost-benefit calculations? (2) If separately owned inputs into the production of damage take place sequentially over time, what is the correct economic methodology for determining the allocation of rights? (4)
3. Why is the following argument unacceptable on economic grounds? Since the nuisance was there first, the victims willingly consented to it by establishing residences nearby. (3)
4. In *Bove v. Donna Hanna*, Bove was there first, but the courts did not grant the rights to Bove. But in *Mahlsted v. Indianola*, the courts did grant rights to the party that was first. Why did the courts act differently in these two cases? (4)

5. When is it appropriate to have a nonconforming land use? (4)
6. Explain why the court made Del Webb pay for moving of the smelly feedlot even though when cities expand, cattle feedlots are not compensated for moving costs. (6)
7. What are the advantages and disadvantages of riparian rights versus a system of prior appropriation? (6)
8. What problems arise when the right to a shipwreck goes to the discoverer rather than to the ship owner or the insurance company that insured the wreck? (4)

REFERENCES

Barzel, Yoram. (1997). *Economic Analysis of Property Rights*, 2nd ed. Cambridge: Cambridge University Press.

Blackstone, William. (1776, 1830). 2 *Commentaries on the Laws of England* 402.

Elickson, Robert C. (1989). A Hypothesis of Wealth Maximizing Norms: Evidence from the Whaling Industry. 5 *Journal of Law, Economics, and Organization* 681.

Lueck, Dean. (1995). The Rule of First Possession and the Design of the Law. 38 *Journal of Law and Economics* 393.

Scotchmer, Suzanne. (2004). *Innovation and Incentives*. Cambridge, MA: MIT Press.

VII CONTRACTS AND BREACH OF CONTRACT

If the parties to the contract are rational, which we have assumed all along, then they will tend to write efficient contracts. As a result, economists are loath to argue that a contract should be invalidated. While the legal system is somewhat more skeptical about the ability of the parties to write optimal contracts, the legal system generally assumes that the parties know what is best and that courts should not substitute their wisdom for the contractual specifications.

However, even with the best of intentions, contracts sometimes are breached or are alleged to have been breached. Houses are not built to specifications, items are delivered late or not at all, and marriages end before, not until, death do us part. Part VII provides the economic foundations for determining (a) whether a contract has been made, (b) if the contract has been breached, and (c) what the appropriate legal remedy should be when there is a breach.

Chapter 21 considers the role of courts in filling contracts gaps. After an extensive discussion on how courts determine whether a contract has been breached, the chapter looks at various remedies for breach and explains when one method is chosen over another.

When is an agreement enforceable and when is it not? Chapter 22 first considers the case of *Pennzoil v. Texaco*, where Getty Oil was alleged to have breached its contract to sell its shares to Pennzoil because of tortious interference by Texaco. But was there a contract in the first place? There had been a handshake between the owners of Pennzoil and Getty. Does a handshake mean that there was an enforceable contract? The chapter then takes the opposite perspective and asks when a written contract should not be enforced. Courts will not enforce contracts that promote illegal activity. Also, under very special circumstances, courts will not enforce poorly written and misleading contracts. The chapter provides an economic rationale.

In Chapter 23, we consider contracts and breach of contract within the context of the family. We consider prenuptial contracts and marriage "contracts" more generally, as well as surrogate motherhood contracts and polygamy. Divorce can be seen as a breach of contract, and therefore, we discuss reasons for and determinants of spousal support and property division, including such seemingly arcane subjects as who owns the fertilized embryos after the couple is divorced.

21 Default Rules and Breach of Contract

A. The Role of Contract Law 194

B. Determining Whether a Breach of Contract Has Taken Place 195

C. Remedies for Breach 196

D. Relational Contracts 200

E. Concluding Remarks 202

SUGGESTIONS FOR FURTHER READING 204

REVIEW QUESTIONS 204

REFERENCES 206

As in other areas of law, the objective of contract law is to promote economic efficiency. Because the court generally provides *default rules* that can be overridden by the parties to the contract, the role of contract law is more circumscribed than in other areas such as accident law. If a court rules that drunk drivers are not liable for accidents, then there will be more drunk driving. But in contract law, if a court rules that drunk workers cannot lose their jobs unless the contract allows for this to be the case, then firms will write into their employment contracts that workers can lose their jobs if they show up drunk for work. So the major effect of a court decision is not on how workers perform, but on how contracts are written. The role of the court is circumscribed in a second way, as well. The parties often have a written contract. Because written contracts can have gaps and some element of ambiguity, the parties may disagree about the interpretation of the contract. The court may resolve this ambiguity by defining certain terms in a contract so that the meaning is clear to the parties in this and future contracts. For example, the owner of the World Trade Center was insured against terrorist attacks for up to $3.5 billion "per occurrence." The owner claimed that the attacks on 9/11 were two occurrences, while the insurance companies claimed that this was one occurrence. Ultimately, the courts had to decide the meaning of occurrence (see box page 201). But, in this example as well as in others, the court must use the contract or industry standards as a basis for its judgment; the court cannot create a decision out of whole cloth.

A. THE ROLE OF CONTRACT LAW

In a nutshell, the role of contract law is to minimize the cost of the parties writing contracts + the cost of the courts writing contracts + the cost of inefficient behavior arising from poorly written or incomplete contracts. In this chapter, we will focus on gap filling by the courts. The courts choose those rulings that induce the fewest exculpatory clauses, thereby making contracts as short as possible. A good analogy is to think of a note with an RSVP. If the person giving a party expects most people to come, the note will say reply only if you are not coming; if the person expects most people to refuse, the note will say reply if you are coming. In this way, the cost of replying is minimized.

The law of contracts is essentially the implied long-form contract of any short-form contract actually made by the parties to the agreement. No actual contract can or should cover all contingencies. The transaction costs of doing so would be enormous. For example, suppose that I sign a contract for a person to spray paint my house by a certain date for X dollars. What happens if the painter's wife dies, my house burns down, a hoard of locusts descends on my house, or the city outlaws spray painting? It is unlikely that our contract has been drawn up in such a way as to account for all these contingencies. Indeed if the agreement was verbal, nothing but the price and an agreement to paint the house may be explicit.

Why not a simple statement that the parties should act efficiently? The whole point of the contract and contract law is to guide the parties to act optimally by suggesting efficient behavior under the circumstances – a bright-line rule. So a statement that the parties should act efficiently would be of little help.

B. DETERMINING WHETHER A BREACH OF CONTRACT HAS TAKEN PLACE

Contracts may be breached in many ways. FedEx may have promised to deliver your package overnight, but the plane carrying your package may have crashed. Your contractor may have promised to use galvanized pipe made by one steel firm, but the foreman may have purchased pipe made by a different firm. You thought you were buying a Rolex watch, but you got a Roelicks (a lollipop made out of fish eggs) instead. If you read the fine print, some of these contingencies might have been accounted for. But what happens if the contract did not specify what should be done under the circumstances?

The court first has to decide whether a breach has actually taken place. This is done by careful reading of the contract and then by filling in the contract when the contract does not provide guidance. The court tries to determine what the contract would have looked like if the parties had considered it beforehand. The underlying cost-benefit analysis is the same as employed in other areas of the law, but the issues and legal terminology differ.

To illustrate, let us consider *Tsakiroglou v Noblee Thorl*, A.C. 93 (1962). Tsakiroglou agreed to sell Sudanese peanuts to a German firm. The Suez war erupted, and the canal was blocked. An alternative was to ship the peanuts around the Cape of Good Hope, which was both very expensive and very slow[1] Tsakiroglou refused to ship the peanuts for the agreed upon price. Did Tsakiroglou breach the contract?

The court (House of Lords) undertook a *close* reading of the contract and determined that the contract did not specify the shipping route but did specify that Tsakiroglou would be responsible for paying any charges for insuring the shipment of peanuts. The court extrapolated from what was said and what was not said in the contract – because Tsakiroglou was insuring the shipment, this suggested that Tsakiroglou would insure against other risks, such as the closing of the Suez Canal. Thus the court ruled that Tsakiroglou had breached the contract and should be responsible for shipping the peanuts around the Cape of Good Hope. Of course, if there were cheaper alternatives, such as shipping peanuts from the United States, Tsakiroglou would have done that instead, if Tsakiroglou knew from the get-go how the court would rule.

The court tried to determine from a close reading of the contract what the contract had to say about Tsakiroglou's responsibility if the Suez Canal were to close. The court provided a plausible interpretation, but it is by no means an obvious interpretation (an obvious interpretation of breach would be Tsakiroglou's failure to ship the peanuts if the Suez Canal had remained open, but the price of peanuts had gone up and Tsakiroglou had sold the peanuts to a third party). When the interpretation rests on such a slim reed, an alternative approach is to ignore the contract altogether and ask whether Noblee Thorl would have agreed ahead of time to pay the additional cost of shipping the peanuts around the Cape of Good Hope if the Suez Canal were blocked. I think that the answer is likely to be no. The cost of a trip all around Africa from Sudan to the Mediterranean is likely to outweigh any cost advantage of Sudanese peanuts (which in all likelihood was the low cost of shipping from Sudan through the Suez Canal). Shipping peanuts grown in the United States or West Africa would probably make much more economic sense. It would be easier for Noblee Thorl than Tsakiroglou to find an alternative supplier

---

[1] The actual case was not concerned with the issue of the peanuts being delivered late.

of peanuts because Noblee Thorl, being a purchaser, was likely to be in contact with a number of suppliers before the Suez Canal was closed. Given this analysis, it appears that Nobli Thori would have agreed to buy the peanuts elsewhere if the Suez Canal was blocked. So Tsakiroglou did not breach the contract.

Thus we have two contrary views. One way to determine whether the court was right is to look at contracts made after the court decision and see whether these contracts have clauses requiring (or excusing) performance if the Suez Canal is again disrupted for shipping. If performance is required (excused) in case of a closure, then the court was right (wrong) in its analysis. Unfortunately, I do not have access to such contracts.

C. REMEDIES FOR BREACH

If the court decides that there has been a breach, it has several remedies at its disposal.

An important solution to breach of contract is to require *specific performance.* The breaching party is required to fulfill the contract as stated. For example, if person A has a written contract to sell his house to person B and then A turns around and sells the house to person C, the law requires that the house goes to B. A major reason for specific performance is that courts do not have to waste time estimating damages to B (which would be the case if C were allowed to keep the house). Determining damages would be very difficult in such cases. Suppose that the house sold for $1 million. The court would have to determine how much B valued the house and then subtract the price of the house to calculate B's loss in consumer surplus. It is not easy to determine subjective value; B has reason to exaggerate and there may be little objective evidence to either refute or support such claims. Specific performance saves on the court transaction costs that would be entailed in trying to obtain such information. Specific performance generally works well for things that exist and only a transfer is involved. In the United States, specific performance is confined mainly to exchange of real property, unique items like paintings and patent rights and contracts for the sale of a majority of shares of a corporation; in France, specific performance holds for all transfers.

Sometimes specific performance is not so easy or it cannot be done. This creates great bargaining power for the one party. In such cases, specific performance is not invoked; instead there is some kind of damage remedy (including the possibility of zero damages). The following examples will illustrate.

If FedEx fails to deliver an item (say, because the airplane crashed in the ocean as in the Tom Hanks film), FedEx is not required to satisfy specific performance (in fact, it generally is dismissed from all liability under the doctrine of impossibility). Clearly, in almost all cases, the cost of retrieving the item from the bottom of the ocean would be far beyond the value of the item, itself. FedEx would be at an unreasonably weak bargaining position if it were subject to specific performance. The cost of retrieving a letter from the bottom of the ocean might be $1 million. If the letter writer could demand specific performance, FedEx could be forced to shell out nearly $1 million to avoid such a worthless project. No shipper would want to be put into such a position and no sender of a letter would want to spend the extra amount of money to cover for such a contingency.

Also if Fed ex were required to undertake specific performance, it might undertake excessive precaution from a social cost-benefit point of view. If FedEx were liable of $1 million if the package were lost, it might spend $10,000 on precaution (for example, putting packages in floating containers) to avoid paying that $1 million to the senders of the lost package, even though it might be worth only $100 to the senders. In the end, those who sent packages would pay for this excess precaution, which would not be worth the price paid. The efficient solution is for FedEx to undertake the optimal precaution, which occurs when FedEx is liable for the *true cost* to the party losing the package.

As another illustration, suppose that a contract has specified that a house be built with copper plumbing and the contractor has used galvanized pipes instead. Clearly, it would not be cost-effective to tear down the walls and install copper pipes. So once again, specific performance makes no sense (and therefore it is not even an issue). Even in less dramatic cases, the cost of specific performance may be significantly less than the benefit to the homeowner.

Another reason for not enforcing specific performance is for the court to avoid the cost of supervision. Suppose that you have paid me to paint your portrait. The courts would make me return the money and possibly make me reimburse you for any costs that you undertook in anticipation of my painting your portrait. The court would not force me to paint your picture. The fear is that I might make an unflattering portrait and then we would be back in court. That is why specific performance holds for transfers, but not for services.[2]

As an alternative to specific performance, the court can award money to the victim (plaintiff) for breach to induce optimal behavior by the breaching party (defendant). But how is the award determined? There are various solutions depending on the circumstances. As always, incentives must be taken into consideration.

Sometimes the contract specifies the amount of money to be paid by the breaching party. These are known as *liquidated damages*. In such situations, the court should enforce the contractual agreement because presumably the parties to the agreement knew what they were doing when they wrote the contract.[3] That is, liquidated clauses are likely to be Pareto optimal. Liquidated damages encourage "efficient breach." For example, suppose that the cost to a buyer from late delivery is $25 and that this is the agreed upon amount of liquidated damages. If the benefit to the seller for *not* delivering on time is greater than $25, it makes sense for the seller to breach because the cost of breach ($25 in liquidated damages) is less than the cost of delivering on time. So, liquidated damages encourage on-time delivery if and only if it is efficient to do so.

Note that the buyer would not want to have liquidated damages greater than $25 because the price charged by the seller must cover the cost of delivery and nondelivery. The buyer would not want to encourage the seller to spend $26 to deliver on time since the buyer implicitly pays for this when the buyer makes the purchase in the first place.

Not all contracts have liquidated damages clauses. Therefore, it is up to the courts to determine what the damage remedies are. We will now consider some of the guiding principles.

As was shown in an earlier chapter, the victim is expected to *mitigate damages* when it is cost effective to do so. If a homeowner discovers that the newly installed shower leaks into the rooms below, the contractor is not liable for the damage that occurs from showers taken *after* the discovery (although the contractor is liable for damage that occurred before the discovery of the leak). So the breaching party is never liable for the

---

[2] One exception is that a performer is not allowed to switch the performance venue. Specific performance at the original venue rather than paying damages is the rule.

[3] The courts typically accept the contractual terms; however, there are exceptions, especially when the damages are punitive (beyond the loss to the plaintiff).

damage that could have been mitigated under the doctrine of *avoidable consequences*. This rule is most important for its effect on the breaching party! It is true that we want the victim to mitigate damages optimally, but the victim would also mitigate damages if the victim received zero compensation or any other fixed amount independent of the victim's behavior. What this rule does is create the optimal incentive for the breaching party. If the breaching party were not liable for damages, the breaching party would breach whenever the cost of preventing breach was greater than zero;[4] if the breaching party were liable for all damages, even if not mitigated, the breaching party would not breach, even if the cost of preventing the breach were greater than the cost imposed on the breached party. The only rule that creates the right incentives for both parties is the doctrine of avoidable consequences (or what we called *marginal cost liability*).

Mitigation of damages is concerned with post-breach behavior by the victim. We will now consider *pre-breach* behavior by each of the parties. It is useful to consider the general problem within the context of a particular example. Suppose that a retailer (Y) has hired a software firm (X) to install an accounting program by a certain date. The retailer could *rely* on the software being provided on time and give notice to those workers whose services were no longer needed and hire those whose services would be. If the software was not available on time, the retailer could be in a very serious bind. To forestall such a problem, Y might undertake precaution *y*, such as keeping the unneeded workers and not hiring the new workers until the software was installed, which would mean additional delay as it takes time to hire them. Of course, the extent of precaution by Y depends on the likelihood and degree of X being late (the probability and extent of breach), which in turn depends on the amount of precaution *x* that X undertakes, such as employing extra programmers for the job. As always, the optimal amount of precaution by each party is where the last dollar spent on damage reduction reduces expected damage by $1. All of this can be put in more formal notation.

Let $P(x)$ be the probability of X not delivering the software on time. The larger x, the less likely that this will be the case (that is, the derivative of P with respect to $x = P' < 0$). Let $D(y)$ be the amount of damage given a breach. Greater precaution by Y results in less damage given a breach by X (that is, $D' < 0$). The expected damage is $P(x)D(y)$ – the probability of a breach times the amount of damage given that there is a breach. The parties to the contract want to choose an optimal contract that minimizes total costs – expected damage to Y and the cost of damage prevention by X and Y:

$$C = P(x)D(y) + x + y \tag{21.1}$$

The first-order conditions are

$$P'(x)D(y) + 1 = 0; \text{ equivalently, } P'(x)D(y) = -1 \tag{21.2}$$

$$D'(y)P(x) + 1 = 0; \text{ equivalently, } D'(y)P(x) = -1 \tag{21.3}$$

That is, X should increase his expenditures on precaution (preventing a breach) until the last dollar spent on precaution by X reduces expected damage by $1. And Y should increase her expenditure on reducing possible damage in case there is a breach until the last dollar spent on precaution by Y reduces expected damages by $1. Clearly, the greater the likelihood of breach by X (that is, the larger $P(x)$ is), the greater the

---

[4] Because providers have reputations, they would not be so cavalier in their behavior. See Chapter 24.

precaution that should be undertaken by Y.[5] The optimal amount of precaution is the solution to Equations (21:2) and (21:3) and is denoted by x^{Ω}, y^{Ω}. Contracts are designed to encourage the optimal outcome.

All of this looks very similar to our analysis of accidents and accident law, but the words and emphasis differ. When discussing accidents, D stood for expected damage. Here D stands for damage given a breach so that $D = PD$ (note that the italics distinguish damage from expected damage). Here, the parties have two different roles: X reduces the probability of breach, P(x), and Y reduces the damage, D(y), in case there is a breach.[6] When we discussed accident law, the relationship, D(x,y), was more general because both X and Y could reduce the probability of an accident (the owner of the truck can replace worn tires, the driver of the car can drive with more care) and the extent of damage when there is an accident (the truck owner can install a lower bumper, the driver can fasten the seatbelt). In accident law, a negligence rule was required to insure that both parties behave optimally, but in the breach of contract cases that we consider here, we do not have to worry about contributory negligence of the victim because the victim's precaution does not affect the probability of a breach.[7] Hence, contributory negligence or relative negligence is not a standard concept in contract law. However, as equations (21:1) and (21:3) suggest, the level of damages depends on the pre-breach behavior of the victim. And, as noted in earlier contexts, when the injurer (in this case the party who breaches) is strict liable for all damage, then the victim will not have any incentive to take precautionary care. Contract law resolves this problem by limiting the scope of damage compensation when the amount of the victim's precaution greatly affects the degree of damages. By limiting the scope of damage compensation in such circumstances, the victim's failure to take optimal precaution falls mainly on the victim. Y has the appropriate incentive to take care because Y is responsible for any damage that goes beyond the measure of damages compensated by X. We will now illustrate this abstract argument in terms of more concrete legal cases.

Sometimes, the breaching party is not liable for any consequential damages. If Kodak loses a roll of exposed film, Kodak is only liable for replacing the film, not for the cost of redoing the wedding so that replacement photographs can be made.[8] Such a rule means that the victim will be liable for consequential damages and therefore the victim has the appropriate incentives to reduce them. The victim can reduce the extent of damage from lost film by taking several rolls of film, processing them at different times, etc. This is the y term in our formal presentation. Of course, Kodak has the appropriate incentives to not lose the film in the first place because it has to pay for the replacement and it has a reputation to protect. Now Kodak could offer to insure for consequential damages, but that would raise the price of the film to cover for such eventualities. The fact that Kodak, Fuji, or any film processor does not offer to be liable for consequential damages is strong evidence that consumers are not willing to pay for the extra price that such liability would entail.[9]

---

[5] Note that for Eq. (21.3) to continue to hold as P(x) increases, $D'(y)$ must decrease. $D'(y)$ decreases when y increases because marginal productivity of y is decreasing (that is $D''(y) > 0$).

[6] There are some instances where X could reduce the damages given a breach, but we will ignore them here.

[7] There can be cases of breach of warranty where both sides are inputs, but such cases are more fruitfully explored in the chapter on lawnmowers.

[8] If a specialized part is not supplied on time, the supplier is not liable for lost profits because the part was not available. The general rule is ensconced in *Hadley v. Baxendale*, 156 Eng. Rep. 145 (1854).

[9] Industry custom is a good indicator of efficient allocation of liability in contracts, but not for noncontractual cases such as pollution where bargaining is unlikely and costs can inefficiently be shifted onto third-parties.

Why does the lost-film case only require replacement of the missing film, while the leaking-shower case makes the breaching party liable for consequential damages? There are several reasons. There is little that the victim of the leaking shower should do before the leak is discovered; that is, y^{Ω} is close to 0 so that even if contractor X is liable for consequential (but mitigated) damages, that will not greatly distort Y's precaution from the optimal. Furthermore, the film case is more likely to involve minor harms where self-insurance by the victim makes the most sense. Finally, if Kodak were liable for consequential damages, it would not know the extent of consequential damages Kodak was agreeing to when it agreed to process film. Of course, the potential victim could inform Kodak that this was an especially important roll of film and Kodak might be willing to insure for consequential damages in return for a higher price for processing. But having gone through this negotiation and a determination of the damages that it would be liable for in the case of breach, it would make sense to have liquidated damages rather than merely an agreement to be liable for the consequential damages. In contrast, the contractor can see what he is getting into when he undertakes a project and can adjust the price of the contract accordingly. Indeed, the contractor is likely to be a better estimator (and reducer) of consequential damages than the person purchasing his services. All three of these reasons together make a sufficient argument against consequential damages for film but in favor of consequential damages for poor plumbing.

The example of going to Kodak and negotiating a higher price for added protection may seem unrealistic, but many firms do provide the option for more coverage. You can reduce the probability of regular mail being lost by paying the extra cost to have it registered. As another example, you can insure your FedEx package for several hundred dollars if you pay FedEx the requisite amount. Note that the dollar amount is clearly specified in such cases; FedEx does not state that it will be liable for consequential damages. So this is an example of liquidated damages.

D. RELATIONAL CONTRACTS

Particularly when the relationship between the contracting parties is long term and complex, the legal system is likely to be a poor venue for specifying the substantive terms of the contract. The courts might not be able to observe the relevant information or the issues might be too subtle and nuanced for the courts to handle. Think how hard it would be for the courts to determine whether a faculty member deserves to be rehired. There are no contractual terms specifying the hurdles for teaching and research (and for good reason – it is too hard to specify all the contingencies in making the optimal decision). Instead, many of the contract terms are relational (which side makes the decision) rather than substantive (what the decision should be) – hence, the term relational contract. Under such circumstances, the court no longer fills in substantive gaps; rather, the contractual terms are about process and the court's role is to ensure that the process is upheld and when necessary to fill in gaps regarding the relationship. For example, the university can terminate non-tenure-track faculty (typically lecturers) at will (without an explanation).[10] This greatly reduces the cost of terminating someone in comparison to a situation where the university must demonstrate "just cause." In the latter case, the courts might be asked to determine whether the university had

---

[10] The common law acceptance of at will contracts has been circumscribed by concerns regarding discrimination.

9/11 AND THE ATTACK ON THE WORLD TRADE CENTER

"A word is not a crystal, transparent and unchanged, it is the skin of a living thought and may vary greatly in color and content according to the circumstances and the time in which it is used." Justice Oliver Wendell Holmes in *Towne v. Eisner*, 245 U.S. 418 (1918).

In 2001, Silverstein Properties, Inc. (and related entities), signed a 99-year lease on the World Trade Center. In July 2001, Silverstein obtained insurance from several carriers providing coverage of $3.5 billion "per occurrence." Was the attack on the World Trade Center, one occurrence or two? In December of 2004, a New York jury ruled that for insurance purposes the attack was two occurrences. In May of 2004, involving a different set of insurance companies, a different jury decided that the attack was one occurrence, but in that case, the insurance companies made use of a temporary form that defined a series of closely related events as one occurrence.

CIVIL LIABILITY FOR VIOLATING STATE REGULATIONS

A California jury held that Wal-Mart had violated state law by depriving employees of legally mandated lunch breaks. One hundred sixteen thousand present and former employees were awarded $56 million in compensatory damages and $115 million in punitive damages. This outcome may be altered on appeal. Wal-Mart now has cash registers that stop working when the person is due for a lunch break. See the *San Francisco Chronicle*, December 22, 2005.

"good reasons" for not rehiring. Courts are incompetent to make such judgments, and they are also expensive. So the contract gives the university the property right to make this decision. The situation for tenure is somewhat more complicated. The university has to follow its rules and procedures (for example, a recommendation must be made by a faculty committee after getting outside letters attesting to the person's research potential). Again the courts do not "second guess" the university's decision; rather, the court's role is to make sure that the appropriate procedure was undertaken. As a final university example, course assignments and teaching times are usually left to department chairs, while the number of homework assignments and grading of papers is under the control of the professor. Sometime these contract terms are implicit in that they are not written in a manual but are customary. If a flood closes the university for four weeks, there may be a dispute between the administration and a faculty member about whether a final exam should be given. If the case goes to court, the court would not determine whether an exam should be given under the circumstances, but who should have the right to decide.

Articles of incorporation are, to a large extent, relational contracts. In a dispute between the stockholders and the board of directors concerning whether Coca-Cola should expand into the selling of soy milk, the courts do not decide whether soy milk is a profitable area for Coca-Cola. Rather the courts determine which side has the right to make the decision. In general, the allocation of this decision right is made explicit in the articles, and presumably the right goes to where it is of most value. Only when there is some ambiguity will the court fill in the relational gaps in the contract.

BUILDING WITH PANORAMIC VIEW FOR SALE: $250.000

According to the October 11, 2003, *San Francisco Chronicle*, there is only one draw-back – it is a mausoleum with seven dead people and not any windows. The seller, John Schiffeler, is the last in the line. Schiffeler claims that his ancestors cannot make use of the view. He also says that money is for the living to use, not for the dead to take with them. Should he be allowed to move the bodies elsewhere and sell the mausoleum to someone else? What if the contract his ancestors signed states otherwise?

CAN YOU SUE FOR A BAD PERFORMANCE?

A class action suit against the band Creed charged that the lead singer Scott Strapp "was so intoxicated and/or medicated that he was unable to sing the lyrics of a single Creed song." The plaintiffs wanted refunds for their tickets and reimbursements for parking fees. Defense attorneys for the band Creed argued: "You can't bring a lawsuit against a band for sucking." In agreeing with the defense attorneys, judge Peter Flynn said the precedent was an unsuccessful suit against the Chicago Cubs baseball team. As long as the team or band takes the field, ticket buyers can't get a refund for a poor performance. What do you think would be the result if you could? Or, as some who don't like this kind of music might say, how would you know if the band played poorly.

What if the issue isn't quality, but quantity? Michael J. Young filed a proposed class action breach-of-contract suit in Cook County, Illinois, Superior Court on October 8, 2003. Concertgoers had bought $75 tickets to what was advertised as three full sets by the groups Limp Bizkit, Linkin Park, and Metallica. Young claims that Limp Bizkit left the stage after only seventeen minutes. See *National Law Journal*, October 20, 2003.

E. CONCLUDING REMARKS

When it comes to contracts, courts should write default rules because the contracting parties have a comparative advantage over courts in writing optimal contracts. And for the most part courts do act in this way (the major exceptions involve personal injury cases and enforcement of legislative rulings). But the same does not hold for legislatures. Legislatures impose all kinds of regulations that interfere with the writing of contracts, even though legislatures are at a comparative disadvantage in writing them.[11] Consequently, one should be skeptical when legislatures specify contractual relations, even when the legislation seems reasonable.

Consider for example, the California regulation that workers should have a half-hour lunch break – California Labor Code §800 (2004). I like to take 1 1/2 hour lunch breaks, and perhaps most people would like one hour for lunch. But why should the length of a lunch break be a regulation? It is possible that some people would prefer shorter breaks. It is also possible that a number of businesses would be willing to pay their employees more if they were willing to take shorter lunches and that their employees would be

---

[11] Of course, it makes more sense for legislatures and courts to regulate when there are high transaction costs (which is generally the case for automobile accidents and pollution).

WHO GETS TO DECIDE?

In February 1990, Terri Schiavo entered into a "permanent vegetative state" when oxygen flow to her brain was interrupted for about 5 minutes. In 1998, her husband petitioned the court to have his wife's feeding tube removed. He argued that she had previously indicated that she would not want to be kept alive in this way. Her parents disagreed. In 2000, a circuit court judge ruled in favor of her husband. Her parents appealed. But in 2003, the circuit judges' ruling was upheld and the feeding tube was removed. In response, the Florida legislature passed Terri's Law allowing the governor to override the judge's order. Two hours later, Governor Jeb Bush directed that the feeding tube be reinserted. In January 2005, the U.S. Supreme Court rejected Governor Bush's appeal of the Florida court decision. On March 16, 2005, a Florida appeals court allowed for a March 18 removal of the feeding tube. On March 18, 2005, a House of Representatives panel issued subpoenas for Terri Schiavo and her husband to appear at a hearing, but the trial judge blocked the move, and her feeding tube was removed. The House of Representatives then asked the U.S. Supreme Court to intervene, but the court declined to do so. On March 21, President Bush signed a bill passed by the House and Senate that transferred jurisdiction of the case to a U.S. district court. The district judge denied the parents' request to have the feeding tube reinserted. Her parents then appealed to the circuit court, which found in favor of the husband. Governor Bush tried to take custody of Schiavo and the parents appealed to the Supreme Court, which again refused to hear the case.

In the absence of an advance health care directive signed by the person, what should the default rule be: (1) life prolonged as much as possible; (2) life not prolonged if the person will not regain consciousness; and/or (3) spouse makes the decision; (4) parents make the decision; (5) courts make the decision; (6) person who is willing to pay for maintaining the person in a vegetative state makes the decision; or (7) President Bush makes the decision.

If you want to reduce transaction costs and save surviving relatives from wasting their money on attorney's fees, you can download an Advance Health Care Directive from: http://ag.ca.gov/consumers/general/adv_hc_dir.htm.

willing to accept that trade-off. Employees are not stupid. If an extra 10 minutes for lunch each day is worth $10 a week (but not more) to the employee, then the employee would be willing to give up 10 minutes for lunch each day in exchange for an $11-a-week increase in salary. Businessmen are not stupid either. If a business is not able to get enough employees with the appropriate qualifications when it pays $320 a week and provides 20-minute lunch breaks, then the business will pay its employees $331 a week and provide 20-minute lunch breaks if profits are higher this way (due to less down time) than if it pays its employees $320 and provides 30-minute lunch breaks.

In this chapter, we have discussed breach of contract. It may seem immoral, but economists believe in efficient breach. That is, economists do not want a person to uphold a contract when the cost of doing so is greater than the benefit to the other party. For example, the U.S. mailman is supposed to deliver through rain, sleet, and snow, but perhaps not when there is a hurricane blowing. Because contracts are incomplete and have gaps, a simple reading of a contract that refers only to rain, sleet, and snow may make failure to deliver during a hurricane appear to be a breach. But when the

LIFEBOAT CONTRACTS

Recall the case of the four men in the lifeboat. All four might have agreed to draw lots to sacrifice one of the living because ex ante their life expectancy might be improved from zero to three-fourths. But consider other possible contracts. Suppose that they wanted to sacrifice the weakest because the weakest might die even if he ate one of his fellow passengers. The only way to draw up this contract so that it would be acceptable to all parties would be to sign it before the trip. Once a person knows that he is the weakest, he may argue that the contract conditions for his sacrifice have not been met. So the conditions for sacrifice have to be clearly spelled out ahead of time. The optimal trade-off requires that the sacrifice of one person increases the expected survival rate overall (more precisely, no one should be sacrificed until the marginal reduction in life expectancy of the sacrificed person is less than or equal to the sum of the marginal increases in life expectancy of the others). But how is that point determined and what kind of contract could be written so that ex post the stronger do not interpret the contract in their favor? Remember that the weakest will no longer be around to argue that he was sacrificed prematurely. This issue points out a problem faced in more prosaic documents – the terms and execution of the contract must be capable of being verified by third parties (the courts).

court determines what the contract would have looked like if the parties had ex ante considered this contingency, they may determine that the people receiving mail would not want to pay for the extra cost of mail service during a hurricane. That is, in the completely contingent contract, failure to deliver the mail during a hurricane would no longer be a breach because both parties would agree beforehand that this was the correct decision. In a nutshell, promises are contingent and not all contingencies can be spelled out ahead of time in a contract.

SUGGESTIONS FOR FURTHER READING

Ayres and Gertner (1989) discuss gap-filling. Goldberg (1998) considers other aspects of relational contracts. Posner (2003) provides a critique of the economic approach; see also the responses in the same issue by Ayres and Craswell. Craswell and Schwartz (1994) have assembled a number of interesting articles on contract. Shavell (2004) covers contract in considerable detail.

REVIEW QUESTIONS

1. What is the role of contract law? (2)
2. What is a complete contingent contract? (2) Why don't we see any? (2)
3. Define default rule. (2)
4. In the United States, the default rule is that organs cannot be harvested from a dead body; in many states, the default rule can be overridden when you apply for a driver's license by signing a declaration that you will allow your organs to be donated in case of death.

In Austria, the default rule is the opposite – unless you have signed a document stating the contrary, you are assumed to have consented to having your organs harvested. How do you think that these rules influence the number of organs harvested? (6)

5. What is meant by specific performance? (2) When is it used and why? (3) When is it not used and why? (5)

6. In California, surrogate mother contracts are upheld. If the surrogate mother refuses to give up the baby, the law requires specific performance rather than having the surrogate mother pay damages to the people who contracted with her. Why? (3)

7. What are consequential damages? (2) When is the breaching party responsible for and not responsible for consequential damages and why? (6)

8. In 1999 France passed legislation (since rescinded) requiring employers to reduce the workweek for their full-time employees by four hours – from 39 hours to 35 hours – but to keep the total weekly pay per worker unchanged. The reasoning behind the legislation was that this would reduce unemployment. What do think happened? (4)

9. What is a relational contract? (2) When and why would we expect to see contract terms to be relational rather than substantive? (6)

APPLICATIONS: Find the effect (if any) of the different possible rulings. Answer under the assumption that the rule is a default rule and then under the assumption that the rule is binding.

10. Korean Steel Works promises to deliver steel springs for rabbit dolls to Los Angeles Rabbit Works on November 1. A wildcat strike takes place at the steel works and the springs cannot be delivered in time to the Rabbit Works. The rabbits cannot be made for the Christmas season and Rabbit Works loses $3 million in profits. In this situation, both sides can undertake precaution in case there is a wildcat strike (provide some examples). But only Korean Steel Works can reduce the probability of a strike. Who should be liable for these lost profits? (10)

11. A basketball player for the Los Angeles Lakers orders a size 24 basketball shoe for a game against the Miami Heat. When the shoes arrive, they are only a size 23 and too tight. As a result the player underperforms and the Lakers lose. Should the shoe store be held liable for the loss of the game? (4)

12. A singer catches a cold and is not able to perform at a concert. Do you think that the owner of the concert hall is in general reimbursed for the lost profits or the cost of advertising undertaken by the owner (reliance costs), both or neither? (10)

13. Westinghouse had a fixed-price contract to sell uranium to electrical utilities at $10 a pound. Westinghouse was a "middleman." It purchased uranium from producers and then sold it to the electrical utilities. In 1975, the price on world markets was $40 a pound. Only a small proportion of Westinghouse's obligations were covered by fixed-price contracts with uranium producers. It appears that Westinghouse had bet that the price of uranium would go down (which it did but not until 1982 when the price was $8 a pound). If Westinghouse honored the contracts, Westinghouse would have incurred over $2 billion in losses. It claimed it did not have to honor the contracts with the utilities because of commercial impracticability. Should Westinghouse have had its way? Postscript, the case was settled out of court with the utilities absorbing a lot of the cost. (10)

REFERENCES

Ayres, Ian and Robert Gertner. (1989). Filling Gaps in Incomplete Contracts: An Economic Theory of Default Rules. 99 *Yale Law Journal* 87.

Craswell, Richard, and Alan Schwartz. (1994). *Foundations of Contract Law.* New York: Oxford University Press.

Goldberg, Victor. (1998). Relational Contracts. In Peter Newman (ed.), *The New Palgrave Dictionary of Economics and the Law.* London: Macmillan Reference Limited.

Posner, Eric A. (2003). Economic Analysis of Contract Law after Three Decades: Success or Failure? 112 *Yale Law Journal* 829.

Shavell, Steven. (2004). *Foundations of Economic Analysis of Law.* Cambridge, MA: Harvard University Press.

When Is a Handshake a Contract and When Is a "Contract" Not a Contract?

A. *Pennzoil v. Texaco* 208
  1. When Is a Handshake a Binding Contract? 209
  2. Determining Actual Damages 209
  3. Punitive Damages 210
  4. Epilogue 212
B. Read the Fine Print 212
C. Why Contracts for Criminal Behavior Are Not Enforced 214

SUGGESTIONS FOR FURTHER READING 215
REVIEW QUESTIONS 215
REFERENCES 215

Courts enforce most written agreements but not all. What is the economic rationale for the different treatment? Courts enforce some verbal agreements and not others. Why? This chapter considers three cases – *Pennzoil v. Texaco*, *Williams v. Walker-Thomas*, and *Miltenberg & Samton v. Mallor* – to help in developing answers to these questions.

A. *PENNZOIL V. TEXACO*

In 1984, Getty Oil made a verbal agreement to sell three-sevenths of its stock for $110 a share to Pennzoil (one of the major players in Getty Oil, Gordon Getty, had previously signed a letter of intent). The picture of the handshake was in major newspapers. The next day Texaco offered Getty more money and Getty sold the stock to Texaco for $128 a share for a total of $10.1 billion (at that time, the largest merger ever). Pennzoil sued Texaco in a Texas court for tortious interference in the contract. On November 19, 1985, a jury returned a verdict in favor of Pennzoil, finding actual damages of $7.53 billion and punitive damages of $3 billion. At the time this was the biggest jury award ever (now some tobacco awards have exceeded it). Was there a breach of contract? How would we decide? And if there was a breach of contract, how should damages be determined?

Before we get into the economics, a little background gossip about the major players may help to understand some aspects of the case. J. Paul Getty was a multibillionaire when being a billionaire meant something. He was very cheap. He put a pay phone in his house so that guests were charged for phone calls, and when his grandson was kidnapped, he refused to give the kidnappers any money until they sent him his grandson's ear.[1] When he died, he left the bulk of his estate to the Getty Museum. The directors of the museum needed to sell shares in the privately held oil company to purchase more art and build a new museum. Hence, they decided to sell the stock. Texaco, despite its name, was incorporated in New York. It has a long history of doing stupid things. It supported Hitler before World War II. To look better in the eyes of the public, it then sponsored the Metropolitan Opera Company on the radio for the next 60 years. Several years ago, it was involved in a discrimination suit when one of the vice presidents recorded highly inflammatory statements made by the management. Recently, it has merged with Chevron (and is now being sued for environmental damage in Bolivia). The losing lawyer, David Boies, went on to lose a number of other high-profile cases, including the Microsoft antitrust case and *Gore v. Bush* (nevertheless, he is probably one of the great trial lawyers in the United States). The winning lawyer, Joseph Jamail, went home with $200 million. Jamail was known previously for such feats as convincing a jury that the city of Houston was negligent for planting a tree that his client ran into while drunk.

When Texaco made the offer to Getty, it also promised Getty that it would be liable for any legal bills. That is why Pennzoil sued Texaco for tortious interference with a contract rather than suing Getty for breach of contract. Finally, and perhaps most important, Pennzoil despite its name is not incorporated in Pennsylvania, but in Texas. This certainly explains why Pennzoil sued in a Texas court and why the jury was so sympathetic to its case.

---

[1] It made sense that Getty would not want to pay a ransom as this would encourage kidnapping of his other children and fifteen grandchildren.

1. When Is a Handshake a Binding Contract?

How do we decide as economists (not as lawyers) whether a verbal agreement is a contract or an indication of strong interest?[2] As is often the case, it would be foolish to believe that one could figure this out as an armchair economist. The trick is to look at the market (which might be influenced by the law). In some markets, verbal contracts mean nothing. This is the case in real estate where only signed documents are binding. In other areas, no written agreements take place. In the diamond industry, a handshake is binding. So what we have to do is to first see whether similar transactions usually end in written agreements. If such exchanges almost always require a written contract, that indicates that the handshake was not sufficient and therefore there was not a breach of contract. If such exchanges usually are completed with a handshake, we need to apply a second test. On those occasions when one or the other party wants to back out of the contract, is a penalty customary? In some cases the answer is no. If you shake hands on buying a puppy from someone and say that you will write a check tomorrow and fail to do so, you are unlikely to be sued for breach of contract. And if someone else comes along in the meantime and offers more for the puppy, the seller is unlikely to be sued for selling the puppy to this third party. Getting back to Pennzoil, if the deal was very complicated, such an exchange would usually require a written agreement, in which case there was no breach. If the deal was more akin to buying stock, then the argument for a breach of contract is much stronger, but even here stock purchases still need an initial written agreement.

2. Determining Actual Damages

At the trial, numerous oil geologists and other experts testified regarding the cost of Pennzoil finding and developing new oil reserves equal in amount to the oil reserves sold by Getty to Texaco. Oil exploration is very risky. Drilling is expensive and most wells are dry. The numerical estimates were based on a lot of hypothetical situations, including the cost of drilling, the probability of success, and the extent of the discovered reserves. After considerable testimony, the jury came up with the amount of $7.3 billion in actual damages. But is this a good way to estimate damages? The answer is no.

The best way of determining damages is to not determine them at all. In this case, specific performance (plus an additional charge for lost time) would appear to be the appropriate solution.[3] Just have Texaco give up its ownership of the Getty assets. In this way, the court would not have to estimate value. Specific performance makes sense in breach of contract cases because it just says perform the contract. But recall that this case was tortious interference with a contract. Specific performance is not an established principle in torts because only rarely could it be applied (although it would make sense in this situation if Texaco or Getty were forced to sell stock to Pennzoil for $110 a share).

When specific performance is not an available remedy, there are various ways of estimating the damages to Pennzoil. In economic terms, the best estimate of the cost to Pennzoil was the differential between the price of the stock that Pennzoil paid and

---

[2] Actually, the case is more complicated. As already mentioned, there was a signed letter of intent. So a related question is when is a letter of intent an agreement and when is it just an agreement to try to come to an agreement.

[3] Pennzoil could have asked for an injunction preventing Getty from selling stock to Texaco.

the price that Texaco paid. If there had not been any breach, then Pennzoil would have paid $110 a share for the stock and then probably turn around and sell it to Texaco for $128 a share since Texaco appears to have valued the Getty oil more than Pennzoil valued Getty oil. Our best guess is that the stock was not worth more than $128 a share to Pennzoil. If it were, then Getty would not have sold it for only $128 to Texaco.[4] Thus, the cost to Pennzoil was approximately $18 a share or $1.4 billion. This is less than 20 percent of the jury's determination of the actual damages.

The above analysis has to be slightly modified because Texaco also accepted liability in the event that Pennzoil sued for breach. This indicates that Texaco valued the stock at more than $128 a share since Texaco preferred to pay some settlement and/or trial costs (appropriately discounted for the probability of such an event occurring) and $128 rather than bargain with Pennzoil directly.

Why is the court's measurement of damages to Pennzoil so far off? The court determined the cost of finding an equivalent amount of reserves less the price saved from not buying the Getty stock. But of course the best (most efficient) way of Pennzoil obtaining that amount of reserves is not by drilling but rather by buying firms with petroleum assets. That is why Pennzoil and Texaco were trying to buy Getty in the first place, rather than drilling. Thus a good estimate of Pennzoil's lost profits is the price that Texaco paid minus the amount Pennzoil had agreed to pay. And if this is not adequate, we can look at publicly traded companies with petroleum assets and ask how much it would cost to buy them. Again we are looking at the market rather than engaging in cost studies (both oil companies had already figured all of that out when they decided to buy a company rather than drill).

As already mentioned, all these methods of estimating loss are inferior to specific performance. So why didn't Pennzoil ask for specific performance (even it the rule was not part of the tort canon)? The following might be an answer: oil stocks dropped dramatically soon after the purchase by Texaco. So in hindsight Texaco did Pennzoil a big favor. And that is why Pennzoil did not ask for specific performance. It is hard to explain why Texaco did not suggest specific performance. Perhaps such an argument might have cut into their claim that there was no breach. Alternatively, they might have thought that the jury might accept Texaco's cost estimates.

3. Punitive Damages

We next turn our attention toward the issue of punitive damages. Actual damages are payments to the plaintiff for harm suffered. Punitive damages are meant to punish the defendant beyond the implicit punishment of paying for the harm. In general, punitive damages are employed when there is little or no social benefit to the activity being punished and therefore the objective is to minimize the activity. For example, punitive damages might be assessed against a driver who was drag racing when the accident happened to discourage racing on city streets. In general, competitive offers are seen as socially desirable unless it involves something illegal such as bribes.

---

[4] One must always consider symmetric arguments in economics. Texaco did not think that Pennzoil would sell the stock for less than $128 a share; otherwise, it would have purchased the Getty stock indirectly from Pennzoil.

How do we decide the optimal amount of punitive damages in case of a breach? The best way is to observe the industry standard. In writing a contract, the parties to the agreement would want to choose an optimal level of punitive damages. Thus, we might want to look at liquidated damages for similar kinds of breach and see whether these damages go beyond compensation for harm. There are two problems with this approach. The first is that punitive damages are not allowed in breach of contract cases (presumably for good reason) so one cannot look to the market in this case. The second problem is that the case was tortious interference by Texaco rather than breach of contract by Getty (although distinguishing between the two is difficult as Getty willingly entered into the agreement with Texaco).

So let us try to a different approach to assessing punitive damages. Let us see why punitive damages are used in addition to compensatory damages. We have already considered one reason – to discourage socially unredeeming activity. The following are other possible reasons:

1. The party inflicting the damage is rarely punished. Thus, for example, the charge for theft is not merely the cost of the stolen items since the thief is rarely caught. Such a low level of punishment would not sufficiently deter theft. This does not apply in this case where the Texaco's identity is known and the existence of the breach is apparent.
2. The benefits to the party inflicting damage outweigh the damage to any one victim but not to the set of victims. For example, there may be many victims from antitrust behavior by a monopolist. Thus, to encourage the victims to pursue a case, there are treble damages. This is closely related to 1. Again this rationale does not apply here.
3. "Double your money back" if unsatisfied is a way of warranting the quality of the product being sold. Again this is not applicable to the case at hand.
4. To discourage the use of the court instead of the market, punitive damages might be added. But the cost of the using the court was not $3 billion or even $300 million.
5. Certain actions such as fraud and extortion have no redeeming qualities and therefore we want to deter such activity. Being an aggressive competitor does not fit neatly into this category.

Only point 4 provides a rationale for punitive damages in this case, and, as already noted, point 4 does not justify the high amount of punitive damages.

The punitive damages to Texaco appear to be about five to six times the benefit of the breach to Getty. What would the effect be if this ratio of punitive damages to profits were universally held? To be sure, there would be fewer breaches. But this comes at a cost because the line between tortious interference in a contract and being a good competitor is not clear. Thus, the potential breacher will expend considerable resources to make sure that the competitive offer is not a breach and may withhold an offer altogether. This increases transaction costs. Furthermore, it is possible that very high punitive damages will encourage more litigation as it becomes more worthwhile for people to sue for breach of contract in questionable cases on the hope that they will receive huge amounts.

4. Epilogue

Because of Texaco's threat of appeal to the federal court, Pennzoil was not guaranteed that it would get the $10.5 billion that the jury awarded.[5] Both sides were spending enormous sums on legal costs. Pennzoil and Texaco eventually settled with Texaco paying $3 billion to Pennzoil.

B. READ THE FINE PRINT

Going from the rich and famous, we turn to a case involving Ora Lee Williams, who with her seven children was living on $218 a month in welfare payments in the 1960s. There is not much more I can say about her, except that her legal case with Walker-Thomas Furniture is famous and covered in nearly all casebooks on contract law.

Walker-Thomas Furniture, like many other furniture companies, allowed its customers to pay in installments; the customers were given loans for purchasing the furniture, and the furniture itself was used as collateral. Often customers bought different items of furniture at different times on the installment plan. When they did, the terms of the contract included the following: "the amount of each periodical installment payment to be made by [purchaser] to the Company under this present lease shall be inclusive of and not in addition to the amount of each installment payment to be made by [purchaser] under such prior leases, bills or accounts; and all payments now and hereafter made by [purchaser] shall be credited pro rata on all outstanding leases, bills and accounts due the company by [purchaser] at the time each such payment is made." You probably had a hard time understanding this last sentence, and you would have had a harder time understanding it when it was buried in a lot of other detail and written in much smaller print. So I will explain it via a simple example. Suppose that you bought a chair for $200 and promised to pay $10 a month for 24 months. If you did not pay in full, the furniture company could repossess your chair. Suppose at the end of twenty-three months, you bought a second chair for $200 so you would owe in total $220. You would then be expected to pay $11 a month for the next two years. But here is the kicker. If you defaulted on your payment anytime in the next two years, say one year later, both chairs could be repossessed. In *Williams v. Walker-Thomas Furniture Co.*, 350 F. 2d 445 (1965), Williams had paid off all but $164 on $1,800 worth of furniture when she bought a stereo on credit, on which she subsequently defaulted. Should the contact be upheld?

Courts should be very hesitant to overturn contracts. If contracts can be overturned because they are unfair, then contracts are made by the courts rather than by the contracting parties, who are in a better position to determine relative value. If contracts can be overturned when the plaintiff claims the contract is hard to understand, then plaintiffs will not bother to understand contracts and contracts will be unenforceable. Either way, the parties would not know what kind of contract they made until the courts made their decision. Furthermore, Walker-Thomas contracts may have enabled the borrower to obtain a loan at a lower interest rate. All of these reasons suggest that the contract should be upheld.

---

[5] Texaco had appealed to the state court. See 729 S.W.2d 768 (1987).

However, efficiency requires that key parts of the contracts be clear and understandable so that people understand the bargain that they are making. Otherwise, the agreement may not be a Pareto improvement. The Walker-Thomas contract was harmful to the furniture company's most reliable customers – those who buy furniture over several years and paid out most of their loan. This suggests that if Williams understood the contract, she probably would not have signed it in the first place and instead she would have purchased the stereo from another store where she would only have lost the stereo in case of default. Because important conditions were buried in the middle of the contract and hard to understand and because the conditions appeared to be so unreasonable, it would make sense to make an exception in this case to not enforce the contract as written.[6] Such a ruling would encourage future contracts to be written in a language understandable to both parties with the key terms of the contract being prominently displayed.

As is true for many of the cases I consider, the appellate court in the Walker-Thomas case made a ruling similar to my recommendation (it said that the lower court could choose not to enforce the contract if the conditions warranted that conclusion), but the court's argument was different. The appellate court concentrated on the conditions for a contract to be unconscionable (unfair), thereby justifying its not being upheld.[7] One condition was lack of competition. Competition increases information (e.g., our firm offers better financing terms), rendering the lack of clarity in a firm's contract less of a problem. But the rest of the analysis, although couched in economic terms, was not consistent with the arguments presented in this chapter.[8]

So why should the courts accept industry custom in the Pennzoil case but not here? In the Pennzoil case, all the parties had lawyers. In contrast, Williams was not a sophisticated buyer. This reasoning has been used by the courts. For example, in *Kluger v. Romain*, 59 N.J. 522, 544 (1971), the court said: "The need for application of the [unconscionability] standard is most acute when the professional seller is seeking the trade of those most subject to exploitation – the uneducated, the inexperienced and the people of low incomes."

It should be realized that while *Williams v. Walker-Thomas*, as well as *Henningsen v. Bloomsfield Motors* (mentioned in footnote 6), are mainstays of law school curricula, the vast majority of contracts are upheld by the courts. Indeed most cases never get to the courts because it is clear to all involved that the contract will be upheld. The argument here is that only in the most egregious cases – where important conditions are difficult to understand and buried in the contract, these conditions are so unreasonable that it is extremely unlikely that the person would have knowingly agreed to them ahead of time, the person is unsophisticated, and there is little competition – that the contract should be ruled invalid.

[6] See *Henningsen v. Bloomfield Motors*, 161 A.2d 69, 92 (1960), where the court said the seller's use of fine print was to "promote lack of attention rather than sharp scrutiny" and *Kinney v. United Healthcare Services*, 7 Cal.App. 4th 1322, 1332 (1999), where the court said that the arbitration clause language was "so extensive as to render it difficult for a lay person to read and understand."

[7] If you are stranded in a desert and a driver offers to rescue you for a million dollars and you agree to the terms, a court will not uphold the agreement if you renege once you get home

[8] Also the decision has at times been treated as a ban against cross-collateralization, while the argument here is that cross-collateralization is acceptable if the conditions are made clear to the buyer.

PUNITIVE DAMAGES FOR BEDBUGS

In 1998, an extermination service discovered bedbugs in several rooms in a Chicago Red Roof Inn Hotel and offered to spray all 191 rooms for $500. The hotel rejected the offer but continued to rent rooms where the bugs had been found. The plaintiffs got one of these rooms. In a biting decision, the jury awarded punitive damages that were thirty-seven times the compensatory damages. The amount is above the single-digit multiplier for punitive damages that the Supreme Court in *State Farm Mutual Ins. Co. v. Campbell*, 123 S. Ct. 1513 (2003) suggested would not violate the due process requirements of the Fourteenth Amendment.

In *Mathias v. Accor Economy Lodging*, 347 F. 3d 672 (2003), the appellate court said that the hotel's failure to warn the guests in the $100-a-night rooms amounted to fraud and probably battery – willful and wanton conduct that supported an award of punitive damages. Judge Richard Posner (a founding father of the economic approach to law) provided several justifications for the appellate court's allowing the large multiplier. If a tortfeasor "is 'caught' only half the time he commits torts, then when he is caught he should be punished twice as heavily in order to make up for the times he gets away." Also, in the absence of a multidigit multiplier it would be difficult to finance litigation that only had a prospect of negligible compensatory damages. Finally, punitive damages are particularly justifiable because the defendants had increased the cost of litigation by filing "a host of frivolous evidentiary motions despite the modest stakes."

C. WHY CONTRACTS FOR CRIMINAL BEHAVIOR ARE NOT ENFORCED

The legal system enforces agreements. It thereby facilitates cooperation between parties by making contractual commitments more credible.

However, courts do not enforce contracts that promote criminal behavior. The reason is straightforward. Most contracts are not only Pareto improving for the parties to the contract, but wealth maximizing for society as a whole. But criminal activity generally imposes costs on others – the murder victim suffers a negative externality. Society does not want to promote wealth-reducing activities (even theft, which involves a transfer, reduces wealth as the victim will undertake costly behavior to avoid theft and the thief will undertake costly behavior to successfully carry out the theft). Enforcing a contract for criminal behavior would increase the likelihood that the contract will be carried out. But it is in society's interest to reduce criminal behavior. So it does not enforce such contracts.

An interesting case in this regard is *Miltenberg & Samton v. Mallor*, 1 A.D. 2d 458 (1956). The plaintiff buyer asked Miltenberg & Samton, a food broker, to label cans of herring as mackerel. M&S pasted new labels on the old, which Mallor observed when he picked up the cans. Rather than taking off both labels and starting from scratch, the parties agreed that M&S would be liable for any losses if the deception were discovered, which indeed was the case. The plaintiff sought to collect a penalty from the defendant as stipulated in their contract. However, the court did not uphold the contract.

SUGGESTIONS FOR FURTHER READING

There are other interesting issues concerning the existence of contract. For example, if your uncle promises to give you $10,000 in four years, this is not a legally enforceable contract; but if your uncle promises to give you $10,000 in four years if you quit smoking and you do, then the courts will enforce such a contract. See Posner (2003) for an economic explanation. Polinsky and Shavell (1998) provide a thorough analysis of punitive damages. For a more extensive discussion of the diamond industry, see Bernstein (1992). For more gossip on the Getty family, see Hewins (1961) and Pearson (1995). For more on personal debt contracts, see Chapter 30 on Bankruptcy.

REVIEW QUESTIONS

1. How does one determine whether handshakes imply a contract? (6)
2. In *Pennzoil v. Texaco*, how did the court determine the cost of the breach to Pennzoil? What are some superior methods? Why are they superior? (6)
3. What problems arise if a contract is ruled null because it was hard for the plaintiff to understand. What is the benefit of such a ruling? (6)
4. Why aren't contracts for criminal activity upheld? (2)

REFERENCES

Bernstein, Lisa. (1992). Opting out of the Legal System: Extralegal Contractual Relations in the Diamond Industry. 21 *Journal of Legal Studies* 115.

Hewins, Ralph. (1961). *J. Paul Getty: the Richest American*. London: Sidgwick and Jackson.

Pearson, John. (1995). *Painfully Rich: J. Paul Getty and his Heirs*. London: Macmillan.

Polinsky, A. Mitchel, and Steven Shavell. (1998). Punitive Damages: An Economic Analysis. 111 *Harvard Law Review* 869.

Posner, Richard A. (2003). *Economic Analysis of Law*. New York: Aspen Publishers.

23 Marriage as Contract: Family Law

A. Marital Relations 218

B. Spousal Support 219
   1. Why Spousal Support? 219
   2. Lump-Sum or Periodic Spousal Support? 219

C. Property Division 220

D. Prenuptial (Antenuptial) Contracts 222

E. No Fault Divorce versus Fault 222

F. Should the Engagement Ring Be Returned if the Marriage Is Called Off? 223

G. Polygamy 224

SUGGESTIONS FOR FURTHER READING 227

REVIEW QUESTIONS 227

REFERENCES 227

Marriage can be viewed as a long-term contract between two people who are emotionally attached to each other, and divorce can be viewed as a breach of the marriage contract. Economics analysis as a descriptive theory of law is relatively weak in explaining family law. The law regarding divorce varies greatly across states and between countries, especially in comparison to the other areas of law that we have investigated. For example, in most, perhaps all countries, a drunken driver who smashes into a pedestrian is liable for the harm. In some countries, however, divorce is not allowed (divorce was not legal in Ireland until 1995), some states do not allow alimony, most states have no fault, and others allow divorce only for fault. Furthermore, in some state, such as California, there is community property (assets generated in marriage are split equally, unless the assets are clearly defined as separate property), while in other states there is separate property, except under specified circumstances. Of course, there may be economic explanations for some of these variations. For example, separate property may be more likely in societies where a higher percentage of wealth is inherited rather than being a joint product of the marriage.

Despite the wide variation, there are still some characteristics that are common. Furthermore, we can always find the economic implications of the law even if we cannot always find the economic justification.

A. MARITAL RELATIONS

Marriage is like a partnership, and like any partnership the potential for conflict is high. The marital market reduces conflict in two ways. First, there is considerable search for partners where (for whatever reason) conflict is likely to be low and productivity is likely to be high.[1] Second, there is typically a greater emotional bond between a married couple than between business partners. The conflict between two people who love each other is likely to be less than the conflict between two people with greater self-interest.

With some exceptions (contraception and abortion, physical harm, terminating the partner's life), the law does not enter into the marital relationship. One spouse cannot sue the other for being a spendthrift, not doing the chores, committing adultery, or even for harm from a lawnmower accident. As long as the couple is still married, the married couple is presumed to be able to resolve differences more effectively than the courts. That is, the couple is treated as a unit.[2]

This hands-off attitude changes when the marriage is dissolved. In the absence of a prenuptial contract, the court is often asked to determine the allocation of property, children, and income (spousal support and child support). We will now turn our attention to some of the issues that arise when there is a divorce.

---

[1] People also search for a productive partner to maximize the returns to marriage. The Cobb-Douglas production function, $Q = AK^\alpha L^\beta$, where K stands for capital and L for labor, also characterizes the marriage relationship where K stands for Karl and L stands for Lucy. Notice that the relationship between K and L is multiplicative so that the higher the one, the more productive the other. This means that there will tend to be positive assortative matching – high-quality males will tend to marry high-quality females. An example is the positive correlation of educational attainment between spouses.

[2] There is the case of *Oreste Lodi v. Oreste Lodi*, 173 Cal. App. 3d 628 (1985), where the litigant tried to sue himself! Needless to say, the appellate court had fun with this case.

B. SPOUSAL SUPPORT

1. Why Spousal Support?

Spousal support (alimony) is most common when one of the spouses, typically the woman, has specialized in household production (e.g., raising children), while the other spouse has specialized in marketable production. Having children is an important reason for marriage. But those women who have forgone market employment to have children face great risk when a marriage is dissolved. They have fewer marketable skills and the demand for them as marriage partners may be reduced. If the woman is not insured via spousal support, she may continue her career and postpone having children during the marriage. Both spouses might prefer that the wife specialize in having children and that she receive spousal support in case of divorce. That is, the husband who is able to bear more risk would be willing to promise spousal support in the event of a divorce to persuade his wife to have (more) children. In the absence of such an implied agreement, the appropriate level of specialization would not take place. The risk-averse party is insured so that the optimal amount of risk is undertaken.[3]

The factors determining spousal support generally coincide with the theory outlined above. Those women who have few job skills, have young children, and have been married a long time to high-income earners tend to get more than otherwise.

Ever since Adam Smith, economists have extolled the virtues of specialization. Think of how poor we would be if everyone of us had to grow our own food, assemble our TV sets, and make our own clothes. Nature has specialized fetus-growing in women. So some division of labor in the household is inevitable, but over time the division of labor is less within the household than across households. Education and childcare are to a great degree done by specialists. There is day care, nursery school, and primary education. Food comes prepared, takeout is common, and microwaves are ubiquitous. Wealthier people hire maids and gardeners to assist with household production. Thus, over time there has been less need for nonmarket specialization by the woman, and as a result the role of spousal support has diminished.

2. Lump-Sum or Periodic Spousal Support?

Spousal support is typically paid in monthly installments. Sometimes spousal support lasts until the spouse receiving alimony is able to establish a career; sometimes it lasts until the person receiving alimony gets remarried.

In principal, a lump-sum amount could be based on expectations regarding the periodic amount. A person who had low prospects of being remarried would receive a greater lump-sum than a person who was likely to be remarried in the near future. According to Smartmoney.com, Jane Fonda got $10 million in Time-Warner stock when she married Ted Turner in return for not getting anything more if they divorced (by

---

[3] See our discussion of insurance in Chapter 27. Cohen (1987) argues that spousal support is a way to prevent opportunism by the husband. He views marriage as a long-run relationship: the wife specializes in child-rearing while young in return for the husband supporting her when they are old. Because the wife performs her part of the bargain early in the marriage, there is great potential for the husband not fulfilling his part of the bargain. As men and women age, the opportunities in the marriage market improve for men vis-à-vis women (the ratio of men to women decreases and men's fertility declines less rapidly). Therefore, men may opportunistically seek divorce. To either discourage this opportunism or minimize its effect, husbands are required to provide spousal support when their ex-wives have specialized in raising children.

that time, the stock was worth $70 million). In general, alimony is not lump-sum, however. There are a number of reasons why. (1) Unlike Ted Turner, most people's wealth is in human capital rather than physical capital. So the average person does not have enough wealth to pay off a lump-sum amount equivalent to the present expected discounted value of a stream of alimony payments. The person paying the alimony could borrow the money. But borrowing the money is very costly. Capital markets are not perfect, especially when it comes to human capital. (2) If alimony is collected by some person who has custody of the children, then periodic alimony payments gives the alimony payer economic leverage in seeing the children without recourse to the courts. (3) Lump-sum payments increase the risk to the spouse who is less capable of bearing risk (the woman in most cases) and reduces the risk to the party better able to bear the risk. From the opposite perspective, periodic alimony payments until remarriage reduce risk to the person who is receiving alimony and presumably the party less capable of bearing risk. If the supported spouse marries earlier than expected, the spouses gets less than she would have received if she had received a lump-sum, but her need for the money is less (assuming her new spouse brings more wealth than expenses); if the supported spouse marries later than expected, her need for money is greater than expected, and the supported spouse gets more than she would have gotten from a lump-sum payment.

Like most insurance policies, there is some *moral hazard* where the insured does not take the optimal amount of precaution (as is the case under strict liability where the victim is insured against damage). When the payments are periodic, the supported spouse is deterred from remarrying because this induces loss of spousal support. There is also moral hazard with regard to work effort. Periodic support payments are typically adjusted over time according to the earnings of both spouses. The more the supported spouse makes, the less the supported spouse gets in support; the more the support-ing spouse makes, the more the supporting spouse has to pay the supported spouse. Therefore, both parties are deterred from making more money, as they have to share the increase with their former spouse. Of course, there are laws that try to reduce the moral hazard problem. A number of states deny continued spousal support to those who are cohabiting (see, for example, In re *Marriage of Sappington*, 478 N.E.2d 376 (1985) and Cal. Fam. Code §4323(a)). To encourage optimal work effort, the supported former spouse has to make "best faith efforts" to get a job. On the other side, the supporting party cannot absolve his/her financial responsibilities to the supported party by quitting his/her job and becoming a monk.

C. PROPERTY DIVISION

When a business partnership dissolves, in general, each partner keeps the assets that he/she brought into the partnership; only the assets acquired during the partnership are divided. For similar reasons, property brought to the marriage is often treated as separate property.[4] The major exception is the family home, which in some places is treated as community property even if one party brought it into the marriage.

---

[4] This appears to be somewhat cross-cultural. For example, in the event of dissolution, the dowry may revert to the woman.

It is often hard to divide property fairly ex post. The method used by the courts is a good approximation, but it does not encourage truthful revelation of preferences. Take, for example, the valuation of a house. Suppose that it is the wife who has the option of buying the house. She will argue to the court that the house is falling apart, while the husband will argue that it is a palace. Therefore, one tries to find outside "neutral" experts to estimate its true value. But there is still a problem. If the expert underestimates the value of the house, then the wife exercises her option and takes the house at the estimated value. If the expert overestimates the value of the house, then the wife can decline the option. As a result, the house will be sold with the proceeds being shared by the former husband and wife. So there is a bias in favor of the wife. In general, the market is the best method of revealing true value. Either side bids for the house or they sell the house to a third party. Money bids elicit honest revelation of preference (as long as there is at least one other person bidding in the auction). But market transaction costs are not trivial. Putting up the house for sale involves time showing the house and commissions to realtors. The transaction cost involved in determining the true value of the house outweighs the benefit of a more accurate assessment.

What happens if a husband works to put his wife through medical school and then they divorce?[5] How much should he get for his investment in her medical career? This is a very complicated question, especially if he has received some of the benefits from her higher earning power. So let us consider the simple case, where divorce takes place when the wife graduates from medical school. Even this "simple" case is quite complicated, and so far the field has provided only a very rudimentary understanding.

Human capital markets are not very efficient. If you borrow money for your education and you do not pay the money back because you are a failure, the bank cannot repossess either your money or your education. Spouses are more capable than banks in monitoring the qualities of their marriage partners, and therefore spouses may be in a better position to make educational loans. But what rate of return should they get on their loan? If they get too high of a rate, then there will be underinvestment in medical education; if they get too low of a rate, then there will be overinvestment in medical education.

If the man did not put his wife through medical school, the woman would have to borrow the money. So we might want to use the cost of borrowing money. However, we might want to use the rate of return of the husband's money if used elsewhere (lending to a bank). If capital markets were efficient and had no transaction costs, then the interest rate would be the same for borrowing and lending. They are not; so we are stuck with these two imperfect measures.[6] But at least we have an upper and lower bound. It suggests that the husband's *property* ownership in the wife's medical practice is limited to the return on the loan rather than attributing part of the value of the medical practice to the husband solely because they were married at the time. Of course, the

---

[5] In the past, it was often the case that the wife put the man through medical school, but today there are more women than men in medical school.

[6] An additional problem is that some of the money that the husband made while his wife was going through medical school was consumed by both of them. So, there needs to be a determination of how much was actually borrowed by the woman either for her consumption or for her investment in a medical career.

husband my still get spousal support based on the success of his former wife's medical practice, but here we are talking about property division.

D. PRENUPTIAL (ANTENUPTIAL) CONTRACTS

Marriage is a contract. The court provides default rules regarding spousal support and property division. Couples have the alternative to write their own prenuptial contract. In this way, they can divide property and determine support based on their own needs.

Although premarital agreements date back to the 2,000-year-old Ketubah, an ancient Jewish premarital agreement, they did not become popular in the United States until the 1980s. Initially, U.S. courts were quite skeptical of such agreements, but over time, the courts have been more accepting of prenuptial contracts. In general, they are likely to accept the contract if it is written, both parties have had sufficient time to review the contract before the wedding, and both sides have had the opportunity to consult a lawyer. The reason for requiring written contracts is clear. Because so much might be said in the privacy of a couple's relationship, the courts would have a hard time determining the nature of the verbal contract. Thus a written contract is required if the courts are to uphold a prenuptial contract.

In the previous example regarding medical school financing, we assumed purely market measures. There is a problem here in that the man might have had the opportunity to marry someone else who would have provided him with an annuity of X dollars. Hence his opportunity cost in marrying the medical school student is X dollars. There is also the opportunity cost for the wife – perhaps someone else offered to put her through medical school and not get anything in case of divorce. Both parties have assets (character, personality, looks) that are not fully realized in the job market although perhaps positively correlated with market income. Prenuptial contracts allow both parties to take everything into account.

With regard to marriage, it's caveat emptor (buyer beware). Suppose that a person has stated that he has a bachelor's degree when he never graduated from college. This is neither grounds for divorce, nor grounds for suing for fraud. If a person claims that he (she) is a virgin, then a discovery that the person has had sex before marriage with someone else is not grounds for divorce in those states that require fault. Although a written contract declaring that the person has never been married will be grounds for fraud if the person has been previously married.

E. NO FAULT DIVORCE VERSUS FAULT

In California there is no-fault that extends to the issue of alimony; that is, fault has no effect on alimony payments. As suggested earlier, no-fault reduces court costs. Here we will investigate the advantages of having fault.

In our discussion of liability rules, we argued that the negligent party should be liable for the damage. Under a fault rule for divorce, if one spouse engaged in criminal activity or had extramarital affairs, then that spouse is deemed to be at fault and therefore ordered to pay more alimony (or receive less). Thus laws regarding fault encourage optimal behavior. However, in practice such a system is impractical. Marriage is a complicated relationship rather than an isolated accident. So fault is more difficult to determine when there is a divorce than when there has been an automobile accident.

Furthermore, in societies with different values, it is difficult to have a consensus on relative fault within a marriage. Therefore, in modern societies no-fault has superseded fault.[7]

F. SHOULD THE ENGAGEMENT RING BE RETURNED IF THE MARRIAGE IS CALLED OFF?

Ben Affleck gave Jennifer Lopez a 6.1-carat pink-diamond engagement ring. The marriage was called off; should Jennifer return the ring?

If Jennifer returns the ring, then both parties are back to the same position as they were before the engagement. This is akin to the reliance rule in contract law. But here the reliance rule makes more sense than in contract law. In contract law, it is relatively easy to determine which party breached the contract. When it comes to personal relationships, courts are at a severe disadvantage in determining which party did the breaching. Therefore, one side should not be disadvantaged, as would be the case if Jennifer got to keep the ring.

Suppose instead that the person ending the engagement is labeled the breaching party, and the courts award the ring to the other person. This would create the wrong incentives. A person (X) who wanted to end the engagement might make life miserable for the other person (Y), thereby getting the other person to break off the engagement. In this way, X would end up with the ring. A subtler rule would award the ring to the person who was better behaved during the engagement. This would be akin to a comparative negligence rule. However, this rule is very difficult to implement. Different people have different attitudes and expectations, and more important, both parties are likely to have known each other's faults before they were engaged. If they got engaged despite these faults, then why should these same faults be used as the reason for the other party breaking off the engagement? So these alternatives have serious problems.

Another approach is to ask who would end up with the ring if transaction costs were low. If the ring were the man's family heirloom, the ring would almost always be more valued by the man. In her book of etiquette, Emily Post said that such heirlooms should be returned. If the ring were bought at Costco (perhaps in a package of three, like other items sold in the store), the answer would not be as obvious. The woman could wear the ring (but it might be more difficult to do so if she married someone else), convert it to a pendant, or sell it; the man might use the ring again (although the recipient might feel uncomfortable wearing someone else's engagement ring) or sell it. In the end, it seems that the man has more use for the engagement ring than the woman.

Law and etiquette regarding the return of rings has changed over the last 100 years. In the 1930s, the aforementioned Emily Post suggested that the woman keep the engagement ring (unless an heirloom). Now according to US Weekly etiquette expert Peter Post, Jennifer or any other woman has to give back the ring. Why the change? Seventy years ago it was more common for women to be virgins until they were engaged. The harm from breaking off an engagement fell mainly on the woman. Therefore, to equalize

---

[7] It should be noted that Islam does not require fault.

WHO ARE THE PARENTS?

Robert and Denise went to a fertility clinic where they had Robert's sperm fertilize donor eggs, some of which were then implanted in Denise's uterus. Their daughter Madeline was born in February 2001. Susan, a single person, went to the same clinic. She wanted an anonymously donated ovum fertilized by an anonymously donated sperm to be implanted in her uterus. Her son Daniel was also born in February 2001. Unfortunately, the ovum implanted in Susan had been mistakenly fertilized by Robert's sperm. Robert and his wife did not want the embryos fertilized by Robert's sperm to go to anyone else. When Robert found out, he and his wife Denise went to court so that could have custody of Daniel. Who should have custody?

Using economic analysis and ignoring legal precedent, Susan should have custody. If Robert and Denise do not get custody of Daniel, the cost to them from the mistake is one less ovum. If need be, the lost egg can be replaced by another donor and fertilized with some new sperm from Robert. That is, there is a relatively cheap substitute. The cost to Susan of not having custody is having a second pregnancy to gain one child. Essentially, Robert and Denise were asking Susan to be a surrogate mother, which is much more costly than asking Robert and Denise to give up a fertilized donated egg.

Now, for the court decision: in 109 Cal. App. 4th 1109 (2004), the appeal court ruled that Robert and Susan have joint custody! Denise is out of the picture.

the harm and to ensure that the man's promises were credible, the woman kept the engagement ring. Sexual mores have changed and the harm from a broken engagement is not so one-sided. Indeed, engagement rings appear to be less common even though people are wealthier.

I suppose you would like to know whether Jennifer returned the ring. I can't tell you. The ring was returned to Harry Winston, the New York jeweler, and he would not say who returned it.

G. POLYGAMY

Polygamy (or more appropriately, but less commonly used word, *polygyny*) means that men may have more than one wife (as opposed to *polyandry*, which means that a woman may have more than one husband).[8] Although polygamy has been portrayed as a situation, which benefits men at the expense of women, other things being equal, the reverse tends to be true.

Consider a regime, where men may have two or more wives, but otherwise the legal regime is the same, in particular, women can divorce their husbands. This increases the demand for women and hence their implicit price. So on average women benefit as there is more competition for them. And if a woman does not want to share her husband with other women, she can always choose to be with a man who will have only one wife because no more than one-half the men can practice polygamy. Of course, this man

---

[8] Polygyny is more common than polyandry. One possible reason is that under polygyny all parents know who their offspring are, but under polyandry, males do not know which children are genetically related to them.

WHO ARE THE PARENTS?

In *re Baby M*, 109 N.J. 396 .2D 1227 (1988) involved a sperm-donating father and a surrogate (but natural) mother who refused to give up the baby when it was born, as required by the contract. The woman had been hired for $10,000. This was perhaps the first case involving surrogate motherhood, and it made quite a sensation at the time. The New Jersey court ruled that such contracts are not enforceable but that the best interests of the child suggested that the father should have custody with visitation rights of the surrogate mother. Neither parent was allowed to sell movie rights without prior approval of the court. Since then, courts and legislatures have responded to surrogacy in a variety of ways. Some states uphold such contracts (e.g., California, see *Johnson v. Calvert*, 851 P.2d 776 (1993)) and others do not (e.g., Louisiana).

Should the contract be upheld? The following is one way to go about answering the question. Fathers want to hire someone who will deliver as promised. If the surrogate mother can unilaterally break the contract, then the father will not be able to distinguish between those women who are sure that they won't want to keep the child and those who are not so sure. It is no.

WHO OWNS THE EMBRYOS?

If a couple divorces, who owns the rights to the frozen fertilized embryos? The former wife wanted the frozen embryos to become a mother; the former husband did not want to be the father. Here is what the court said in *Davis v. Davis*, 842 S.W.2d 588 (1992): "If no prior agreement exists, then the relative interests of the parties in using or not using the pre-embryos must be weighted. Ordinarily, the party wishing to avoid procreation should prevail, assuming that the other party has a reasonable possibility of achieving parenthood by means other than the use of pre-embryos in question. If no other reasonable alternative exists, then the argument in favor of using the pre-embryos to achieve pregnancy should be considered."

The more difficult (that is, costly) it is for the woman to produce new embryos, the more likely the court will rule in favor of the woman. Using a cost-benefit analysis, what would be your decision?

WHEN SHOULD GIFTS BE RETURNED?

Dear Abby: My husband of 10 years recently left me for another woman. My mother-in-law e-mailed me today telling me to return . . . all anniversary and Charistmas [gifts] for the last 10 years. . . . what is the best way to respond?

Stewing in Seattle

Dear Stewing: . . . [I]gnore her outrageous e-mail.   (February 27, 2006)

Britney Spears got married on New Year's Eve 2003, but the marriage was annulled soon afterward. Suppose that the bride and groom received gifts. Should they return the gifts if they were opened? What if the gifts were unopened? Suppose that the dissolution took place one month, six months, or one year later. Would your answer change?

BARRY BONDS SCORES AT THE CALIFORNIA SUPREME COURT

Barry Bonds and Susann "Sun" Bonds met in August 1987. Barry was a major league baseball player making $100,000 per year. Sun was unemployed. They became engaged in November 1987. In December, Barry told Sun that they would have to sign a prenuptial agreement. Sun agreed. The day before the wedding in February 1988, Barry's attorneys presented Sun and Barry the proposed agreement. Sun was advised to seek independent counsel. She declined. Sun signed the agreement and the couple married.

When Barry filed for legal separation in 1994, Sun challenged the validity of the prenuptial agreement. The trial court ruled the agreement was valid and found that Sun signed it voluntarily, uncoerced by any threats: In re Marriage of Bonds, 24 Cal. 4th 1 (2000), the California Supreme Court upheld the lower court. The Supreme Court found that although a party's representation by independent counsel is one factor to be considered in determining the voluntariness of a premarital agreement, it is not determinative.

Shortly thereafter the California Legislature changed the rules regarding prenuptial contracts. From now on, the prenuptial contract must be presented at least two weeks before the wedding. Times have changed since J. Paul Getty had one of his wives sign a prenuptial contract written in Spanish, a language that she did not speak.

WHO GETS TO NAME THE CHILD?

The father wanted to name the 10-month-old boy "Samuel Charles." The mother, to whom he wasn't married, had named the child "Weather'by Dot Com Chanel Fourcast." Here is the mother's explanation for the unusual name. She knew little about the father's family names and so hadn't much to work with; the father was a weather forecaster. The woman liked the last name Weatherby, and thought that it would make a good first name; this was her fourth child, and therefore she spelled his name "fourcast" instead of "forecast." And she liked Chanel perfume and therefore spelled "channel," "chanel." In *Sheppard v. Speir*, 85 Ark. App. 481 (2004), an Arkansas state appellate panel affirmed a trial court's renaming of the child, Samuel Charles.

What do you think the mother will call the little boy when she wants to get his attention?

might have only one wife because he is less desirable on other grounds. So a majority of men are hurt by polygamy because the demand for them is decreased and possibly a majority will have no wives (if at least a quarter of the men have two wives or if at least an eighth have four wives). It is even possible that some men with multiple wives might not benefit from a regime of polygamy. The reason for this possibility is that some men with two wives might prefer to have one wife with more desirable characteristics than two wives with less desirable characteristics, but the women with these more desirable characteristics are all married to more desirable men with more than one wife. So in the end only a small percentage of men benefit from a system where polygamy is allowed.

We note that polygyny was outlawed in the United States when only men had the right to vote.

I have said that, other things being equal, women benefit from a system of polygamy. In this case, other things being equal, seems not to hold. Women tend to have more power in Western industrialized societies where polygamy has long been outlawed than in other places where polygamy is still practiced (many Muslim societies) or practiced until relatively recently (China early in the twentieth century). Furthermore, polygamy often involves child brides who cannot be considered consenting adults. Renegade Mormon marriages at times involve 14-year-old girls, while Iranian law allows 9-year-olds to marry.[9]

SUGGESTIONS FOR FURTHER READING

Levmore (1995) compares marriage to partnerships. Landes (1978) and Cohen (1987) provide alternative explanations for alimony. Dnes and Rowthorn (2002) and Smith (2003) consider various contractual relationships regarding divorce (for example, whether divorce should require the agreement of both spouses rather than the present arrangement where marriage but not divorce requires the agreement of both spouses). Borenstein and Courant (1989) and Meighan (1997) discuss division of property when one spouse has gained human capital in the marriage. Wittman (2003) includes two articles on baby selling (by E. Landes and R. Posner and by Prichard) as well as an article on rings and promises (by Brinig). For a discussion of surrogacy, see Hatzis (2003). Brinig (2000) covers many of these topics with a more jaundiced view of the contribution of economics to our understanding of the issues.

REVIEW QUESTIONS

1. Why is alimony given for specific investment? (4)
2. What is the difference between lump-sum and periodic payments until remarriage. What are the factors that determine when one is more appropriate than the other? (6)
3. If the engagement is called off, should the woman get to keep the ring? What if the man had an affair with an old flame? (6)
4. Using economics, who should be the parents of Daniel B. (discussed in the box)? (6)
5. Explain who wins and who loses under polygamy in comparison to a situation outlawing polygamy. (6)
6. Many women seek abortions. Other couples seek children to adopt. It is generally the case that buying babies is illegal, but couples may pay for medical care expenses faced by the pregnant mother. What would happen if baby selling were made legal? (4) When baby selling is illegal, supply and demand still operate, but in different ways. Explain. (6)

---

[9] At the time of writing this book, Kansas, which does not have polygamy, allowed 12-year-olds to marry with the consent of their parents.

REFERENCES

Borenstein, Severin, and Paul N. Courant. (1989). How to Carve a Medical Degree: Human Capital Assets in Divorce Settlements. 79 *American Economic Review* 992.

Brinig, Margaret. (2000). *From Contract to Covenant.* Cambridge, MA: Harvard University Press.

Cohen, Lloyd. (1987). Marriage, Divorce and Quasi-Rents, or "I Gave Him the Best Years of My Life." 16 *Journal of Legal Studies* 267.

Dnes, Anthony, and Robert Rowthorn (eds.). (2002). *The Law and Economics of Marriage and Divorce.* Cambridge: Cambridge University Press.

Hatzis, Aristides N. (2003). "Just the Oven": A Law and Economics Approach to Gestational Surrogacy Contracts. In Katharina Boele-Woelki (ed.), *Perspectives for the Unification or Harmonisation of Family Law in Europe.* Antwerp: Intersentia.

Landes, Elizabeth M. (1978). Economics of Alimony. 7 *Journal of Legal Studies* 35.

Levmore, Saul. (1995). Love It or Leave It: Property Rules, Liability Rules, and Exclusivity of Remedies in Partnership and Marriage. 58 *Law & Contemporary Problems* 221.

Meighan, Katherine W. (1997). For Better or for Worse: A Corporate Finance Approach to Valuing Degrees. 5 *George Mason Law Review* 193.

Smith, Ian. (2003). The Law and Economics of Marriage Contracts. 17 *Journal of Economic Surveys* 201.

Wittman, Donald (ed.). (2003). *Economic Analysis of Law: Selected Readings.* Malden, MA: Blackwell Publishers.

VIII HARMS ARISING BETWEEN CONTRACTING PARTIES

Part VIII flows naturally from Part VII on contracts and breach of contract. Here we are concerned with damage from leaking pens, exploding soda bottles, and lawnmower accidents, as well as the breakdown of automobile engines. All of these might be covered in a contract and the product failures could be viewed as breaches or alleged breaches of implied warranty.

From another view, Part VIII can be seen as the low transaction-cost variant of Part V on torts and liability rules. In Part V, we showed that if drivers are not liable for harm to pedestrians, then drivers will provide less than the optimal level of precaution toward pedestrians. Does the same logic hold for the producers of automobiles? If they are not liable, will automobile manufacturers provide less safe automobiles? The logic of Part V suggests yes, but Part V covered high transaction costs cases, while Part VIII covers low transaction cost cases. As we will see, the answer is no.

Part VIII also clears up other common misperceptions. For example, those who root for the consumer might rejoice when the court finds the manufacturer liable for damage. But, as we will see, the consumer ultimately pays for the manufacturer's liability. In the long run, the legal system is incapable of shifting wealth from suppliers to demanders or vice versa. Indeed, we show in Chapter 26 that forcing the producer to be strictly liable may make both sides worse off.

As is the case throughout the book, we use cost-benefit analysis. When physical injury and death may be involved, it may seem distasteful to undertake such an analysis. But all of us implicitly put a price on life when we buy cheaper but less safe cars or vote for fewer highway patrol officers to cut down on taxes.

24 | Exploding Coca-Cola Bottles[1]

A. **Exculpatory Clauses Allowed** 232

B. **The Effect of Liability When Exculpatory Clauses Are Not
    Allowed – Symmetric Information** 234

   1. Consumers and Producers Equally Good Insurers 234
   2. One Side Has a Comparative Advantage in Insuring 235

C. **Concluding Remarks** 236

SUGGESTIONS FOR FURTHER READING 237

REVIEW QUESTIONS 237

REFERENCES 238

---

[1] Some might find it valuable to read Chapter 27 on insurance before reading this chapter.

You buy a pen from Wal-Mart. It leaks and ruins a new suit. Should Wal-Mart be liable? Should the manufacturer be liable? Or should you be liable? You buy a bottle of Coca-Cola and it explodes in your face. Should the manufacturer be found liable? You buy some TNT and it explodes in your face while you are setting it into place. Should the manufacturer be liable? You go to a doctor and she does not check for glaucoma because you are young and unlikely to get it. Later you find out that you have glaucoma, and it has seriously progressed because it was untreated. Should the doctor be liable? You get AIDS from a blood transfusion. Should the hospital be liable? Should the donor be liable? Should the Red Cross be liable? Or are you uncompensated for the harm? You get herpes from your sexual partner. Should your partner be made liable or should you be stuck with uncompensated damage?

To answer these questions, we have to first ask a different set of questions – what difference does the assignment of liability make on the behavior of the participants. For example, if Coca-Cola is not liable for the damage when their bottles explode, will they produce less safe bottles? Most students answer yes to this last question, but, as we will show, "no" is in general the correct answer.

The theoretical analysis will be in terms of polar cases: in this chapter, we consider exploding Coke bottles, a situation where the behavior of the consumer (except for purchasing the Coke in the first place) has *relatively* little influence on the likelihood or extent of damage.[2] In the next chapter, we consider malpractice by doctors, again a case where the consumer's behavior (in this case, the patient) has little role in the likelihood that that the doctor will make a mistake. In the chapter after that, we will discuss lawn mower accidents where the behavior of the consumer is an important input into the production of damage.

A. EXCULPATORY CLAUSES ALLOWED

An *exculpatory clause* allows the negation of a legal ruling (*default rule*) if there is some kind of express consent by the parties to the contrary. For example, in the absence of an agreement to the contrary, laundries might be liable for clothes left over thirty days. This is the default rule. By posting a notice that they will not be responsible for clothes left over thirty days, laundries can overrule the unstated expectation. This is the exculpatory clause. On the other side, a manufacturer is not liable by law for an automobile engine lasting fifty thousand miles unless there is a warranty (exculpatory clause) assuming liability for fifty thousand miles.

It should be noted that many ostensible exculpatory clauses are either invalid or redundant. For example, a sign saying that a parking lot will not be liable for damage to your car does not exclude the company from being liable for negligence. The message on the side of a box of Kodak film that states that when the film is defective, Kodak is only liable for the cost of purchasing a new role of film is not an exculpatory clause because that is the law even if the message were not on the box.

If exculpatory clauses are allowed, the final assignment of liability does not depend on the initial allocation of liability. If the default rule is that Coke is liable for exploding bottles, but Coke's profits are higher if it is not liable, then Coke will print a label on the bottle saying that it is not liable. If it is more profitable for Coke to be liable, it will have

---

[2] The key word is *relative*. A consumer could wear goggles and a flak jacket when picking up a bottle of coke.

no need to print anything on the Coke bottle. Thus, the only effect that the rule has when exculpatory clauses are allowed is on the amount of printing or other costs required to write the exculpatory clause (transaction costs). This is just another application of the Coase theorem: when transaction costs are low, the ultimate assignment of rights is independent of the initial assignment.

Why might it be profitable for Coke to assume liability? It is possible that Coke can produce two kinds of bottles: a fat Coke bottle that never explodes and a slim one that explodes one out of a million times causing $20,000 in damage, which on average is 2 cents damage per bottle. If buyers are risk averse, then they would prefer to pay 2 cents extra (or even more) for the fat bottle. If Coke can produce the fat bottle for less than 2 cents, then it can make more profit by producing the fat bottle and accepting liability (which in this example would be zero).

Even if Coke can only produce the slim bottle, it may be profitable for Coke to assume liability if Coke is risk neutral (the likely case) and some of its customers are risk averse (again, the likely case). By assuming liability, Coke might be able to sell its slim bottle for 3 cents extra to risk-averse buyers even though it only costs Coke on average 2 cents per bottle extra for damage payments when it is liable. Both sides are better off than if Coke produced the bottle without assuming liability.

Of course, if some customers are risk neutral or risk preferring, Coke can offer two kinds of bottles: one with liability by Coke and one without. Just as there is sugar-free Coke, there may be liability-free (for the consumer) Coke and liability (for the consumer) Coke, the latter selling for less. This is similar to the option for an extended warranty on new cars and appliances for an added price. By assuming liability, Coke is providing an insurance policy to the consumer. It is a tied product. The consumer buys both Coke and a specialized insurance policy.

In a nutshell, Coke will provide the warranty (insurance policy) if it can charge more for the warranty than it costs Coke to provide the warranty.

Whether Coke is a monopolist or a perfect competitor, when *both sides are informed*, profit maximization will lead to the optimal allocation of liability.[3] If the cost to Coke from assuming liability is 2 cents and the benefit to the consumer is 3 cents, then Coke will assume liability. Even if Coke is a monopolist trying to exploit the last penny from the consumer, it will offer additional amenities, including insurance, if this increases its profitability. If it increases its profitability, Coke is better off; and if consumers are willing to pay more for the insured bottle than the uninsured bottle, then those consumers buying the insured bottle are better off, also.

Of course, it is possible that Coke's cost of insuring consumers is greater than the benefit accruing to them. In such cases, Coke will not want to be liable and will either disavow liability (if the default rule says that Coke is liable) or not print anything regarding liability on their bottles (if the default rule says that consumers are liable).

Note that lack of liability by Coke does not imply that Coke does not have the proper incentives to provide the optimal amount of safety. If safe bottles are cost effective (that is, their cost is less than the expected damage reduction from their use), then Coke will provide safe bottles whether Coke is liable or not. The incentive to provide safety is no different from the incentive to provide other characteristics. Coke will provide more fizz, easy-to-open bottles and cans, and safe bottles if people value these amenities more

---

[3] In the next chapter, we will discuss the issue of information in greater detail.

than their costs. People cannot sue Coke for excessive time spent trying to open hard-to-twist bottle caps; yet, Coke still has an incentive to provide easy-to-open bottles. The same holds true for safe bottles. They will provide safety if it is cost effective. Safety is a tie-in good. Cars come with batteries and tires, but not always with stereo equipment or antitheft devices and rarely with driving gloves and sunglasses. Amenities cost something. Firms provided additional amenities if consumers are willing to pay for them.

B. THE EFFECT OF LIABILITY WHEN EXCULPATORY CLAUSES ARE NOT ALLOWED – SYMMETRIC INFORMATION

Sometimes exculpatory clauses are not allowed. Here we investigate the differing outcome when one side or the other is made liable and exculpatory clauses are not allowed either way.[4] That is, either the law requires that Coke be held strictly liable for the damage or the law does not allow Coke to be held liable.

1. Consumers and Producers Equally Good Insurers

If consumers are *informed* about the risks of exploding bottles and they can obtain insurance for the *same* price as Coke obtains insurance, *nothing is changed* when liability is shifted from Coke to the consumer except that the consumer no longer buys an insurance policy with his Coke. In turn this means that the consumer will pay less for Coke (if the bottle has a positive probability of exploding).

Consider first the possibility that only one type of bottle can be produced and that either Coke or the consumer can purchase insurance at an actuarially fair price. If the bottle on average causes 2 cents harm, then the consumer will pay an extra 2 cents when Coke is liable; when Coke is not liable, the person will pay Coke 2 cents less but put the money in the kitty (or buy the insurance separately from another party for 2 cents a bottle). Note that when Coke is liable, the price of Coke is higher, but that does not mean that the demand for Coke is less (in fact, it is unchanged). This is because the higher price reflects the added insurance.

Let us stick with the assumption that the average harm from exploding bottles is 2 cents a bottle. If two types of bottles can be produced and the nonexploding Coke bottle cost only 1.5 cents more to make, then the nonexploding bottle will be produced whether the consumer or Coke is liable (because it is cheaper than producing and insuring the exploding bottle). For example, if the consumer is liable, Coke might offer the safer nonexploding bottle for 1.8 cents more than the exploding bottle. Consumers would pay 1.8 cents more for the nonexploding bottle because they would on average save 2 cents a bottle in damage. Therefore, the consumers would be better off, and Coke would be too. In a nutshell, even though Coke is not liable, it has the same incentives as it does when it is liable. Of course, under the present assumptions, when Coke is liable, it will also produce the safer bottle.

To make sure that we understand the logic, it is useful to consider the symmetric possibility – that it costs 2.5 cents more to produce the nonexploding bottle. If consumers

---

[4] It is extremely rare that the producer of a product is prevented by law from assuming liability and providing insurance (blood donors may be a counterexample). We assume it here to demonstrate the difference from the symmetrically opposite situation. For analyzing the case where exculpatory clauses are allowed one way but not the other, just combine the analysis from last section and this section.

can purchase insurance for 2 cents a bottle, then they will buy the exploding bottle and insurance rather than paying 2.5 cents additional for a nonexploding bottle. If producers are liable, they will produce the exploding bottle and divvy up 2 cents on average for damage rather than produce the nonexploding bottle for an additional 2.5 cents. In turn, consumers will pay 2 cents more for a bottle.

Thus, when both sides are equally good insurers and both sides are informed about the risks, the outcome is the same whether the producer is liable or not. Note that this equivalence result holds even though the liability cannot be shifted (via an exculpatory clause, for example).

2. One Side Has a Comparative Advantage in Insuring

We next consider the case where one side or the other may be a cheaper insurer.[5] Other things being equal, we want the cheaper insurer to provide the insurance. If the law makes a mistake and requires the side that is a more costly insurer to be liable (provide insurance), then, faced with higher cost, the consumer will substitute either less-explosive bottles or different products entirely.

Let us start with an easy case. Only the exploding bottle can be made and on average, the harm from exploding is 2 cents per bottle. If it costs the producer 3 cents per bottle to insure and the consumer 2 cents a bottle to insure, we want the consumer to be liable because the total cost to the consumer will be less in this way. And of course if the numbers are reversed, we would want the producer to be liable.[6]

Now, let us consider a more interesting case. To make the analysis as concrete as possible, the following assumptions will be made: the additional cost to Coke in producing the nonexplosive bottle is 2.5 cents; the average damage from the explosive bottle is 2 cents; the insurance cost to Coke per explosive bottle is 2 cents; the insurance cost to the consumer per explosive bottle is 3 cents; and the risk averse consumer prefers to pay 3 cents a bottle for insurance rather than face the risk of an uncompensated explosion.

In this example, Coke is the cheaper insurer. If it were liable, it would produce the explosion-prone bottle and pay 2 cents per bottle for insurance (yielding greater profit than paying 2.5 cents for an explosion-proof bottle). If the consumer were liable, the consumer would purchase the nonexploding bottle because the additional cost of the nonexploding bottle is 2.5 cents, which is less than the additional cost of the insurance (3 cents) for the exploding bottle. Therefore, making the consumer liable will result in the more expensive (safer) bottle being produced. *Precaution* (less-explosive bottles) *is a substitute for insurance.* If insurance costs are relatively greater for consumers, then consumers will tend to substitute the more expensive but less explosive bottle or buy different products entirely. This argument runs contrary to what most people would expect because making Coke liable would result in the lower-quality bottle being produced (Coke saves 2.5 cents in production costs by producing the prone-to-explosion bottle but only pays 2 cents more in insurance costs). On average, both the consumer and the producer are worse of in comparison to the case where Coke is liable (since Coke is the cheaper insurer, by assumption).

For completeness, let us consider the contrary case, where the consumer is the cheaper insurer – the cost of insurance being 2 cents to the consumer and 3 cents to the producer.

---

[5] The reasons for one side being a cheaper insurer than the other will be discussed more thoroughly in Chapter 27 on insurance.

[6] If liability by the manufacturer involves court costs and these court costs are high, then the consumer may be the cheaper insurer even though the consumer's behavior has no effect on the damage rate.

If the law requires Coke to be liable, Coke will substitute the safer but more costly bottle. Once again there may be substitution away from Coke and both the manufacturer and the consumer are worse off than would be the case if the consumer were liable.

All these examples should demonstrate that making Coke liable does not redistribute wealth from Coke to consumers since the consumer pays for the insurance via a higher price. At most, making Coke liable redistributes income from those who do not have bottles exploding in their faces to those who do but would not have purchased insurance if Coke were not liable. When Coke is liable, everyone pays a higher price for the Coke because of the added insurance. Only those consumers who have bottles exploding in their faces benefit from this insurance (and only if they would not have purchased insurance on their own if they were liable).

C. CONCLUDING REMARKS

In an earlier chapter, we considered automobile accidents where the choice of liability rule is extremely important because the participants cannot bargain beforehand. In such high transaction cost situations, when the injurer is not liable, the injurer has little incentive to take care. Therefore, the legal system needs to impose some form of liability on the injurer (negligence liability if the activity is justified; strict liability if it is not clear whether the activity should be undertaken in the first place).

In this chapter, the Coke bottle example yields a contrary intuition. We have assumed that only Coke can affect the likelihood and severity of an exploding bottle. Nevertheless, when Coke is not liable for the damage, Coke still has the appropriate incentive to provide the optimal amount of care as long as consumers accurately judge the expected damage. The Coase theorem works with a vengeance. Even when reputations are not completely accurate, these incentives still exist. There is less need to protect the victim via regulation or strict liability when the participants are engaged in an implicit or explicit contractual relationship.

To illustrate the argument, we have used an example of an exploding bottle of Coca-Cola. The explosion may result in personal injury, in a rug being stained, or merely in the bottle of Coca-Cola being no longer useful for consumption. A similar analysis can be applied to less-explosive situations. An air-conditioner may stop working or catch fire; and a contractor may not finish a job on time. In all of these cases, there is some kind of harm.

For the most part, courts have used default rules when there is no personal injury. That is, the courts allow the contracting parties to rewrite the contract if the parties believe that the default rules are suboptimal. But when an item is manufactured and a person is injured, the courts are more likely to impose their will and not allow default rules. Sometimes, the producer is liable only if there is a design defect. This sounds like a negligence rule, and, if applied properly, such a rule makes sense – we want the producer to be liable when the producer has taken less than the optimal amount of precaution in its design. However, at other times, the court may insist on strict liability by the producer in the absence of contributory negligence by the victim. The overriding rationale is that the manufacturer is the cheaper insurer as it can spread the risk of injury over its many customers.

The logic is clearly elucidated in *Escola v. Coca-Cola Bottling Co.*, 150 P.2d 436 (1944). Escola, a waitress in a restaurant, was injured when a bottle of Coca-Cola broke in her hand. Judge Traynor stated in a concurring opinion: "Even if there is no negligence... public policy demands that responsibility be fixed wherever it will most effectively reduce the hazards to life and health... Those who suffer injury... are unprepared to meet its consequences.... Against such a risk there should be general and constant protection and the manufacturer is best situated to afford such protection.... The risk of injury can be insured by the manufacturer and distributed among the public as a cost of doing business.... The manufacturer's liability should, of course, be defined in terms of the safety of the product in normal and proper use."

In a nutshell, Judge Traynor argued that when it comes to exploding soda bottles, the manufacturer is the cheaper insurer. However, it is not at all clear that this is in fact the case. The consumer can buy a medical and/or disability policy that insures the consumer against injury from a variety of risks – manufactured, genetic, and just plain clumsiness. Making the manufacturer liable may be a more costly method of insuring the consumer, especially because manufacturer liability often involves lawyers (we will get back to this issue in later chapters). Finally, if Coke were truly the least-cost provider of insurance, Coke would not have to be forced to provide it.

SUGGESTIONS FOR FURTHER READING

Klein and Leffler (1981) and Rogerson (1983) discuss the importance of reputation in promoting quality. For a critical review of Judge Traynor's argument in *Coca-Cola v. Escola*, see Epstein (1985). All the articles in this issue of the *Journal of Legal Studies* are devoted to products liability and are also of interest. Many special rules have been established for determining whether the producer is liable. Boyd and Ingberman (1997) consider products liability rules (such as "customary practice" and "state of the art") and their effect on safety.

REVIEW QUESTIONS

1. Define: default rule (2) and exculpatory clause (2). Provide some examples. (2)
2. When exculpatory clauses are allowed, why are courts virtually incapable of affecting either the distribution of wealth or the outcome? (2)
3. Compare a legal regime that says that the producer is strictly liable for actual damage to the consumer to a regime that says that the producer is not at all liable for damage to the consumer. Compare levels of safety under the two regimes; also discuss who pays for insurance. Assume that the consumer's behavior has no effect on the probability of damage (e.g., a Coke bottle).
   (A) Assume that exculpatory clauses are allowed and consumers and producers are perfectly informed about all risks. (4).
   (B) Assume that exculpatory clauses are not allowed, that consumers and producers are perfectly informed about all risks, and that each side is able to obtain insurance at the actuarially fair rate (that is, it costs x dollars in insurance premiums to cover x dollars in expected damage). (10)
   (C) Assume that exculpatory clauses are not allowed, that consumers and producers are perfectly informed about all risks, and that one side is able to obtain insurance at the actuarially fair rate but the other cannot. (10)

4. A flu epidemic forces the schools to close. Should the teachers or the school district be liable for the lost wages? What difference does it make if exculpatory clauses are allowed? What differences does it make if exculpatory clauses are not allowed either way? Explain. (10)

5. In *Helling v. Carey*, 519 P.2d 981 (1974), the court found ophthalmologist Carey liable for Helling's undiagnosed and therefore untreated glaucoma. Defendant Carey testified that the standard for the profession was to not test for glaucoma for people under 40 years old, as the incidence for this age group was 1 in 25,000. Helling was 32 at the time of her visit. Suppose that harm to people under the age of 40 when they have glaucoma and are not treated is $1 million. Suppose further that cost of the test is $20. Who should be liable under these assumptions? (5)

REFERENCES

Boyd, James, and Daniel Ingberman. (1997). Should Relative Safety Be a Test of Product Liability? 26 *Journal of Legal Studies* 433.

Epstein, Richard A. (1985). Products Liability as an Insurance Market. 14 *Journal of Legal Studies* 645.

Klein, Benjamin, and Keith B. Leffler. (1981). The Role of Market Forces in Insuring Contractual Performance. 89 *Journal of Political Economy* 615.

Rogerson, William P. (1983). Reputation and Product Quality. 14 *Bell Journal of Economics* 508.

25 The Role of Asymmetric Information

A. Neither Side Is Informed 240

B. Consumers Differ in their Knowledge 241

C. Adverse Selection 241

D. Malpractice 242

    1. Patients Are Fully Informed 242
    2. Patients Cannot Identify Negligent Doctors 243

E. Concluding Remarks 243

SUGGESTIONS FOR FURTHER READING 244

REVIEW QUESTIONS 245

REFERENCE 245

In the previous chapter, we demonstrated that even when no exculpatory clauses are allowed and hence there are limits on free contracting, the law is incapable of redistributing income from Coke to the consumers or vice versa. The law only determines which side will be the insurer. If both sides are equally good insurers, then the law has no effect on the allocation of resources either. The assignment of liability has no affect on the safety of the bottles produced. However, if one side is a better insurer and the law requires that the inferior insurer be liable (that is, provide insurance), then there will be an inefficient allocation of resources in comparison to a regime where the superior insurer provides the insurance. This is an important result. It says that court-imposed *mandatory* rules regarding liability can never make the outcome better than it would be in the absence of mandatory rules, but mandatory rules may make things worse.

These results are based on a model. Like any model, certain simplifying assumptions are made to make the analysis easier. For example, we have assumed that consumers know the likelihood of damage. But consumers may not have this information. Consider the example of the person who chooses a surgeon out of the yellow pages. This person may not know that in the past the surgeon has operated on a patient's left leg when it was the right leg that needed surgery (see box later in this chapter). This chapter is devoted to exploring issues arising from consumer lack of information.

Before proceeding, one caveat is in order. The issues considered in this chapter should be seen as refinements of the basic model discussed in the previous chapter rather than as a substitute analysis. The results of the basic model are a good first-order approximation and the starting point for a more complicated analysis. The burden of proof is on those who want to overthrow the model. It is not sufficient to show merely counterexamples. One needs to show that the basic model does not have a major role in explaining behavior.

As a general rule, economists like exculpatory clauses or free contracting because utility-maximizing individuals should be allowed to contract for what is best for them. The most efficient allocation of resources is likely to occur. One can argue that exploding Coke bottles have few third-party effects (e.g., moral externalities) so that government intervention on the behalf of third parties is not necessary.[1] In the absence of third-party effects, what might be the reason for not allowing exculpatory clauses? The best reason is asymmetric information.

A. NEITHER SIDE IS INFORMED

Before discussing the problem of asymmetric information, it is useful to consider the possibility that neither side is informed. In the absence of Coke being liable, neither the producer nor the consumer might know the probability of damage. Some or most of the consumers might not notify Coke of damage from the exploding bottle if consumers were not compensated. In this way, liability by the producer might produce more information for both sides than no liability. That is, the legal system in general and lawyers

---

[1] Insurance may cause third-party effects. If people have hospitalization insurance, they may not be as cautious in choosing soda bottles because some of the cost of the explosion falls on the other members of the insurance pool. These "others" would prefer that the appropriate bottle be chosen in order to keep down their insurance rates. One method is to not insure people who drink from cheap bottles (just as sky divers are often not able to obtain life insurance). Alternatively, the members of the pool might want laws to be passed that prevented cheap bottles from being sold.

and their clients in particular may encourage the production of useful information. Of course, such information is costly to obtain and one always needs to weigh such costs against the benefits and at the same time ask whether there are cheaper ways to obtain the information.

B. CONSUMERS DIFFER IN THEIR KNOWLEDGE

Consider the case where Coke has an accurate assessment of the likelihood and extent of damage, but half the consumers believe that there is a zero chance of damage and the other half believe that the probability of damage is twice as likely as it really is so that on average consumers have an unbiased estimate of the expected damage. Despite my comments in Section A, this asymmetric information in favor of Coke is probably realistic. I worked in a soda-bottling plant and bottles exploded on occasion; so, Coke would not be surprised that consumers have bottles explode in their face, as well.

Again, for expositional purposes, let us assume that the safe bottle never explodes. Assuming that Coke has the requisite information, if Coke is liable and exculpatory clauses are *not* allowed, it will provide the most efficient outcome, which might be a safer but more expensive bottle or a less safe bottle with higher insurance costs. Either way, the full cost of Coke is reflected in the purchase price.

If Coke is liable but exculpatory clauses are allowed, those consumers who overestimate the expected damage will still want to have Coke liable (and Coke will provide either the safer bottle or the less-safe bottle with insurance). However, those consumers who underestimate the expected damage will mistakenly buy the uninsured slimmer bottle with an exculpatory clause, making themselves liable because they do not think that the extra cost of either a fatter bottle or an insured bottle is worth the price. At the time of purchase, they underestimate the cost of Coke because the damage comes later. Not allowing exculpatory clauses prevents these overly optimistic people from making a mistake when they fail to buy insurance. This is a paternalism argument: exculpatory clauses are not allowed to prevent a minority of people from making mistakes. *Other things being equal, we want the more informed party to make the decisions and this will be the case when the more informed party is held liable.*

C. ADVERSE SELECTION

Asymmetric information can also take place across brands. Assume that Coca-Cola produces bottles that never explode and that Coke has a 50% share of the market for soft drinks and that Croaka-Cola (not a registered trademark), which has cornered the other 50% of the market, produces bottles that explode .0004% of the time causing $10,000 worth of damage (otherwise, the brands are identical).[2] Assume also that the consumers cannot distinguish between Coke and Croak and think that bottles from both companies are likely to explode .0002% of the time. This is known as adverse selection. If consumers are liable and they self-insure, then they will not be able to determine

---

[2] To keep the analysis as simple as possible, assume that only Coke knows how to produce the safer bottle and that it does not cost Coke anything extra to produce the safer bottle. Again for heuristic purposes, assume that pricing is competitive with price equal to marginal cost. In this way, we need not worry about downward sloping demand curves.

the relative safety of Coke and Croak.[3] The cost of damage will only be revealed after purchase, when the bottle either does or does not explode. Half will be buying Croak, although they would not if they were fully informed. If the manufacturers are liable, Coke will sell for 4 cents less than Croak (because the cost of insurance is reflected in the price), allowing the consumers to make the correct choice. Hence, one might want to argue that soft drink manufactures should be liable and that no exculpatory clauses should be allowed.

However, there are counters to this argument. Coke itself might advertise that its bottles are safer, and if its advertising were not believed, it might offer liability insurance to its customers. Croak would not be able to match the offer at the same price.

In a nutshell, when there is asymmetry in knowledge in favor of the producer, there is greater reason for the producer to be liable. But the argument in favor of liability is probably as not as strong as one might think at first because even in the absence of forced liability, the safer producer will want to offer the consumer insurance if it is cost effective to do so.

D. MALPRACTICE

The exploding Coke bottle is a paradigm for those cases where the consumer's behavior (beyond the purchase itself) has little effect on the outcome. Other examples include the transmission of HIV in blood transfusions and the removal of the wrong organ by a surgeon.[4] Doctors often complain about the negative impact of malpractice claims, and they have considerable antipathy toward the lawyers that pursue such claims in court. But what does economics tell us? Our answer will proceed from the simple to the complex.

1. Patients Are Fully Informed

Assume first that legal transaction costs are minor so that the transaction cost of doctors insuring patients is low and that patients are informed regarding the quality of their doctors.[5] This is parallel to the first Coke example in the last chapter. Under this assumption, the existence of malpractice liability does not affect the price of medicine to any significant degree. Malpractice is basically just another word for negligence. Regardless of who is liable, doctors, in general, would want to undertake cost-effective prevention; that is, they would have the appropriate incentives to be nonnegligent.

In the absence of malpractice liability, those doctors who are known to be negligent (perhaps they are incompetent) would have to charge less for their services. If their negligence caused greater damage than the benefit from their doctoring, negligence-prone doctors would go out of business.

In the presence of malpractice liability, patients are willing to pay higher fees to substitute for the patient self-insuring, purchasing insurance, or facing uninsured risk. Suppose that patients do not have a separate insurance policy. Then the main effect

---

[3] If consumers buy their insurance from some other party and the insurance is specifically targeted toward the purchase (unlikely) as airplane accident insurance is, the insurer might know the relative risk for Coke and Croak. This would be reflected in insurance rates and consequently the asymmetric information would disappear.

[4] Malpractice is in a different area of law from products liability, but the underlying economic logic is the same.

[5] We ignore the issues that arise because of the pervasive existence of health insurance (e.g., people may be insensitive to price, when their insurer pays all).

of malpractice liability is a shifting of the burden from the few patients harmed to all patients of the negligence-prone doctors. Under malpractice liability, patients pay an implicit insurance premium when they visit negligence prone doctors in comparison to a situation of no liability by the doctor (however, the patients would not want to pay more than they would for doctors that are never negligent). Doctors who are never negligent would not be affected by the patient's right to sue for malpractice. Negligence-prone doctors would either have an incentive to improve their performance or, if incompetent, go out of business if the damage and subsequent liability was greater than the benefit from being a doctor.

2. Patients Cannot Identify Negligent Doctors

To grasp the underlying logic, we initially assumed that patients could identify negligent doctors. But this assumption is not always realistic. Although patients may ask their own doctor and other patients about the reliability of a surgeon, this information is costly to obtain and imperfect. As a consequence, it is often difficult for patients to distinguish between good doctors and negligence-prone doctors. Thus, there is the potential for adverse selection.

Suppose that doctors could not be sued for malpractice. If patients *cannot distinguish between good and bad doctors*, then in the absence of malpractice liability, negligent doctors could shift the cost of their negligence onto their unsuspecting patients (and indirectly onto nonnegligent doctors). Patients would pay the same price for both types of doctors but face greater risk from the negligence-prone doctor.

In contrast, when doctors are liable for malpractice, negligent doctors face the cost of their negligence. Thus, malpractice liability by the doctor not only serves as an insurance policy to the patient but also provides clearer incentives to the doctor. If malpractice insurance premiums paid by the doctor are reasonably experience rated or based on monitoring of the particular doctor's qualifications and behavior, then inefficient behavior by the doctor will result in higher insurance cost to the doctor.[6] In this way, incompetent doctors pay for their inefficiency – the problems arising from asymmetry in information are reduced when the informed (in this case, the incompetent doctors) must pay for their incompetence.

E. CONCLUDING REMARKS

In the absence of malpractice liability, patients might have a hard time distinguishing between Dr. Coak and Dr. Croak. Malpractice liability improves the ability of patients to distinguish between the two. When patients are imperfectly informed, malpractice liability also improves the incentives for doctors and hospitals to take care. But this insurance system involves high court costs.[7] Lawyers are expensive and legal error may arise (juries may find nonnegligent doctors "negligent" and negligent doctors "not negligent"). In turn, this means that doctors and hospitals may undertake "defensive medicine" (that is, excessive care). All these costs are ultimately reflected in the price of the medical services. If the costs are too high, the service may not be offered at all

---

[6]   Malpractice insurance is generally experience rated to the class of practitioners rather than the individual doctor. However, excessively bad experience may possibly prevent the doctor from obtaining malpractice insurance.

[7]   To avoid some of these excessive court costs, hospitals may require patients to arbitrate certain disputes.

TAKE CARE IN CHOOSING YOUR DOCTOR

Ricardo Romero was having back trouble. So he went to Dr. Merrimon Baker, an orthopedic surgeon. Unfortunately, Dr. Baker did not disclose the following to Romero: that he left a surgical sponge inside one patient's body, operated on another patient's left leg instead of the right leg, and operated on the wrong hip of a third patient. Nor were there any signs in his office stating that his ex-wife divorced him because he was addicted to painkillers, that he had been sued for malpractice numerous times, or that he had lost privileges to perform surgery at two hospitals.

In 1998, Romero went into the hospital to have a herniated disk repaired by Dr. Baker. The operation went awry and he nearly bled to death on the operating table, suffering serious brain damage. Now, he can barely walk or see and needs help feeding himself. Romero and his family sued several entities, including the hospital in which the surgery was performed. Romero alleged that the hospital "acted with malice by credentialing Baker to practice medicine at the hospital – even though it knew that he abused prescription drugs and was an incompetent surgeon." The jury awarded Romero a total of $40 million. The hospital was found liable for $12 million in punitive damages and for more than $11 million in actual damages. The hospital appealed, claiming that no sufficient legal or factual evidence was presented to support a claim of malicious credentialing. In *KPH Consolidation, Inc. v. Romero*, 102 S.W.3d 135 (2003), the Texas Appeals Court agreed with the hospital and reversed the awards for punitive and actual damages and sent the case back for a retrial.

Update: In May 2005, the Texas Supreme Court backed the appellate court decision. Dr. Baker is still affiliated with several hospitals in the Houston area. Some Web sites claim that Romero found Dr. Baker in the yellow pages, but the appellate record says that Romero got a referral from another doctor.

because patients (or their insurance companies) may not be willing to pay for the high price.

Although doctors and hospitals are subject to malpractice (negligence), they are not subject to strict liability as is more or less the case for Coca-Cola. Suppose that they were. Then, as we have argued throughout these last two chapters, the patient would have to pay for this insurance policy. Hospitals would have to spend time evaluating the prospects for each patient to determine the appropriate price. Patients who were likely to die would have to pay enormous sums for medical care, and if they did die, the money would go back to their estate. The law is not always efficient, but it is unlikely to be so absurd.

Finally, one should always be aware of the symmetry in our analysis. Although the examples in this chapter assume that the producer or provider is better informed than the consumer, it is possible that the consumer has superior information (see the following chapter). In which case, the symmetric argument applies.

SUGGESTIONS FOR FURTHER READING

See Landes and Posner (1987) who claim that consumers tend to be misinformed about low probability events. They argue in favor of strict liability when there is a risk of serious injury and the consumer has little effect on the probability of an injury occurring.

REVIEW QUESTIONS

1. Compare a legal regime that says that the producer is strictly liable for actual damage to the consumer to a regime that says that the producer is not at all liable for damage to the consumer. Compare levels of safety under the two regimes; also discuss who pays for insurance and the choice between insurance and greater safety. Assume that the consumer's behavior has no effect on the probability of damage.

   (a) Assume that exculpatory clauses are allowed, that consumers are imperfectly informed about risks (half overestimate and half underestimate) and that producers and consumers are able to obtain insurance at the actuarially fair rate if they choose to do so. (10)

   (b) Assume that exculpatory clauses are not allowed, that consumers are imperfectly informed about risks (half overestimate and half underestimate) and that producers and consumers are able to obtain insurance at the actuarially fair rate if they choose to do so. (10)

2. What problems arise when consumers cannot distinguish the differences in product quality between two manufacturers? How will the high quality manufacturer respond? (10)

REFERENCE

Landes, William M., and Richard A. Posner. (1987). *The Economic Structure of Tort Law.* Cambridge, MA: Harvard University Press.

26 Consumers and Producers Cause Damage: Lawnmowers

A. Efficient Contracts 248

B. The Problem with Strict Liability 249

C. Automobile Warranties 249

D. Monopoly and Exploitation Theories 250

E. Concluding Remarks 250

SUGGESTIONS FOR FURTHER READING 252

REVIEW QUESTIONS 252

REFERENCES 253

A lawnmower accident may occur because the mower was poorly designed or because the person was careless. The lawnmower company cannot ex ante discriminate among buyers.[1] For example, it cannot refuse to sell to careless buyers or charge careless buyers a higher price (as is the case with insurance companies who can either refuse to insure high risks or charge them a higher price).[2] The lawnmower example is thus different in two ways from the Coke bottle example. Here, both sides are important variables in the production of the potential damage, but only one side can choose with whom she does business.

A. EFFICIENT CONTRACTS

Once again, this is a low transaction cost case, and, consequently, when exculpatory clauses are allowed, the (initial) assignment of liability will have no effect on the actual (final) assignment of liability. For example, if the court's default rule assigns liability to the manufacturer and the manufacturer's profits are higher when it does not have a tie-in insurance sale, then the manufacturer will just put a tag on the mower saying that it is not liable.

What would the efficient contract look like? Certainly, it would not make the lawn-mower manufacturer liable for all damage. If the manufacturer were liable for all damage, then the purchaser would be less likely to undertake the optimal amount of prevention.[3] For example, when the manufacturer is liable for all damage to the blades, some owners may exercise less than the optimal amount of precaution in avoiding rocks. If the manufacturer were liable for blades broken in this way, the cost of lawnmowers would be excessively high (the cost to the purchasers would be more than the benefit from not having to avoid rocks).

On the other side, the company might offer an insurance policy for damage arising from certain types of lawnmower failure where the consumer has little impact on the likelihood or extent of damage. If it were relatively cheap for the company to prevent a blade from flying through the air and causing damage and users could do little to prevent such failures, then the company would produce the safe blade and insure customers against damage from flying blades. The cost of the insurance policy would be quite low because flying blades would be quite rare. The insurance policy would be especially good selling point if customers were not able to ascertain the likelihood of flying blades from simple (costless) inspection. Thus we see that there is likely to be some insurance but not complete coverage, the extent of insurance again depending on which side is the cheaper insurer.

If court costs are low, then the allocation of liability between the manufacturer and the customer would be similar to a negligence rule. The manufacturer would be liable for those items in which it was cost effective for the manufacturer to provide precaution (the flying blade), while the customer would be liable for damage that resulted from

---

[1] The seller might be able to distinguish after the accident whether the person was careless or not. For example, a court might be able to determine that the lost toe occurred because the person was mowing the lawn in her bare feet.

[2] The lawnmower company is facing adverse selection.

[3] The suboptimal provision of precautionary measures by the consumer when insured (that is, when the manufacture is strictly liable) is known as "moral hazard."

less than the optimal amount of care by the customer (breaking blades by mowing over rocks).

B. THE PROBLEM WITH STRICT LIABILITY

But what would happen if the manufacturers of lawnmowers were strictly liable (and no exculpatory clauses were allowed)? Then consumers would take less than optimal care when using their lawnmowers ($y < y^{\Omega}$). Those people who were careful would be forced to pay for those who were careless through higher prices for lawnmowers because of higher insurance costs. More important, the manufacturer would at the margin substitute costly design elements that reduce either the probability or extent of damage. While at first blush this might appear desirable, what it means is that the lawnmower is of higher quality than is appropriate on efficiency grounds ($x > x^{\Omega}$). In a nutshell, if lawnmower manufacturers were strictly liable, individuals would not take as great a care as they should, particularily so when the damage is to physical property or the lawnmower itself, because the cost is shifted onto others (moral hazard). The careful would pay for the careless, not only by paying for the added cost of insurance but also by paying extra for a lawnmower built for idiots. If the cost were too high, consumers might forego the purchase of a new lawnmower and stick with the old dangerous mower (or perhaps get a goat instead).

So, if one really had the consumers' interest in mind, one would prefer a regime where consumers were liable for damage from or to lawnmowers over a regime where the manufacturers were strictly liable! Making manufacturers of lawnmowers strictly liable does not shift wealth to consumers, rather it shifts wealth away from both the average consumer and the manufacturer. Of course, the choice need not be restricted to strict liability or no liability by the manufacturer. Negligent rules such as the following could be applied: the manufacturer is liable unless the consumer was negligent or the consumer is liable unless the manufacturer was negligent (because of a design defect, for example).

C. AUTOMOBILE WARRANTIES

Automobile warranties illustrate many of the arguments made in the previous sections. Manufacturers never warrant that their cars won't run out of gas. Suppose they did. Then drivers would be less likely to watch the fuel gauge and manufacturers would be paying for fuel deliveries. Ultimately, consumers would pay for this warranty. It seems that most drivers would prefer that they not have an unlimited access (even automobile clubs only allow for a very limited number of such calls). The customer is generally liable for all scratches to the paint on the car once the car has been driven off the lot. While the manufacturer could conceivably increase the scratch resistance of paint, it is the customer who is best at preventing scratches. So making the manufacturer liable for all scratches would create the incorrect incentives and the costs would not be worth it to most consumers. However, the manufacturer typically warrants the engine as long as oil is added at appropriate intervals and the car is not used for racing (the manufacturer is liable unless the customer is negligent). Finally, the manufacturer warrants the air-conditioner unless the owner has worked on it. Compared with a paint job, there is little that the owner can do that will affect the working of the air-conditioner (except turning it on) if the owner does not open the mechanism. So it makes sense that the manufacturer would be liable.

D. MONOPOLY AND EXPLOITATION THEORIES

I have used economic efficiency to explain the allocation of liability in contractual relationships. One might want to compare this explanation with the "market power explanation." I use quotes because the market power explanation is often fallacious. The market power explanation says that the lawnmower manufacturers take advantage of the consumer by offering her less than she wants (shoddy goods or inadequate warranties – sometimes termed *contracts of adhesion*). Elsewhere the market power explanation claims that firms force tie-in arrangements (e.g., you have to buy CPU, keyboard, and monitor when you buy an iMac) – more than she wants. However, if the consumer is willing to pay more for something (quality, insurance, or other amenity) than the extra cost of producing it, then the firm will provide it; and if the consumer is not willing to pay for the extra cost, then the firm will not provide it. *If there is market power, it is exploited through price, not through quality.*

The empirical evidence is also strongly against the exploitation theory. The ordinary consumer with little countervailing market power often gets a warranty, although those with considerable market power often do not, despite the fact that they can get products for lower prices than ordinary consumers. For example, consumer warranties on washing machines often expressly state that the warranty does not hold if the item is used for commercial purposes. Laundries have more market power than consumers as laundries may buy dozens of washing machines at a time, but they do not get similar warranties. Of course, this makes sense. Commercial washing machines are used much more intensively than family washing machines and therefore are more likely to break down.

The same holds within the legal system. Although some have argued that large corporations control the legal system at the expense of the ordinary consumer, the evidence is to the contrary for product liability cases. Company A may not be liable to company B for damage arising from the use of A's products, although company A may be liable to consumer C for damage arising from the use of A's products. The exploitation theory would predict the opposite – that A would be liable to B but not to C, but this rarely, if ever, occurs. Again there are good reasons for the differential treatment. Consumers are not expected to be as knowledgeable as those who deal with equipment as professionals.

E. CONCLUDING REMARKS

To a noneconomist, it may seem amoral to make cost-benefit calculations when the choice involves the possibility of death or serious injury, but individuals, governments, and businesses make such calculations every day. Individuals decide whether to drive

SHOULD CAR TRUNKS HAVE INTERNAL RELEASE MECHANISMS?

In *Daniell v. Ford Motor Co.*, 581 F. Supp. 728 (1984), the plaintiff tried to commit suicide by locking herself into the trunk of a Ford LTD. She changed her mind about the suicide, but she remained in the trunk for nine days, suffering psychological and physical damage. Daniell argued that not having an internal release mechanism was a design defect. The court held that it was virtually impossible to unintentionally lock oneself into a trunk, and therefore it made no sense for Ford to account for such a possibility in its design.

The above is an easy case to solve. But consider the following: hundreds of people have jumped off the Golden Gate Bridge. A netlike barrier could be placed below the bridge to save people trying to commit suicide. Should the relatives of the suicide victim be able to sue the Golden Gate Bridge authority for not installing such a barrier?

RIDING A LAWNMOWER IN REVERSE

A father who ran over and injured his son while riding backward on a lawnmower sued the manufacturer, Sears Roebuck, alleging strict liability and negligence. In *Brown v. Sears, Roebuck & Co.*, 328 F.3d 1274 (2003), the 10th Circuit agreed with a Utah federal court that Sears was entitled to summary judgment (a summary judgment occurs when the facts are so clear and one-sided that a trial is not needed). The trial court found that Sears had provided clear warnings about the potential for accidents involving small children, that expert testimony concerning safety devices refuted the defective design theory, and that the operator was at fault.

with worn tires or cars without airbags. Few people drive tanks although they are safer in most crashes. Governments could hire more traffic police, thereby making driving safer, but they choose to spend their revenues elsewhere.

Although businesses do not like to make it public, they often explicitly engage in such cost-benefit analyses. According to court documents, General Motors calculated that putting a shield on some gas tanks would cost $13 more per car, but save only $5 per car in liability due to fewer burns from exploding gas tanks.[4] Although GM tried very hard to hide the fact that they undertook such cost-benefit calculations[5] and many

---

[4] Unfortunately for General Motors their figures were way off – when they chose not to put in the shield, their additional liability was much higher than $13 per car.

[5] In *Cameron v. General Motors*, No. 3-93-1278-07 (D.S.C.), GM shredded important documents and GM lawyers, including Kenneth Starr (the special prosecutor of President Clinton), were alleged to have engaged in obstruction of justice to hide the relevant cost-benefit calculations. In a 1999 California case, *Anderson v. General Motors*, the jury was so disgusted with the same cost-benefit calculations that the jury awarded $4.9 billion in punitive damages. The trial judge later reduced the punitive damages to $1.09 billion. G.M. threatened to appeal and the sides settled for an undisclosed amount.

In an earlier case, Ford Motor Company paid punitive damages for making such cost-benefit calculation when designing the Pinto. Ford had calculated that it would cost $11 per vehicle to prevent its gas tank from being susceptible to fire and explosion in case of a crash. Ford treated the cost of a death at $200,000. The resulting cost-benefit calculations suggested that the savings in production costs would outweigh the increase in liability. These calculations came out in a trial when a boy with burns over 90% of his body sued Ford. The jury awarded the boy $2.5 million in compensatory damages and $125 million in punitive damages (later reduced to $3.5 million by the judge). See *Grimshaw v. Ford Motor Company*, 119 Cal. App. 3d 757 (1981).

LAWNMOWERS USED AT DUSK

A 7-year-old child lost function in his thumb and sustained disfigurement to his hand when it was caught in the air-intake screen of a lawnmower engine. The parents claimed that a $9.50 metal guard placed over the engine of the Dixie Chopper riding lawnmower, made by Kohler Co., would have covered all of the moving parts and prevented the accident. Kohler argued that it had sold more than nine hundred thousand of its engines without any problems, that the manufacturer of the lawnmower, Magic Circle Co. (which settled before trial), was at fault for failing to install a safety guard, and that the boy's mother should not have operated the lawnmower at dusk with her young child nearby. In January 2004, a Florida jury awarded the boy $2.6 million. The verdict was reduced because of comparative negligence and settlement setoffs. The jury found Kohler 75% at fault and Magic Circle 25 percent at fault. *Marcotte v. Kohler Co.*, No. 98-30113-CA-02 (Miami-Dade Co., Fla., Cir. Ct.).

were outraged by such calculations when they were made public, the argument here is that such cost-benefit calculations should always be made.

SUGGESTIONS FOR FURTHER READING

Further discussion of the ideas in this chapter can be found in Epple and Raviv (1978) and Priest (1981). See Geistfeld (2000) for a survey of many other issues surrounding warranties. Reform of products liability has been of great interest to economists. For different solutions, see Rubin (1991) and Viscusi (1993). For a complete survey of lawnmower accidents, see Costilla and Bishai (forthcoming). Using data from the *National Hospital Discharge Survey 1996–2003* and the *National Electronic Injury Surveillance System 1996–2004*, they found that there were more than 70,000 lawnmower accidents a year that resulted in a hospital or emergency room visit. These include injuries from flying objects, severed toes and back strain.

REVIEW QUESTIONS

1. Lawnmower manufacturers cannot distinguish ex ante between high- and low-risk consumers, but consumers can distinguish quality and safety of the lawnmower either by inspection or by reputation. Why does this make a difference? (6)
2. If exculpatory clauses are allowed, what difference does the legal regime (liability for the manufacturer or not) make on the type of lawnmowers produced, the degree of care exercised by the consumer, and the nature of the insurance policy (if any) provided? (6)
3. If exculpatory clauses are not allowed, what difference does the legal regime make on the type of lawnmowers produced and the degree of care exercised by the consumer if both sides are risk neutral and consumers are knowledgeable about the risks involved in lawnmower use. (20)
4. Should a person be liable for giving another person herpes? (10)

REFERENCES

Costilla, Vanessa, and David M. Bishai. (forthcoming). Lawnmower Injuries in the United States: 1996 to 2004. *Annals of Emergency Medicine.*

Epple, Dennis, and Artur Raviv. (1978). Product Safety: Liability Rules, Market Structure and Imperfect Information. 68 *American Economic Review* 80.

Geistfeld, Mark. (2000). Reforming Products Liability. In Boudwin Bouckaert and Gerrit De Geest (eds.), *Encyclopedia of Law and Economics.* Cheltenham: Edward Elgar. http://users.ugent.be/~gdegeest/

Priest, George L. (1981). A Theory of the Consumer Product Warranty. 90 *Yale Law Journal* 1297.

Rubin, Paul H. (1993). *Tort Reform by Contract.* Washington, DC: American Enterprise Institute.

Viscusi, W. Kip. (1991). *Reforming Products Liability.* Cambridge, MA: Harvard University Press.

IX INSURANCE AND THE LAW

Until now, our main focus has been on how the law provides the right incentives for people to undertake the optimal amount of precaution. But there may be other objectives such as allocating risk, especially when allocating risk to the party that is better able to bear such risk does not interfere to a great degree with the optimal amount of precaution being undertaken.

Risk is ever present – a person may be paralyzed from an automobile accident, die from a bee sting, or lose his or her house in a fire. Insurance reduces *monetary* risk by shifting wealth from uncertain good states of the world to uncertain bad states of the world. Thus, insurance is a much broader concept than what most people think of as insurance – buying medical or life insurance. For example, strict liability insures the victim from harm, while no liability insures the injurer from paying for damages. The takings clause insures people from the risk of their property being taken without compensation and warranties insures consumers from the risk of product failure.

In Chapter 27, we cover the essentials of insurance. For insurance to be viable, risks should not be correlated, the behavior of the insured should not change greatly in the presence of insurance (when behavior does change, it is known as moral hazard), the insurer should be able to identify those in higher risk categories, and the insurance should be provided without large administrative costs.

French and California law mandate royalties for artists when their paintings are sold for a higher price. In Chapter 28, we show that royalties insure investors but increase the risk for artists. We then show why royalties are inappropriate for the art market but are sensible for the book market.

Most states regulate insurance. In Chapter 29 we show the problems that arise when states try to regulate the automobile insurance industry so that "good drivers" pay lower premiums. We show that governments cannot abolish market forces; they just reappear in a more costly fashion.

Bank depositors in the United States are insured so that the depositors get their money back even if the bank goes bankrupt. In Chapter 31, we discuss the problems of insuring savings institutions from the perspective of the ideas developed in Chapter 27. This provides considerable insight into the banking crises that have rolled through the United States, Japan, France, and a host of other countries in recent years.

Of course, to understand fully such banking crises, we need to understand the incentives of the various actors under bankruptcy. Hence, in Chapter 30 we discuss the conflict of interest between stockholders and creditors under bankruptcy. In particular, we show that once a firm is in bankruptcy, the stockholders are insured from further loss. This creates the moral hazard discussed in Chapter 27.

27

The Market for Insurance

A. Insurance Companies Aggregate Uncorrelated Risks 258

B. Insurance Companies Try to Control for Moral Hazard 260

C. Insurance Companies Try to Control for Adverse Selection 261

D. Insurance Companies Try to Control Administrative Costs 263

**E. Insurance Companies Provide the Coverage
   That People Want** 263

   1. Nonpecuniary Damages 264
   2. Ex Ante versus Ex Post 264

F. Concluding Remarks 266

SUGGESTIONS FOR FURTHER READING 267

REVIEW QUESTIONS 267

REFERENCES 268

When most people think of insurance they think of life insurance and medical insurance, but whenever one side is liable for damage, they are insuring the other party. Hence, the question of who should be liable is often answered by determining which side is the cheaper insurer. In turn, this determination requires an understanding of the market for insurance.

Most people are risk averse when there is a potential for a *large* downside loss. Consider the following gamble: a 50% chance of losing $10,000 and a 50% chance of winning $10,002. Even though a person can expect to win $1.00 from such a gamble, few people would undertake such a bet and most would be willing to pay for insurance against having to face such a gamble. For example, a person might be willing to pay $30 to avoid this gamble. In contrast, a risk preferring person would prefer the gamble to a sure thing of $1.00; while the risk neutral person would be indifferent between the gamble and a sure thing of a $1.00. In the simple example presented here, a trade would take place between the risk neutral (or risk preferring) person and the risk averse person if the transaction costs were not too high.

Insurance shifts income from uncertain good states of the world to uncertain bad states of the world. When you buy fire insurance on your house and your house does not burn down, then you are worse off having bought insurance because you paid the premiums. If your house burns down, you are better off having bought the insurance than you would be if you had not purchased any insurance. The market for fire insurance exists because insurance companies have a comparative advantage in risk spreading and the transaction costs are relatively low. These two concepts are key to our understanding of insurance and we will now investigate them in greater detail.

A. INSURANCE COMPANIES AGGREGATE UNCORRELATED RISKS

Insurance companies try to aggregate *uncorrelated* risks. The law of large numbers makes the risk of an average loss less than the risk for a single loss. This can be illustrated by the following simple example. Suppose that there is a 50% chance of my losing $100 and a 50% chance of my losing $0 with an expected loss of $50. See the top row of the Figure 27.1. Suppose that there is another person who faces the same set of possibilities, but their outcomes are independent of mine (think of this as two independent tosses of a coin). By pooling our risks and agreeing to share equally in each other's loss, there is 25% chance of our average loss being $100, a 25% chance of our average loss being $0 and a 50% chance of our average loss being $50. Again the expected loss is $50, but the risk profile is reduced – each party is half as likely to face the $0, $100 gamble. See the second row of Figure 27.1. With four people in the insurance pool, the risk profile converges further toward the center (see the third row). This reduced risk profile means higher expected utility to the risk averse. When the number of people is one thousand, the expected loss is still $50, but the chance that the average loss is greater than $60 is very slight because the risk profile converges on the expected value. Risk-averse people prefer a less spread out risk profile and therefore will want to join in insurance pools even if there is some cost to forming them.

For mathematical clarity, we have treated the risk of a house burning down as being 50%. However, the intuitive understanding is clearer if we consider a 1/1000 chance of a $100,000 house burning down. Risk-averse people would rather be in a large insurance pool, where they would expect to pay somewhere in the neighborhood of

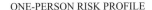

ONE-PERSON RISK PROFILE

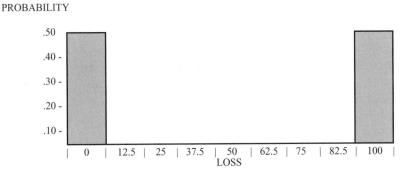

TWO-PERSON RISK PROFILE

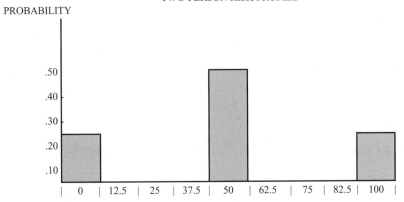

FOUR-PERSON RISK PROFILE

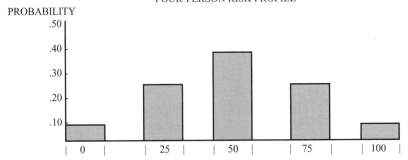

Figure 27.1. Insurance pools reduce risk.

$110, depending on whether there were fewer or more fires (the extra $10 would be for the administrative costs), than to face the uninsured risk.

Insurance companies reduce risks by pooling them and this is how they make money: they sell risk-reduction. Individuals have a much harder time diversifying their portfolio of risks. One may have a job, drive a car, own some stock and a house. The risks associated with these are likely to be uncorrelated, but the diversification is very limited. Insurance will not be purchased unless the provider of insurance has a comparative advantage in diversifying its portfolio into uncorrelated risks.

It is difficult to insure when risks are correlated. Insurance companies do not sell insurance on your house for destruction by atomic bombs even though the probability of your house being destroyed in a war is less than the probability of it burning down. This is because the risk profile for the insurance company is the nearly the same as for the individual: when there is no war, no houses are destroyed in warfare; when there is a war (especially an atomic war), if one house is destroyed by bombs, most of the other houses are likely to be destroyed also. Trade takes place only when one side has a comparative advantage. There is little advantage to pooling risk when the risk is highly correlated across individuals, as it would be for insurance against damage from war. And of course if there is a war, the assets of the insurance company could be destroyed as well, making payment difficult if not impossible.[1] In order to reduce their exposure to correlated risks, insurance companies often sell part of their portfolios to re-insurers.

For similar reasons, the smaller the downside loss (when it does occur), the less likely that it will be insured. Individuals are much better at diversifying their own portfolio of mild bad luck. My shirt ripped, but the milk in my refrigerator did not sour as soon as I expected it to. The main reason for not insuring against such contingencies is that the insurance companies are unlikely to have a significant comparative advantage in diversifying such risks, and the transaction costs of paying premiums and filing claims is likely to swamp any remaining benefits from risk reduction.

B. INSURANCE COMPANIES TRY TO CONTROL FOR MORAL HAZARD

Insurance may create inefficient incentives. Consider what might happen if your car were fully insured against theft. Because the harm falls on the insurance company rather than on you, you might leave your car door unlocked or not park it in the garage, even though you would not be so careless if you were liable and risk neutral. The insurance term for this behavior is *moral hazard*. Moral hazard exists *when the presence of insurance reduces the person's incentive to take care below the optimal*. Earlier we saw how strict liability by drivers reduces precaution by pedestrians.

Insurance companies try to control moral hazard by requiring appropriate behavior, experience rating, and by having deductibles and coinsurance. Warranties for automobile engines hold only if the owner has serviced the engine at appropriate intervals. Many states have the rule of comparative negligence, which reduces the amount that the accident victim can collect from negligent injurers (e.g., drunken drivers) when the victim herself has been careless. Insurance companies may also monitor the inputs and charge higher prices if the person has not taken optimal precaution. For example, a house with dead bolt locks and fire alarms may have lower rates on theft and fire insurance than a house without these devices.

Insurance companies may also experience rate – those policyholders with a history of filing claims will pay a greater premium. In this way, the insured ultimately pays for her carelessness.

Health insurance companies have coinsurance when they pay only 80 percent of the doctor bills. Because some of the cost of going to the doctor falls on the patient, the patient will be more careful (than in the presence of full insurance) in deciding whether

---

[1] There are other problems with insuring a house from war damage. The probability of war can change very rapidly due to changing political circumstances and is hard to estimate the actual risks.

to go to a doctor and in choosing high-priced medical care. A deductible in an insurance policy means that the first x dollars of cost fall on the insured. If the owner of a car has a $200 deductible on his theft insurance, he will be more careful to prevent theft than he would be if there were no deductible.

The insured also want moral hazard to be controlled. When a person is engaging in moral hazard, the reduction in prevention cost is less than the increase in expected damage. The damage however is paid by the insurance company and ultimately by all of its policyholders so the person does not face the full cost of her inefficient behavior. All of the insured would prefer that there was less moral hazard by everyone because their insurance rates would be reduced by more than the benefit from their own moral hazard.

The above methods reduce but rarely eliminate moral hazard completely. Furthermore, these methods often involve a social cost – monitoring is not free. The insurance company reduces moral hazard until the cost of reducing it equals the benefit.

In analyzing the purchase of fire insurance from Allstate, it is clear that Allstate is the insurer and the homeowner is the insured. Consequently, it is moral hazard by the homeowner that must be controlled. However, in many issues in this book, and in the last three chapters in particular, either side may be the insurer. The issue then becomes: on which side is moral hazard more easily controlled. If consumers are insured by Coke against damage, then consumers may be less careful in the way they handle Coke bottles (although we have assumed in our earlier discussion that consumers had no effect on either the probability or the extent of damage). If consumers insure soft drink manufacturers against having to pay for the damage arising from exploding bottles, then soft drink manufacturers *may* face moral hazard (if they are not experience rated by the consumers) and provide cheaper but prone-to-explode bottles. So either way there is a potential for moral hazard.

Even when Coke is not liable for damage and consumers are, moral hazard by Coke is likely to be relatively small. Coca-Cola sells millions of bottles of Coke. If their bottles are likely to explode, Coke will develop a reputation for being unsafe, and consumers will shift their purchases to other brands to avoid damage. Coke, realizing this to be the case, will provide the appropriate level of care in the first place.

It is harder to prevent moral hazard on the consumer side. If some consumers are careless, Coke will not know about it ahead of time and therefore Coke will not be able to refuse selling to these careless customers or charge them a higher price. Coca-Cola might be able to determine after the fact that a consumer was careless, but such investigations are costly and not always feasible.

C. INSURANCE COMPANIES TRY TO CONTROL FOR ADVERSE SELECTION

Suppose that everyone could buy a life insurance policy for the same price and that this price was based on the average life expectancy of a 50-year-old male. Those who were older than 50 and/or expecting to die in the relatively near future would rush out to buy the insurance, and those who were young and in good health would avoid purchasing it. This is known as *adverse selection – when an insurance company does not distinguish between individuals with different levels of risk, and consequently people with higher than average expected risk, who produce a negative expected profit for the insurance company, purchase insurance more often than people with lower than average risk.* Of course, in this particular example, the insurance company could easily distinguish between high and low risk by charging more for older people and those in poor health. However, it is often difficult for the insurance company to determine whether an applicant is high or low risk. The problem of adverse selection arises when the applicant knows her risk type but not the insurance company.

It is easy to confuse moral hazard and adverse selection. Moral hazard is the change in behavior brought about by the presence of insurance. Adverse selection concerns types of people purchasing insurance. High-risk people are more likely to buy insurance even if their behavior does not change when insured.

Insurance companies try to control adverse selection by separating people into different risk pools – higher risks pay higher premiums. Life insurance companies require medical exams before someone is put in their low-risk, low-premium pool. They also ask whether the applicant is facing litigation (because losers in lawsuits are prone to commit suicide). Automobile insurance companies charge more for male drivers under age 25 because they are more likely to be in an accident.

Such separation into risk pools is inevitably imperfect. The individual typically knows more about his or her own characteristics than does the insurance company. High-risk individuals can get "cheap" insurance if the insurance company mistakenly believes that the individuals are moderate or low risk. While the insurance company can monitor ex ante (for example, have a doctor give a medical exam for those wanting to buy life insurance) or ex post (charge higher prices for those who have collected on their insurance in the past), such monitoring is costly and subject to diminishing marginal productivity.

Competition between insurance companies constantly creates the potential for adverse selection. Insurance companies try to skim off below-average risks leaving the above-average risks to other insurance companies.[2] If one insurance company discovers that young male drivers with a grade-point average of B or better in school have fewer accidents, the company can offer this group a policy at lower rates than for other young male drivers. If another insurance company does not institute the same program, they will discover that their policyholders have higher average accident costs because the low-cost policyholders with high grade-point averages have gone elsewhere.

Adverse selection can be so severe that there is complete *unraveling* and the market fails to exist. Consider bankruptcy insurance. Each company has better information than the insurance company on whether it will go bankrupt – the cost of the insurance company investigating each company's financial records and future prospects would be prohibitive. Suppose that if all firms were insured against bankruptcy, the average cost to the insurance company would be $10,000 a year. If the insurance company charged $10,000 a year for the insurance, firms with below-average expected loss would be unlikely to purchase the insurance while those with above-average expected loss would purchase the insurance, making the average loss to the insurance company greater than $10,000, say, $15,000. If in response to this situation, the insurance company raised its rates to $15,000, firms with expected bankruptcy losses below $15,000 would drop out. In response, the insurance company would again have to raise its rates. Without being able to distinguish between high- and low-risk types, the market for

---

[2] This is known as cherry picking. Just as customers in a store will sift through the cherries to get the best-tasting ones, insurance companies sift through the set of possible clients and choose those with the lowest risk.

bankruptcy insurance is likely to unravel completely so that the insurance company will always lose money no matter how high a price it charges as long as it has any customers. Hence, there is a complete absence of bankruptcy insurance outside the financial sector.[3]

The potential for adverse selection arises wherever there is insurance. When the producer is liable for damage, the producer *might not* be able to distinguish between high- and low-risk consumers, although the consumers know in which category they fall. When the consumer is liable for damage, the consumer *might not* be able to distinguish between high- and low-risk producers, although the producers know in which category they fall. Hence part of the answer to which side is the cheaper insurer depends on the comparative advantage in controlling adverse selection.

D. INSURANCE COMPANIES TRY TO CONTROL ADMINISTRATIVE COSTS

Insurance companies try to reduce the costs of administration. One method is to control the cost of damage assessment. Some manufacturers offer a seven-year warranty on their cars. They do not say that if your car breaks down before 70,000 miles you can take them to court. Stockbrokers require you to sign an agreement that disputes will be arbitrated rather than taken to court. The reason is obvious. Courts are a very expensive method of damage assessment. Insurance administrative costs are typically less than 10 percent of the amount insured. That is, more than 90 cents out of each dollar of insurance premiums goes back to the insured. In tort cases, administrative costs (mainly legal fees for both sides) are about 58 cents out of each dollar. That means that only 42 cents out of each dollar goes to the insured.[4] Usually, administrative costs are reduced still further if the person who might be hurt self-insures rather than collecting from someone else.

Insurance companies also try to contain the costs of assignment to risk pools. Insurance companies could ask drivers to undertake a drivers' test before purchasing automobile insurance. They could then charge less-skilled drivers higher rates. But this would be costly and for the most part ineffective as people would drive more carefully under test conditions. Thus such tests are rarely, if at all, administered.

Finally, insurance companies try to contain administrative costs by insuring relatively rare events. The rarer the event, the less the paperwork.

E. INSURANCE COMPANIES PROVIDE THE COVERAGE THAT PEOPLE WANT

Insurance shifts wealth from good states of the world to bad states of the world. The extent of this transfer should optimize the insured's expected utility. In private markets, an insurance company will not provide extra coverage if marginal cost to the insurance company is greater than the marginal benefit to the consumer.

One can develop a considerable amount of intuition regarding insurance if insurance companies are viewed as cooperatives trying to maximize the utility of the insured because that is what competitive pressures force profit-maximizing firms to do.

---

[3] The reason banks insure against bankruptcy is that all federally chartered banks must purchase insurance from the Federal Deposit Insurance Corporation. So the problem of adverse selection does not arise.
[4] See Tillinghast-Towers Perrin (2002). Of course, not all cases go to court.

1. Nonpecuniary Damages

Because of decreasing marginal utility of income (risk aversion), people often try to smooth out their consumption stream. That is why people save for a rainy day and buy insurance. These are pecuniary (money) motives.

The tort system often provides compensation for *nonpecuniary* damages, such as pain and suffering, even though we rarely observe similar insurance being purchased in the private sector. For example, if a child falls off a roller coaster, the parents may sue the amusement park and collect money for their child's death. Yet, we rarely observe people taking out life insurance policies on their minor children's lives. Insurance takes money from the good state (child alive) and transfers it to the bad state (child dead). Being able to sue the amusement park for the death of a child will raise the price of the tickets and thereby reduce the amount of money available when the child is alive. In general, parents would rather spend the money on their child than spend money on themselves, in the absence of the child. The tort system requires parents to pay more for amusement park tickets to cover the required insurance even though parents would prefer that their children's lives not be insured. Of course, once the tort system is in place, parents would prefer to collect the money.

While people often buy medical insurance, it is rare that they buy insurance for pain and suffering. For example, rarely, if ever, do people buy an insurance policy that provides them with a million dollars beyond the cost of medical care if they are confined to a wheelchair. Evidently, shifting of wealth to the bad state of the world reduces expected utility. That is, the person prefers to be poorer when confined to a wheelchair and richer when not confined rather than vice versa. However, in the United States, the tort system does provide such insurance by compensating for pain and suffering. So the tort system is providing insurance, which people do not want to purchase ex ante.

So why can one sue for pain and suffering even if people do not purchase such insurance otherwise? The key to understanding is to look at high transaction cost situations such as automobile accidents. To make the analysis as simple as possible let us look at cases where the victim was acting optimally (for example, those cases where automobiles hit pedestrians who were walking on sidewalks). If drivers were not charged for all of the costs that they impose on pedestrians (including nonpecuniary costs), then drivers would not undertake sufficient care. So the purpose of charging drivers for damage is not to compensate the victims (that is, provide insurance) as much as it is to encourage the driver to act optimally. Suing for nonpecuniary damages makes sense in high transaction cost cases because we want the injurer to undertake the optimal amount of precaution.

However, in the amusement park case (and in contractual cases, more generally), the owner of the amusement park already has the appropriate incentive to take care. The compensation is just serving as insurance and, as we already noted, the victim's family does not want to buy such insurance. So collecting for nonpecuniary harms makes no sense in this case.

2. Ex Ante versus Ex Post

Insurance companies provide the insurance coverage that people want to pay for ex ante and not necessarily what they want ex post. This issue is highlighted by considering medical insurance coverage by health maintenance organizations (HMOs). The debate over HMOs has been quite rancorous. Doctors tend to dislike them and politicians spend time trying to regulate them. What does economics tell us?

Health maintenance organizations can provide "Cadillac" coverage where expensive drugs are provided over marginally inferior substitute drugs, there are twenty free visits to mental health practitioner rather than five, Viagra and other drugs enabling enhanced sexual performance are provided, and high-cost experimental therapies are insured. Not surprisingly doctors and mental health care workers prefer Cadillac coverage, but what about the insured? It appears that most of the insured do not want to pay for this Cadillac coverage. HMOs are not intrinsically against providing these services. They would be willing to offer them if the increase in premiums covered the cost of the services. Evidently, those who pay for the insurance do not want to pay for such expanded coverage. Of course, it is perfectly rational to push for expanded coverage when you are actually in need of such services.

Now much of medical insurance is provided by employers, who want to save money on insurance costs, but they ultimately must deal with their employees. Employers are basically indifferent to paying $1,000 more in insurance for Cadillac coverage and $1,000 less in wages or sticking to the old Volkswagen coverage. So it is the employees that decide.

Sometimes there are a few coverage options available (where the employee pays the extra cost of the added coverage), but often only one coverage is available. In such cases, the coverage is more or less determined by the preferences of the average or median employee and those who want more or less coverage are dissatisfied. Those who want more coverage tend to be the most dissatisfied, often because they know that they need the extended coverage.

So why aren't a variety of coverage options available to satisfy the desires of the various individuals? We are back to our old nemesis, adverse selection. All employees are eligible for all plans and cannot be screened out or charged a higher insurance premium based on their medical history. Those who are willing to purchase the Cadillac coverage are most likely to need the coverage. This raises the rates above what they would have been in the absence of adverse selection. Now with the higher rates, the low end drops out again, raising the rates still further. The price may be too high and continue to unravel. For example, at the University of California, in 1999, the "Volkswagen" HMO coverage (which is closer to a Cadillac than a Volkswagen and in any event Volkswagens aren't all that cheap anymore) cost the employer $1,750 a year and the employee nothing; the "Cadillac" non-HMO health insurance policy (which still has many restrictions on medical procedures but not on the doctors chosen) cost the employer $1,750 a year and the employee $9,084. We can see adverse selection at work by looking at the recent history of this non-HMO plan. In 1995, the yearly employee cost was $3,240, but the plan lost money and the company increased its rates; in 1997, the yearly employee cost was $4560, so the low-risk employees dropped and switched to the cheaper HMO plan; by 1999, the yearly employee cost was $9,084. During this same time period the HMO premiums increased by only $192.[5] The adverse selection occurs because the

---

[5] In 2006, the employee contribution for the HMO family plan was about $244 a *month* while the non-HMO high-option plan was $4,120 a month (or nearly $50,000 a year). During this time, medical costs rose and the composition of these plans changed, but these numbers are indicative.

$70,000,000 LEGS

According to the February 6, 2005, edition of *Parade Magazine* and a number of gossip Web sites, soccer star David Beckham's legs are insured for $70 million. If true, the insurance policy could be more than a publicity stunt as Beckham's income depends to a great extent on his legs. Such insurance reduces his income risk.

THE MIRROR OF ADVERSE SELECTION

Recall that in many states a homeowner is *required* by law to notify the buyer of latent defects (such as leaking roofs). Suppose that there was no such law. How would the outcome change? In the absence of transaction costs, there would be no difference! The seller of the house wants to get the highest price possible. Those who own houses without latent defects would offer to sign a contract stating this to be the case. In this way, the owner would get a higher price than otherwise because the buyer would no longer face the risk of needing to repair for such defects. Sellers who do not offer to sign such contracts implicitly admit that their houses have such defects. Potential buyers can infer this to be the case and will pay less for houses that do not come with such contracts. But some homes have more costly defects and others have less costly defects. Sellers of homes with below-average defects will want to distinguish themselves from sellers of homes with above-average defects by providing contracts listing all the defects. In this way, such homeowners will get more than they would if they had not done so (but still less than they would have gotten if the home had no defects). This process will continue until all homes with latent defects, except for the very worst, have provided contracts listing the defects. And of course, all buyers can infer the level of latent defects for the exception. This unraveling is the mirror of adverse selection. In this example, the good risks distinguish themselves to the buyer by their willingness to sign a contract. The unraveling assumes that all people will act in the manner suggested; because this need not be the case, unraveling will be promoted if the law requires disclosure.

insurance company cannot charge high-risk employees more than low-risk employees for company-wide insurance plans.

F. CONCLUDING REMARKS

Insurance reduces risk but at a cost. Whenever there is insurance, there is the potential for moral hazard and adverse selection; also, there are administrative costs. As we saw in earlier chapters, a major justification for products liability is to insure the consumer against risk. But the high cost of insuring people via the courts suggests that this is not a very good method of insuring people. Furthermore, individuals are not inclined to buy the kinds of insurance provided for in products liability, such as pain and suffering. This means that consumers are often paying for insurance that they do not want.

The issue of insurance arises in many areas of the law and in the next few chapters we will make use of the basic framework provided in this chapter to analyze some of these areas in greater detail.

TAKINGS

Recall from an earlier chapter that the U.S. Constitution requires the government to compensate owners for taking private property. One reason for doing so is that such compensation insures citizens from risk. Private companies insure against all kinds of risk. So why not have these private insurance companies insure against government takings instead of the government? The answer is adverse selection. In comparison to insurance companies, city residents are more likely to know which property the city government plans to take. Those residents who are likely to be affected would buy the takings insurance from the insurance company; while others would not bother buying such insurance. Another reason for having the government pay for the taking of private property is that this encourages the government to take into account the costs of its actions.

Government compensation generally ignores moral hazard. The government compensates for improvements to the land even if such investments should not have taken place because a taking was imminent. As a result, property owners may undertake improvements even when it is not economically efficient to do so.

SUGGESTIONS FOR FURTHER READING

Kenneth Arrow's essays on insurance and risk (1974) is the seminal work on the subject. George Akerlof (1970) showed the problem of adverse selection and unraveling in the used-car market (and, by analogy, in other markets, as well). In particular, he showed why used cars tend to be "lemons" and why used cars sell for much less than new cars even if they are nearly brand new. By the way, this Nobel Prize–winning article was rejected by three journals before it was accepted. Priest (1987) provides a detailed discussion of insurance and the problem with third-party insurance.

REVIEW QUESTIONS

(1) Define insurance. (2)
(2) Define and provide examples of moral hazard, adverse selection, and correlated risks. Why do insurance pools try to avoid them? How do they avoid them? (15)
(3) Define and provide examples of nonpecuniary damages. (4) Why might we not want to insure for nonpecuniary damages? (4)
(4) Define and provide examples of self-insurance, experience-rated insurance, and input-monitored insurance. (8)
(5) Suppose that scientists could determine whether you will get cancer by an analysis of your DNA. Assume furthermore that it is not perfect and that 10% of the time a person who will get cancer will be told that she will not and that 10% of the time a person who is told that she will not get cancer, will. How would the market for cancer insurance differ among the following various scenarios? Which scenario has adverse selection? In which scenario would the two different groups be put into two different risk categories?
 a. The test is outlawed.
 b. The test can be undertaken by the individual or at the request of the insurance company.

    c.   The test can be undertaken by the individual and it is confidential. The insurance company cannot ask for the results or request that the test be taken. (15)

(6) Why don't private companies insure against the taking of private property by the government? (4)

(7) Explain the unraveling problem in adverse selection. (4)

REFERENCES

Akerlof, George A. (1970). The Market for "Lemons": Quality Uncertainty and the Market Mechanism. 84 *Quarterly Journal of Economics* 488.

Arrow, Kenneth J. (1974). *Essays in the Theory of Risk-Bearing.* New York: American Elsevier.

Priest, George L. (1987). The Current Insurance Crisis and Modern Tort Law. 96 *Yale Law Journal* 1521.

28

Royalties for Artists and Insurance for Investors

A. Artists Pay to Have Royalties 270

B. Royalties for Authors 272

C. Market Answers 274

SUGGESTIONS FOR FURTHER READING 274

REVIEW QUESTIONS 275

REFERENCES 275

All of us have read stories about starving artists (such as Van Gogh) who sold their paintings for a low price, only to have someone else make millions when the painting was sold later. It seems unfair that someone else should makes so much at the expense of the artist who created the work. As a consequence, laws have been enacted so that visual artists share in the success. For example, continental European law and California law require that royalties be paid to the artist for the increase in the value of the artist's painting or sculpture when it is resold.[1] This seems like a winning formula for artists – when the price of their painting goes up, artists collect royalties, but when the price of their painting goes down, they do not lose. Here we show that the law is misguided and its effect is to the detriment of artists.

A. ARTISTS PAY TO HAVE ROYALTIES

Who should be liable for the appreciation of an artist's work, the artist or the investor? The analysis is virtually the same as the Coke bottle case, except that the random event is a good rather than a bad. And, of course, the failure to appreciate can be seen as a random bad, so even on these grounds, there is not much difference between bottles that may or may not explode and art that may or may not explode in price.

Under the old system, the artist did not gain royalties on the appreciation in value. Under the new law, the artist gains if there is an appreciation in the value of the artwork but does not have to give money back to the investor if the painting depreciates. Yet, the artist does not gain and probably loses because he has to pay for getting into this one-sided bet. The price of a painting today is based on the value that the painting is expected to yield in the future. Assume that a painting is expected to be worth $220,000 one year from now (and that no pleasure or pain is derived from ownership). If interest rates are 10%, and there are no royalties, then the artist will sell the painting for $200,000 today. The investor will be unwilling to pay more (since she could get a better return, 10%, by investing the money in a bank) and the artist will not be willing to sell it for less (because he would get a higher return holding on to his painting). Now few people have such a crystal ball that they can foretell the future with such clarity. So assume that both the artist and the investor believe that there is a 50% chance of the painting being worth $120,000 one year from now and a 50% chance of the painting being worth $320,000 one year from now. The expected value is again $220,000. If both sides are risk neutral and the artist does not receive any royalties, then the price will still be $200,000 today.

Because I want to emphasize the role of risk rather than present value, I will slightly alter the problem. Assume that a few hours after purchasing it, the investor will sell the painting at a lottery where there is a 50/50 chance of the painting being worth $100,000 or $300,000. Again the price before the lottery is $200,000 if the investor gets to keep all the proceeds and all the participants are risk neutral (risk neutrality is assumed to make the calculations easier). But what if the law requires that the artist receive half the gain in appreciation. (I start with this assumption because the mathematics is easier.) The artist will get $166,667 (the calculations will be revealed later). Half the time, the painting will go down in value and the artist will receive no royalties. But half the time the painting will go up in value. The artist will receive half the increase after appreciation – $.5(300000 - 166667) = .5(133,333) = $66,666$. Thus, by the end of the evening the artist will either

---

[1] Civil Code §986. The law only applies to works of art selling for more than $1,000.

have $166,667 or $233,333, each being equally likely. On average, the artist will receive $200,000. The after-purchase return to the investor is lower than in a regime without royalties and thus the investor is willing to pay less to begin with. Of course, with risk neutrality, the *total* expected payment to the artist is the same under a royalty regime and a nonroyalty regime. The equation for the maximum that the investor is willing to pay is: $P = .5(100000) + .5[300000 - .5(300000 - P)]$.

The relationship to the exploding pop bottles is illustrated via the following more complex example. Assume that the artist is Andy Warhol and that he paints realistic pictures of soda bottles. One out of every 100 paintings will explode in value tomorrow and be worth $100,000. The other paintings will be worth nothing. Initially assume that no one can determine which painting will be successful. If the investor gets the full value of the appreciation, she will be willing to pay up to $1,000 per painting (if she could exploit the artist she might only pay half as much). If the artist now gets 50% of the return on the appreciation, the artist will receive $.50 [100000 - P]$ dollars on the paintings that explode (where P is the price that the investor pays to the artist), while the investor will receive $100,000 - .50[100000 - P] = .50[100000 + P]$ dollars on the paintings that explode. Because only 1/100 paintings explode, the investor's expected profit over all possible states of the world is $[1/100][.50][100000 + P] - P = 500 - .995P$. Hence, the most that the investor is willing to pay for any painting is slightly more than $502.50. Hence, 1/100 times the artist receives approximately $49,750.00 in royalties, or $497.50 on average. So once again the artist makes an average of $1,000 per painting. Of course, if the investor can exploit the artist, the per painting average may again be reduced to $500.

More typically, both the probability and the extent of future success vary more across artists than within an artist's collection of paintings. But these probabilities are *anticipated* and therefore are reflected in the price of the original painting. The price of a Donald Wittman painting goes for less than the frame reflecting rational expectations in the art market. The higher price of an Andy Warhol painting reflects expectations about the future, but it is the variation around the mean expectation that interests us here.

In the Coke bottle case, it was a question of who would buy the insurance against a bad. In the artist case, it is who will buy the lottery ticket for the good. When the investor buys the whole painting (that is, there are no royalties), she is reducing the risk to the artist. When the artist buys part of the appreciation, he is adding risk to himself but taking away risk from the investor. Thus the investor is buying an insurance policy from the artist. When things are good, the investor does not collect as much as she would if there were no royalties; but when things are bad and the painting does not appreciate, then the investor is richer than she would have been if there were no royalties and she had paid a higher price for the painting.

As in other cases, the law does not redistribute income from buyers to sellers or vice versa but rather among the artists and/or among investors. Thus, the law redistributes wealth from the unlucky to the lucky artist (controlling for anticipated income) – possibly just the opposite of what we might want on distributional grounds!

Hence, once again we need to ask who is the better insurer (including the transaction costs of having the insurance policy). We try to answer this question by considering some of the more important issues regarding insurance. We first ask which side is better at bearing risk. The artist is not – all his wealth is tied up in his own talents. Under a

CAN AN ARTIST'S WORK BE ALTERED?

In 1958, a private collector donated Alexander Calder's mobile, *Pittsburgh*, to Allegheny County, Pennsylvania, for installation in the Greater Pittsburgh International Airport. The mobile was originally black and white, but when it was installed, it was painted green and gold, the official colors of Allegheny County. Calder protested, but the work was not restored to black and white during his lifetime. Should Calder, as the creator of the work, have the right to prevent its alteration? In France, artists have "moral rights" to prevent such alteration. Although the moral rights of artists were expanded under the Visual Artists Rights Act of 1990, the rights of artists are much more limited in the United States.

royalty system, wealth is shifted from the unlucky to the lucky artist. If he is unexpectedly good, he will win a lot, but otherwise he will lose. In contrast, the investor can spread her risk by diversifying her portfolio of artists. Furthermore, if the artist wants risk, he can withhold paintings from the market (as Picasso did). Because an artist's paintings tend to go up and down as a group, the artist can hold onto 1/20 of his paintings in order to achieve an equivalent effect to a 5% royalty rate.

Transaction costs are also quite high. Many paintings are sold to individuals and it may be very hard to establish whether the painting was resold to another individual. Also, paintings may be swapped in groups, making it hard to establish the price paid for the work of particular artists. Furthermore, if the work is not sold, the artist does not collect royalties even if the painting has appreciated in value.

B. ROYALTIES FOR AUTHORS

It might be useful to ask why it makes sense for writers of books to get royalties but not artists. In the first place, the transaction costs of the book royalty system are to a large degree a by-product of the accounting that takes place in running a publishing company. The company needs to know how many books were sold to determine whether to print more books or even to know its profitability.

The ability of the purchaser to determine value is much harder in the publishing world. Much of the value of the art is determined by how much the work is valued intrinsically by the purchaser. In contrast, publishers value a book by how many copies can be sold. This is often quite hard (read costly) to determine. The publisher can eliminate this cost by just having a royalty schedule. A royalty schedule means that the publisher can save the cost of estimating the number of books sold. So the existence of royalties in the book publishing industry is not to shift the risk onto the author but to save on the cost of estimating book sales. Incurring such costs would for the most part be a loss to both the publisher and the author.

Sometime, authors are not paid royalties, but instead are paid all of the money up front. This may arise when the author is writing in a series where the number of books sold can be reasonably estimated (for example, ghost writers in the *Nancy Drew* mystery series are likely to be paid a fixed amount). Also, estimation costs are likely to be swamped by other considerations when the book is worth millions. A royalty system insures the publisher. With large sales, the potential for moral hazard by the publisher increases (for example, it may alter its advertising budget). Therefore, the author may prefer an outright sale of his rights.

CONTINGENCY FEES

Lawyers often take tort cases on a contingency fee basis – the lawyer only collects if the plaintiff wins or the case is settled out of court for a positive amount. A contingency fee shifts risk from the plaintiff to the plaintiff's lawyer. The plaintiff is partially insured because if the plaintiff losses, the plaintiff does not have to pay for the lawyer's time; while if the plaintiff wins, the plaintiff on average gets less than would be the case if the plaintiff had paid the lawyer on an hourly basis. Contingency fees of 30% may seem high, but if the lawyer wins 50% of the cases, the return is only 15%. There are a number of reasons for contingency fees. Lawyers have a diversified portfolio of cases and are likely to be more risk neutral than their clients (unless the client is a corporation, in which case, the corporation is more likely to use its own in house lawyers, who are paid on an hourly basis). Furthermore, many clients do not have the wealth to pay for a lawyer if the case loses. They could try to borrow from a bank, but a bank is at a comparative disadvantage in comparison to lawyers in evaluating the expected return from litigation.

The alternatives to contingency fees are either an hourly wage contract or a fixed-price contract. There are several problems with an hourly wage contract: (1) it is hard for the client to monitor the hours (unless the lawyer is in house); (2) there is a tendency for the lawyer to work more hours than necessary (this is a type of moral hazard), especially if reputation is hard to establish; and (3) it is risky for the client. A fixed-price contract is also risky for the client. In addition, the lawyer would have an incentive to shirk (yet another form of moral hazard) as the lawyer would not be paid more if the lawyer spent more time increasing the probability of success.

In contrast, contingency fees align the interests of lawyer and the client as the harder the lawyer works, the more the lawyer and the client are likely to receive. Even with contingency fees, the lawyer's and the client's interests are not perfectly matched. Efficiency dictates that the lawyer should undertake an extra dollar of work time if that increases the payoff to the lawyer and the plaintiff by a dollar; but the lawyer is more focused on the return to the lawyer. Thus, the lawyer may want to settle rather than go to trial because the cost of going to trial fall on the lawyer alone, but the lawyer receives only a share of the extra return (if any) from going to trial. This last problem is sometime overcome by having a stepped contingency fee with a greater share going to the lawyer if the case goes to trial.

Given all these problems, why don't lawyers just buy the case from the plaintiffs? That is, why don't they get 100% of the proceeds from settlement or trial in return for paying the plaintiff a fixed amount of money regardless of the outcome? In this way the problems of co-ownership of the asset (the return on the case) would be eliminated, as the benefits of the lawyer's work would be captured by the lawyer. Again, there are several reasons for this not happening. First, it is illegal; indeed, in many countries, any contingency fee is illegal. Second, it would create an incentive for the lawyer to lie about the value of the case and say that it was worth very little. Lawyers understand the law; clients cannot independently determine the true value. The client's best defense would be to go to many lawyers and essentially auction off the case. The problem is that there would also be a great incentive for the plaintiff to lie about the case as this would generate a higher price. The only protection for the lawyer would be to do a large investigation before agreeing to the contract. Finally, having sold off the case, the client would be less interested in testifying and helping with the litigation. Some of this could be overcome by a contract, but the incentives for the plaintiff to cooperate would in all likelihood be smaller than would be the case if the plaintiff shared in the award. All of these problems would greatly increase the transaction costs. So some level of contingency fee seems appropriate.

C. MARKET ANSWERS

Usually, we look to the market to tell us what is the most efficient contract. If most art sales have a provision for royalties in the contract, that would tell us that royalties were generally preferred; if most sales do not have a provision, that would tell us that the benefit to the artist was less than the cost to the buyer. What does the art market tell us about whether royalties are desirable? Unfortunately, the art market can tell us very little. In the United States there is *privity of contract* (the major exception involves the sale of land). When X sells to Y, X cannot put any restrictions (such as a royalty) on Y's sale to Z.[2] We would not observe the market choosing royalties, even if it were efficient to do so, since such a thing is not allowed. If it were allowed and we did not see it happening, that would be strong evidence against such a royalty scheme. In most Continental countries royalties are required and cannot be overridden by a contract (however, royalty agreements are rarely in excess of the level required by law).

Even in the absence of privity of contract, economies of scale might be another reason for not seeing royalty agreements on a particular painting or sculpture. If setting up a royalty system is expensive, but once it is done the average and marginal costs are small relative to the benefits, then individual decisions might not lead to the right collective decision. However, there are two counters to the counterargument. First, there is no reason to believe that there are great economies of scale in a system of royalties for visual artists. Second, if there were economies of scale, why wouldn't a company capture these economies of scale by setting up a royalty system (as is the case in music where royalties on broadcast music are minor per play, but collectively very large).

An important measure of the sensibility of this law is to see whether the sale of art in California (which does not allow exculpatory clauses) has increased or decreased since the implementation of the law in the mid-1970s. I know of no studies regarding this question.[3] I therefore must rely on anecdotal evidence from related markets. The great art markets are in London and New York. Why not Paris? After all some of the greatest artist of the twentieth century, including Picasso and Monet, lived in France. Part of the answer is the rights given artists. There are numerous regulations hampering the sale of art in France, including the royalty requirement. Therefore, major items tend to be sold elsewhere.

SUGGESTIONS FOR FURTHER READING

Hansmann and Santilli (1997) and Landes (2001) consider the Visual Artists Rights Act of 1990 but come to opposite conclusions. Hansman and Santilli emphasize the negative externalities that arise when artists lack moral rights, while Landes argues that the law just increases transaction costs. Both of these articles also have important insights regarding intellectual property, a subject discussed in an earlier chapter.

[2] Privity of contract does not allow split ownership of rights to go beyond those making the initial contract. As argued in Chapter 11, privity of contract makes sense for most transactions because the initial seller of an object is unlikely to care how future buyers use the object and the cost of setting up a registry to enforce the seller's restrictions on its use would swamp the benefits, if any, accruing to the original seller.

[3] A study by Landes (2001) shows that artists living in states with expanded rights for artists do not have significantly different incomes. But this would be expected if artists can migrate from one state to another.

REVIEW QUESTIONS

1. Should the law require investors to pay royalty fees to artists when they sell paintings for higher prices than the investors paid for them? What difference does it make to artist income? (10)
2. Why do authors often get royalties for original books even though book publishers have a comparative advantage in risk bearing. (4)
3. Why do lawyers often work on a contingency fee basis? What are the economic reasons for the lawyer not buying the case outright? (8)

REFERENCES

Hansmann, Henry, and Marina Santilli. (1997). Authors' and Artists' Moral Rights: A Comparative Legal and Economic Analysis. 26 *Journal of Legal Studies* 95.

Landes, William M. (2001). What Has the Visual Artists' Rights Act of 1990 Accomplished? 25 *Journal of Cultural Economics* 283.

29 Automobile Insurance

A. Eliminating Zip Codes 279

B. Epilogue 280

REVIEW QUESTIONS 282

Voters (through referenda) and legislatures often try to change the pricing policies of insurance companies. Many states have active state insurance commissions that put caps on insurance premiums. California has been on the forefront in devising new insurance regulations. In the 1990s, the legislature tried to force insurance companies to provide low-cost earthquake insurance. The major result of this experiment was that a number of insurance companies refused to provide any homeowners insurance in the state (and, as a further consequence, a number of people could no longer purchase homes because they could not buy homeowners insurance). In this chapter, we will focus on California Proposition 103, whose purpose was to alter the structure of automobile insurance rates.

Traditionally, automobile insurance companies have used zip codes to determine rates for automobile insurance. Proposition 103, promoted by Ralph Nader and passed by the voters in 1988, did not allow insurance companies to use zip codes, age, or gender in rate determination. Instead, Proposition 103 required that the driver's record be the primary determiner of rates, with good drivers given 20% discounts. A person qualifies for a good driver discount if she or he meets all of the following criteria – licensed to drive a motor vehicle for the previous three years, has not had more than one violation point during the previous three years, and was not a driver of a motor vehicle involved in an accident that resulted in death or in damage exceeding $500 and was principally at fault. The proponents of the proposition claimed that its passage would result in a decrease in insurance rates.

Now on the surface this seems like a good idea. Why should good drivers have to pay for bad drivers, and why should where I live have anything to do with my insurance rates because it does not have anything to do with my care as a driver? Of course, this idea is not so original that it did not occur to insurance companies also. In a competitive situation, an insurance company could skim off the good drivers and give them a better rate based on these criteria. But they did not, presumably, because such a method is not economically viable. Perhaps the cost of separating into good drivers is greater than the reduction in damage payments. More likely, driver history is not as good a predictor as knowing the zip code. Because accidents are not that likely, a history of no accidents and no more than one traffic violation is not an adequate screen. Furthermore, the likelihood of damage and the cost of repair are higher in some places (like Los Angeles) than others (rural counties).

The above analysis does not change much if insurance companies collude. Suppose insurance companies collude and want to extort as much money as possible from automobile drivers. Insurance companies will still want to charge bad drivers more than good drivers. There is no reason to suppose that insurance companies want to collude in favor of bad drivers. Nor is there any reason to believe that allowing rates to be based on zip codes increases the ability of the insurance companies to collude. Although the proponents of Proposition 103 argued that there was collusion among the insurers to set higher rates, this argument was preposterous. There are too many insurers in the state to form an effective cartel. And many of the biggest insurers are mutuals, where any "profits" are returned to the insured.

Basically, what this law does is to try to shift the cost of insurance from cities to rural areas – from zip codes with high insurance costs to zip codes with low insurance costs. The vote totals reveal this: the tendency was for urban areas to vote for the proposition and rural areas against (and it is not because "good drivers" live in cities and bad drivers in rural areas). Other shifts depend on the insurance commissioner's interpretation of the proposition. For example, at one time, the insurance commissioner ruled that young males with good driving records should not pay any more for insurance than young females with good driving records. Because the former still have a higher rate of accidents, this was an attempt to make young females subsidize the insurance cost of young males.

Our analysis of the proposition is in two parts. The first part asks what would have happened if the proposition had been strictly interpreted. The second part discusses how much of the proposition was eviscerated.

A. ELIMINATING ZIP CODES

State laws do not make the economic laws of supply and demand obsolete. The same competitive forces exist but in different contexts. If Proposition 103 had been strictly implemented, these forces would have greatly undermined the intent of the law to shift the cost of insurance from urban drivers to rural drivers. Furthermore, the cost of automobile insurance would have *increased*.

A strict interpretation of the proposition does not allow a particular insurance company to charge differential rates based on zip codes. However, this does not prevent those insurance companies that sell in rural areas from charging lower rates than those insurance companies that sell in urban areas. Under a strict interpretation of Proposition 103, competitive forces would promote the creation of auto insurance firms devoted to certain market niches. Statewide insurance companies would start to be undersold in rural areas by local insurance companies who only sell insurance to residents of rural counties. For example, a farmers' cooperative might provide auto insurance. Because, rural areas have lower insurance costs, the farmers' cooperative could charge lower rates than those firms that have many urban residents and are not allowed by law to have differential pricing. Therefore, statewide insurance firms (State Farm) would lose business in rural areas to those companies that specialize in rural areas (Rural Farm). Other insurance companies would sell only to high-cost zip codes and charge higher rates (they would not be competitive in low-rate areas). This is just one more example of adverse selection at work. When a firm does not differentiate between high and low risks, the low risks will select out and purchase from firms who have more narrowly defined risk pools. In the end, we would see the same pattern of costs, but a break up of insurance companies into smaller units. These changes would be inefficient and would increase the average cost of insurance. Firm size and specialization pre–Proposition 103 yielded the minimal cost of providing auto insurance – if statewide insurance companies existed, that means that zip code–specific insurance companies could not undersell them because their costs were too high. Now, under a strict interpretation of Proposition 103, the high-cost zip code–specific firms would enter the industry and undersell statewide insurance firms in rural areas. The rates these firms charge would be higher than statewide firms charged to rural residents pre–Proposition 103.

Despite my earlier arguments, some might argue that the insurance industry is not competitive but collusive. For the sake of argument, let us suppose that the insurance industry is collusive. Ignoring the other changes in Proposition 103, the same collusive forces exist after the elimination of zip code rate setting, and, if anything, are magnified.

Thus if, for whatever reason, zip code rate setting enabled the cartel to maximize joint profits, then the cartel would try to institute zip code rate setting in the presence of Proposition 103. One method would be to assign territories coinciding with zip codes. So one firm would sell high-priced insurance to urban-area zip codes, while another firm would specialize in rural areas. Because this option was available earlier and not undertaken, it suggests that this option may be more costly than the earlier method of collusion. Furthermore, because firms cannot compete across zip codes with greatly differing cost configurations, collusion is made easier when firms are implicitly assigned to territories. So, once again, the average cost of insurance is raised.

Now this forecast holds only to the extent that the zip code format is undermined. However, there was strong pressure preventing the complete overturn of the zip code formula. The insurance commissioner initially ruled that the insurance companies could use urban density, repair costs in the area, and so on to establish rates. These are substitutes for zip codes but are clearly more costly because insurance companies did not use them in the past, even though they were allowed to do so. They are more costly either because they are poorer predictors than zip codes or because the cost of collecting and analyzing the data outweighs any benefits from improved prediction. So once again we see that Proposition 103 raises the costs of providing insurance.

So what is the major effect of the law? If the law were rigorously enforced, the basic result would be to raise the cost of insurance.[1] The rules against zip codes would not shift money from insurance companies to consumers. There might be some shifting of wealth from rural to urban automobile owners, but for the most part this would be mitigated as insurance companies tried to control adverse selection by selling only to certain zip codes. Because this control of adverse selection is more expensive than using zip codes in setting rates, this would increase insurance costs.

B. EPILOGUE

It has now been 17 years since Proposition 103 was passed. Initially, there was considerable confusion. A number of insurers stopped providing automobile insurance. There were various lawsuits and somewhat contradictory interpretations of the proposition by the insurance commissioner. Insurance practices are now being adjusted to the requirements of the law.

The law as interpreted is not as Draconian as expected by the writers of the proposition. Initially, zones were substituted for zip codes. Recall that a zone can be based on local repair costs, for example. So there was still differentiation, but it was not as finely tuned. Now zip codes have not only returned, they are required, but they are weighted less. Drivers in Los Angeles pay significantly more for automobile insurance than drivers in Eureka, even when they are purchasing from the same company. The insurance industry has not had to reorganize – State Farm still sells throughout the state.

Before Proposition 103, male drivers under age 25 paid very high insurance rates. Proposition 103 does not allow insurance premiums to depend on age. Like many other parts of the proposition, this "requirement" was only partially implemented. So now

---

[1]   Under Proposition 103, the insurance commissioner must approve all rate changes. This too increases the cost of insurance.

DON'T HIDE YOUR VALUABLES IN THE FIREPLACE

In *Harria v. Poland* (1941), 1 K.B. 462, the plaintiff, in an attempt to deter theft, hid her jewelry under some wood on a grate. Unfortunately, she forgot that she had done so and lit a fire. Should she be allowed to recover this loss on her fire insurance policy?

In this case, the court ruled yes, but in general the courts have ruled against recovery. Now most fire insurance policies exclude coverage for such an event.

AUTO INSURANCE OR HOUSE INSURANCE?

As he was nearing his house, X pressed the button on his garage door opener so that he could drive into the garage. Unfortunately, Y was on a ladder painting the second story of X's house above the garage, and fell down when the garage door opened and hit the ladder. X had two policies, a homeowner's policy and an automobile insurance policy that covers all actions incidental to driving the car while the car is in motion. Which insurance company should be liable? *Armed Forces Insurance v. United Services Automobile Association*, California 6th District Court of Appeal, unpublished opinion, 2005.

---

premiums depend on experience. All drivers with less than nine years driving experience pay higher rates ($25 - 16 = 9$), and males still pay higher rates than females.

Proposition 103 said that rates would drop by 20% for good drivers. Insurance companies are in business to make profits not to subsidize "good" drivers who have not had a major accident in three years. Undertaking such a pricing policy would have resulted in insurance company losses. The courts ruled that insurance companies are entitled to a fair return on their investments. In the intervening years, payouts by insurance companies went down and returns on their investments were high because of the stock market bubble and improvements in automobile safety. Insurance companies could afford the 20% discount for good drivers and rates were low. Since the stock market bubble burst, returns to insurance companies declined, and they have had to increase their rates. The original supporters of Proposition 103 are trying to revive the original interpretation and have threatened to have a new proposition.

Postscript: In December 2005, California State Insurance Commissioner John Garamendi announced that he would introduce new regulations that require insurers to base auto rates primarily on a driver's record and not on zip codes. In his announcement, Garamendi said: "I want to end the unfairness and the confusion. Auto insurers in California must base their rates primarily on how you drive and not on where you live."[2] By Garamendi's logic, fire and earthquake insurance premiums on my house should depend on how well I take care of my home, not on where I live (an earthquake zone). After all, according to Garamendi it is not my *fault* if an earthquake destroys my house. And taking Garamendi's logic one step further, the state should pass a law equalizing rents in urban and rural areas.

---

[2] http://www.insurance.ca.gov/0400-news/0100-press-releases/0080-2005/release-120-05.cfm.

REVIEW QUESTIONS

1. If zip codes (and substitutes) could not be used for determining automobile insurance rates, what would be the effect? (10)
2. Suppose that zip codes could not be used for determining automobile insurance rates, but imperfect substitutes could be. Explain the effect on prices. (2)

30 | Bankruptcy

A. Corporate Bankruptcy 284

   1. Conflict of Interest 284

   2. Creditor Priority 286

   3. Creating a Unity of Interest 288

B. Personal Debt Contracts 289

C. Personal Bankruptcy 290

SUGGESTIONS FOR FURTHER READING 292

REVIEW QUESTIONS 293

REFERENCES 293

When commitments to creditors exceed the ability of the debtor to pay, the person or firm faces bankruptcy. Bankruptcy often involves numerous creditors often from different states with conflicting interests, and typically there are a series of ongoing decisions rather than a single decision as in most court cases. As a result, in the United States, there are special federal bankruptcy courts.

A. CORPORATE BANKRUPTCY

If a firm goes into chapter 11 bankruptcy, it is reorganized.[1] Reorganization may mean a restructuring of the firm's debt and change of people in control (the previous board of directors may be replaced by representatives of the lenders). Firms in bankruptcy are no longer obligated to pay interest to prebankruptcy lenders; but with the court's approval, they may borrow more money and pay off their newly made loans. If the firm goes into chapter 7, the assets of the firm are sold off.

In recent years, a number of prominent firms have gone to bankruptcy court. These include WorldCom (MCI) in 2002 with $103 billion in assets, Enron in 2001 with $63 billion in assets, and Kmart in 2002 with $14.6 billion in assets (note that the assets are listed with the bankruptcy court and may not be accurate). But most bankruptcies do not make headlines in the newspapers. In an average year, more than thirty thousand firms file for bankruptcy in the United States.

1. Conflict of Interest

Bankruptcy law literally fills volumes. Here we will focus on one issue – the conflict of interest among claimants. We will consider three major parties: (1) Stockholders (also known as holders of equity): they are residual claimants, meaning that they only have claims on resources after all other claimants have taken theirs. (2) Secured debt held by lenders: a mortgage on a house or an automobile loan from a bank is secured debt. The lender owns the property in case of default. (3) Unsecured debt.[2] The debt is unattached to any particular item. When you purchase a shirt from Macy's with their credit card or go to the doctor and pay later, this is unsecured debt. Macy's will not repossess your shirt and the doctor will not repossess your thymus. Unsecured debt by a firm includes wages and items received by the firm but not yet paid for. Lenders of unsecured debt have priority of payment before stockholders but after holders of secured debt. We will discuss the reason for this priority system in the following pages.

The conflict of interest among parties can be illustrated via the following simple example (see Table 1). The firm has assets worth $100 (in present value terms) and liabilities of $150 to an unsecured creditor, the bondholder. The firm can take three courses of action. Action A has 100% chance of increasing the value of the firm by $50. That is, there is a 100% chance that the expected value of the assets will be $150. Under action B, there is a 50% chance that the expected value of the assets is $180 and a 50% chance that the expected value of the assets is $100. Action C has a 50% chance of assets being worth $170 and a 50% chance of $140. The bondholders

---

[1] Individuals face chapter 13.
[2] Debt (secured or unsecured) is a fixed obligation to pay interest (and principal, usually) at certain times, regardless of the profitability of the firm.

Table 1

Expected value of assets	Stockholder expected return	Bondholder expected return
A.	$1 \times 150 = 150$	0	150
B.	$.5 \times 180 + .5 \times 100 = 140$	$.5 \times 30 + .5 \times 0 = 15$	$.5 \times 150 + .5 \times 100 = 125$
C.	$.5 \times 170 + .5 \times 140 = 155$	$.5 \times 20 + .5 \times 0 = 10$	$.5 \times 150 + .5 \times 140 = 145$

Table 2

Expected value of assets	Stockholder expected return	Bondholder expected return
A.	$1 \times 1150 = 1150$	1000	150
B.	$.5 \times 1180 + .5 \times 1100 = 1140$	$.5 \times 1030 + .5 \times 950 = 990$	$.5 \times 150 + .5 \times 150 = 150$
C.	$.5 \times 1170 + .5 \times 1140 = 1155$	$.5 \times 1020 + .5 \times 990 = 1005$	$.5 \times 150 + .5 \times 150 = 150$

prefer action A because they will always get their $150 back. The equity holders prefer action B because they have a 50% chance of profiting by $30, and their expected profit is $15. Yet action C maximizes the expected return to the assets because the expected value of the assets is $155.

Although there is always the potential for conflict of interest between stockholders and creditors, the conflict is greatest when bankruptcy is a very likely. Consider the opposite case where the initial assets of the firm were $1,100. Then the bondholder would be indifferent between A, B, and C and the stockholder would prefer C to A to B (see Table 2). That is, the stockholders maximization problem would then be identical to maximizing the value of the assets.

The objective of bankruptcy law should be to maximize the value accruing to the assets (even if this means that the assets are sold off).[3] As in other areas of the law, we ask what would be done if there was a complete merger with one person owning all the assets and liabilities. Because of the conflict of interest among the various parties this may not be done.

Why doesn't the Coase theorem come to the rescue? That is, why don't the participants bargain and in the process shift rights to the highest use? To some degree this does take place, and to some degree bankruptcy law is designed for this to take place. However, there may be many creditors and the free rider/monopoly holdout problem arises when any one creditor can demand payment or force the firm into bankruptcy. For example, assume that there is an assembly line, and the first machine is the security for creditor A, the second machine is the security for creditor B, and the third machine is the security for creditor C. All three machines are needed for production. Without the protection of bankruptcy law, unanimous agreement is needed by the three lenders if the firm is in arrears in its payments. Each lender will want to extort the most for itself and hold the others hostage – the problem is analogous to trying to build a freeway without eminent

---

[3] Others have also argued that the objective should also be to punish the managers, thereby reducing the ex ante probability of bankruptcy.

domain. More generally, in the absence of bankruptcy law, there would be a rush by creditors to be the first in line to get paid off, even if the costs to others were greater than the benefits to the particular creditor. A creditor does not care whether an otherwise viable firm fails because she demanded that some critical assets to be sold so that she could get her money back. If the assets as a whole are worth more than the parts, it would make sense to disallow such a rush by the creditors. On the other side, it might make sense for the bankrupt firm to borrow more money. Perhaps it is getting close to Christmas and if the firm borrows more money to buy items for resale, it would be more profitable and less in the red. In the absence of bankruptcy law, each creditor might try to be a free rider and have the other creditors extend more credit. Bankruptcy law also helps to solve this free rider problem.

Ex ante agreements between the debtor and all its creditors regarding bankruptcy could be made in theory, but the complexity and recontracting necessary as the debt structure changes makes such a contract illusory. Hence, we have bankruptcy law.

There are two interrelated questions to ask. (1) What is to be done to the firm (sell the assets piece by piece, keep running the business, or sell it to a third party)? These are the same set of questions that a firm asks even when it is not in bankruptcy – where are the assets valued the highest. (2) Who gets the proceeds? Presumably, the allocation of the proceeds should not interfere with the decision implied by question 1. Ultimately, the ex post bankruptcy allocation should not interfere with the optimal ex ante borrowing. As always, the best guess of optimal ex ante borrowing is found in the ex ante contracts.

2. Creditor Priority

Bankruptcy law has been overhauled in recent years. One question that arose is whether secured debt should have priority over unsecured debt when the firm is in bankruptcy. Consider the case where the firms assets are $150 and its debts are $100 to the owner of secured debt and $100 to the owner of unsecured debt. Under the priority system, the secured creditor would receive $100 and the unsecured creditor would receive $50. If there were no priority, all creditors would receive 75 cents on the dollar (in this case, $75 each). Now, if there were no transaction costs, either system would involve the same total costs. Under the priority system, secured creditors would be facing less risk than under the no priority system and therefore would lend at lower interest rates. But this would be exactly matched by the increased interest payments demanded by unsecured creditors when the system shifted from no priority to priority for secured creditors because the latter has greater risk for unsecured creditors.[4]

However, transaction costs are not zero. Secured creditors have collateral (ownership in particular property). By having ownership (such as in a car), their need for monitoring is reduced. So, those who have a comparative disadvantage in monitoring choose collateral. By having collateral, they are willing to lend at lower rates. If the rights of secured creditors were not recognized in bankruptcy, then firms would have to borrow at higher rates in the first place. The cost of unsecured debt would go down (because it is less risky without priority to secured debt), but the average cost of debt would rise because there would be greater monitoring costs (everyone would have to monitor with the less efficient monitors monitoring more and the more efficient monitors monitoring

---

[4] This is just a variant of the Modigliani-Miller theorem.

less because their loans were not at as great a risk). Essentially, not giving priority to secured debt destroys a market – there is no (or almost no) market for secured debt because creditors are not differentiated.

Typically, secured debt is for a long period of time and therefore lenders with secured debt are unlikely to have relevant information when the firm is nearing bankruptcy (the original loan may have been made many years before). In contrast, creditors holding short-term unsecured debt typically have recent knowledge of the firm as they observe the firm when they make the loan. So short-term lenders are able to monitor at lower cost.

Even if there were no comparative advantage in monitoring, there might be some benefit to differentiating risk classes. A firm before bankruptcy has the option to have no secured debt. The fact that it has chosen to differentiate its debt into secured and unsecured suggests that its total interest bill is less when it differentiates than when it does not differentiate.

Sometimes secured debt is owned by two different entities. For example, a firm may have borrowed $100,000 from person 1 in 1991 and $100,000 from person 2 in 2001. The firm may have used the same $240,000 machine as collateral. If the machine, were worth at least $200,000 at the time of bankruptcy, there would be little problem. But what if there was an unusually high rate of depreciation of the machine so that it was worth only $150,000 in 2003 when the firm declared bankruptcy (rapid depreciation because of overinvestment happened in the telecommunications industry at the end of the twentieth century)? Three priority schemes are possible: (1) The first lender has priority; that is, lender 1 receives $100,000 and lender 2 receives $50,000. (2) The second lender has priority; lender 1 receives $50,000 and lender 2 receives $100,000. (3) Neither has priority; each receives $75,000. Bankruptcy law has implemented the first scheme. This reduces the need for monitoring by the first lender, although it increases it for the second creditor (who should have a comparative advantage in monitoring since she can see the more recent activity and viability of the firm). This also prevents an easy way for the firm to transfer the rights of the first creditor to a friend at a cheap price. If the second party lends a little and gains one-half of the asset, which is now only worth three-fourths of the original value, and the original creditor has the other half value, the original creditor would only have three-eighths of the asset instead of one-half. Thus giving the first creditor the rights to the asset first, means that later creditors and the debtor cannot postcontract alter the value of the secured debt. If the first creditor shared instead of having priority (or was second in line), then the first creditor would probably insist on a new contract whenever the asset had a second creditor. This would raise transaction costs.[5] When the second creditor is second in line, she always knows what the bargain is when she steps into it. ·

There are also priorities with regard to government taxes, workers versus management, postbankruptcy lenders versus prebankruptcy lenders, and so on. In general, they give priority to those who know the least about the welfare of the firm. For example, hourly workers are paid before managers. This example runs counter to the view that the law enables the powerful to exploit the workers. Postbankruptcy lenders have priority over prebankruptcy lenders. Otherwise, who would lend if they were last in line.

---

[5] Bondholders may require that no more leveraged debt be floated without their permission since this increases their risk.

3. Creating a Unity of Interest

As we have seen, when a firm is facing bankruptcy, there is no longer a unity of interest in maximizing the value of the firm's assets. Stockholders are willing to take bad bets as long as the expected return to the stockholders is positive. So there is a problem if stockholders are left in charge. We now consider various methods of creating the desired unity of interest.

a. Liquidation.   Under chapter 7, the assets of the firm are auctioned for cash and then distributed according to the prespecified priority of creditor claims. If the firm is auctioned off either piecemeal or as a whole, then the assets will go to the highest bidder. For a given priority, all creditors and stockholders would want the highest price for the assets. So there is a unity of interest. Economists who believe in the market, generally prefer chapter 7, the auction market, to chapter 11 where legal intervention and bargaining by the participants is supposed to lead to highest value. How much is a Van Gogh painting or a bankrupt firm worth? One can argue at length, but the best test is the market test. Under chapter 7, the firm will remain intact if the benefits from the synergies of human and physical capital are sufficiently positive that the firm is worth more as a whole to the one bidder than it is worth in parts to the other bidders.

b. Structured Bargaining.   Under chapter 11, there are several ways of creating a unity of interest. The standard solution is to make a change in the board of directors to reflect the relative interests of the creditors and stockholders. The parties then negotiate and come up with a reorganization plan. Problems still exist because individual members have different goals. So while the interests more accurately reflect the creditor interest, there is not a unity of interest. Under chapter 11, all classes of creditors must approve a reorganization plan (by one-third majority in the amount of claims and by a simple majority in the number of claims). This gives bargaining power to classes that are otherwise less important. The bankruptcy judge has to approve of the plan according to the "best interest of creditors" test, which means that each class of creditors receives at least as much as it would have under liquidation. Of course, the voting rule already insures this to be the case. Sometimes all classes of creditors do not agree, in which case the judge can "cram down" a reorganization plan on a class of unwilling creditors. However, in such cases, the cram down comes with a minimal guarantee to those who have been forced into the bargain.

c. Appointment of a Trustee.   The court may appoint a trustee to maximize the return on the asset (this method is commonly used in France and England). So unity of interest is created by having a single trustee that is beholden to neither the creditors nor the stockholders. Of course it may not always be easy to find a skilled and knowledgeable trustee to undertake such a task.

d. Convert All Creditors into Stockholders.   Another way to create unity among creditors is to make all of them into stockholders – if they are all stockholders, then they all want to maximize the value of their stock.[6] The number of shares that creditors get then depends on what they would have expected to receive if the firm were liquidated.

---

[6]   Roe (1983) has been a strong advocate of this approach.

If in liquidation the firm is unlikely to have any assets beyond those assets that are secured, then the secured creditors get virtually all the shares in the reorganized firm. If the outlook is more promising, unsecured creditors gain a greater percentage of the shares than otherwise. But this kind of agreement as well as reorganization itself (which keeps secured creditors at bay) is not costless. In the first place, it is costly to determine the terms of trade and the rules of behavior under bankruptcy. In the second place, making secured debt less secure will ultimately increase the initial cost of borrowing on secured debt.

B. PERSONAL DEBT CONTRACTS

When individuals cannot make payments on furniture or cars, these items may be repossessed. At times there has been concerted effort to make repossession more difficult – it is easy to be sympathetic to a person who needs a car for work and nevertheless is about to have his car repossessed. To understand the implications of such a policy, let us consider an extreme variant. Suppose that a lawyer is arguing that banks should not be allowed to repossess cars purchased by college students. Also assume that you are the judge and that you are not interested in economic efficiency; rather, your only interest is to promote the welfare of college students. Would you rule in favor of the plaintiff and against repossession?

Ruling against repossession would help those college students who already had loans and were in arrears. But the key consideration is the long-run effect. Clearly, laws against repossession would hurt those students who were applying for loans. By not being able to repossess cars owned by students, banks and auto dealers would be facing greater risks in lending to them. In response, they might not lend to students at all or else raise the interest rates charged to students. In this way, college students as a group would pay more ex ante.

To the extent that banks could not differentiate between students who were good credit risks and students who were bad credit risks, students who were good credit risks would end up paying (through higher interest rates) for students who were poorer credit risks. There would be no redistribution of income from banks to students because the banks would charge for the increased risk of default. There would however be a redistribution of income from one set of students to the other.

As a group, students would be hurt by a rule against repossession. Some will no longer be able to borrow money for purchasing an auto. The lenders are also hurt by such a law. A law against repossession puts a limit on *free contracting*. To the extent that the parties to the contract were rational and contracting costs were low, we would expect the parties to come to an agreement that was Pareto optimal. After all, if one party could have been made better off without hurting the other party by a change in the contract, why wouldn't the contract change have been made?

Preventing repossession creates *improper incentives*. Since there are no costs to the students from defaulting on their loans, they will have greater incentive to default.

Preventing repossession also destroys the ability of the market to *separate* good risks from bad risks. The collateral is lost when the bank repossesses the automobile. Those students who are unlikely to default, can signal this to the market by putting their car at risk. This is a method of creating incentives for *honest revelation* of intentions. If banks are allowed to repossess, those borrowers who intend (or are merely likely) to default

WHY DOES O. J. SIMPSON LIVE IN FLORIDA?

Why does O. J. Simpson, the former football player and the man found innocent of killing his former wife Nicole Brown Simpson and her friend Ron Goldman, live in Florida? Not because he thinks that he can find "the real killer" there. He is there because he owes $33.5 million from civil suits brought by the Goldman and Brown families. Federal bankruptcy law protects his $4.1 million National Football League pension from being used to pay off the civil suit. Bankruptcy law also allows a homestead exemption – the amount of the exemption depends on each state and only two states, Florida and Texas, put no limit on the value of the home. Not surprisingly, wealthy people facing bankruptcy often move to Florida and buy multimillion-dollar homes. But why does Florida want to attract such people? The answer: Florida has no income tax, but high property taxes.

will be hesitant to put up collateral.[7] Preventing repossession destroys this signaling device.

As a general rule, individuals have better information about their ability and intent to default. Preventing repossession would force banks to *substitute* more costly methods of determining a person's credit riskiness. Banks would have to investigate people more thoroughly and be more cautious in their lending policies. These substitutes for repossession are costly and would be passed on to college students. Note that the role of substitution is very important. It is not just the substitution of Hydrox cookies for Oreos typically considered in beginning economics courses. Here the substitute for collateral is a more costly method of separating poor credit risks from good credit risks – a more thorough investigation.

Thus preventing repossession creates a Pareto inferior outcome. In the long run, the best way to help college students is to enforce the contract.

C. PERSONAL BANKRUPTCY

Approximately 1.5 million people file for bankruptcy each year in the United States. In 2005, President Bush signed the Bankruptcy Abuse Prevention and Consumer Protection Act. We will now consider some of its main features.

As noted earlier, when it comes to corporate bankruptcy, economists tend to prefer chapter 7 (liquidation) over chapter 11 (reorganization). But when it comes to personal bankruptcy, economists generally prefer chapter 13 over chapter 7. The reason for the reversal is simple – incentives. When a corporation is liquidated under chapter 7, all of its assets are put up for sale (and the market decides the value and the use of these assets). When a person goes into chapter 7, the person's debts are discharged, but not all of the person's assets are seized, even if the debts exceed the assets. For example, if the value of the person's house is below the state's homestead limit, the house cannot

---

[7] Because of transaction costs, the borrower rarely gets all her money back. To illustrate, assume that you have borrowed $10,000 on a $12,000 used car (so there is no depreciation from your use). The bank that repossesses your car will sell it wholesale, but you paid for it retail. So you will not get all of your $2,000 back. The bank does not have to sell the auto retail because there is a cost to the bank of selling retail and they would have to charge you for this.

WHAT IS DUE TO THE HOLDER IN DUE COURSE

In *United States Finance Co. v. Jones*, 229 So.2d 495 (1969), the seller provided a loan for installing aluminum siding on Jones's house. The siding turned out to be tarpaper sprayed with paint instead. The purchaser decided to hold back payments, but the money owed was not to the siding company as it had sold the note to someone else (the holder in due course). Should the consumer have to pay the finance company?

Holding back payments is often a low-cost way of insuring that the contract is satisfied (for example, a building contractor is not paid the full amount before the job is completed). This is a much cheaper way of enforcing agreements than suing the person for breach of contract in court. If the siding company had kept the loan, nonpayment would be a good method of enforcing the contract. However, siding companies tend to specialize in siding and loan companies tend to specialize in loans; it makes sense for the siding company to sell off the loans, especially so when the siding company is engaging in fraudulent behavior.

In common law, the holder of due course had to be paid regardless of how fraudulent the initial sale had been. Purchasers did not gain any extra leverage by borrowing instead of paying cash. This allowed for greater market liquidity because the purchaser of the note did not have to investigate the originating firm or its product. The written loan contracts were consistent with the common law, suggesting that the common law was correct. In 1968, the U.S. Congress passed the Truth in Lending Act, which led to a partial overthrow of the common law.

The court argued that the financing company would be a better monitor of the aluminum siding company than the buyer. Therefore, the borrower should be able to withhold money from the finance company (which would then have the incentive to monitor the siding company). Congress has enacted similar legislation for credit cards. If you buy an item with a credit card, you can refuse to pay the bill if you purchased the item in your state and it cost more than $50. Of course, Visa and MasterCard do not want to be in the business of monitoring the quality of purchases. Consequently, their contract with stores requires the store to pay Visa and MasterCard back if the purchaser refuses to pay on a credit card because of a problem with the merchandise.

be seized. Most important, the person's human capital cannot be seized.[8] This means that the cost of liquidation may be small when the person has relatively few seizable assets. In turn, this means that, in comparison to chapter 13, the person might not have sufficient incentive to avoid bankruptcy in the first place. Hence, the economist caution in using chapter 7 as the primary way to deal with personal bankruptcy. The Bankruptcy Act of 2005 makes it more difficult for a person to choose chapter 7 (for example, not allowing liquidation if income minus certain expenses is greater than $167 a month).

As is the case for corporations, there is a creditor priority. First priority goes to domestic support obligations. As noted in an earlier chapter, the supported spouse is less capable of facing risk than the supporting spouse. And definitely, children (whose

---

[8] Under Roman law, debtors could be sold into slavery.

HOW NOT TO GET RID OF YOUR STUDENT LOANS

A Georgia lawyer funded his A.A., B.A., J.D., and L.L.M. degrees with student loans totaling more than $114,000. He then started a law practice, which was unsuccessful. Quitting the practice, he took a job with his brother's landscaping company, where he earned $24,000 per year. He applied for bankruptcy protection, claiming he could not pay off the loans without suffering undue hardship. Rejecting his arguments, the bankruptcy court found that the ex-lawyer did not establish "undue hardship" as contemplated by the bankruptcy code §523[a][8]. In *re Cox*, 338 F.3d 1238 (2003), the appellate court upheld the bankruptcy court decision because the lawyer did not demonstrate that his current financial situation was permanent.

TYSON BITES OFF MORE THAN HE CAN CHEW

OCTOBER 2003 – According to his personal and corporate bankruptcy filings, Mike Tyson is about $30 million in the red. On his expense schedule filed in U.S. Bankruptcy Court in New York, Tyson allocated $18,680.18 monthly for clothing. This is the single largest recurring expense on his monthly bill, which totals $56,732.12 and includes combined child support payments of nearly $10,000. http://www.thesmokinggun.com/archive/mgtpayment1.html.

welfare depends on a parent receiving child support payments) are not capable of bearing risk. So they come ahead of other "creditors" who are more capable of bearing risk. Claims assigned to the government come ahead of claims assigned to private parties. Private lenders are best able to monitor the condition of the borrower (by checking on a person's credit), and therefore the burden on private parties should be the greatest.

To mitigate moral hazard, the following cannot be discharged by going into chapter 7: debts obtained through fraud; debts made for luxury goods and services owed to a single creditor totaling more than $500 and made within sixty days of filing; and debts incurred to pay fines and penalties.

However, not all provisions of the act create the right incentives. For example, if the person's income after expenses is between $100 and $167 a month, then a person with a large debt could choose chapter 7; this option would not be available to a person with a small debt. This rule encourages people to have larger debts. So why is the rule implemented if it encourages greater debt? It is because of postbankruptcy incentives. If a person must pay too large a share of his/her income to creditors, then the incentive to work may be undermined.

SUGGESTIONS FOR FURTHER READING

For an overview of the economics of bankruptcy law, see White (2005). Baird and Jackson (1984) is a classic paper on secured debt. Kanda and Levmore (1994) discuss creditor priority (also see the other authors in the same symposium). For a contrary view, see Bebchuk and Fried (1996). Bhandari and Weiss (1996) cover a number of interesting issues on the economics of bankruptcy.

REVIEW QUESTIONS

1. What is the difference between chapter 11 and chapter 7? (4) What is the difference between a bondholder and a stockholder? (4) What is the difference between secured debt and unsecured debt? (4)
2. Illustrate via an example how the conflict between stockholders and bondholders may arise when a firm is facing the possibility of bankruptcy. (5) Also show why this conflict is reduced when the firm becomes very profitable. (2)
3. From the viewpoint of this book what should be the objective of bankruptcy law? (2) When should a firm be reorganized? When should it be liquidated? (2) Why can't we rely on the creditors to come to a value maximizing agreement? (3)
4. What is the priority of bankruptcy creditors? Provide an economic explanation for the following order of priority (secured creditors before unsecured creditors before equity holders; and workers and worker pensions before managers and manager pensions). Why not give priority to the first people who file for claims? (10)
5. Explain the fallacy in the following argument: Giving priority to holders of secured debt lowers the rate of interest paid by the firm for secured debt but at the same time raises the rate of interest paid on unsecured debt. Therefore, there is no advantage to giving priority to holders of secured debt. (6)
6. If a debtor has used the same collateral for two creditors, which creditor should have priority – the first or second creditor? (4) Note that the debt to each creditor is usually significantly less than the total value of the asset.
7. How do the bankruptcy courts create unity among the conflicting interests? (6)
8. Why do economists tend to prefer chapter 7 over chapter 11 for corporate bankruptcy, but have more qualms about chapter 7 in personal bankruptcy? (4)

REFERENCES

Baird, Douglas G., and Thomas H. Jackson. (1984). Corporate Reorganizations and the Treatment of Diverse Ownership Interests: A Comment on Adequate Protection of Secured Creditors in Bankruptcy. 51 *University of Chicago Law Review* 97.

Bebchuk, Lucian A., and Jesse M. Fried. (1996). The Uneasy Case for the Priority of Secured Claims in Bankruptcy. 105 *Yale Law Journal* 857.

Bhandari, Jagdeep S., and Lawrence A. Weiss (eds.). (1996). *Corporate Bankruptcy: Economic and Legal Perspectives*. Cambridge: Cambridge University Press.

Kanda, Hideki, and Saul Levmore. (1994). Explaining Creditor Priorities. 80 *Virginia Law Review* 2103.

Roe, Mark J. (1983). Bankruptcy and Debt: A New Model for Corporate Reorganization. 83 *Columbia Law Review* 527.

White, Michelle. (2005). Bankruptcy Law. In A. Mitchell Polinsky and Steven Shavell (eds.), *Handbook of Law and Economics*. Amsterdam: North Holland.

31

Deposit Insurance and Banking Crises

A. Monitoring Failure 296

B. Higher Risks Did Not Pay a Higher Price 297

C. Excessive Market Risk 298

D. Improper Incentives under Bankruptcy 298

E. Fraud 299

F. Epilogue 299

G. Japanese Banks 300

SUGGESTIONS FOR FURTHER READING 301

REVIEW QUESTIONS 301

REFERENCES 301

At present, Japan's banking industry is just crawling out of a financial crisis. In the 1980s, there was a significant savings and loan crisis in the United States. A large number of savings and loans (S&Ls) went bankrupt and the insurance pool, FSLIC (Federal Savings and Loan Insurance Corporation), set up to pay off debts of bankrupt savings and loan institutions, faced bankruptcy. Congress sponsored a multibillion-dollar bailout of the industry. Estimates of the taxpayer financed bailout are between $150 billion and half a trillion dollars (the Japanese crisis is much larger). The analysis developed in the sections on bankruptcy and insurance can be used to provide insight into the causes of these crises. Some of the insights can be applied to the East Asian currency crisis, more generally

We will focus on the American savings and loan crisis. Before we begin, it is useful to explain the difference that existed between a savings and loan and a commercial bank in the 1980s. Savings and loans were specialized institutions whose main purpose was to provide long-term mortgages to homeowners. They were regulated by the Federal Home Loan Bank Board and insured by the FSLIC. In contrast, commercial banks had checking accounts and financed automobile purchases, commercial developments, and business ventures. Commercial banks were insured by the Federal Deposit Insurance Corporation (FDIC). Although commercial banks were also in trouble during the late 1980s, the problems were not as severe.

A. MONITORING FAILURE

The stockholder(s) of S&Ls put up very little capital for a savings and loan. By far, the major source of money for loans comes from depositors. But deposits are insured for up to $100,000. Therefore, depositors do not have much incentive to either monitor the behavior of S&Ls or choose those institutions that are unlikely to face insolvency. This is just another example of moral hazard when people are insured. For reasons that will become clear in a short while, the stockholders could not be relied on to protect the interests of the FSLIC. Therefore, it was up to the FSLIC and other government agencies to monitor S&Ls and to regulate their behavior so that the natural enemies of insurance, moral hazard, and adverse selection, did not arise. However, for a number of reasons, the government regulators failed at this task.

The first reason for failure was an inadequate regulatory system. Some of the inadequacy is historical. The regulatory system was set up at a time when S&Ls devoted the fast bulk of their activity to financing and refinancing homes. However in the 1970s, S&Ls were allowed to greatly increase the scope of their lending. The increased scope was designed to remove inherent problems in the savings and loan industry – their deposits were all short term (depositors can withdraw their money at any time), while their loans were typically long term (housing mortgages may be for 30 years). This made the savings and loan industry riskier because short-term rates might be unanticipatedly higher than the interest rates gained on long-term loans made earlier – this could mean that S&Ls were borrowing at higher interest rates than they were lending. The increased scope of lending allowed for greater spread in the term structure. Unfortunately, this increased scope also increased the potential for inappropriate behavior by the savings and loan industry. The old regulatory apparatus was not able to cope with these new problems (monitoring a variety of risky investments is more difficult than monitoring home purchases). Also deregulation was a major force during the Reagan era – there was considerable political pressure to let S&Ls do what they wanted. The idea was that regulation hurts profits. However, whenever there is insurance, monitoring and regulation is required to prevent severe problems of moral hazard and adverse selection from occurring.

Proper monitoring and regulation to prevent bankruptcy is inherently difficult. This may account for the virtual absence of bankruptcy insurance beyond that provided by independent agencies of the federal government such as the FDIC. Either because of the inherent difficulty or adding to it, FSLIC accounting requirements were extremely inadequate. Consider, for example, the valuation of a property where the owner is in arrears. It may be that the property is worth less than the original loan (the severe drop in oil prices greatly undermined property values in Texas in the early 1980s where most of the S&L failures took place), but for FSLIC regulators the original value was used.[1] Because historical prices rather than current market values were used, the FSLIC regulators did not even know whether the S&L was solvent.

B. HIGHER RISKS DID NOT PAY A HIGHER PRICE

A second problem arose because of the peculiar nature of insuring S&Ls and other thrift organizations. FSLIC regulated behavior rather than charging higher premiums for those institutions at greater risk. Although in theory perfect regulation might make all S&Ls equal, in practice they do not.[2] So low risk (of bankruptcy) institutions implicitly subsidize high-risk institutions because they all pay the same premium. This makes high-risk institutions more profitable and more prevalent than otherwise.

It is useful to consider the issue of risk in greater detail. Savings and loans are required to put up a certain amount of capital for every thousand dollars of loans. In this way, even if some of loans do not get paid back, it will come out of the hides of the stockholders rather than the depositors or the insurer of these deposits. The more capital the stockholders put up, the more FSLIC is protected. But S&Ls do not get lower rates if they have more than the minimal capital requirements. Similar arguments hold regarding the diversification of the loan portfolio. Other things being equal, the more diversified the portfolio, the less risk. But the insurance rates do not go down when the S&L diversifies beyond the requirements of the regulators. This is certainly not the way that automobile insurance liability works. When you get a traffic ticket, your insurance rates go up. If an insurance company did not implement such a plan, dangerous driving would increase, there would be more accidents, and the insurance company would go broke from adverse selection because other insurance companies would skim off the lower-risk drivers without traffic tickets.

For the regulators, it is not always a trivial task to determine the riskiness of the loans made by the savings institutions. However, there are substitutes for monitoring. One important method is to shift the risk onto the S&Ls by requiring more capital from them. The increased collateral has the same effect as using your car as collateral on a

---

[1] Proper cost accounting would be expensive (although one might expect that savings and loans would do it as part of good business practice). Another strange accounting practice was the treatment of loans from the Federal Home Loan bank. There are two main headings for assets: stockholder capital and money borrowed from depositors. Money borrowed from the Federal Home Loan Bank is treated as capital rather than as a loan.

[2] Consider the analogous regulation for fire insurance. If all houses were required to be built out of the same materials, be the same distance away from fire stations, and not be built in areas where there were thunderstorms or extreme drought, then the cost of fire insurance per square foot of home might be the same throughout the United States. Alternatively, one can place homes in various risk classes and choose the appropriate insurance rate for each class.

loan. But the capital requirements not only did not vary by the riskiness of the S&L, they were too low in general and significantly lower than the FDIC required from banks.

C. EXCESSIVE MARKET RISK

A third problem arises from market risk. An S&L may try to diversify its portfolio, but diversification is costly because it requires more information. An S&L is more adept at monitoring local debtors then distant ones. Hence, even if its portfolio is spread across homes, apartment buildings, and development projects, all of its loans may be at risk if the local economy is in bad shape. This is what happened in Texas after the downward oil shock.

Now there are other methods of diversification. A holding company may own institutions in several states. But there were rules against such diversification. For example, holding companies with institutions spread across several states did not pay lower premiums to FSLIC. Also, there had been federal restrictions against nationwide savings institutions. This prevents optimal diversification. Since the S&L crisis, Congress relaxed some of these restrictions, enabling national banks and a concomitant diversification. Such diversification is not costless – the owner of the nationwide institution still has to monitor her managers to ensure that they are maximizing profits, but the limits to diversification are no longer merely legal rather than economic.

Savings and loans may also sell their mortgages to third parties, but third parties may need to engage in extra monitoring in order for the third party to be assured of not being sold poor risks. Since the savings and loan crisis, the increased use of standard loan requirements and mortgage contracts has greatly enlarged the secondary market in mortgages.

D. IMPROPER INCENTIVES UNDER BANKRUPTCY

The fourth problem is the most serious. Combined with the first three, it is a recipe for disaster. As shown in the previous chapter, stockholders are often insensitive to the extent of bankruptcy since the cost falls on the creditors. In ordinary markets, creditors monitor the behavior of the firm and charge higher interest rates when the firm undertakes riskier behavior. But depositors (creditors) do not monitor, and the resources of the regulatory agency were stretched thin (and subjected to political manipulation). Therefore, the owners of the S&Ls were relatively free to pursue their own goals without serious consequences. They tended to make higher-risk loans with insufficient diversification, which increased the risk still further. When things went well, the S&L would make lots of money; when things went bad, FSLIC paid for it.

When a firm faces bankruptcy the interests of the stockholders and its creditors diverge most widely. When an S&L faced bankruptcy, its owners were likely to undertake riskier and riskier behavior. They invested in more speculative projects (for example, purchasing an inadequately diversified portfolio of junk bonds) with potentially higher wins and higher losses, even if there was a negative expected return. The losses did not count because they fell on FSLIC, but FSLIC and other agencies were not performing their watchdog role adequately.

Furthermore, to pay off its bad bets, an S&L would raise its interest rates to get more deposits. This strategy either stole away depositors from other institutions (adverse selection) or forced these other institutions to raise their interest rates, making the whole industry less profitable. Between 1980 and 1988, deposits with S&Ls more than doubled (because of high interest rates), when they should have been shrinking. Moral hazard created perverse economic incentives so that the weak tended to undermine the strong. The weak were playing with someone else's money and therefore tended to be more competitive by offering higher interest rates to depositors and lower interest rates to borrowers than more solvent institutions. This undermined marginal S&Ls, which then undertook similar high-risk behavior. The whole thing started to snowball.

E. FRAUD

I have not spent a lot of time on fraud. Outright fraud makes for more sensational headlines than adverse selection (which will never make the front cover of *Time* magazine) but is only marginal in terms of the huge losses faced by FSLIC. Of course, fraud became easier when the regulatory oversight was reduced and made still easier when politicians dissuaded regulators from doing their job.

It is not clear that a private insurer would have done better. Some agency would still have to regulate the insurer to see that it would not go bankrupt – that is, its assets were sufficient to cover failed thrifts. And because there is some correlated risk (a bad recession may hurt all savings institutions simultaneously), the insurance company has a relatively high chance of facing bankruptcy, itself.

F. EPILOGUE

A number of changes have been made. The FDIC Improvement Act (FDICIA) of 1991 affected both S&Ls and commercial banks and resulted in the following changes:

Capital requirements were increased. This put more of the burden on stockholders. This larger collateral requirement means that the stockholders are more cautious and the insurer has less to lose.

Previously, FDIC helped solvent institutions purchase all the liabilities of insolvent banks. For example, bank B might owe $2 billion to its depositors, owe $1 billion to its bondholders (banks can issue bonds) with only $1.5 billion in assets. FDIC would give bank C $1.5 billion to take over bank B. This meant that uninsured bondholders were implicitly insured. Now bondholders are no longer guaranteed such protection. Bank C is given half a billion dollars and the obligations to the bondholders are dismissed. This gives incentives for bondholders to monitor more carefully and reduces the cost to the FDIC of insuring insolvent banks.

There are now broad categories of risk so that institutions in higher risk categories pay higher premiums. However, the pricing system still does not look like the private sector pricing for risk. So low-risk banks still subsidize higher-risk banks.

Regulators do a better job of estimating the current market value of the loans so that regulators can assess risk more accurately. However, there is still room for improvement.

Regulators intervene more rapidly instead of allowing an insolvent bank to do as it wants for a long period of time. This gambling with other people's money created the greatest losses for the FSLIC.

There was also elimination of some restrictions against nationwide savings institutions (thereby encouraging greater diversification and less risk).

GAMBLING WITH SOMEONE ELSE'S MONEY

As noted earlier, the primary business of S&Ls is to make home mortgage loans. But when Seapointe Savings and Loan of Carlsbad, California, failed in 1986, it had not made any home loans since opening in 1985. Instead, it had sold $10 billion of *naked call options*. A naked call option is a promise to sell at a future date an asset (in this case bonds) that the person does not own at a given price if the buyer decides to exercise her option. The seller sells the option to the buyer and hopes that the actual price of the bond in the future will be less than option price so the buyer will not exercise her option to buy. In this way, the seller makes money by selling the option. However, if the actual price in the future is greater than the option price, the buyer will exercise her option, and the seller will lose money because he will have to buy the bond at the high price and sell it to the buyer at the low price. Bond prices went up and Seapoint lost 75% of its assets, most of these assets being federally insured deposits. Of course, if bond prices had gone down, the stockholders of Seapointe would have made a fortune.

G. JAPANESE BANKS

The banking crisis in Japan occurred when the bubble in real estate prices collapsed resulting in the banks being owed more than the property put up as collateral was worth. In the 1980s, many of the largest banks in the world were Japanese. Now most of these have negative value.

The Japanese government has been much slower to act than the U.S. government reacted to its banking crisis. The Japanese government has been unwilling to shut down insolvent banks or to do many of the changes incorporated under FDICIA. This has been one of the major reasons for Japan's long recession.

An interesting exception to the dismal record of the Japanese banks is Takefuji, a consumer credit company that makes unsecured loans but not in real estate. I have argued that having a loan secured with collateral allows the lender to lend at lower interest without the need of much monitoring. Because Takefuji does not make use of collateral, the firm must be adept at monitoring. And Takefuji is a casebook illustration of this argument. When Mr. Takei founded the company in 1966 as a one-person lending agency, he devised his own manual for evaluating risk. He would peak into prospective borrowers mailboxes to see if they promptly picked up the mail; those that did, tended to be better credit risks. Similarly, prompt payment of rent and clean toilets were also positively correlated with being a good credit risk. On the other side of the ledger, people who wore Rolex watches, were not conversant with their occupation, or held a full-time and a part-time job were poor credit risks and were not lent money.

Others in the consumer-lending business resorted to violence to insure that borrowers paid back their loans. Takei denies that he engaged in the practice, but in the beginning, his firm did engage in harassment of delinquent borrowers by shouting at them, making late-night calls, or sending around people who dressed like gangsters. The positive side is that this allowed the firm to lend at lower rates than otherwise because their loans were more likely to be paid back.

In the late 1990s, Takeifuji's profits were double those of any of the top twenty banks in Japan.

SUGGESTIONS FOR FURTHER READING

White (1991) and Benston and Kaufman (1997) provide analyses and cures for the U.S. financial crisis, while Hoshi and Kashyap (2004) have a less-detailed account of the Japanese financial crisis.

REVIEW QUESTIONS

1. Thoroughly discuss the reasons for the savings and loan crisis. (20)
2. What kinds of reforms of deposit insurance were undertaken and why? (20)
3. In the absence of collateral, what kind of action did Takefuji undertake to ensure that it did not make bad loans? (6)

REFERENCES

Benston, George J., and George C. Kaufman. (1997). FDICIA after Five Years. 11 *Journal of Economic Perspectives* 139.

Hoshi, Takeo, and Anil K Kashyap. (2004). Japan's Financial Crisis and Economic Stagnation. 18 *Journal of Economic Perspectives* 3.

White, Lawrence J. (1991). *The S&L Debacle: Public Policy Lessons for Bank and Thrift Regulation*. Oxford: Oxford University Press.

X | GOVERNANCE AND ORGANIZATION

Much of the preceding analysis has been about prices. Examples include determining the appropriate damage remedies for breach of contract, the appropriate fine for criminal behavior, and the appropriate liability for automobile accidents. In Part X, our attention is directed toward governance and organization. When is production organized in markets and coordination achieved through prices, and when is production organized in firms and hierarchy used for coordination? Why are worker-managed firms rare and investor-owned firms common? Why do franchises exist?

In Chapter 32, we argue that organizations work best when conflict of interests among those who govern the organization is minimized. Whenever there is specialization of labor, there is a conflict of interest among workers, making worker governance very difficult. In contrast, corporations are governed by their stockholders, all of them interested in maximizing the return on their stock. We show that one reason for having limited liability for holders of equity is to maintain a unity of interest among the stockholders. We also provide a transaction cost explanation for limited liability of stockholders.

While corporations reduce governance problems, they increase agency problems. Agency problems arise in corporations because the operation of the corporation is done by managers, who are agents of the stockholders. Managers may have different interests from maximizing the return to stockholders. Chapter 33 shows how the interests of the manager are aligned with the interest of the stockholder. Tender offers and the threat of tender offers are particular potent ways of creating an alignment. Tender offers are not available to other forms of organizations such as mutuals.

In Chapter 34, we consider an oft-alleged agency problem in corporations – insider trading where the managers buy or sell stock based on inside information regarding the future performance of the company. We suggest that the way to decide whether this is a problem is to see whether the market for incorporation is a race to the bottom or a race to the top. We argue that the latter holds.

An electrical-generating firm can purchase coal on the spot market, have a long-term contract with a coal supplier, or own a coal mine. Purchasing on the spot market is as the name implies a market solution, the long-term contract is a contract solution, while the third method is a hierarchical solution. Each of these methods involves a form of transaction cost. For example, control within the firm involves agency costs. In Chapter 35, we argue that the organizational form chosen is the one that economizes on opportunism and other transaction costs (both within and across firms). Using a similar argument, we explain why McDonald's is a franchise rather than being a collection of independent restaurants, and why Safeway stores are all owned by Safeway rather than being a franchise. Along the way, we explain criminal organization and the way criminal syndicates control opportunism in the absence of legally enforceable contracts.

In Chapter 36, we discuss the internal organization of legislatures. We show how agency and common pool problems are overcome. In Chapter 37, we investigate federalism. Here there is a joint sharing of power somewhat akin to franchising. We show the important role of competition in explaining the tax and revenue structure.

Chapters 32–35 dealt with the internal structure of the firm. Chapter 38 deals with the internal structure of family relations. The chapter argues that property rights should be maintained within the family to reduce threats and retaliations and other transaction costs. The chapter also shows that the analog to a liability rule is preferred to punishment, the analog of a Pigovian tax.

32 | The Governance of Organization

A. Types of Organization 306

B. The Cost of Governance 306

C. The Nature of Private Property and the Role of Community 308

D. Limited Liability of Stockholders 309

E. Debt versus Equity 310

F. Concluding Remarks 311

SUGGESTIONS FOR FURTHER READING 311

REVIEW QUESTIONS 311

REFERENCES 312

In this and in the following three chapters, the organization of firms and markets will be discussed, and questions like the following will be answered: Why are there franchises? When should we expect to see vertical integration of firms? Why don't the customers own grocery stores? Why don't the workers own automobile firms, and why were collective farms in Russia and China such a failure?

A. TYPES OF ORGANIZATION

In the United States and Europe, manufacturing is dominated by the corporate form. The owners of the corporation are stockholders, whose liability is limited to the value of the stock purchased. In a corporation, the stockholder-investors are the ultimate source of decision making and power in the firm. Stockholders exercise their power through voting (for common stock, it is generally the case that there is one vote per share). Voting is by majority rule. Stockholders determine who will be on the board of directors who in turn (1) hire and fire the major officers, (2) choose what the firm will produce, and (3) decide how much of the profits will be reinvested instead of being returned to the stockholders.[1]

In a worker-cooperative, the workers decide what and how the firm produces, and it is the workers who are the claimants to any residual profits of the firm. A worker-owned business is a romantic ideal of socialists and communists; yet, in the United States, there are few proletarian worker-cooperatives (the most prominent are plywood-manufacturing companies in the Northwest). Instead, the worker cooperative is most common in the bastion of capitalism – investment banking, accounting, and law firms. These are generally termed *partnerships*.

Outside of the financial industry, there are very few businesses that are consumer-owned. REI (a provider of recreational equipment) is probably the most prominent. At one time, there were a significant number of cooperative grocery stores in the United States. Now there are food and bookstore co-ops on some college campuses, but otherwise they have, with few exceptions, disappeared from the scene. However, there are a great number of credit unions and consumer-owned insurance companies (known as mutuals, as in State Farm Mutual and Mutual of Omaha). We will come back to mutuals in a later chapter.

Finally, there are a number of producer-owned cooperatives, including Visa and MasterCard (owned by the banks) and Sunkist oranges, Ocean Spray Cranberry (owned by the growers), and, until 2005, Diamond Walnuts.

B. THE COST OF GOVERNANCE

Why do we observe these different governance structures under different circumstances? As in the rest of economics, the answer depends on costs and benefits. Here the key components are the cost of governance and the cost of monitoring (each is a kind of transaction cost). When there is a unity of interest, the cost of governance is greatly reduced.

The clearest contrast is found by first comparing a worker-owned automobile firm to an investor-owned automobile firm and then comparing the worker-owned automobile

---

[1] How stockholders control the managers of the corporation is discussed in the next chapter.

firm to an accounting partnership. Suppose that the workers owned the automobile firm. There would be endless disputes regarding the amount of pay and the characteristics of the work for each job. Should a machinist make more or less money than a line operator? Should older workers make more than younger workers? Which workers should be assigned night shifts? Naturally, each worker would argue on his or her own behalf. If the worker could no longer own part of the firm when he or she retired and could not sell the stock to a new worker, then those who were about to retire would try to grab the wealth of the firms for themselves. So this would be another source of conflict between the worker-owners.

While some of these issues would arise in corporation, the issues would arise in a different arena – bargaining between union and management and within the union itself. Furthermore, the range of issues negotiated between union and management is more limited than the free-for-all that would occur in a worker-owned firm. In contrast stockholders have a unity of interest.[2] While they may disagree regarding what is the best strategy, they all gain the same amount per share owned when the stock rises in value or dividends are paid.

Let us now turn our attention toward accounting firms. The accountants, not the secretaries or other workers, are the partners. So there is a much greater unity of interest than there would be in a worker-owned manufacturing firm. The scheme for dividing up profits to the partners is relatively simple.

Sometimes the profits are shared equally among the partners. This makes sense given that the work is relatively similar across the partner accountants. The major problem in such an arrangement is shirking. An accountant could go fishing or daydream rather than work hard. This is partially mitigated by the following: accountants do not become partners unless they have demonstrated a strong work ethic. Unlike manufacturing, where the output is a team effort (many people produce a car) and therefore effort has to be monitored, the output of the partner is easily measured and understood by the fellow accountants. And therefore the partner is less likely to be able to shirk without being observed.

At other times, the shares depend on the amount of money each partner brings into the firm (such as billable hours). In comparison to automobile production, which requires the output of a team, the amount that one accounting partner brings to the firm is relatively independent of the effort of other partners. Problems may arise under this scheme as well, as those partners who provide other returns for the firm (such as bringing in new clients, managing internal conflicts, etc.) may not be appropriately awarded. But again relative to other forms of organization and other types of production, the costs are relatively small.

Further insight is garnered by considering ESOPs (employee stock ownership plans). Almost always either this stock does not come with voting rights or the workers own only a very minor share of the firm. Again this is to reduce governance costs – workers do not have a unity of interests with each other or the other shareholders.

The importance of unity of interest is also revealed by considering agricultural-producer co-ops. Ocean Spray is a co-op of cranberry growers. They sell their cranberries to Ocean Spray and then Ocean Spray produces and markets cranberry products. The

---

[2] Recall that from the chapter on bankruptcy that much of bankruptcy law is devoted to creating a unity of interest among creditors.

cranberry growers all benefit when Ocean Spray cranberry juice sells at a high price. Of course, those of you who like the tart taste of cranberries will say that they also produce cranberry-raspberry, cranberry-grape, and so on. Ah, but the growers of raspberries and grapes are not part of the cooperative. If they were, there would no longer be a unity of interest. So the cranberry cooperative just purchases the raspberries. And the same goes for the other cooperatives – they all specialize.

So, given all these reasons against worker-cooperatives, why do they exist in the plywood industry? There are three answers: (1) these worker-cooperatives are very small – they involve about a dozen workers; (2) plywood manufacturing is a simple process and all jobs are rotated among the members, thereby unifying interests; and (3) most of them have disappeared, either stopping altogether or being converted into investor-owned enterprises.

C. THE NATURE OF PRIVATE PROPERTY AND THE ROLE OF COMMUNITY

Communists saw communal property as an ideal that somehow fostered community (notice the same root used three times in a row). At the same time, they saw private property as the root of all evil. Nowhere was this devotion to communal property greater than in agriculture where farms were forcibly collectivized. The question we address here is (1) whether communal ownership of farmland is a good idea and (2) what are its costs and benefits.

The answer to 1 is obvious. Overwhelmingly, when given the choice, people choose single ownership of separate parcels over collective ownership of the whole. Most farmland in the United States is owned by individual families. Most of the remaining farmland is owned by corporations. Even the strongest cases for collective ownership rapidly dissolve into separate ownership. Consider first the case where there are several children who could inherit the land. One possibility is that all the children jointly inherit the land; the second is that one child inherits the land, and the third possibility is that the land is subdivided. The first possibility has historically been rare and is especially rare when the siblings must jointly work on the land (making it less of an investment and more like a worker cooperative). Our other example is the kibbutz. Some of the early Israeli settlers were fervent socialists, and they created joint ownership of the land. Several generations later, most of the kibbutzim have been converted into single ownership, and many of the remaining employ idealistic volunteers from other countries.

The problem of joint governance of agricultural production is enormous. The communal owners have to make decisions about the allocation of their own time (do they all do the same thing or does each specialize). Unlike stockholders who want to maximize profit or a single owner who wants to maximize utility, there is little unity of interest because profit and work are inextricably entwined and thus worker/owner preferences are bound to be in conflict. Furthermore, Workers/owners need to monitor one another's behavior to see that the other is doing their fair share. Why work hard if you will collect your share of the output (profit) whether you work hard or not.

So given all these problems, how and why do the few communal efforts succeed? Let us take a look at the Hutterites, whose twenty-eight thousand members do engage in communal ownership of land and have done so ever since they first came to the United States over 150 years ago. They create a unity of interest in the following ways. They have very similar religious beliefs (it is not like saying you are Catholic and then using birth control) and a hierarchal system where the elders (all men) are quite powerful. Housing and other amenities are identical, and they limit the size of their communities to 120, including children. They do not own TV sets or radios and speak in a Tyrolean-German dialect, which further insolates them from outside divisive influences. They meet for religious services every evening and eat communal dinners. This not only maintains a unity of interest but also can be seen as a governance cost as they work out disagreements at mealtime.

D. LIMITED LIABILITY OF STOCKHOLDERS

Shareholder liability in corporations is limited to the value of the share; if the firm goes bankrupt, the creditors cannot make claims on stockholders' assets such as bank accounts and stock owned in other firms. There are two reasons for this. The first is to create a unity of interest, and the second is to reduce transaction costs. Before considering the second reason, let us briefly consider the first. If there weren't limited liability, then stockholders with greater wealth would be subjected to greater losses. Their interests would therefore diverge from those with less wealth and governance of the firm would be more difficult.

The second and more important reason is to reduce the transaction costs in buying and selling stock. If liability were unlimited, then the value of the stock would not only depend on the value of the corporation but also on the wealth of the stockholders. When the other stockholders have less wealth, then owning stock is riskier as your assets may have to pay for any debts owed by the firm. Hence, you will need to constantly monitor the wealth of the other stockholders, which would be quite difficult if there are many of them. The benefits of a diversified portfolio would greatly decrease, and, as already noted, the value of a stock would not only reflect the value of the firm, but also the wealth of the owners of the stock. So stock prices would no longer be a clear signal of firm value.

It should be noted that limited liability of the stockholders reduces stockholder risk but at the same time increases the risk to others, for example, banks that lend to the corporation. But banks are in a superior position to take on the additional risk when there is limited liability by stockholders because they are monitoring the firm's health when they decide to lend, and there is no need for them to monitor the wealth of the stockholders, which we have already said is very difficult and costly to do.

Lloyds of London is an insurance group without limited liability.[3] If insurance payments are unanticipatedly high, the names (as the investors are called) may have to sell off their houses, paintings, and so forth. Of course, to be a name, the person must have a lot of wealth. So there are greater information costs in this type of arrangement. But given its traditional clubby atmosphere, this information is relatively cheap to obtain. The reason why the names are willing to undertake such a risk is that the return on their investment is very high. Indeed, because they do not have to put up any capital (just a promise) to get a return, they do very well, except when things go bad.

---

[3] Actually, liability is still limited by the degree of risk that Lloyds is willing to undertake. If they insure a ship and it sinks, the underwriters' liability is limited to value of the ship and its contents.

THE LUSTY LADIES WORKERS' COOPERATIVE

The July 17, 2004, *New Yorker* magazine reported on a strip club in San Francisco that is owned by the workers (mostly female exotic dancers). Previously, it was an investor-owned club, and the exotic dancers worked as independent contractors. As independent contractors, each dancer paid the club about $200 a night to use the facilities. In exchange, the dancers got to keep the money that customers paid to see them perform. There are a variety of reasons that the dancers were independent contractors rather than employees of the firm. It allowed the parties to get around certain employment regulations that were not wealth maximizing (that is, the cost of the regulation to the club was greater than the benefit to the dancers). More important, the dancers were the residual claimants. This means that the benefit of improved performance went to the performer. When the club became a workers' cooperative a number of problems arose. Recall that workers' cooperatives try to create a unity of interest by avoiding specialization in work tasks. Unfortunately, not everyone is equally good at bookkeeping, and the male cashier (one of the cooperative owners) did not want to become an exotic dancer. So specialization crept back in with an accompanying increase in disagreements among the co-owners. The dancers were now on a salary. This resulted in them standing around too much rather than engaging in the more exotic aspects. Effort is reduced when the returns go to someone else.

One might wonder whether Lloyds of London is a counterexample to the earlier argument that there needs to be a unity of interest when there are multiple owners. We have already noted that the only participation by the names is to provide capital when the insurance costs outweigh the premiums collected and to receive the income when the reverse is the case. So there is less likely to be conflict among the owners than there would be in a worker-cooperative, for example. Nevertheless, there is less unity of interest than in limited liability corporations because variation in wealth among the names means that they face different risk. Lloyds gets around this problem by having a very unusual structure. It is not a unified company at all. It is a bunch of syndicates. A set of names (syndicate) insures one ship; another set of names insures another ship. There is no governance structure beyond the one arrangement. Once again, the exception is not an exception to the general rule, after all. In recent years, Lloyds has partially switched to a limited-liability setup.

E. DEBT VERSUS EQUITY

As noted in the previous section, stockholders (holders of equity) have voting rights. Why not bondholders (holders of debt with fixed-interest obligations) as well? Stockholders and bondholders do not have a unity of interest; so we would not expect both to have voting rights. Nor would we expect bondholders to have voting rights instead of stockholders. Obligations to bondholders are fixed; so bondholders would have little interest in maximizing the profits of the firm when the firm is profitable. In contrast, when the firm is facing bankruptcy, bondholders have a very strong interest in the welfare of the firm; and thus it is common to have bondholders and other debt holders to have a say in the firm's governance (see the bankruptcy chapter).

EMPLOYEE STOCK OWNERSHIP PLANS

ESOPS are used most often when the firm cannot raise money elsewhere and would be extremely rare if not for special tax breaks. United Airlines is an interesting illustration. United was facing bankruptcy. It could not raise capital to pay for the pilot salaries, and because the pilots were receiving quasi rents (if they quit their jobs, their alternative salaries would have been much lower), the pilots implicitly provided the capital by accepting lower salaries in return for owning the firm. A similar rationale explains why start-ups provide stock options. Outsiders (including venture capitalists) may know less than the workers about the viability of the firm. Because of this asymmetric information, it may make sense for the employees to take on the added risk of gaining stock options rather than being paid a salary; otherwise, the cost of financing would be too high. Furthermore, the employee must be with the firm for a specified length of time before they can actually take advantage of the options. This keeps employees with the firm at a critical time.

ESOPS are appealing to those who see worker ownership as a way to mitigate the evils of capitalism. But in general, ESOPS are a bad idea for workers. Rather than diversifying his/her portfolio, ESOPs put workers at great risk by linking their job and their investments. If the firm goes belly-up, the worker loses his/her job and the value of the stock in the firm. While not formally an ESOP, Enron required its employees to own stock in the firm as part of its retirement package. The workers lost all around when the firm declared bankruptcy.

F. CONCLUDING REMARKS

It is much easier to govern an organization when there is a unity of interests among those who govern. As we have seen, there are a number of methods of creating a unity of interests. But in some organizations, such unity is difficult, if not impossible to create. We will consider one such organization, the U.S. Congress, in a later chapter.

SUGGESTIONS FOR FURTHER READING

Hansmann (1996) and Ellickson (2000) are the inspiration for many of the ideas in this chapter. Both make interesting reading. Woodward (1985) discusses the rationale for limited liability of stockholders.

REVIEW QUESTIONS

1. Why are there few worker-owned businesses in manufacturing? (6)
2. How do worker-owned businesses try to create a unity of interest? (4)
3. Why is there limited liability for holders of stock? (4)
4. Why are the Hutterites able to have communal farms? (10)
5. Why don't bondholders govern firms rather than stockholders? (4)
6. Why are producer cooperatives successful but not worker cooperatives? (6)
7. What is an ESOP? What limits are put on an ESOP? Why? (4)

REFERENCES

Ellickson, Robert. (1993). Property in Land. 102 *Yale Law Journal* 1315.

Hannsman, Henry. (1996). *The Ownership of Enterprise.* Cambridge, MA: Belknap Press.

Woodward, Susan E. (1985). Limited Liability in the Theory of the Firm. 141 *Journal of Institutional and Theoretical Economics* 601.

33

Corporate Law and Agency Problems

A. Private Choice as a Guide to Optimal Choice 315

B. Comparative Advantage 317

C. Tender Offers 317

D. Proxies 318

E. Mergers 319

F. Concluding Remarks 319

SUGGESTIONS FOR FURTHER READING 321

REVIEW QUESTIONS 321

REFERENCES 321

In standard intermediate microeconomics texts, profit maximization by firms is a relatively simple thing – the firm produces until marginal revenue equals marginal cost. Much of corporate law is devoted to a different aspect – how stockholders ensure that managers maximize the value of the firm.

Agency costs are the costs incurred by a corporation because its top management (agent) is not the same as its stockholders (the principals) – the separation of ownership and control. Stockholders want the value of the stock to be maximized but managers may have other goals such as keeping their jobs, even if others are better managers. Managers may be lazy, like to run large but less-profitable corporations, or may be incompetent. Agency costs arise because management has information that stockholders do not and management is empowered to make decisions on behalf of stockholders. Therefore, managers' behavior may go in a direction contrary to the interests of the stockholders without the managers having to pay for it.[1]

Agency costs are mitigated by aligning the interests of the agent with the interests of the principal. *Legal rules* impose fiduciary duties that require managers to act in the best interest of the stockholders. Stockholders can sue managers in civil court for egregious behavior such as self-dealing and embezzlement. However, criminal and civil liability cannot be used for more subtle failures to maximize profits (such as excessive diversification of the product line). Judges are incapable of making such judgments; if they could, they would be running the corporations themselves.[2] Some firms *tie salary incentives to the performance of the company;* some compensate management with stock or stock option plans. These align stockholder wealth with management income, but there is still a misalignment of interests because managers face risk from variation in the firm's stock price that stockholders with their diversified portfolios do not. The *competitive market for managers* rewards the better ones with new job lopportunities and more pay and prestige. But outsiders may have a harder time measuring management quality than the corporation's board of directors or stockholders. If management and the board of directors are not maximizing shareholder value, stockholders can wage a *proxy fight,* take control, and oust them. Such a strategy is difficult, however, and falls prey to the free rider problem. Alternatively, an outsider may overcome the free rider problem by making a *tender offer* and buy a majority stake in the firm. Note that the threat rather than the actual execution of a takeover may be sufficient to encourage managers to maximize profits. Later, we will consider some of these methods in greater detail.

Before we proceed, it is useful to ask the following question: if corporations with diversified stock ownership have such agency problems, why don't other organizational forms transplant the corporation. For example, entrepreneurs could raise funds through debt financing (bonds) rather than by equity (stocks). There are two basic answers. (1) The benefit of reduced risk from a diversified stock portfolio may compensate for increased agency costs. The stockholders have a comparative advantage in risk-taking and the management has a comparative advantage in decision making. The benefits of this specialization may overcome the agency costs. (2) Parallel problems to agency

---

[1]   Known contrary behavior is reflected in lower salary for management. For example, large perquisites (extended vacations, cars, and planes) are a substitute for higher salaries. Our analysis in this chapter is focused on publicly held corporations rather than closely held corporations where the managers are typically the major stockholders and the firm is incorporated to limit liability rather than to diversify risk.

[2]   Hence judges do not second guess managers. This is known as the "business judgment rule."

costs arise in other organizational forms. Suppose that managers borrowed the money themselves; then the lenders would have to monitor the managers so that they did not squander the lenders' money.

An interesting question is when one of these organizational forms is more likely to appear than another. Corporations are the preferred business form when large amounts of outside capital need to be generated. Typically, in accounting and law firms, there is little need for outside capital; most of the costs are the labor services, which are billed to the clients. Therefore, a partnership makes more sense in these circumstances (and in the United States, law firms cannot be investor-owned corporations).

A. PRIVATE CHOICE AS A GUIDE TO OPTIMAL CHOICE

In trying to determine the optimal set of corporate laws, our best guide is the corporate charters and bylaws actually chosen, the laws of the state where the corporation was chartered, and the legal rules of the exchange where the corporation is listed. This parallels the argument regarding the allocation of liability for damage between contracting parties – the market choice under free contracting is in general the best guide to the optimal choice.

Consider the situation where the owner of a firm is deciding to incorporate. If the articles of incorporation have inefficient rules (for example, not allowing auditing or guaranteeing lifetime jobs for managers), then long-run profits will be reduced. Therefore, investors will pay less for the stock in the first place. If the original owner wants to maximize her own profit from the sale of stock, she will choose efficient rules that maximize the profitability of the corporation when it is owned by the purchasers of the stock. Not surprisingly, no corporate bylaws outlaw external audits.

Since articles of incorporation and bylaws do not include all possible rules, some of the unstated provisions are determined by the rules of the state where the firm is incorporated. The original owner of the firm will choose to incorporate in that state whose rules maximize the return to the original owner, and, as already noted, this is where shareholder return is maximized. States can gain from incorporation when the incorporation fees are larger than the costs, to the state of incorporation (including court costs and filing costs).[3] So states compete for incorporating firms by providing corporate rules that maximize shareholder value. This is known as a "race to the top."[4]

The same logic holds true for the choice of stock exchange. Firms will register with that stock exchange (New York, NASDAQ, etc.) whose rules regarding trading of the stock and accounting requirement maximize the value of the firm's shares.

These competitive forces do not eliminate all agency costs. As in other areas of economics, rules are implemented until marginal cost (of enforcement due to extra monitoring, for example) equals marginal benefit (of reduced agency costs).

---

[3] Delaware, where nearly one-half of the largest firms are incorporated, derives 16% of its revenues from corporate franchise fees. Delaware also provides special expertise: corporate law cases have their own special court so that the judges who specialize in corporate law are more knowledgeable and their decisions are more predictable.

[4] Ralph Nader, "the consumer advocate" along with his co-authors Green and Seligman (1976), claimed that state charters are a race to the bottom and therefore federal regulation is preferable. His confusion derives from his lack of understanding regarding competition. Suppose that it were a race to the bottom, then the stock of corporations incorporated in Delaware would be low. Corporate raiders would then buy the cheap stock, incorporate elsewhere, and make a killing.

It is possible that the original owner of the firm has different objectives than profit maximization. Perhaps she wants to be the head of the firm even though profits might be higher under different management. She would then write into the articles of incorporation that she is to remain as head of the corporation even though stockholders might prefer someone else. This would result in less money being offered for the stock in the first place and would only be done if the original owner valued managing more than the loss of profits from her management. Of course, such rules also maximize joint value but would be a poor guide to those businesses where the original owner has no particular attachment to running the firm.

Actual charters and bylaws would be a poor guide under the following three scenarios: (1) agency failure – managers rather than owners decide the nature of the articles of incorporation; (2) asymmetric information – investors are prone to mistakes; and (3) third-party effects.

The first scenario is extremely unlikely. The original owner has a great deal to lose from an inefficient charter; the original manager may gain little from an inefficient charter (he may not have anything to do with the incorporated firm) and always gains less than the original owner loses.[5] And furthermore, if the charter were inefficient, the firm would be ripe for a takeover – with a lower stock price because of an inefficient governing clause, another firm could take it over, change the governing structure and increase the value of the stock.

There are also problems with the second argument that investors are prone to mistakes and choose firms with inefficient corporate charters. Unwise investors will tend to lose money, and wise investors will tend to gain. Those with the largest and most influential investment portfolios will tend to be the most informed (and possibly the luckiest). So survival-of-the-fittest investors implies survival-of-the-fittest corporate charters. Furthermore, numerous institutions arise to provide information to the uninformed investor. Investment counselors develop the requisite information to guide potential purchasers of initial public offerings (IPOs);[6] firms specialize in the underwriting of the stock and develop reputations for choosing good risks; exchanges, too, develop reputations. Purchasing mutual funds means that the investor need only study the return on the fund itself rather than knowing about all the items in the market basket. Of course, those potential investors with a comparative advantage in analyzing growth potential might not rely on these modes and instead offer venture capital directly to the firms.[7]

Market choices yield bad outcomes when there are third-party effects and high transaction costs prevent these effects from being internalized. Consider the possibility (contrary to fact) that the place of incorporation also determined the liability of the corporation regarding pollution. If this were true, North Dakota might allow shipping companies to be free of liability from oil spills on the high seas. Shipping companies would then incorporate in North Dakota. Thus, competition would lead to an inefficient

---

[5]   This counterargument may be less persuasive for those situations where the charter is being amended. However, at the time of incorporation, the firm could make certain kinds of amendments harder to make if stockholders are worried about ex post rule changes.

[6]   Many of the Wall Street shenanigans that were recently revealed showed that the major investors were able to get first in line for the IPOs.

[7]   Although all of these institutions reduce the risk to the uninformed, they may not eliminate it entirely. For example, there may be a special market niche for the gullible.

result.[8] But this scenario cannot happen because corporate law is about the internal rules of the corporation. Thus, corporate law is unlikely to have such third-party effects although some have argued that laws of incorporation for one company may undermine investor confidence in the market as a whole.

B. COMPARATIVE ADVANTAGE

In deciding whether there should be a government regulation rather than free contracting, one should always consider the issue of comparative advantage. In ordinary economics, comparative and absolute advantage suggests that Florida oranges are shipped to Minnesota in exchange for wheat rather than having Minnesota grow oranges and Florida grow wheat. The concept of comparative advantage can be used to analyze legal issues as well. Consider rules regarding insider trading by management. There are federal regulations against managers of a corporation short-selling stock in the corporation.[9] Assume, for the sake of argument, that insider trading is "bad." The question then becomes who is best able to deal with this bad, firms or the federal government. Managers are capable of many bads. They may sleep on the job, hire attractive and incompetent rather than unattractive but competent underlings, or get paid more than they are worth. In general, stockholders are felt to have a comparative advantage over federal regulators in determining the employment contract. We would therefore want to know why stockholders were relatively less competent with regard to curbing opportunism that arises from short selling.

Comparative advantage also takes place between the firm and the stockholders. As already noted, stockholders are better at diversifying risks and managers are better at managing. Using the insight of Coase, we would expect that rights would be allocated to managers if and only if these rights were more valuable to the managers than to the stockholders. Equivalently, rights are granted to managers if and only if the allocation increases the wealth of stockholders.

C. TENDER OFFERS

Tender offers present shareholders with the opportunity to sell some or all of their stock at a premium above the market price. The people acquiring the stock hope to gain a majority of the stock and take a controlling interest in the company, thereby overcoming the problems of diffuse ownership. Once in charge, the new owners can make changes in the board of directors and in management, more generally. If they make wise decisions, the value of their shares will increase.

The reason why stock is not just bought individually and (surreptitiously) on the open market at market prices is that there are federal laws against one person or entity having more than 5 or 10% controlling interest in a firm without a public announcement.

---

[8] Such a race to the bottom is found in the registry of ships. Ships are registered in those countries with the least stringent requirements (e.g., no minimum wage; no pollution standards, etc.). This is why ships are usually registered in Liberia, Panama, and Bermuda rather than the United States and England, for example.

[9] Selling short means that the person promises to sell stock, which she does not presently own, at a specified price at a future date. The seller is betting that the price will be less than the market predicts. We will consider insider trading in greater depth in the next chapter.

Even without this reason, the supply of shares put for sale does not necessarily go up when the price goes up since the higher price reflects higher value.

Tender offers typically take place when the managers are hostile to a merger. Tender offers involve high transaction costs – they require newspaper advertisements, services of an investment banker, and considerable legal services.[10] However, the offer can prevent holdouts because the offer can be made contingent and it need not result in 100% of the shares being purchased. For example, the offer can be "I promise to buy 60% of the shares at $50 a share if and only if stockholders are willing to sell me 60 percent of the shares at that price."

One might think that stockholders would want to encourage tender offers because tender offers are above the market price. But, in fact, many corporate charters include defensive tactics that discourage such offers These may include staggered terms for new directors, which serves to delay effective control, supermajority requirements so that more than half of the shares are required for a merger, and "poison pills" stocks, which mature once any person owns more than x percent of the shares and entitles their owners (except the bloc holder) to purchase additional shares at a discount or sell at a premium to the majority owner.

Now it is possible that this resistance increases the collective bargaining power of present shareholders. However, at the same time, these defensive tactics (1) increase transaction costs by raising legal barriers and (2) loosen the control over managers by making takeovers more difficult. Takeovers are a way to make sure that managers are behaving and maximizing shareholder value. The threat of a takeover keeps the manager maximizing; reducing the takeover threat increases the possibility of agency problems.

Economists have argued endlessly about the relative merits and demerits of poison pills without reaching a consensus. We therefore fall back on our earlier argument that the market is making the right decision. Many corporate charters (but not all) and many states (but not all) allow poison pills. So at least in some circumstances poison pills are likely to be value maximizing.

D. PROXIES

Suppose that the firms managers perform poorly, then those investors with a nontrivial amount of stock in the firm (pension funds, Warren Buffet, etc.) can organize a rival slate of directors and ask for proxies (assignment of their votes) from other shareholders. Proxies are felt to be less effective than tender offers because the returns to those organizing the fight are smaller; most of the benefit falls on passive stockholders not waging the proxy fight. Leaders of the proxy typically hold a smaller share of the firm than would be the case if they acquired the firm through a tender offer. However in acquiring the firm through a tender offer, they may have to pay a premium price.[11] So the choice between a proxy fight and a tender offer depends on the circumstances.

---

[10] Tender offers are costly and unwieldy instruments. The group making the tender offer must provided an expensive disclosure document with the Securities and Exchange Commission (SEC). It must offer all stockholders the same deal, and the offer must remain open for twenty business days. Some of the rules come under the Williams Act (15 U.S.C. §§78m(d), (e), 78n(d)–(f)).

[11] It is often the case that a firm that intends to make a tender offer will first buy a significant number of shares in the corporation so that part of the increase in share value brought on by the tender offer is captured by the firm making the tender offer.

CLASS ACTION SUITS AND AGENCY PROBLEMS

Sometimes the harm to any one victim is quite small so that it does not pay the victim to hire an attorney and go to court to collect damages, but the collective harm to all the victims is quite large (for example, pollution from a smoking factory). Under such circumstance, were the legal system to rely on individuals to bring suit, there would be too little litigation and too much harm (assuming that the harm should be mitigated by the actions of the injurer). There are two solutions to this problem. One is to impose government regulations that reduce harm (such as pollution) to the optimal level. For example, in the twentieth century, government regulation including zoning usurped the role of private nuisance suits as a way of controlling pollution. The second method is the class action suit, where the claims are bundled into one suit so that it becomes worthwhile to litigate. At the same time, such class action suits eliminate duplicative trials where the same factual and legal issues are covered.

Class action suits are not without problems, however. The lawyer is an agent for plaintiffs with only modest interest in the lawsuit because of the small harm and small potential award to any individual plaintiff. The lawyer may choose a strategy that maximizes his/her fees rather than maximize the expected return to the plaintiff (for example, the lawyer may settle a case for a small amount if the settlement provides for large fees to the lawyer or prolong the suit if that increases the lawyer's fees). Because of the small amounts of money that an individual plaintiff can expect to receive, no one on the plaintiff side has the incentive to monitor the lawyer to make sure that the lawyer is representing the interests of his clients. Of course, there might be another lawyer who might take on a class action suit against the first lawyer for not representing his clients appropriately.

E. MERGERS

A merger takes place with the consent of both boards of directors and stockholders in contrast to a tender offer where only the target firm's shareholders need to approve. The transaction costs are much lower for a merger than for a tender offer. This means that the takeover firm may offer the incumbent managers a better deal (promising not to fire the managers or giving them golden parachutes) to gain their acquiescence. But the offer is bounded by the transaction-cost savings.

F. CONCLUDING REMARKS

Ultimately, it is the market for corporate control via proxies, merger, and tender offers that maintains the alignment of manager behavior with the shareholder interest in maximizing the return on their investments. Corporate rules of governance and the courts are too unwieldy to insure profit maximization by themselves.

The great expansion of the corporate form of organization is a testament to its ability to satisfy the owners of capital and at the same time please the customers of the firm. Insight can be gained by considering a different organizational form within a particular context – consumer-owned grocery stores (food co-ops). Such grocery stores are so rare

A RACE TO THE BOTTOM

I have argued that when it comes to corporate charters, competition between the states is a race to the top. However, when it comes to welfare, the opposite is the case – it is a race to the bottom. It is typically the case that taxpayers of a state would like to shift the burden of welfare onto other states. This is accomplished by providing fewer benefits to welfare recipients than other states provide to their welfare recipients. Even if the taxpayers of a state would like to be generous to those of its citizens who are on welfare, they cannot prevent residents of other states from migrating to the state to take advantage of the more generous assistance. In *Shapiro v. Thompson*, 394 U.S. 618 (1989), the Supreme Court found unconstitutional a Washington, DC, requirement that welfare recipients be residents for a year immediately before their application for assistance. The district had argued that the without such a requirement that the taxpayers of the district would face an unfair financial burden. However, the court ruled that this requirement ran contrary to the constitution, which requires that all citizens be treated equally. Because the provision of welfare by the states is a race to the bottom, the federal government, rather than the states, should be responsible for welfare. And to a great extent this is the case (see the chapter on federalism). In contrast, corporate law, being a race to the top, suggests that the states should have their way with minimal federal interference.

in the United States that it is necessary for me to describe their operation. The customers determine who is on the board of directors, and the board of directors determines the policy of the stores. "Profits" are returned to the customers based on the amount the customer has purchased during the year. Co-op grocery stores are not very successful in competition with investor-owned grocery stores even though these cooperatives are ostensibly set up for the customer while the investor-owned companies are organized to maximize the profits of their shareholders. This lack of success at first sight might seem puzzling. First, the "profits" of a co-op go to the customers rather than to the investors; so other things being equal, the customers of co-ops would be paying lower prices for their food in a co-op. Second, the co-op is organized to satisfy the interests of the consumer while the investor-owned supermarket is organized to promote stockholder interest. One might think that a firm that was run to please customers would be more successful than one that was run to please its stockholders. The reason for the general lack of success of grocery co-ops is the absence of a well-functioning market for corporate control. The consumer interest is almost always very diffuse so that it makes little sense for individual consumers to exercise control over managers. The problem of diffuse interest would be compounded if a consumer cooperative tried to take advantage of economies of scale by servicing many cities. Furthermore, inefficient co-ops are not targets of opportunity by other firms. As a result, the firms are less efficient.[12]

While there is a large supply of critics of the corporate model and there are compelling cases of corporate failure (Enron being a highly visible example of fraudulent behavior

---

[12] So, given the above argument, why do we see agricultural cooperatives? As shown in an earlier chapter, agricultural cooperatives (such as Ocean Spray) are simple organizations composed of likeminded producers. Although there may be some free riding, there are incentives for members to closely monitor the management because each member's wealth depends to a great extent on the success of the cooperative. In contrast, the benefit to any individual consumer from monitoring the management of a food co-op is very small.

by some of its managers), it should be noted that in the United States over large periods of time, the return to stockholders has been much greater than the return to bondholders or depositors in savings institutions. At the margin there is room for improvement, but fundamentally the corporate mode is a giant success.

SUGGESTIONS FOR FURTHER READING

Jensen and Meckling (1976) is a classic paper relating the structure of the firm to agency problems. Winter (1977) and Romano (1993) emphasize the role of state competition. Easterbrook and Fischel (1991) provide a comprehensive understanding of U.S. corporate law, while Kraakman et al. (2004) deal with corporate law in a comparative (cross-national) context. Bebchuk and Fried (2004) have a more negative view of corporate law – they believe that the stockholders have insufficient control over managers.

REVIEW QUESTIONS

1. What are agency costs in corporations? (2) Why do they arise and how are they mitigated? (8)
2. Why is state incorporation a race to the top? (6)
3. Define tender offers. (2)
4. What are the arguments pro and con about facilitating tender offers? (8)
5. Why is welfare a race to the bottom? (4)
6. Lawyers are agents of their clients. Why are lawyer agency problems particularly severe in class action suits? (4)

REFERENCES

Bebchuk, Lucian, and Jesse Fried. (2004). *Pay Without Performance: The Unfilled Promise of Executive Compensation*. Cambridge, MA: Harvard University Press.

Easterbrook, Frank H., and Daniel R. Fischel. (1991). *The Economic Structure of Corporate Law*. Cambridge, MA: Harvard University Press.

Jensen, Michael C., and William H. Meckling. (1976). Theory of the Firm: Managerial Behavior, Agency Costs and Ownership Structure. 3 *Journal of Financial Economics* 305.

Kraakman, Reiner, Paul Davies, Henry Hansmann, Gerard Hertig, Klaus J. Hopt, Hideki Kanda, and Edward Rock. (2004). *The Anatomy of Corporate Law: A Comparative and Functional Approach*. Oxford: Oxford University Press.

Nader, Ralph, Mark Green, and E. Joel Seligman. (1976). *Constitutionalizing the Corporation: The Case for the Federal Chartering of Giant Corporations*. New York: Norton.

Romano, Roberta. (1993). *The Genius of American Corporate Law*. Washington, DC: AEI Press.

Winter, Ralph K., Jr. (1977). State Law, Shareholder Protection, and the Theory of the Corporation. 6 *Journal of Legal Studies* 251.

34 Insider Trading

A. The Market Answer 324

B. Types of Insider Trading Not Allowed by Corporate Charters and State Rules 325

C. Selling Short 325

D. Why Insider Trading Is Good 326

    1. More Information Reduces Volatility 326
    2. Insider Information Is Cheaper Than Outsider Information 327

E. Concluding Remarks 327

SUGGESTIONS FOR FURTHER READING 328

REVIEW QUESTIONS 328

REFERENCES 328

At present there are federal regulations against *insider trading*. Although the term, insider trading, refers to all kinds of insiders (including lawyers who represent the firm and printers who print firm announcements) and all kinds of trading (including the buying of land), in this chapter, we will focus on regulations concerning the buying and selling of stock in a publicly held corporation by its directors and officers. For example, corporate officers are not allowed to sell *their* firm's stock short (promising to sell stock that they do not presently own at some time in the future), nor are they allowed to both buy and sell stock within a 6-month period even if the transactions were not a result of insider information.[1] Finally, these insiders cannot buy or sell stock if any inside information remains undisclosed. This is how Martha Stewart got into trouble. It was originally alleged that she obtained inside information albeit indirectly from Sam Waksal, the CEO of Inclone, who had just found out that a promising drug was not so promising after all. Before the news became public, Waksal's parents and children sold stock worth hundreds of thousands of dollars. Stewart heard about the sales and traded on this information as well. Waksal is in prison for seven years. Stewart was found guilty of lying to investigators (not about trading on inside information) and was sent for a short stay in prison.

Arguments against insider trading include the following: Because there is not a "level playing field" public confidence in the stock is undermined and investors will pay less for the stock in the first place; it encourages managers to invest in areas where managers have more opportunity for insider trading rather than investing in areas that maximize stockholder return; and managers may manipulate the performance of the firm to make good on their bets regarding the fall of the stock when they have sold it short (this is akin to a basketball player missing a few baskets when he has bet on his team losing). Of course, these latter two reasons imply the first.

A. THE MARKET ANSWER

Now, one can find arguments both for and against insider trading (arguments in favor will come at the end), but what does the competitive market tell us about where the balance lies? Most state laws of incorporation do not have similar rules against insider trading today nor did most of them have such rules before the 1960s when such insider trading was prohibited.[2] States make money from having firms incorporate in the state. Competition among states gives potential corporations (stockholders) the best deal.[3] The fact that most states did not outlaw insider trading suggests that such insider trading

---

[1] This kind of insider trading should not be confused with insider purchases of stock in *another* corporation that is the intended target of a takeover. See our discussion later in the chapter.

[2] *Goodwin v. Aggassiz*, 186 N.E. 659 (1933), argued that insiders did not have to disclose any information if trading were impersonal and not face-to-face. The Securities Exchange Act was enacted in 1934, but not until *SEC v. Texas Sulphur Co.*, 401 F.2d 833 (1968), was Securities and Exchange Commission Rule 10b-5 interpreted as preventing the selling of stock by corporate insiders. Thereafter, the need to put such a prohibition in state charters and corporate bylaws was reduced.

[3] The competitive argument holds more generally. Different politicians compete to provide efficient state (and national) rules. This holds for both regulation of production and the design of state corporate law. However, the competition for corporate charters is fiercer than the competition for production. A firm physically located in one state can choose to incorporate anywhere. Compare this to state regulation of production. If Texas has an inefficient law regarding the extraction of oil, the firm cannot move its oil drilling to Iowa, and a move to Oklahoma may be quite expensive.

did not harm stockholders. Similarly, if we look at individual corporate charters and bylaws, we do not typically observe firms incorporating with rules against this type of insider trading.[4] If insider trading were bad for stockholders, that is, it reduced the return on equity, then corporate charter and bylaws would disallow insider trading in order to raise more capital in the first place.

Salaries, bonuses, office size, and other terms of employment are generally assumed to be best left up to private negotiation. Most people would agree that government agencies do not have a comparative advantage in making these decisions. We rely on the competitive market to prevent managers from commanding exorbitant salaries, so why not rely on the market to prevent insider trading if that is a problem? Even if the federal government has a comparative advantage in detection and in enforcing the agreement (making it a criminal offense rather than a civil penalty), one would at least expect the stockholders to have some rule against it. Especially since we observe other rules against malfeasance by the corporation officers.

B. TYPES OF INSIDER TRADING NOT ALLOWED BY CORPORATE CHARTERS AND STATE RULES

The following rule is typically seen in state charters and in corporate bylaws. If corporation A intends to make a tender offer for corporation B, an insider of corporation A is not allowed to buy stock in corporation B. Such insider trading just raises the cost of purchase to the corporation as the insider and outside followers raise the price of the target stock. There is also unnecessary double transaction involved in a sale (to the insider) and then resale (to corporation A). Furthermore, the ability to make profits on such a transactions may influence the manager's choice. Similarly, an insider is not allowed to buy land that the corporation intends to purchase.

We also observe state and corporation rules against insider trading for accounting firms (and allied professions) and business newspapers, such as the *Wall Street Journal*. In these latter cases, the rules against insider trading are to protect customers from insider trading and not the stockholders: if people thought stories were printed in the *Wall Street Journal* to manipulate the stock market on the writer's behalf, then the *Wall Street Journal* would not have customers.

If corporations are smart enough to protect themselves from these types of problems by insiders, why aren't they smart enough to protect themselves from the other type of insider trading? Perhaps, because there is no problem.

C. SELLING SHORT

The greatest potential problem from insider trading is selling short (betting that the market price will go down).[5] The manager may throw a monkey wrench in the works

---

[4] A counterexample is Microsoft. It does not allow insider trading.

[5] It may be useful to describe selling short in greater detail. Person S (in this case the manager) promises to sell the stock to person D at a certain price in the future. The seller does not own the stock at present. She is betting that the price will go down so that she can buy the stock some time in the future and then sell it at the higher price at the agreed upon date. The buyer, of course, is betting that the stock market price will be higher in the future and that he is getting a bargain.

to make sure that the price of the stock will go down – the firm may be manipulated in order to make good on a bet. But obviously the manager will have a hard time keeping his job if others detect such behavior.[6] Since any manager is only one part of a management team, the likelihood of nondetection or perfect collusion by the team is remote. Despite the theoretical possibility of managers undermining their companies to make good on their short sales, there have been no recorded cases (even when short selling was allowed).

Furthermore, short selling in other firms may create similar problems; yet, there are no rules against this type of behavior. For example, the managers of Dell computers could sell Gateway computer stock short, then underprice Dell computers, thereby undermining the profitability of Gateway (and Dell). Or the managers of Dell could buy stock in their competitors and then throw a monkey wrench into Dell, making the competitors more profitable.

There is, of course, prohibition of short buying and selling in sports – betting by the players is not allowed. But this proves the point. There are no specific federal rules against players betting on outcomes of their own teams. The leagues themselves outlaw the behavior. If owners of teams are smart enough to see the potential bads from betting, why aren't the owners of corporations smart enough to prohibit short selling of stock when they think that short selling will be costly to the firm?

D. WHY INSIDER TRADING IS GOOD

Heretofore, the analysis has been on whether insider trading is bad. I will now shift the focus of the analysis and show why it may be desirable. There are two beneficial results: (i) It tends to make the stock less volatile and therefore, on average, higher priced. (ii) The cost of information acquisition by stockholders is reduced and therefore stockholders are better off.

The Coase theorem applies here. Who should have the property right to insider trading? Economic efficiency dictates that it should be the one who values it the most. By allowing an exchange (instead of making an inalienable right of stockholders), it will go to its highest use.

1. More Information Reduces Volatility

The more informative the price of the stock, the less the risk and the greater the return to the *original* stockholders. If the price is not fully informative (some information does not get translated into price), then buyers of stock need a higher expected return either to overcome the greater risk or to compensate for the costs of obtaining information about the stock. This means a lower purchase price of the stock.

Managers can make announcements or put their money where there mouth is. Clearly, we are much more likely to believe the latter, and either as a result of their purchases or by others following their lead, the price of the stock will tend to mirror the beliefs of the inside traders.[7] A public announcement without inside trading is a poor

---

[6] Although this may not be a serious threat if he is about to retire.

[7] Arguments can be made that managers cannot make any excess profits from insider trading if others know that they are insiders. Why sell stock to an insider? This must mean that the stock is worth more than you think it is. Therefore, the only effect of insider trading is to alter the market price, but no trade will be made!

substitute. Some things cannot be announced (for example, "we are about to secretly buy some undervalued land"). Also the announcements are lumpy and hard to interpret (something like an Alan Greenspan announcement) unless they are in the following form: "the stock price should be two dollars higher." Even in this form the announcement may not be believed (perhaps the firm is trying to get lower rates from bondholders). With continuous insider trading, the stock price is more informative. In turn, the more informative the stock, the less the fluctuation in the price of the stock.[8]

The main counterargument is that the firm can engage in buying and selling of its own stock without recourse to "insider trading." That is, the benefits of insider trading would still accrue if the managers bought and sold stock on behalf of the firm.

2. Insider Information Is Cheaper Than Outsider Information

If the managers do not provide inside information, others such as stock analysts can spend time obtaining special information (e.g., monitoring shipments from a company), thereby making an "unlevel" playing field. Clearly, this is much more costly, and, more important, the average stockholder is "hurt" even more by outsider's information than insider's information. This is because managers will be paid less if managers can accrue additional income from inside trading. Outsiders do not benefit the firm in this way.

E. CONCLUDING REMARKS

This is, by far, the most controversial chapter in the book. Even if you are not convinced by the argument (sometimes even I worry about it being right though I have found no convincing argument to the contrary), the following is worth remembering: There is a limited role for economists. It is not up to the economist to find the costs and benefits of insider trading. Rather, it is up to the economist to determine whether the market has the appropriate incentive structure for choosing the optimal outcome. If the market does not have the appropriate incentive structure, then the economist can ask whether the regulatory market does.

The discussion of the regulation against insider trading provides many economic insights, but it is misleading in one important way. The basic argument is that there is little need for federal regulation of corporations. And in fact there are relatively few federal regulations – rules regarding insider trading is one counter-example. Another area of federal regulation regards the issuing of stock and the information that must be provided. More recently in response to the Enron accounting scandal, the Sarbanes-Oxley Act of 2002 was enacted. This is probably the most important change in U.S. securities law since the New Deal; among other things, it requires the CEO to certify that the accounting was done properly, provides for criminal sanctions, and bans personal loans to executive officers and directors (some have called it a full

---

[8] The actual proof is complicated, but the intuition is that there should be smaller swings because of the smaller changes in information and a higher level of information. Insiders might try to get around the public trading disclosure rules. If insider trading were legal, it might be difficult to track the trading of insiders (they certainly would want to hide their identity before the trade was consummated). For example, they might swap information and trade on the other person's information.

CAN OUTSIDERS TRADE ON INSIDE INFORMATION?

Suppose that you as an outsider eavesdrop on a conversation by insiders about a proposed tender offer. Should you be allowed to trade in the stock if this information is not public knowledge? In *United States v. O'Hagan*, 521 U.S. 642 (1997), the Supreme Court ruled no. The court upheld SEC rule 14e-3, which prevents trading on tender offers of undisclosed information.

employment act for accountants). But the other areas of corporate law are left to the states. Despite Ralph Nader's arguments that corporate law should be federalized, rules regarding incorporation should be and are, in general, left up to the states and the corporations.

SUGGESTIONS FOR FURTHER READING

This chapter is based on the work of Manne (1966) and Carlton and Fischel (1983). There have been a number of papers that have attempted to undermine their arguments. Perhaps the best is Ausubel (1990). Among other things, he argues that we wouldn't have laws against insider trading unless someone is hurt by them. He is correct on this point, but the parties hurt by insider trading are the stock market professionals. These professionals are hurt by the superior competition of the true insider and the lack of opportunities for extraordinary profits when the market is working efficiently because of insider trading. Ausubel then provides a model where there are two types of players, insiders and outsiders, and two periods. Because outsiders are afraid that insiders will take advantage of them in the second period, investors will pay less for the stock in the first period. But the problem with his model is that he has again not accounted for the stock market professionals – the third set of players. If insider trading is outlawed, then the stock market professionals will take advantage of the average stockholder in the second period, but, as we have noted in the chapter, the cost of the stock market professionals obtaining the requisite information is high and their gains are not offset by lower management salaries (as would be the case if management were allowed to engage in insider trading). For a comprehensive history and overview of insider trading, see Bainbridge (2003). For a spirited defense of Michael Milken, the junk-bond king, who was accused of insider trading, but plea bargained to lesser charges that resulted in a prison sentence and payment of $600 million (see Fischel, 1995).

REVIEW QUESTIONS

1. What is insider trading? (2) What is the basic approach to analyzing whether insider trading should be allowed? (4)
2. A number of economic arguments have been brought forth in favor of and against government regulation against insider trading. Provide a coherent argument of your own one way or another. (10)

REFERENCES

Ausubel, Lawrence M. (1990). Insider Trading in a Rational Expectations Economy. 80 *American Economic Review* 1022.

Bainbridge, Stephen M. (2003). The Law and Economics of Insider Trading: A Comprehensive Primer. http://ssrn.com/abstract=261277.

Carlton, Dennis W., and Daniel R. Fischel. (1983). The Regulation of Insider Trading. 35 *Stanford Law Review* 857.

Fischel, Daniel R. (1995). *Payback: The Conspiracy to Destroy Michael Milken and his Financial Revolution.* New York: HarperCollins.

Manne, Henry G. (1966). *Insider Trading and the Stock Market.* New York: Free Press.

35

Organizational Response to Opportunism: McDonald's, the Mafia, and Mutual of Omaha

A. The Potential for Opportunism and Some Solutions 332

B. Franchising 334

C. Organized Crime 336

D. Mutuals 337

E. Concluding Remarks 337

F. Postscript 338

SUGGESTIONS FOR FURTHER READING 339

REVIEW QUESTIONS 339

REFERENCES 340

Individuals and firms may act *opportunistically*. A coal-fired electrical generating plant could be built next to a coal mine to take advantage of the low shipping costs; but once it is built, the mine might raise the price of coal. If not supervised, a salaried employee might work less hard than she would if she were an independent contractor on piece rate; but if she were an independent contractor on piece rate, she might produce inferior quality goods if it were difficult for the buyer to determine quality without observing the care taken in producing them. Opportunism is just a variation of moral hazard – whenever the costs (or benefits) of someone's action do not fully fall on the person, the person may undertake less than the *socially* optimal amount of care. Within the firm, opportunism can be seen as an agency cost, more broadly conceived. The worker is an agent of the manager who is an agent of the CEO who is an agent of the stockholders.

Contracts are devised to improve coordination and align incentives. But all contracts are imperfect in this regard. These imperfections mean that the potential for opportunism remains. Firms can be viewed as a nexus of contracts. Thus choosing to organize relations within firms instead of within a market may not eliminate opportunism entirely but change the nature of the opportunism (as our example of piece rates illustrates).

So what do McDonald's, the Mafia, and Mutual of Omaha Insurance have in common, besides starting with M? As we will see, they are all organizational forms that arise to combat opportunism. But first we will discuss the problem of opportunism in greater detail.

A. THE POTENTIAL FOR OPPORTUNISM AND SOME SOLUTIONS

In standard economic textbook treatments of markets, consumer A buys an apple from supplier B. However in the real world, exchanges are often much more complicated, especially when future performance is involved (so that there is not an immediate exchange), there is the potential for opportunistic behavior.

To illustrate, let us consider a real-world example of an electrical-generation plant being built next to a coal mine. The Navajo Generating Station is the largest coal-power electrical-generating plant west of the Mississippi; it cost $650 million to build. It is located near Peabody Western Coal Company's Kayenta mine, which was developed to provide coal for the electrical generating plant. This was done to minimize transportation and inventory costs, but at the same time, this puts the coal mine and the electrical power plant at the mercy of each other since all the output of the coal mine goes to the electrical power plant and all the coal for the power plant comes from the Kayenta mine and neither has close substitutes. That is, each side has undertaken *specific investment*.

Once the specific investments were made, the situation turned into a *quasi-bilateral monopoly* situation (as the generating plant had no alternative source of coal and the coal plant had no other buyer), even though the preinvestment situation was characterized by perfect competition (for example, the electrical generation could have located near another coal mine). Because of the monopoly situation, the potential for opportunism was great. For example, the coal mine could have charged an extremely high price for the coal. There are a number of methods of mitigating the opportunism problem, each with a different cost configuration. We will now consider each in turn.

As was shown in the chapter on Coke bottles, *reputation* is one solution to the problem of opportunism. If the mining company wanted to induce other companies to build electrical power plants nears its coal seams, it would not want to have a reputation for price gauging. However, reputation is costly to establish and to discover. And in this case, where the likelihood of the same situation arising in a different location is slight, reputation would be a very weak force.

One side or the other may reduce the potential for opportunism by *reducing its specific investment*. For example, the power company could have placed its electrical-generating plant halfway between two coal mines. In this way, it would no longer be subject to the *holdup* problem. Similarly, the mining company might have chosen a coal mine location closer to other buyers. Of course, these methods are costly.

Another method of reducing opportunism is to *allocate the cost of the specific investment onto the side that is prone to act opportunistically*. For example, consider the situation where a firm wants its employees to develop skills so that the employees will be more productive. If these skills are not be transferable to other firms and if the firm is not sufficiently worried about its reputation, the firm might not sufficiently reward its employees for the specific investment that they have undertaken. Therefore, the employees would be reluctant to undertake the investment in the first place. To encourage their employees to invest in such specific assets, the firm might pay for cost of the investment. This is why the learning of firm-specific skills is often subsidized by the employer, while general investment in knowledge with transferable skills (for example, the kind of learning done in college) is more often paid for by the individual. If a firm were to subsidize general investment, employees might behave opportunistically and work for another firm soon after gaining the skills unless the employment contract required former employees to reimburse the firm for the investment. Getting back to the coal mine – electrical-generating plant problem, suppose that it is the mining company that is likely to behave opportunistically. It might build the power plant and lease it for short periods of time so that there is no need for the electric power company to undertake specific investment, and as a result the power company would not be subjected to opportunistic pricing. But this solution seems particularly farfetched.

In this case, a complicated *long-term contract* detailing the amount supplied and the prices paid was negotiated. In this way, neither side was subjected to ex post bargaining over prices. If there were many coal mines nearby, a long-term contract might not have been negotiated. For example, in the northeastern part of the United States where there are many coal mines and coal power plants, long-term contracts between the two are rare.

Sometimes, the legal system is a poor venue for enforcing the terms of the contract. Perhaps the courts cannot observe the relevant information or it is costly to do so., especially, when performance is multifaceted and ongoing, courts are blunt instruments. And lawyers are never cheap. Under such circumstances, *the residual rights to control may be rearranged*. For example, the firms might *vertically integrate* (the electrical generating plant purchases the coal mine or the coal mine purchases the generating plant). In this way *hierarchy* is substituted for the *market*. In this case, price is easy to observe and other issues are easily resolved via a long-term contract. So vertical integration between the coal mine and electric power company is not in the cards.

The rationale for vertical integration is nicely illustrated by considering its varied application within agriculture. Agricultural land is often leased for use as pasture and growing annual crops but rarely for growing grapes or fruit trees. That is, in the latter case, vertical integration (the farmer not only grows grapes but also owns the land) is much more common. This is to be expected as it would be very difficult to write a long-term contract that accounted for the various contingencies and yet was easy for the courts to observe. Hence, the potential for opportunism between the grape grower and the landowner would be too great. From another point of view, valuable investment opportunities might not be fully exploited. Of course, hierarchy has its own kinds of transactions costs (workers can behave opportunistically as well) and such costs of hierarchy must be weighed against the benefits.

B. FRANCHISING

McDonald's is a franchise. Most of the McDonald's hamburger outlets are not owned by McDonald's Corporation but rather by individual owners. Franchising is an interesting example of a complicated long-term contract. It is a two-headed beast. There are two profit maximizers, McDonald's Corporation, the franchisor, and the local owner, the franchisee. The local owner pays McDonald's Corporation a significant amount of money, and, in return, the franchisee gets training and the use of the McDonald's name. McDonald's Corporation collects royalties on sales of hamburgers and fries. McDonald's Corporation can also terminate the contract with the franchisee and buy back the franchise.

An interesting question arises: Why doesn't McDonald's Corporation either (1) own all of its outlets rather than franchising, or (2) sell off the right completely so that each McDonald's outlet is a completely independent store?

Under a franchise agreement, the franchisee, not the franchisor, raises the capital for a new outlet. An early but incorrect answer to the first question was that firms franchise to raise capital. While this looks like an economic explanation, it involves poor economic logic. McDonald's can diversify its portfolio by investing in numerous outlets. A creditor that lends 1/100 of the cost of 100 outlets faces less risk of default than a creditor that lends 100% of the cost of one outlet. Therefore, creditors of an undiversified franchisee would demand higher interest to cover their greater risk.[1]

The basic reason for McDonald's Corporation not hiring managers to run their outlets and instead selling off the right to manage is because of comparative advantage and transaction costs. Essentially, McDonald's Corporation is better at training and engaging in collective advertising while the local owner has a comparative advantage in managing. The reason for this comparative advantage is transaction costs. Suppose that McDonald's Corporation owned all its outlets. It would want its managers to work as hard as to be expected given the going wage. They would not want the manager to shirk on the job (shirking is a kind of opportunism). But how would McDonald's know whether their manager was shirking? They would have to monitor the person's work effort, which would be difficult given the dispersed nature of the McDonald's outlets, and, in any event, this would require McDonald's Corporation to hire a supervisor. And to prevent the shirking of the supervisor, they would have to hire another supervisor to supervise the supervisors. Instead McDonald's sells off the right to manage to the owners of the outlets. The owners of the outlets are now the residual claimants to

---

[1] One creditor would save on monitoring costs (here the cost of evaluating the loan) by looking at only one outlet rather than 100, but the total cost of monitoring 100 is virtually the same whether they are monitored individually or collectively.

profits and will work harder than a poorly supervised manager. Both sides are better off. McDonald's Corporation gets the same (or more) in payments and royalties as it would have made in profits if it owned the outlet, while the owner-manager is better off because she doesn't have to implicitly pay for the supervisor and instead gets the full return of her nonshirking rather than having to share it with McDonald's.

This monitoring explanation suggests that when there are company outlets they tend to be where supervision costs are relatively low – densely located in one geographical area and typically close to corporate headquarters.[2]

There is another way of understanding this arrangement. By putting up money, the owner-managers are signaling that they are high-quality managers. If McDonald's is hiring its own managers, everyone will claim that he/she is of high quality, even if they know that they are not. If McDonald's instead says that a person has to put up money to be the owner-manager, then only those who can raise that amount of money and expect to have a positive profit (after opportunity cost) will purchase the right. So this is a method of eliminating low-quality managers and preventing adverse selection.

On the other side of the coin, why doesn't McDonald's Corporation sell off the right completely. The reason is to prevent opportunism by both the franchisor and the franchisee. The cost of an inferior product falls not only on the particular franchisee, but on other franchisees as well. A bad experience at one McDonald's outlet is likely to discourage a return to other McDonald's outlets. All the franchisees are better off in an ex ante way if they commit to police themselves. Essentially, McDonald's Corporation is doing quality monitoring on behalf of the franchisees and also on behalf of itself so that it can sell more franchises in the future. So the owner manager is not completely independent and faces the possibility of losing her franchise if she does not provide the appropriate quality. McDonald's Corporation receives royalties on the sales of food at McDonald's outlets. It is therefore interested in continuing to provide subsidiary services such as advertising, developing new products, and monitoring franchisees for quality.[3] If it received all of the money upfront, the franchisees would have to rely on the courts to enforce the contract rather than self-interest.

I have argued that the franchisor can often be seen as working on behalf of the franchisees to ensure that they do not engage in opportunistic behavior. At the same time, there is always the possibility that the franchisor may behave opportunistically. One way out of this latter problem is to have the franchisees own the franchisor collectively. This is the case for MasterCard and Visa where the banks issuing the cards are franchisees, but the banks as a collective are the franchisor. Originally, Bank of America was the franchisor of Visa, but the extraordinary conflict of interest between being the credit card operator and being a bank that competed with other banks, resulted in the sale of the operation.

In explaining why fast-food outlets are often franchised, it is also important to explain why hardware and grocery stores are not. Ace Hardware Stores are independently owned stores that share in advertising and purchasing. Why aren't they a franchise?

---

[2] Internationally, they are legal issues that also determine the structure of ownership. At present, about 27% of McDonald's outlets worldwide are owned by the corporation. But in early 2006, the company announced that a significant fraction of these were scheduled for refranchising or conversion into direct licensing because of underperformance. See Dow Jones Newswires 01-24-06.

[3] Monitoring quality is easier than monitoring effort. Spot checks of bathrooms is easier than ensuring that the manager is working to full capacity. McDonald's maintains quality by insisting that meat comes from certain suppliers rather than the owners of the outlet buying meat on the open market.

Most hardware store business is local. A bad experience with an Ace Hardware store in Boston is unlikely to dissuade a person from using another Ace Hardware store in Miami (because the person is unlikely to be in need of a hardware store while visiting Miami). Because there are so few negative spillover effects, there is no need to have a special enforcement mechanism to keep the independent hardware stores in line. Furthermore, the quality of the products sold in the hardware stores is more dependent on the manufacturers, where brand name may be important. This is in contrast to a McDonald's outlet, where the quality of the meat, the amount of time the hamburger has been lying around before it is served, and the cleanliness of the toilets would all depend on the individual owner if the outlets were completely independent.

But why are Safeway grocery stores centrally owned rather than being either a franchise or being completely independent? Isn't it true that a bad experience in one is likely to dissuade someone from using another? Yes, but most of the quality control for Safeway stores (making sure that the fruits are not spoiled and the stores are stocked with items) is located in the more centralized distribution network. So franchising the individual outlets would not yield as many benefits as a fast-food franchise where the fries must be hot and served as quickly as possible. At the same time, the central distribution system makes an independent network more costly to run.

C. ORGANIZED CRIME

Criminals and criminal organizations cannot rely on the courts for the enforcement of their contracts – illegal contracts cannot be enforced (see Chapter 22 for the economic explanation). Therefore, substitute mechanisms must be used to prevent opportunism.

Members of criminal organizations often have family and grammar school ties. Frequently, initiation requires an honor code and a lifetime commitment to the organization. Opportunism is less likely in long-term relations, where any immediate gain is likely to be outweighed by the loss from the long-term relationship being terminated.

Initiation into a criminal gang usually requires the person to carry out a crime; sometimes the crime is murder. This is a good way to determine whether the person is an undercover agent. It also means that the initiate is vulnerable to blackmail, which helps to keep the initiate's behavior in line with the criminal organization's interest.

Vertical integration is another method of controlling opportunism, but vertical integration is likely to be limited in criminal organizations. Vertical integration requires monitoring and a two-way flow of information to prevent shirking. Because criminal organizations are illegal, it would be dangerous to have monitoring and information flow that law enforcement agencies might tap into. As a result, the illegal drug trade depends to a great extent on independent contractors rather than on a central organization directing the production of coca, the importation of cocaine into the United States, and its distribution. Those people selling cocaine on street corners are neither on an hourly wage nor on a salary.

As in legitimate businesses, the cost of monitoring determines the nature of the contract. A criminal organization is unlikely to have a profit-sharing agreement with a bar owner that it is extorting because the bar owner can keep two sets of books. Instead, the organization is likely to force the bar owner to buy liquor from its distributor at an inflated price (liquor purchases being easier to monitor). Here too, the arrangement is more like an independent contractor – the bar owner is not an employee of the criminal organization.[4]

Perhaps the most important way of curbing opportunism in the criminal world is the use of physical violence, including murder, for breach of contract. The threat of being shot with a Glock 35 is definitely a "high-powered" incentive. However, it is also the case that murder is a way to breach. Unlike the legal world, there are no neutral third-party enforcers of illegal contracts. As a result, murder is much more likely in criminal dealings than it would be if criminal contracts were legal.

Organized crime may try to reduce competition by organizing a cartel. Indeed, an important role of the Mafia is to manage *horizontal* problems between competitors. But this is difficult to do because the returns to taking over a competitor are very high. This is often done by "rubbing out" the competition.

D. MUTUALS

Organizational form and contractual relations are a response to the potential for opportunism. An interesting example is the governance of life insurance companies. In the nineteenth century, almost all life insurance companies were mutuals. A mutual is an organizational form where the customers own the company – the customers are the residual claimants. Thus, if insurance premiums are above the payout rate, policyholders get a rebate. Most life insurance and many auto insurance companies are mutuals (for example, Northwestern Mutual and State Farm Mutual) rather than being investor owned. Why? There is a great potential for opportunism in the life insurance business. The person pays for his/her insurance today, but only collects sometime in the future. The temptation for the investor-owned insurance companies to risk their policyholders' money to maximize their stockholders' return is very high. Because of their diversified portfolios, investors are risk neutral, and therefore maximize expected return. In contrast, people who buy insurance are risk averse and therefore are willing to trade-off expected return for less risk. This creates a conflict of interest. In the nineteenth century, consumers did not trust investor-owned organizations. Today, with strong reputations, and strong regulations regarding capital requirements, consumers are willing to purchase insurance from investor-owned firms. Indeed, mutual insurance companies such as Prudential and Metropolitan Life have turned themselves into investor-owned corporations.

E. CONCLUDING REMARKS

Depending on the legal structure and the locus of opportunism and its severity, different organizational forms arise to combat the opportunism. For example, when there is a bilateral monopoly between a producer of electricity and the provider of fuel, then a long-term contract is needed. If the legal regime is weak or the contract cannot be written in such a way that courts can determine whether a breach has taken place, then either the market will fail or there will be vertical integration – the fuel supplier and

---

[4] The argument here is not that there is no vertical integration – some bars and waste management firms may be owned by the Mafia (if we believe the HBO series *The Sopranos*) – but rather that the Mafia's direct control is unlikely to go very deep.

IS THE FRANCHISEE OR THE FRANCHISOR RESPONSIBLE?

In *Miller v. D. F. Zee's, Inc.*, 31 F supp. 2d 792 (1998), Christine Miller and three other employees filed a suit against D. F. Zee's (the franchisee) and Denny's (the franchisor). The plaintiffs alleged that they were victims of sexual harassment by employees of the restaurant. The essence of their argument against Denny's was as follows: Under the franchise agreement, Zee's agreed to train and supervise employees in accordance with Denny's *Operations and Food Service Standards Manuals*. Denny's regularly sent inspectors to assess compliance and reserved the right to terminate the franchise for noncompliance. Hence, Denny's should have terminated the franchise (Denny's was aware of the problem). Denny's filed a motion for summary judgment (that is, the case against Denny's should be dismissed without even going to trial) because a franchisor cannot be held liable for harassment by franchise employees. The court denied the summary judgment and instead held that the franchisor could be held vicariously liable because the franchisee and its employees were agents of Denny's. There is a tendency for the courts to make separate entities more entwined. This was seen earlier in the holder-in-due-course example.

electrical producer will merge. Of course, vertical integration will take place only if opportunism and transaction costs, more generally, are less within the merged firm than between the two firms.

F. POSTSCRIPT

I have argued in this and other chapters that efficiency determines the organization of production and ownership patterns (for example, whether there is a firm or a market, corporation or partnership, central ownership or franchise, equity or bond financing). Of course, firms are interested in maximizing profits, not necessarily economic efficiency, more generally. In the examples I have provided, the two tend to coincide. But there is one important area where the firm structure that maximizes profits does not necessarily maximize economic efficiency overall – when the firm is liable to parties not doing business with the firm such as victims of automobile accidents and pollution. A corporation can limit its and the industry's exposure to tort liability by creating smaller subsidiaries or selling off the business to smaller firms. These "independent entities" and smaller firms may be judgment proof against large awards, where the larger firm might not be. To illustrate, consider shipping. There could be (1) one large firm composed of many ships; (2) an umbrella organization, where each ship is incorporated separately; or (3) a large number of totally independent firms. Suppose that a ship, the *Independent Valdez*, is found liable for spilling oil in Prince William Sound in Alaska and causing $2 billion worth of damage. If the firm is composed of only one or two ships' worth in total, $200 million, then the firm can avoid all liability beyond $200 million. However, if the ship were the *Exxon Valdez* and part of a much larger firm, then the firm would be liable for much more.[5] Now Exxon had actually undertaken the middle strategy where each ship was incorporated separately but under the corporate

---

[5] The ship is now known as the "Sea River Mediterranean." The spill took place in 1989, but the punitive damages were still being appealed in 2006.

directorship of Exxon. However, the court pierced through the *organizational veil* and made Exxon Corporation liable. When courts behave this way, firms will not change the ownership structure to avoid liability to third parties.

There are other ways that the law can undermine attempts by businesses to reduce liability to third parties. For example, the law can require shipping firms to buy adequate insurance or post bonds; therefore, a firm cannot reduce the liability of the shipping industry by creating separate entities or selling off to independent firms. Once again, although not perfectly so, the interests of the firm are aligned with the interests of society; the choice of structure is for the most part independent of the issue of liability.

SUGGESTIONS FOR FURTHER READING

Coase (1937) is a classic paper on the theory of the firm. In this article, Coase explained when production is organized within a firm rather than between firms in a market setting – the former is limited by the entrepreneur's ability to control, while the later is limited by the transaction costs involved in contracting. During the past thirty years, there has been an incredible amount of interest in the topic. Klein et al. (1978) introduced the issue of bargaining over quasi-rents. Joskow (1985) discusses long-term contracts between coal producers and coal-burning providers of electricity. Milgrom and Roberts (1992) consider the problem of incentives and coordination within the firm. Among many other things, they show that high-powered incentives may be counterproductive if unmeasured actions are important for the success of the firm. Hart (1995) provides a property rights perspective. Holmstrom and Roberts (1998) and Gibbons (2004) provide recent overviews. Rubin (1978) is an important early paper on the franchise relationship. See also Hadfield (1990). For more on mutuals, see Hansmann (1996) and Pottier and Sommer (1997). Gianluca and Peltzman (1995) and Dick (1995) are good places to start if you are interested in the economics of organized crime.

REVIEW QUESTIONS

1. What is meant by the phrase specific investment? (2)
2. Explain four ways of curtailing opportunism. (8) Each method involves a cost. Explain (4)
3. Who typically pays for specific investment – the worker or the firm? Why? (4) Who typically pays for general investment – the worker or the firm? Why? (4)
4. Under what circumstances is vertical integration most likely? Provide an example. (4)
5. Why do we have franchising in the first place rather than outright ownership by the franchisees? (4)
6. Why doesn't McDonald's Corporation own all of its outlets?
7. Why are actual franchise contracts asymmetric in that most of them are devoted to preventing opportunistic behavior by the franchisee? (5)
8. How does organized crime try to reduce opportunism? (6)
9. Why were life insurance companies in the United States first organized as mutuals?
10. Why did the courts rule that Exxon Corporation was liable for the oil spill from the *Exxon Valdez* rather than treating *Exxon Valdez* as a separate company? (4)

REFERENCES

Coase, Ronald. (1937). The Nature of the Firm. 4 *Economica* 386.

Dick, Andrew R.. (1995). When Does Organized Crime Pay? A Transaction Analysis. 15 *International Review of Law and Economics* 25.

Fiorentini, Gianluca, and Sam Peltzman (eds.). (1995). *The Economics of Organized Crime.* Cambridge: Cambridge University Press.

Gibbons, Robert S. (2004). Four Formal(izable) Theories of the Firm? *MIT Department of Economics Working Paper No. 04-34.* http://ssrn.com/abstract=596864

Hadfield, Gillian K. (1990). Problematic Relations: Franchising and the Law of Incomplete Contracts. 42 *Stanford Law Review* 91.

Hansmann, Henry. (1996). *The Ownership of Enterprise.* Cambridge, MA: The Belknap Press.

Hart, Oliver. (1995). *Firms, Contracts, and Financial Structure.* Oxford: Oxford University Press.

Holmstrom, Bengt, and John Roberts. (1998). The Boundaries of the Firm Revisited. 12 *Journal of Economic Perspectives* 73.

Joskow, Paul L. (1985). Vertical Integration and Long Term Contracts: The Case of Coal Burning Electric Generating Plants. 1 *Journal of Law, Economics and Organization* 33.

Klein, Benjamin, Robert G. Crawford, and Armen Alchian. (1978). Vertical Integration, Appropriable Rents, and Competitive Contract Process. 21 *Journal of Law and Economics* 297.

Milgrom, Paul, and John Roberts. (1992). *Economics, Organization and Management.* Englewood Cliffs, NJ: Prentice Hall.

Pottier, Steven W., and David W. Sommer. (1997). Agency Theory and Life Insurer Ownership Structure. 64 *The Journal of Risk and Insurance* 529.

Rubin, Paul H. (1978). The Theory of the Firm and the Structure of the Franchise Contract. 21 *Journal of Law and Economics* 223.

36 The Organization of Legislatures

A. Electoral Competition Controls Agency Costs 343

B. The Coase Theorem Applied to Legislatures 343

C. Mitigating the Common Pool Problem 344

D. The Endogeniety of Committee Structure
   and Committee Assignments 345

E. Concluding Remarks 347

SUGGESTIONS FOR FURTHER READING 348

REVIEW QUESTIONS 348

REFERENCES 348

While we have concentrated much of our attention on courts, legislatures also make laws. However, here our interest is not on the laws that legislatures make but rather on the organization of legislatures, and in particular the organization of the U.S. Senate and House of Representatives. Many of the issues raised in previous chapters reappear in this chapter. First is the agency problem. Legislators are the agents of the voters. How are agency costs mitigated? The second and third problems are related. As noted earlier, governance costs increase dramatically when there is not a unity of interest. This is definitely the case in legislatures where different legislators represent populations with different ideologies and concerns. Furthermore, legislatures make collective decisions, and, as also argued earlier, coming to a collective agreement may involve high transaction costs. So how is the legislature designed to economize on both of these problems? Finally, there is the potential for opportunistic behavior by a subset of legislators at the expense of other legislators and their districts. One manifestation of this is known as the *common-pool problem* or more prosaically as pork-barrel politics. The benefits of a project may fall on a few districts, but the taxes that pay for such projects are shared by all districts. Therefore, a legislator from any given district is likely to ignore the costs that are imposed on other districts. This is the problem of the commons reappearing in legislatures. How is the legislature structured so that such behavior is mitigated?

Before delving into legislative organization, it is useful to briefly consider democracy more generally and compare it to totalitarian governments.

Because governments have the power to coerce, much of politics is about the distribution of the pie.[1] The tax system may be progressive (people with larger incomes pay a greater percentage of their income in taxes), neutral or regressive. And subsidies can be made to special groups such as veterans, sugar growers, or blind people at the expense of other taxpayers.

Democratic politicians gain office by getting the most votes. A presidential candidate with a platform composed of an inefficient set of policies can be beaten by a candidate with a Pareto superior platform as no one is made worse off and some are made better off by the second candidate. In this way the second candidate will get more votes, than otherwise. Indeed, one might say that politics is all about creating coalitions that are not Pareto dominated. Of course, those who lose in the political process will not be soothed by knowing that their losses were efficiently redistributed. But because democratic politics is majority rule politics, those who are dissatisfied will be in the minority.

Now let us turn our attention to authoritarian regimes. In a dictatorship there is some force for efficiency. Other things being equal, the dictator would like to grab as much pie for himself; there is no benefit to the dictator in a pure distribution game when some of the pie is wasted and not consumed by anyone. However, this is a weak force. First, if the dictator is incompetent in this regard, he is unlikely to give up power willingly; and replacing him against his will often involves high transaction costs. So the forces of competition are greatly attenuated. Second the dictator may either have a great taste for control or require control to remain in power. Control may greatly reduce economic wealth. To prevent competing sources of power, trusted cronies may be appointed to run organizations while other entities may be stifled. Finally, there is little rule of law so that agreements are unlikely to be upheld. When property rights are dependent on who is in power rather than the rule of law, investment will be less than

---

[1] The phrase "rent-seeking" is often used to characterize such activities.

otherwise because promises may not be honored by the next dictator. In particular, an agreement to buy out the dictator if he will hand over the reins of power to the next dictator may not be enforced. The life of dictators once they are no longer dictators is much shorter than the life of ex-presidents.

A. ELECTORAL COMPETITION CONTROLS AGENCY COSTS

Turning our attention back to the legislature, legislators try to appeal to the voters of their own district. If they don't, opposition candidates will take their place. So this is how agency costs by legislators are mitigated – legislators lose their jobs if they stray too far from the interest of the median voter. The opposition keeps close track of the incumbent's voting record and statements, ready to inform voters of any possible missteps. There is no need for voters to pay attention to the incumbent's voting record. The incumbent will argue her strengths and the opposition will argue her weaknesses during the election campaign.

Elections are essentially zero-sum games as only one candidate can win. As a result, the competition is much fiercer than in ordinary markets. Foster Farms may claim that their chickens taste better than any other, but they will not accuse Imposter Farms (not a registered trademark) of selling tainted chicken because some consumers might be concerned that all chickens are tainted and choose to become vegetarians instead. This problem does not arise in elections as the candidates are only interested in vote shares. Not surprisingly, there is more mudslinging in elections than in ordinary markets.

B. THE COASE THEOREM APPLIED TO LEGISLATURES

Congress is structured to reduce transaction costs. Most legislation requires only a majority. Majority rule instead of a unanimity rule reduces negotiation costs by preventing monopoly holdouts. Negotiation is also enhanced by the fact that Congress is very small in comparison to the overall population of the United States. Furthermore, there are many rules of procedure that enhance the legislature's ability to come to an agreement. For example, the rules of the House prohibit amendments of a subject matter different from the text under consideration. This rule, commonly known as the germaneness rule, is considered to be the single most important rule of the House of Representatives because of the need to keep the focus of a body the size of the House on the subject at hand (too bad one can't use the germaneness rule at the dinner table). Political parties also reduce transaction costs by facilitating trade among their relatively like-minded members. Winning coalitions are created within the context of the party platform rather than on an ad hoc basis.

Coase demonstrated that when there are well-defined property rights and low negotiation–transfer costs, economic market failures disappear. For example, the ostensible divergence between private and social cost or "externality" that arises when ranchers have the right to let their cows trample farmers' corn is eliminated when farmers pay ranchers for nondamage. In much the same way, low transaction costs can overcome many of the externality argument explanations for democratic market failures.

Political markets are inefficient when one group of actors does not account for the costs or benefits to another group of actors. An oft-cited example of the divergence between private and social costs is the majority's shifting of costs onto an unwilling minority. But when political transaction costs are low, any inefficiency is likely to be negotiated away. Consider Coase's classic example in the context of a legislature, where a majority represent ranchers and a minority represent farmers. Even though ranchers have the right of the majority to pass laws allowing their cows unlimited freedom to trample farmers' corn, the law will only allow the optimal amount of damage. Of course, part of the legislative deal would require the farmers to pay for nondamage, possibly through higher taxes. The only difference between this version and Coase's is where the deals are made. In his version, they are made in the private sector; in this example, they are made in the public sector. But in both versions the outcome is wealth maximizing.

An independent corroboration of this example has been uncovered by Kantor (1998). He studied the closing of open range in Georgia after the Civil War. The traditional agricultural practice had allowed animals to roam the countryside freely. This put the burden on farmers to erect fences around their crops. All unfenced land was considered common pasture and could be used by anyone. According to Kantor's estimates, closing the range would have generated large benefits for many counties in the state, especially those with improved acreage. However, the existence of a commons created high transaction costs so that voluntary agreements to close the commons were impossible. In 1872, the Georgia legislature partially resolved this problem by allowing county referenda on stock law (closing the range). Voting on the referenda reduced the transaction costs considerably since the unanimity required in private bargaining to close a commons was no longer required. This still did not lead to many counties adopting the stock law. A majority of voters would lose if such a referendum passed even though the gains to the minority would be greater than the losses to the majority. In 1881, the legislature passed a law that promised to enforce side payments between expected winners and losers if the new law were adopted at the local (subcounty) level. By law, tenants (who typically used the commons for grazing their cows) were provided free use of pasturage for land enclosure. This changed stock laws from a losing to a winning coalition and many more stock laws were approved.

C. MITIGATING THE COMMON POOL PROBLEM

Congress members are relatively unconcerned with the welfare implications of their policy decisions on other districts since only their constituents can influence their chances of reelection. Thus, each congressman pushes for policies of benefit to his constituency (political pork) regardless of the financial cost to other districts. So how does Congress mitigate this common pool problem? There are three answers: the small size of Congress, the party system, and the structure of Congress (this last point will be covered in a separate section).

As already argued, the small size of Congress reduces transaction costs, thereby allowing Pareto-improving trades and bargains. An inefficient method of transferring wealth from one district to another can be defeated by an efficient transfer. Politicians do not win reelection by maximizing the amount of pork that comes to their district, but rather by maximizing the welfare of some set of actors within their district. If these actors gain less pork (before-tax income), but at the same time, pay much less in taxes so that their after-tax income is greater, the representatives will increase their probability of winning by instituting a lean omnibus bill that eliminates most of the pork.

Logrolling (vote trading over issues) occurs only if the parties to the agreement are made better off. The essence of logrolling is the bundling of minority interests into a majority package. Inefficient costs are unlikely to be shifted onto third parties (other districts) because these third parties would then enter into the negotiations and strike a deal to make all of the participants better off than they would be under an inefficient regime.

Furthermore, a political party is designed to overcome this problem and to take credit for universal policies (for example, foreign policy). National political parties internalize the negative externalities that might arise from local interests trying to shift costs onto other districts. The political party is a coalition that facilitates Pareto improving trades within the party and puts restraints on opportunism by its members – party leaders can assign committees, allocate campaign funds, and so on. Although some authors have argued for the declining importance of political parties in the United States, the party label provides information and has an important influence on the vote tally. Few independents win congressional elections, indicating that the party label is a valuable commodity. A political party that promotes unpopular policies will discover that its candidates lose more elections than otherwise.

D. THE ENDOGENIETY OF COMMITTEE STRUCTURE AND COMMITTEE ASSIGNMENTS

Both houses of Congress have committee systems. For example, the House of Representatives has an Agriculture Committee, Armed Services Committee, Veterans' Affairs Committee, and a Budget Committee. Congressmen volunteer for committee assignments, and allocation is often but not always according to seniority. In general, but again not always, committees decide what legislation gets to the floor of the House for a vote.

An extensive literature views congressional committees as centers of power and the prime source for political market failure. In this section, I argue to the contrary. Committee structure and assignments are not exogenously determined. Rather the structure of Congress and the staffing of committees should be seen as efficiency-enhancing arrangements under the control of the political parties and the congressional majority.

Appointments to committees are predominately determined by individual congressman's preferences. Not surprisingly, members of the agricultural committee come from agricultural rather than urban districts. However, assignments to committees are ultimately the responsibility of the political parties. That is, the political party exerts hierarchical control in making committee assignments. The party would not make assignments that would result in negative-sum legislation for its members. An important method of party control is to make transfers to major committees partially dependent on past behavior on minor committees. Those who have voted with the leadership on key votes in the past are rewarded with choice reassignments. More important, committees also have a greater percentage of members from the majority party, thereby controlling for the possibility of defection.

While Congress has a committee structure, which could be seen as representing special interests (for example, Agriculture), it also has control committees such as Budget and Appropriations, which oversee the more specialized committees. In particular, these committees balance the competing demands of the various specialized committees by

DICTATORS AND TRANSACTION COSTS

As we have seen throughout this book, institutions arise to reduce transaction costs. In this chapter, for example, we have discussed the role of political parties and voting rules in reducing the cost of bargaining and coming to an agreement. In contrast, dictators often increase transaction costs for the would-be opposition. Freedom of assembly and independent newspapers and television stations are not allowed. While some have argued that this is to increase the effectiveness of government propaganda, few people believe the propaganda, except possibly the dictator's entourage. Rather, these restrictions on information and exchange are imposed so that it is difficult for the opposition to coordinate its antigovernment activity. If you do not know that there are antigovernment demonstrations in cities, X, Y, and Z, you are less likely to demonstrate in city W.

HOMEOWNERS' ASSOCIATIONS

Developers of large-scale housing tracts provide single and multiple residences in styles and quantities that maximize profits. They also provide rules and regulations (known as restrictive covenants) that homeowners desire. Regulations might require cars to be parked in garages rather than driveways, roofs to have wood shingles instead of asbestos, and houses to be stained rather than painted.[2] The problem with rules is that overtime conditions change, and the rules and regulations need to change also. For example, concern for fire might result in ceramic tiles being preferred over wood shingles. Homeowner associations are set up to deal with such problems. To reduce transaction costs, voting on many of the regulations are by majority or supermajority rule. However, to prevent rent-seeking, there are limits on what the homeowner association can do. For example, a majority of homeowners cannot decide to sell someone's house against their will.

Zoning boards can be seen as a parallel solution to homeowner associations when the parcels are separately owned and the transaction costs of merger are prohibitive. The reason why zoning boards rather than courts decide spatial arrangements is that there are multiple rather than two sides involved.[3] Single housing units, duplexes, apartment houses, as well as grocery stores and office buildings all have to be located somewhere. Courts are set up to decide two-sided disputes. Multiple-sided disputes need a different forum. Hence, there has been a withering away of the common law of nuisance and a shift to city councils and their appointed bodies as arbiters of spatial arrangements.

limiting the amount of total expenditures. Membership on control committees are much more likely to reflect the preferences of the median congressman in the party, there being less potential for opportunism when the goals of the agent and the principal coincide.[4] Finally, passage by a committee is not sufficient; Congress can always vote down a committee bill.

---

[2] I am not making this up. These are the rules for my development (albeit not always enforced). I am also not allowed to put up a basketball hoop or have two dogs.

[3] Zoning is prospective while court decisions are often retrospective. So zoning may also help individual planning.

[4] Cox and McCubbins (1993) show that these control committees (universal, in their terms) are more representative of Congress than special committees such as agriculture.

IRRATIONALITY OF MAJORITY RULE AND ROBERTS RULES OF ORDER

One requirement of rationality is that preferences are transitive. That is, if X prefers A to B and B to C, then rationality requires X to prefer A to C. Unfortunately, as shown in chapter 3, collective decisions need not be rational even if individuals are. Consider the following preference relationships by voters X, Y, and Z:

	X	Y	Z
1	A	B	C
2	B	C	A
3	C	A	B

Under majority rule, an election between A and B would find A to be the winner; an election between B and C would find B to be the winner, but an election between A and C would find C to be the winner. Hence, there is cycling rather than transitivity.

If there were no rules regarding voting on resolutions at a meeting, there would be endless cycling as first B would be offered as a substitute for C with B winning the ensuing vote, then A winning over B, C over A, B over C, and so on. *Robert's Rules of Order* for deliberative assemblies does not allow such substitutions, thereby ending the cycling. This however gives great power to the agenda setter.

The Constitution grants the legislative branch the right to determine the rules of its own proceedings, so rules and procedures should be seen as endogenous and designed to serve the majority. We should not expect Congress to design a committee system that is inefficient. Even after committees have been set up, Congress has considerable power. The House can shift jurisdictions of committees, refer certain bills to several committees, and impose procedural rules (for example, minority members can choose witnesses).

More fruitful than merely listing methods available to Congress for controlling committees are the predictions regarding when and where these controls will be implemented. The following two hypotheses follow directly from maximization when control is costly: (1) the more important the committee, the more control that Congress will exert over it; and (2) the more deviant the committee members' preferences are from those of Congress, the more controls that Congress will put on the committee.

Turning to confirming evidence, the Budget Committee is very important since it balances all the competing needs by the more specialized committees and therefore is a likely candidate for greater control by the party leadership. This is, in fact, the case. Members are handpicked, and tenure and seniority norms observed for other committees do not apply.

We next consider the second hypothesis, regarding preference outliers. The more extreme are a committee's members' preferences relative to those of the House, the lower will be the committee's probability of receiving restrictive rules for its bills. And the more extreme a committee chairman's preferences relative to the House, the greater the restrictions put on the chair.

E. CONCLUDING REMARKS

Congress members will try to organize Congress in a way that maximizes their reelection. The structure may grant greater power to some than others (e.g., seniority rules), but the distortion is limited by the desire of each legislator to win re-election. The committee assignments and organization cannot be against the interest of the majority of members, and ultimately, each member's behavior cannot go against the interest of a majority of the voters in the member's district.

SUGGESTIONS FOR FURTHER READING

Much of the argument presented in this chapter is based on Wittman (1995). Legislative organization is a fertile research area and many people have written on the topic from a variety of perspectives. Cox and McCubbins (2005) show the importance of political parties in organizing congress. Their work treats political parties as the fundamental institution of Congress and committee structure as a way for the dominant political party to implement its will. A contrary view is undertaken by Weingast and Marshall (1988), who treat congressional committees as being autonomous. They view the committee structure as a credible commitment device for enforcing agreements and solving the problem of intransitivity. Sheplse and Weingast (1995) is a compendium of arguments on legislative organization. Cox (2006) shows how voting procedures in legislatures are structured so that plenary time is managed.

REVIEW QUESTIONS

1. How are agency costs of representatives mitigated? (2)
2. What is the common pool problem in legislatures? (2) How is it mitigated? (4)
3. How can the Coase theorem be applied to legislatures? (4)
4. Explain how the structure of committees in Congress and their assignment is endogenous. (6)

REFERENCES

Cox, Gary W. (2006). The Organization of Democratic Legislatures. In Barry Weingast and Donald Wittman (eds.) *The Oxford Handbook of Political Economy*. Oxford: Oxford University Press.

Cox, Gary W., and Mathew D. McCubbins. (1993). *Legislative Leviathan: Party Government in the House*. Berkeley and Los Angeles: University of California Press.

Cox, Gary W., and Mathew D. McCubbins. (2005). *Setting the Agenda: Responsible Party Government in the US House of Representatives*. Cambridge: Cambridge University Press.

Shepsle Kenneth, and Barry Weingast (eds.). (1995). *Positive Theories of Congressional Institutions*. Ann Arbor: University of Michigan Press.

Weingast, Barry R., and William Marshall. (1988). The Industrial Organization of Congress. 96 *Journal of Political Economy* 132.

Wittman, Donald A. (1995). *The Myth of Democratic Failure: Why Political Institutions are Efficient*. Chicago: University of Chicago Press.

37 | Federalism

A. **The Role of the Central Government** 351

   1. Maintaining Free Trade 351
   2. Reducing Cost Shifting unto Other States 352
   3. Dealing with Conflicting State Laws 352

B. **The Benefits of State and Local Government Competition** 353

C. **Redistribution and Political Structure** 354

SUGGESTIONS FOR FURTHER READING 355

REVIEW QUESTIONS 355

REFERENCES 355

The United States, Brazil, Germany, and many other nations are federal governments, where the central government has certain powers and the state and local governments have a different set of powers. Even countries that are not considered federal have city governments that make independent decisions. Why do we have federal governments? And in federal governments, which activities are allocated to the central government and which activities are allocated to the state and local governments? Not surprisingly, if you have been paying attention to this book, transaction costs broadly defined provide much of the answer.

A major benefit of centralization is to *take advantage of economies of scale* (especially, military) without having to rely on contract and constant renegotiation. One could have fifty independent states agreeing to have a joint military. But the problem with such an arrangement is that one or more states might want to opt out of a military engagement (offensive or defensive), sometimes because the state thought it was a bad idea, but almost always because the state could then shift the cost onto the other states and take a free ride. Furthermore, there would be continual threats to break up the alliance because of disagreements over both the composition of the military and the proper share of the defense budget shouldered by each state.

A related benefit of centralization is to *promote coordination and prevent prisoner dilemma games* that might arise if the states were completely sovereign. An example, that we will come back to in greater detail, is preventing tariffs and other restraints of trade between the states. Another example is to control pollution that might drift from one state to several others. Although, some problems of pollution might be resolved between the states by contract, this is not always easy. First, in the absence of a central government, there is not a third party to enforce the agreement. Second, in the absence of a central government, property rights are established in a situation of anarchy where any state can do what ever it wants to another state as long as it does not fear retribution. This makes an optimal settlement more difficult to achieve than when there is a central authority dictating the resolution and/or establishing a sensible baseline from which to negotiate.

However, uniting states composed of different people with different preferences and endowments increases the problem of governance. As noted in an earlier chapter, governance works best when the parties have similar interests. Bargains are easier to make and rent-seeking is reduced. Furthermore, centralization increases the *monopoly power* of the center to impose its will on people with opposing preferences. If a citizen does not like government policy, it is more costly for the citizen to emigrate when the country is composed of formerly independent states. Since December 1845, those who do not like U.S. policy can no longer flee to the Republic of Texas (in fact, some might say that that in 2006 the opposite exists – if you live anywhere in the United States, you are under control of the Republic of Texas).

Federalism is an institution that tries to achieve simultaneously the advantages of small and large governmental units – strong enough to resist external enemies and coordinate actions between the states, but limited enough so that the center does not intrude on local autonomy. The key to understanding the organization of a federal government is to determine which activities belong in the center and which activities are best left to the subunits. It is obvious that the central government should be in charge of waging war and printing money. We now turn our attention to more subtle issues.

A. THE ROLE OF THE CENTRAL GOVERNMENT

Federalism is a form of dual sovereignty, whereby the federal government and states have control over their own spheres of authority. This is akin to our previous discussion of the franchise arrangement, where the franchisee is in charge of the local decisions and the franchisor is in charge of providing public goods (such as advertising) and controlling negative externalities among the franchisees. Local governments will have better information than distant central governments about local conditions and preferences and greater incentives to satisfy them. Thus zoning is left to local governments while defense (and other activities that require coordination between the states) is left to the central government, rather than vice versa.

Like multilayered firms, federations will not function effectively unless incentives are properly structured. The central design challenge is to structure incentives so that local politicians have strong incentives to serve their constituents, while minimizing incentives and opportunities to shift costs onto other constituencies.

1. Maintaining Free Trade

The interfering and unneighborly regulations of some States, contrary to the true spirit of the Union, have, in different instances, given just cause of umbrage and complaint to others, and it is to be feared that examples of this nature, if not restrained by national control, would be multiplied and extended till they became not less serious sources of animosity and discord than injurious impediments to the intercourse between the different parts of the Confederacy. Hamilton 22 (p. 144) *Federalist Papers* complaining about the Articles of Confederation.

Economists love free trade both within and among countries. But the ability to enforce free trade within a country is easier than among countries. For example, there has been free trade within the United States for more than 200 years, but only in recent years has there been such free trade between the United States and Canada (and still there appear to be many barriers to cross-county trade between the two). This may be because hierarchy is more effective than contract between two sovereigns (especially when there is no third-party enforcer) or because the political pressure for and against free trade is more likely to balance out in favor of free trade within a country than across countries. From a transaction cost perspective, having separate countries reduces within country transaction costs but increases cross-country transaction costs.

One role of the federal government is to maintain free trade within the federation. Article II, section 10 of the U.S. Constitution disallows states from imposing export or import duties without the consent of Congress unless absolutely necessary for executing inspection laws.

States and other jurisdictions may enact legislation that affects interstate commerce when these regulations serve valid goals such as safety. However, the courts are likely to find unconstitutional "state efforts to protect local economic interests by limiting access to local markets by out of state suppliers" (*Dean Milk Company v. City of Madison, Wisconsin et al.*, 340 U.S. 349, 1951). In this case, the court struck down a municipal ordinance forbidding the local sale of milk that had not been pasteurized and bottled at an approved plant within five miles of the center of the city. This ordinance clearly was economically inefficient.

Courts have consistently struck down those state taxes, which unjustifiably benefit local commerce at the expense of out-of-state commerce. For example, in *Hale v. Bimico Trading, Inc.*, 300 U.S. 375 (1939), the court held unconstitutional a Florida statute, which imposed an inspection fee sixty times the actual cost of inspection on cement imported into the state because that statute excluded locally produced cement from all inspection and inspection fee requirements.

One might ask why the court does not allow the states to decide since presumably the states would be interested in promulgating optimal contracts. In the absence of such a proscription by the court, there would be some tendency for states to engage in efficient contracting with each other. Unfortunately, there are relatively high transaction costs between the states and among the citizens. There might be numerous attempts to gain a bargaining advantage by threatening to pass tariffs and other restraints of trade in order to increase the rents accruing to the citizens. Hence, it is more efficient to outlaw inefficient behavior, in the first place.

2. Reducing Cost Shifting unto Other States

Consider the following problem. An accident between a U.S. government vehicle and a New York driver takes place in New York State. The New York driver sues the U.S. government in a New York state court. The jury may be inclined to rule against the U.S. government because most of the money is paid by taxpayers of the other states and the benefits go to a citizen of New York. To forestall such a problem, the U.S. Tort Claims Act requires that the trial be held in a federal court where the judge is not beholden to the people of New York.

Now a similar problem arises if the accident involved a vehicle owned by a Texas corporation instead of the US government. New York juries would tend to favor the New York litigant while Texas juries would favor the Texas litigant.[1] If all such incidents were resolved in a Federal court, state courts would atrophy and federal courts would be overinvolved in state law. The solution (albeit an imperfect one) is that the plaintiff must choose a state where the defendant has some kind of presence, physical or financial (such as having Internet customers in that state), so that the potential bias is mitigated.[2] A situation where this requirement was not met was in *World-Wide Volkswagen Corp. v. Woodson*, 444 U.S. 286 (1980). In this case, a New York resident bought a Volkswagen from a New York dealer. While driving through Oklahoma, the purchaser had an accident. The case was brought to trial in Oklahoma, where the purchaser claimed that the Volkswagen was defective. The Supreme Court ruled that the case could not be tried in Oklahoma.

3. Dealing with Conflicting State Laws

Which state's laws should take precedent when the laws of different states are in conflict? Again, a transaction cost analysis provides the answer. Federalism is based on territory. And in many cases, making territory the basis for rule-of-law choice minimizes information costs. Suppose for example, that a driver from Alaska runs into a pedestrian from Florida while both are in California. Which state's rule should be operative? California is

---

[1] We alluded to this possibility in our discussion of *Pennzoil v. Texaco.*
[2] Note that the Class-Action Fairness Act of 2005 shifts multistate class-action cases to the federal courts.

the obvious choice. If not, drivers and pedestrians would constantly be looking at license plates to determine which state law applied. Because pedestrians do not identify themselves by state, the most reasonable expectation is that the pedestrian is from California even if the stereotype is that Californians don't walk. Furthermore, California law is adapted to California driving conditions more than to Alaskan driving conditions. Not surprisingly, the courts have upheld the view that the place of the automobile accident determines the prevailing law.

For similar reasons, there is a general rule that estates are administered under the law of the decedent's domicile, not the heirs'. Suppose that the opposite were true. Wills would have to be rewritten every time one of the potential heirs moved; and if there were more than one potential heir, it would be unclear which state law would prevail.

The laws that regulate a married couple's relationship (say community property) are the state of domicile, not the state where they happen to invest (*Veazey v. Doremus*, 510 A.2D 1187, 1986). And if one spouse moves to a new state, that unilateral act cannot change the legal relationship – the law of the original common home state continues until both spouses move elsewhere. Again this makes sense. In the absence of such a rule, neither spouse would know the marriage contract, and one spouse could unilaterally change the contract by moving to a different state.

Not all such choice of law cases are so transparent. Phone orders may simultaneously involve two states. Since consumers are unlikely to know the state (if an 800 number), let alone state law, it makes sense that the location of the consumer tends to be the operative factor. This reasoning is especially persuasive if the seller specializes in phone orders so that the cost of learning state law is amortized over many customers and the price can vary to reflect the differential in product liability law among the different states.

Another solution to choice of law would have the federal government choose the better law. But this would undermine the whole structure of federalism since there would no longer be different laws for different states (see *Erie R.R. v. Tompkins*, 304 U.S. 64. 1938).

B. THE BENEFITS OF STATE AND LOCAL GOVERNMENT COMPETITION

Whenever there is not a perfect match between individual tax burdens and benefits from government expenditures, there is a potential for inefficiency as those who benefit more than they pay might not take into account the tax burden on others and those who pay more in taxes than they gain in government expenditures might not take into account the benefit to others. This is a more general version of the common-pool problem introduced in the previous chapter.

Under centralization, the center has *monopoly* power over the tax base and the common-pool problem becomes most acute. While competition between the political parties may reduce egregious inefficiencies, a high level of forced redistribution is possible. Under decentralization, governments *compete* for mobile citizens and firms. Jurisdictions that do not provide the kinds of services that mobile taxpayers want will lose these taxpayers to other jurisdictions that do. In equilibrium, jurisdictions will reflect the preferences of their constituents. People with high demand for public services would be drawn to localities with high levels of public services and high levels of taxation, while people with low demand would be drawn to localities with low taxes and low spending. School districts that spend a lot per pupil will be more attractive to families with young children than to retirees. An extreme example is a large retirement community (such as Del Webb's Sun City, which we encountered in Chapter 20) where people under age 52 are not allowed and no taxes are needed to support local schools since there are no children. Instead, taxes and/or association fees are used to fund golf courses and fitness centers (http://www.delwebb.com).[3] This competition and sorting provides constituents with a powerful preference revelation mechanism beyond voting and lobbying.

Competition among jurisdictions means that a local jurisdiction's ability to tax *mobile* factors is very limited. Capital mobility, for example, implies that heavier taxation on capital will in the long-run drive capital to other jurisdictions unless the taxes are devoted to expenditures complementary to capital such as roads, waste collection, and other infrastructure. This same logic holds for any mobile resource. Ultimately, any tax and expenditure pattern not desired by the mobile resource falls on the immobile resources rather than the mobile resource. Because capital, land and labor are complementary in the production process, any *excessive* tax on capital ultimately hurts the relatively immobile resource such as land (and possibly labor) even if the proceeds of the tax go directly to the landowners.[4]

In a nutshell, immobile voters would not want to impose taxes on mobile capital, even if the owners of this capital are outsiders with no voice whatsoever in local politics.

C. REDISTRIBUTION AND POLITICAL STRUCTURE

Because capital and labor are mobile, the ability of state and local governments to redistribute income is very constrained.[5] An *individual* jurisdiction may tax the rich to subsidize the poor, but this policy will neither reduce the net income of the rich nor raise the net income of the poor when both groups are completely mobile. This repeats a theme brought up throughout the book regarding the difficulty of redistributing wealth.

Other things being equal, the smaller the geographic scope, the greater the competitive pressure. Hence redistributive politics is shifted upward, to encompass a larger geographical area, where such transfers may be more effective. For example, in the United States, fiscal transfers from the federal government subsidize state administered welfare programs like AFDC (Aid to Families with Dependent Children) and Medicaid. Similarly, to promote greater equality of education between poor and wealthy school districts, school financing has shifted from local property taxes to state income taxes.

---

[3] The retirement communities are an extreme case because younger people are not allowed to enter even if they wanted to. Another methods of exclusion is to have a very large minimum lot size so that only rich people, who do not need welfare services, are able to afford living in the community. More generally, people can choose to live in a city or a suburb, each with its costs and benefits.

[4] An excessive tax is one that taxes more than the rents that accrue to the owner of the capital from being in the location. For example, it may be worth $100 million for a firm to have its warehouse next to city Y's harbor, rather than in another city. This is known as a rent and can be appropriated by city Y via a tax.

[5] When capital and labor are mobile across countries, the ability of central governments to redistribute income is constrained, as well.

SUGGESTIONS FOR FURTHER READING

The Federalist Papers by Hamilton, Madison, and Jay is a magnificent collection of papers on political philosophy as well as being a practical guide to designing the U.S. Constitution. Grofman and Wittman (1989) and Rodden (2006) cover the modern political economy approach to federalism. More extensive discussions of the topics in this chapter can be found in Laycock (1992) and O'Hara and Ribstein (2000), who consider choice of law, Posner (2002), who discusses cost-shifting between the states, and Wildasin (2006), who provides a comprehensive guide to the role of competition between local jurisdictions (the Tiebout hypothesis). Wittman (2000) discusses the trade-offs as the size of the polity increases. Other important work on federalism can be found in the list of citations.

REVIEW QUESTIONS

1. The U.S. Constitution does not allow trade barriers between the states. Why doesn't the Coase theorem (bargaining between the states) obviate the need for such constitutional rules? (4)
2. If a pedestrian from Delaware is hit by a driver from New York in the state of New Jersey, which state law should be in effect? Why? (4)
3. If a couple divorce and the former wife moves from New Jersey to Minnesota, which state's rule applies and why? (4)
4. Explain why competition between jurisdictions means that mobile factors cannot be taxed beyond the rents that the factor gains by being in the particular location. (6)
5. Why is the burden of welfare payments shifted to the central government? (4)
6. In a federalist system, what role should the central government play? (4) Why aren't all decisions shifted to the center? (4)
7. As we saw in earlier chapters, most of corporate law is left to the states. However, most of bankruptcy law is federal law. Explain why this is the case rather than vice versa. (6)

REFERENCES

Brennan, Geoffrey, and James M. Buchanan. (1980). *The Power to Tax: Analytical Foundations of a Fiscal Constitution*. Cambridge, MA: Cambridge University Press.

Grofman, Bernard, and Donald Wittman (eds.). (1989). *The Federalist Papers and the New Institutionalism*. New York: Agathon Press.

Hamilton, Alexander, James Madison, and John Jay. (1788, 1987). *The Federalist Papers*. London: Penguin Books.

Inman, Robert, and Daniel Rubinfeld. (1997). The Political Economy of Federalism. In Dennis Mueller (ed.), *Perspectives on Public Choice: A Handbook*. Cambridge: Cambridge University Press, pp. 73–105.

Laycock, Douglas A. (1992). Equal Citizens of Equal and Territorial States: The Constitutional Foundations of Choice of Law. 92 *Columbia Law Review* 249.

Posner, Richard A. (2003). *Economic Analysis of Law, 6th Edition*. New York: Aspen Publishers.

Riker, William. (1964). *Federalism: Origins, Operation, and Significance*. Boston: Little Brown.

Rodden, Jonathan. (2006). *Hamilton's Paradox: The Promise and Peril of Fiscal Federalism*. Cambridge: Cambridge University Press.

Weingast, Barry R. (1995). The Economic Role of Political Institutions: Market Preserving Federalism and Economic Development. 11 *Journal of Law, Economics and Organization* 1.

Tiebout, Charles M. (1956). A Pure Theory of Local Government Expenditures. 64 *Journal of Political Economy* 416.

Wildasin, David E. (2006). Fiscal Competition. In Barry Weingast and Donald Wittman (eds.), *Oxford Handbook of Political Economy*. Oxford: Oxford University Press.

Wittman, Donald. (2000). The Size and Wealth of Nations. 44 *Journal of Conflict Resolution* 868.

38 The Internal Organization of the Family

A. Boundaries and Codependence 358
   1. Boundaries 358
   2. Joint Responsibility 358

B. Child Rearing 359
   1. The Negligence Rule and Minimization of Transaction Costs 359
   2. The Indifference Principle 360
   3. Sibling Fighting and Joint Outputs 362

C. Concluding Remarks 363

SUGGESTIONS FOR FURTHER READING 363

REVIEW QUESTIONS 364

REFERENCES 364

In previous chapters, we discussed the role of property rights in society and the internal organization of the firm. In this chapter, we consider the internal organization of the family. We will show that the same concepts used throughout the book can be fruitfully applied in designing the optimal rules for household behavior.

Scholars in law and economics typically use appellate court decisions, corporate charters, and the like as their source of empirical evidence. However, there are few, if any, legal documents regarding the internal organization of the family. Therefore, as a substitute for appellate court decisions, I will use statements from best-selling books, such as *Children: The Challenge* by Dreikurs and Solz (1986) and *Facing Codependence* by Mellody et al. (1989).

A. BOUNDARIES AND CODEPENDENCE

The above books use a different terminology from the lexicon used in economics, but as we will see, the concepts are parallel. We start off by introducing the concept of boundaries.

1. Boundaries

Boundary systems are invisible and symbolic "fences" that have three purposes: (1) to keep people from coming into our space and abusing us, (2) to keep us from going into the space of others and abusing them, and (3) to give each of us a way to embody our sense of "who we are. (Mellody, et al., p. 11)

The concept of boundaries and setting limits is fundamental in this literature. Each person in a relationship has to respect his/her own and the other person's boundaries (physical and emotional). People with damaged or nonexistent boundaries have dysfunctional relationships. They may have trouble protecting themselves and saying no, and/or they may violate other people's boundaries.

The leap from "boundaries" to "property rights" is a small one. Boundaries play the same role in personal relationships as property rights play in the economic sphere. Property rights prevent others from trespassing on our land, and property rights prevent us from trespassing on other people's land. The particular bundle of rights defines the nature of the property. When transaction costs are low and property rights are well defined and enforced, productivity and efficiency are enhanced. Parallel results hold for boundaries.

Families work best when everyone sets boundaries or limits. The therapeutic method is to set limits rather than make war. The appropriate behavior within nonmarket small-number relations is to emulate voluntary transactions within a competitive market. If you do not like Ford cars, you do not firebomb their dealerships; you just do not buy their cars. In interpersonal relations, you do not punish the other person (either physically or through guilt trips), and you do not try to control the other person's behavior (via jealousy, servitude, or power). Instead, you set limits so that the other person does not harm you.

2. Joint Responsibility

The aforementioned books argue that people have choices and must take responsibility for being in harmful relationships. If Y continues in a relationship with X even though

X's behavior is harmful to Y, then Y has chosen to be a victim just as X has chosen to be the victimizer. Indeed, Y is labeled a codependent to emphasize the joint responsibility. This *jointness* is greatly reminiscent of arguments made by Coase regarding issues in the law – both the polluter and the pollutee are responsible for the damage to the pollutee. It is misleading to say that the polluter alone causes damage to the pollutee. Similarly, it would be misleading to say that X alone causes the damage to Y when Y chooses to be in a situation where she is harmed by X. If she set limits (which might mean divorce if X is an abusive husband), then she could avoid the harm.

So far the discussion has been at a very abstract level. I will now apply these concepts to child rearing.

B. CHILD REARING

As I have demonstrated in earlier chapters, efficient rules require that a person face the consequences of his/her own decision. The same holds true within the family. In this section, I show how relationships are structured so that externalities are minimized. I discuss how boundaries are implemented in child rearing via the use of a negligence rule. I comment on the child psychologist's concern with long-run incentive effects and show how the notion of joint outputs yields insight into the appropriate method of dealing with fights between siblings.

1. The Negligence Rule and Minimization of Transaction Costs

> It is important to understand the difference between "behavior and consequences" and "Crime and Punishment." The consequences should be, if possible, a reasonable follow-up related to what happened . . . (Mellody, et al., p. 140)
>
> Let us say your son in junior high starts to forget his lunch every day. He calls you, his mother, and you take his lunch. To stop this behavior pattern, you sit down with him and say: "Look Charley, the normal consequences of not making arrangements for lunch is that you go hungry." Then when he forgets his lunch the next day and calls you again, you say. "I'm sorry. . . . The normal consequences of your not taking lunch with you is for you to be hungry. I am not bringing your lunch." (Satir, 1972, quoted in Mellody, et al., p. 140).

In this example, the recommended method is for the mother to set limits and let the consequences fall on her son.[1] The mother chooses a negligence rule. The victim (her son) is liable if the mother is not negligent. That is, if she has chosen the optimal (appropriate) level of care from her perspective, then the full cost of her son's behavior falls on him. As we will see, this is more efficient than the mother continuing to bring her son's lunch to school and then either hectoring him about it all the time or threatening to not let him watch television for a week.

Once the mother has done her job, she is out of the picture. The mother does not try to control Charley's behavior (or let him control her). She does not watch that he goes to school with his lunch; she does not use force by physically making him pick up

---

[1] Rousseau was an early proponent of the doctrine of natural and logical consequences. Sometimes the parent structures the logical consequences. For example, a parent cannot let a small child run into the street and face the natural consequences. However, the parent can warn the child that if the child runs into the street, then for the rest of the day the child will have to stay inside where the child is in less danger. This is not a punishment, but a consequence of the parent protecting the child.

his lunch; she does not threaten to harm him if he forgets his lunch; and she does not threaten to harm herself ("if you keep on forgetting, I will kill myself"). All these latter methods involve transaction costs. Neither parents nor psychologists had to hear from Coase to know that monitoring, threatening punishment, and actual punishing are all costly. And they may not work – hectoring by mom may bring her a sore throat, but Charley may just tune out.

More important, the method respects Charley's boundaries so that Charley learns what his boundaries are and how to make decisions and take responsibility in the absence of others. His motivation to remember bringing his lunch should not be based on whether his mother will be upset and will threaten to kill herself. Boundaries and private property exist because the effects on third parties are minimal allowing optimal choices to be made while ignoring the concerns of others. If Charley's mother overly involves herself in making sure that Charley brings his lunch to school, then she is enmeshing her own issues onto something that is essentially Charley's issue. Of course, the well-meaning mother wants Charley to learn responsibility. But hectoring and punishing him is no way to make him responsible because then his mother is responsible for the punishment, not Charley.

2. The Indifference Principle

The child psychologist's message is (1) parents should change their own behavior rather than try to change their child's behavior and (2) parents should not punish and control but instead provide choices. At first sight, the rationale for such recommendations seems contrary to economic intuition. After all, punishment is a type of incentive, and the child always has the choice of whether to behave, thereby avoiding punishment. Furthermore, it is not immediately obvious why trying to change the other person's behavior might not be cost effective. But as I will now show, the psychologist's words are not mere sophistry. The underlying economic logic provides a strong theoretical explanation for their recommendations.

A good starting point for insight is to assume that a price system is feasible. Then the mother could charge Charley a price for her delivering lunch equal to the opportunity cost of her time plus driving expenses. In this way, the mother would be *indifferent* to Charley's choice.[2] Charley would be free to choose whether he forgets his lunch, while the mother sets the appropriate baseline – she makes his lunch but does not deliver it unless she receives adequate compensation. This system thus mirrors liability rules (which, in principle, try to make the victim whole and therefore indifferent to whether there is damage) more than Pigovian taxes or punishments (which try to change the "criminal's" behavior but leave the victim uncompensated and desiring greater deterrence).

Charley may not have enough money to bribe mom. But there may be close substitutes. Perhaps mother could have Charley dig in the garden for an hour, which might compensate her for the time to deliver lunch. This would not be a punishment but treated as a charge for mother's time. Charley would then be given the option of whether his mother delivers lunch when he forgets it.

Unfortunately, a price system may not be feasible (the child's allowance may be too small), so the work of the child psychologist is much more difficult than that of the

---

[2] Economic equilibria create indifference at the *margin*.

economist who only has to say that price should be set equal to opportunity cost. The psychologist needs to be much more creative in making a nonmonetary system behave in the way a price (liability rule) system would. As is readily seen, the psychologist's recommendation in this case (do not deliver the lunch) closely emulates a price system in its effect. Once again, the mother is (almost) *indifferent* to whether Charley takes his lunch because she does not deliver when he forgets. And once again Charley can choose to forget.

Now compare this to the punishment alternative. Mother delivers the lunch and then, as punishment, does not let him go out on the weekend. Having Charley stay at home on the weekend does not compensate mother. Therefore, mother is no longer indifferent to Charley's choices. If he forgets his lunch and she delivers it, she faces an uncompensated social cost. Charley's choice is imposing a negative externality on mother. Mother is strongly against this alternative from happening. Hence her interest is in controlling Charley's behavior, not in giving him a free choice. Almost by definition, a punishment system involves a *dead-weight social cost.* Preventing Charley from going out on the weekend does not compensate mother; so, she is choosing to be punished when she delivers the lunch.[3]

The first theorem of welfare economics requires no externalities if there is to be economic efficiency. But a punishment system generates externalities. If the mother continues to bring Charley his lunch, then Charley is imposing an externality on his mother when he forgets, and she imposes an externality on him when he gets punished. Thus, punishment is inherently a system riddled with externalities. Child psychologists help parents organize the household responsibilities so that such externalities and dead-weight social losses are minimized.

Optimal domestic organization suggests that the mother structures the choice set available to Charley so that she is indifferent as possible to his choices. I will label this as the *indifference principle.* In a system where people are indifferent to other's choices, no externalities exist.

Psychologists are also very concerned with avoiding child-parent contests of power (or will) and win/lose situations. In such situations there is strategic game playing, domestic warfare and other behavior seeking to alter the utility of the other player. Each party is trying to change the other person's behavior rather than his/her own. All of these involve high social cost and the possibility of suboptimal outcomes, and all of these arise because the mother is not indifferent. To illustrate, consider a solution that child psychologists dislike and where the indifference principle is violated – mother delivers forgotten lunches and Charley is punished by not being allowed to go out on the weekend. Mother is trying to control Charley, but Charley can avoid being controlled by his mother by controlling and punishing her – making her deliver his lunch. This kind of warfare creates winners and losers and encourages strategic behavior. If Charley does not like losing the contest, he may purposely "forget" his lunch to impose a cost on his mother; although he is getting punished, Charley is victorious for having defied her. He can now prove that the threat of punishment does not work. Outcomes now depend on how each can manipulate the other person rather than the immediate and direct effect on their own utility functions. Each side is attempting to establish a reputation

---

[3] The threat of punishment may not be credible if it requires additional costs such as monitoring the punishment.

for toughness by imposing negative externalities on the other even though there is a cost to oneself.[4] And once there is war, escalation is always possible.

Compare this to the case where Charley's mother does not bring the forgotten lunch. Because his mother is indifferent between both alternatives (Charley remembering and forgetting), Charley cannot make his choice to affect his mother's welfare or influence her behavior. Therefore, he cannot engage in strategic behavior. Mother and child are not in a win/lose situation or in a situation that is a test of power, so Charley will make the decision based on his own wants and needs not on others'. Because she is indifferent, Charley's mother will not try to influence his behavior either. A similar analysis holds if Charley's mother is fully compensated for the cost her time if she does deliver the lunch.[5]

The economic solution to Charley's forgetfulness is not solved by finding the optimal level of punishment when mother delivers Charley's lunch – parents need not call on an economist to derive the first-order conditions.[6] Instead, the solution is found by structuring the situation so that the mother is indifferent to Charley's choice. By withdrawing from the situation entirely, mother not only stops considering the optimal level of punishments and rewards, she stops engaging in other high transaction cost activity, including the need to negotiate with Charley on the issue.

Hence, the psychologist creed: change your behavior instead of trying to change the other person's behavior. If mother does not like bringing lunch, she stops bringing lunch rather than trying to change Charley so that he will bring his own lunch instead. Of course, his behavior may change: once she stops bringing, he may stop forgetting. But even if he continues to forget, she does not try to change his behavior.

3. Sibling Fighting and Joint Outputs

> In a fight it is difficult to establish who is guilty. It is not the result of the misbehavior of one child – they all contribute equally to the disturbance, which is the result of their combined effort. . . . The children are . . . coordinating their efforts whether for the welfare of the family or for the furtherance of its tensions and antagonisms. (Dreikurs and Solz, 1987, p. 261).

Many of the ideas presented in the earlier sections are embodied in how to handle fighting between siblings. The basic advice by child psychologists is to stay out of it. Fighting is a joint output. Putting the blame on one child because he did the hitting or because he is older and therefore should know better is a failure to recognize this jointness. If the parents protect the child that ends up crying, then children will use crying to get their way; that is, they will learn to manipulate their parents, rather than learning to resolve problems.[7] If the parents protect the abuser, then children will learn

---

[4] Anger may be used as a weapon by the parent to punish or control the child, but the child may control the parent by provoking the anger.

[5] Of course, the real world is never as simple as the simple characterizations in the child-rearing text. Charley may choose to scream at his mother for not delivering his lunch, thereby complicating the simple game tree. But the same idea holds – mother sets limits instead of punishing.

[6] The first-order conditions must consider the supply of offenses when the punishment involves a dead-weight loss. Seé the chapter on crime.

[7] If the parents blame the older child or stand up for the seemingly "abused" one, then the parents "reinforce the 'victims' feelings of inferiority and teach the victim how to use deficiency and weakness to gain special consideration, thus augmenting the very predicament the parents want to eliminate" (Dreikurs and Solz, 1987, p. 213).

to abuse others' boundaries rather than find shared solutions to problems. Furthermore, by interfering the parent may also be an unwitting input. Perhaps both children have motives to get the parent's attention. One child may want to get the other in trouble; the other child may want to get attention, even if it is negative attention. But even if the children do not want to fight, constant intervention by parents shifts the cost of dispute resolution onto the parents and prevents the siblings from learning how to resolve the disagreement by themselves. While the parents might want to give guidance on how to resolve conflicts, it is not up to them to settle disputes or assign blame, unless both siblings ask. "One can, and should, have a friendly discussion about fights, without the least hint of finger pointing . . . and work out with the children the way and means of settling difficulties. However, this cannot be done while the fight is taking place." (Dreikurs and Solz, 1987, p. 214)

But what if an older child truly terrorizes a younger one? Once again, the solution for the parents is to structure the situation so that strategic behavior by the children is minimized. For example, the parents may have rules that the children are in a room at different times. Indeed, whenever feasible, sending children back to their individual rooms is a good strategy. First, withdrawal from conflict (not violating the other's boundaries) is a good lesson for the children to learn. Furthermore, it sets a relatively neutral and non-manipulatable (by the other child) status quo point from which each child can bargain with the other to obtain a positive outcome (for example, playing together in the living room). By sending the children back to their rooms, the parents do not enter the conflict or take part in the quarreling. They are not judges; they are just setting limits and minimizing strategic game playing by their children.[8]

C. CONCLUDING REMARKS

Neoclassical economics assumes that the family unit maximizes joint welfare. This chapter shows how parents foster a functional property rights system so that joint welfare is in fact maximized.

I have shown that the ideal family is much like the ideal economic market. There is no need either for a special language or for a special set of behavioral assumptions when discussing the optimal organization of family relationships. The economic logic used in designing an optimal legal system applies equally well to the design of an optimal set of household rules.

SUGGESTIONS FOR FURTHER READING

A more extensive discussion of family organization is found in Wittman (2005A). Very few other economists have written on this topic. An exception is Becker (1974), who developed what is affectionately known as the "rotten kid theorem." In this article, Becker shows how parents with sufficient income can create the right incentives for children to contribute to the family welfare. Further afield, Lundberg and Pollak (1994) have written about bargaining between spouses, but this reading is more related to the subject of the next chapter, where we discuss bargaining in the shadow of the law. As one

---

[8] The operative word is "minimize" because it is impossible to eliminate all strategic game playing.

could infer from all the citations, Mellody et al. (1989) is a good source for the clinical psychology approach. Seen through the lens of an economist, their advice to the reader is to act like homo economicus – that is, each person should realize that she has control over her own choices and should choose what is best.

REVIEW QUESTIONS

1.   How are Coase's analysis of torts and codependency theory in psychotherapy related? (10)
2.   Why are limits to be preferred over strategic game playing? (10)

REFERENCES

Becker, Gary S. (1974). A Theory of Social Interactions. 82 *Journal of Political Economy* 1063.

Dreikurs, Rudolph, and V. Solz. (1987). *Children: The Challenge.* New York: E. P. Dutton.

Lundberg, Shelly, and Robert A. Pollak. (1994). Noncooperative Bargaining Models of Marriage. 84 *American Economic Review* 132.

Mellody, Pia, A. W. Miller, and J. K. Miller. (1989). *Facing Codependence.* New York: Harper & Row.

Rousseau, Jean-Jacques. (1979). *Emile: Or, On education,* translated by Allan Bloom. New York: Basic Books.

Satir, Virginia. (1981). *Conjoint Family Therapy.* Palo Alto, CA: Science and Behavior.

Wittman, Donald. (2005A). The Internal Organization of the Family: Economic Analysis and Psychological Advice. 58 *Kyklos* 121.

XI BARGAINING IN THE SHADOW OF A TRIAL

Throughout this book we have talked about agreements and bargains. But how do people actually bargain? In this section, we analyze bargaining in the shadow of a trial. The courts are a particularly apt place to study bargaining because court documents are publicly available and there is a clear structure – a trial comes at the end of the process if the case is not settled. Consequently, data on the *outside option* (the trial outcome) and bargaining strategies (demands and offers) can often be obtained. This is in contrast to ordinary economic exchanges where we can observe the agreement, but not the outside option – the outcome when there is no agreement between the two parties which might be agreements with third parties. The facts are also much easier to obtain than bargaining in the shadow of war, where the nature of the disagreement and the conditions for a peaceful resolution may not be known. For all these reasons, bargaining has been studied more in the context of trials than within ordinary economic markets or between countries in the shadow of war.

In Part XI, we explain why very few cases filed with the court end up in a trial. We also explain, how bargaining is affected by the likely outcome of the trial and the cost of trial. Finally, we explain why cases that go to trial systematically differ from cases that are settled.

39

Settlement or Trial?

A. Plea Bargaining in Criminal Cases 368

B. Some Refinements 371
  1. Each Side Must Account for the Possibility That the Other Side
     Has Different Information 371
  2. Both Sides Trade Off Probability of a Settlement for an
     Increased Surplus 373

C. The Selection of Cases for Trial 374

D. Concluding Remarks 375

SUGGESTIONS FOR FURTHER READING 377

REVIEW QUESTIONS 377

REFERENCES 377

Few criminal or civil cases go to trial; most are settled out of court. Why? Is it right that a criminal charged with murder can plea bargain and be sentenced for aggravated assault instead?[1] What kind of inferences about settlements can we make from trial outcomes? In this chapter, we answer these and related questions.

A. PLEA BARGAINING IN CRIMINAL CASES

We initially focus our analysis on criminal cases.[2] Both the prosecutor and the defendant have expectations about the trial outcome. These expectations determine their willingness to settle instead of going to trial. If the defendant believes that the jury is likely to find her innocent of murder, the defendant will not agree to a settlement that results in life imprisonment; if the defendant believes that the jury is very likely to send her to the electric chair, then the defendant will be more willing to settle for life imprisonment (notice that the argument does not depend on whether the defendant actually committed the crime). The same logic holds for the prosecutor. His bargaining position toughens as his perceptions regarding the likelihood of a conviction increases.[3]

But why are the parties willing to settle in the first place? Each side has an incentive to avoid trial because trials are (1) costly and (2) risky. Both sides may prefer the certain outcome of a settlement. We illustrate via a series of increasingly complex examples.

Suppose first that both the prosecutor and the defendant have the following beliefs about the trial: There is a 50% chance that the jury will find the defendant guilty and send the defendant to five years in prison and a 50% chance that the jury will find the defendant innocent (zero years in prison). The expected outcome of the trial is then 2.5 years in prison. Of course, the analysis would be identical if we were considering fines in the thousands of dollars instead of years in prison.

The prosecutor is generally thought to be risk neutral.[4] This is because the prosecutor has a diversified portfolio of cases. Thus a reasonable approximation of the prosecutor's utility function is that his utility is linear in the number of years that defendants go to prison. The prosecutor's utility function is the upward sloping line drawn in Figure 39.1. Since the expected outcome of the trial is 2.5 years, the prosecutor would not settle for less than that. This is why the possibility of settlement arrow for the prosecutor points to the right from 2.5. Another way of understanding the prosecutor's willingness to settle is to see that half the time his utility is 150 (when the defendant is sent to prison for five years) and half the time his utility is zero (when the defendant is found innocent).[5]

---

[1] As we show in a boxed discussion later, former U.S. Attorney General Ashcroft tried to discourage such plea bargaining.

[2] Civil case can be analyzed in the same way, with the word "plaintiff" substituted for the word "prosecutor" and the outcome being viewed as an award to the plaintiff rather than as a punishment for the defendant.

[3] There is strong empirical evidence showing that participants bargain in the shadow of the law. For example, in a study of jury trials involving automobile accidents, I found that the correlation between the defendant's final offer to the plaintiff and the jury award was 83%, while the correlation between the plaintiff's final demand to the defendant and the jury award was 65%. These figures underestimate the true correlation because those cases that go to trial tend to be cases where one or both parties are optimistic and wildly off the mark.

[4] The assumption of risk-neutrality by the prosecutor is not necessary for the analysis, but it does simplify the diagrams.

[5] Recall from Chapter 1 that utility functions and utiles are just convenient ways of expressing preferences.

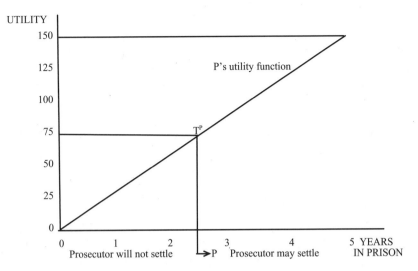

In the diagram we assume that there are no other costs to the prosecutor in going to trial.

Figure 39.1. The prosecutor will not settle for less than 2.5 years.

So the prosecutor's expected utility from going to trial is $T^P = 75$. The prosecutor will settle only if his utility from the settlement is at least 75.

Prosecutors have budget constraints. They can only hire so many assistant prosecutors, and there is only a limited time to prosecute cases. Therefore, other things being equal, they prefer to settle a case since settling the case generally requires less time and expense than going to trial. If the budget is very tight, the district attorney may have to drop some cases and not prosecute them. If he can save resources on one case by settling, the district attorney may be able to pursue cases that might otherwise be dropped. Therefore, it is quite possible that the prosecutor might settle for even less than 2.5 years.

We next consider the defendant's willingness to settle. In Figure 39.2, we have assumed that the defendant is risk averse: the defendant's utility function is the concave (bowed out) curve. When the defendant is risk averse, the defendant wants to avoid the gamble of a trial and therefore might be willing to settle for more than 2.5 years in prison (the expected outcome if the defendant goes to trial). That is, the dashed utility from trial-gamble line (which represents all possible probabilities of conviction from zero in the upper-left-hand corner to one in the lower-right-hand corner) is below the settlement sure-thing line. To understand these two lines, consider the utility that the defendant would get from settling for 2.5 years in prison. This would be $S^{2.5}$ (or more properly, the vertical distance of $S^{2.5}$). Now consider the expected utility from the trial: 50% chance of zero years in prison, 50% chance of five years in prison. To make the analysis simpler, we have calculated the utility in numbers corresponding to percentages.[6] If the defendant goes to trial, half the time she will get 0 years and 100 "utiles"; and half the time she will get five years and 0 utiles. When the defendant goes to trial, her expected number of years is 2.5 and her expected utility is $T^D = 50$ utiles. The defendant would be indifferent between this gamble and the sure thing from a

[6] We have also used the same utility scale for the prosecutor and the defendant so as to not clutter up the page. But the analysis does not require the scale to be the same.

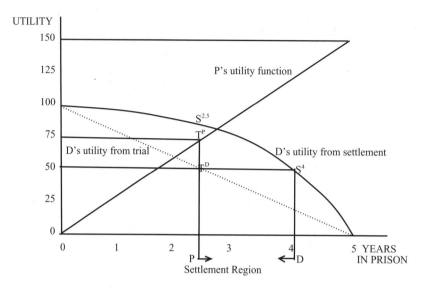

If a settlement takes place, it will be where the arrows overlap (between 2.5 and 4 years).
As the cost of trial increases from 0 (as drawn), the size of the settlement region
increases.

Figure 39.2. A settlement is possible.

settlement of four years (denoted by S^4) with utility $= 50$. Of course, the defendant
would prefer to settle for less than four years and that is why the possibility of settlement
arrow for the defendant is drawn going left from four years.

Now, a trial may be costly to the defendant. She may be paying for her lawyer or she
may not be out on bail (in which case a verdict of not guilty would still mean that the
defendant had served jail time). Because of these costs, the defendant might be willing
to settle for even more than four years given the utility functions as drawn.

In Figure 39.2, a settlement is possible because the arrows overlap. Including the cost
of the trial for either the prosecutor or the defendant would increase the size of the
settlement region because one or both of the parties would like to avoid the cost of a
trial. We next consider situations where a settlement is impossible.

If the defendant is risk preferring, her utility function will be convex (below the
straight line) and a trial will be more likely as the defendant prefers the gamble over the
certainty of 2.5 years of prison. This is illustrated in Figure 39.3, where the defendant
will not accept more than approximately 1.1 years. If the defendant settles for the
1.1 years, she will receive 50 utiles: if the defendant goes to trial, her expected utility
is also 50 utiles. Therefore, the defendant is indifferent between the two choices. The
defendant would not accept any settlement for more than 1.1 years because then the
defendant would be worse off. However, as we have already shown, the prosecutor will
not accept anything less than 2.5 years. As a consequence, there is no overlap and a
settlement will not take place.[7]

If we include the cost of trial, then the minimal demand by the prosecutor moves left
from 2.5 and the maximal offer by the defendant moves right from 1.1. If the numbers

---

[7] If the criminal were truly risk-preferring and if it were legal to do so, then the prosecutor could offer the
defendant a risky settlement – heads, the defendant goes to prison for five years; tails, the defendant goes free.
In this way, both sides would save on court costs. So, in principle, a settlement is possible even if the defendant
is risk-preferring.

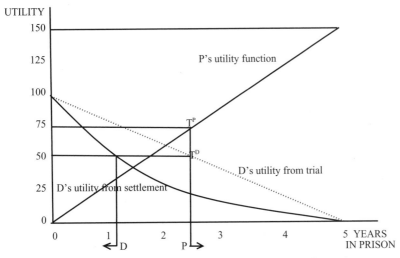

Figure 39.3. No settlement is possible when the defendant prefers risk.

represent thousands of dollars rather than years in prison, then there will be an overlap if the total cost of a trial to both parties is greater than $2,500 − $1,100 = $1,400.

So far we have assumed that both sides have the same expectations. However, it is quite possible that they have different expectations regarding the trial outcome. Both could be relatively optimistic about their chances of winning (meaning that the defendant's subjective probability of her being sentenced to five years in prison is lower than the prosecutor's subjective probability of the defendant being sentenced to five years in prison) or both could be relatively pessimistic (we assume on average, but not necessarily in the particular case, that the two expectations are consistent). If the degree of optimism is sufficient, then a negotiated settlement may be impossible. In Figure 39.4, the defendant's expectations are the same as before (50% chance of five years and 50% chance of zero years) so that her expected amount of time in prison is 2.5 years. To make the analysis easier, we assume that the defendant is also risk neutral. Thus, in this case, she would not accept any settlement that required her to spend more than 2.5 years in prison. But the prosecutor now believes that there is a 90% chance of the defendant being sent to prison for five years so that the prosecutor believes that the expected prison time is 4.5 years. In this case, there is no overlap and no settlement is possible.

Of course, we have ignored court costs. Let us once again convert years into thousands of dollars. Then the *expectation differential* (the prosecutor's expectations about the trial minus the defendant's expectations about the trial) is $4,500 − $2,500 = $2,000. If the total cost of a trial to both parties is greater than the expectation differential of $2,000, then a settlement is possible. Otherwise, it is not.

B. SOME REFINEMENTS

1. Each Side Must Account for the Possibility That the Other Side Has Different Information

In the previous section, we modeled the case where the parties had differential expectations about the trial outcome. In Figure 39.4, the defendant thought that the defendant had a 50% chance of going to prison, while the prosecutor thought that the defendant had a 90% chance of going to prison. However, if each side knew each

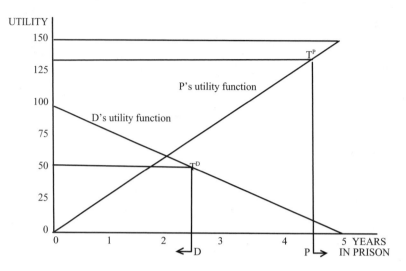

D believes that she has a 50% chance of going to prison. P believes that D has a 90% chance.

To simplify the exposition, we have assumed that the defendant is also risk neutral.

Figure 39.4. A settlement is not possible when both sides are optimistic.

other's expectations, then both would readjust their own expectations so that they no longer would disagree! We illustrate, with the following simple example. Suppose that the number of years that the defendant will go to prison is the average of two rolls of the die and that the defendant has seen the first roll (1) and the prosecutor has seen the second (5). This characterizes a situation where the defendant and the prosecutor each have private information on how well they will argue their own case at trial (their roll of the die), but the trial outcome depends on both arguments.[8] A naïve view would assume that the defendant and prosecutor would never alter their expectations. But if each side could observe the other side's roll, then they would both agree that that the outcome of the trial will be three years in prison for the defendant.

Even if they cannot observe the other side's roll, both sides can form beliefs about the other side's observation and the outcome of the trial. Both sides know that the expected outcome of the other side's roll $= [1/6]1 + [1/6]2 + [1/6]3 + [1/6]4 + [1/6]5 + [1/6]6 = 3.5$. Hence, the defendant should adjust her expectations to $[1 + 3.5]/2 = 2.25$, and the prosecutor should adjust his expectations to $[5 + 3.5]/2 = 4.25$. Both sides adjust their expectations because they realize that both sides have a partial and possibly contradictory understanding of what the jury will decide. Thus the trial expectations considered in the previous section incorporate the possibility that the other side has contrary information.

The legal system has a number of rules that encourage pretrial exchange of information. Prosecutors cannot hide evidence in favor of the defendant. In civil cases, both sides are subject to pretrial discovery. This means that one side can request information from the other. All of this is likely to reduce the differential in expectations, thereby increasing the likelihood of a settlement. But pretrial discovery does not eliminate

---

[8] This characterization is analogous to a common-values auction.

differential expectations entirely. In practice, not all information is conveyed. For example, one side would not reveal that it thought that the judge was biased in its favor. If it did, the other side would ask for a different judge. Thus at the end of the day there is still room for differential expectations, but the thinking is more nuanced. Each side's estimate of the trial outcome factors in not only public information and that side's private information about the strength of its case, but also expectations about the other side's private information.

2. Both Sides Trade Off Probability of a Settlement for an Increased Surplus

The observant reader will have noticed that nowhere have I said that a settlement will take place. Instead, I have shown that when there is no overlap (as in Figure 39.4) a settlement is impossible. When there is an overlap (as in Figure 39.2) a settlement is possible, but it still may not take place because each side is willing to trade off probability of a settlement for a greater surplus when there is a settlement. To illustrate, let us turn our attention toward civil cases and suppose the following situation holds:

1. The defendant only knows that the outcome of the trial will be a roll of the die multiplied by $1,000 (this is the amount that the defendant will pay the plaintiff).
2. The plaintiff knows the outcome of the trial with certainty (she has observed the roll of the die).
3. The defendant makes a one-time take-it or leave-it offer to the plaintiff (if the offer is rejected, then the case goes to trial).[9]
4. A trial costs the defendant $900 and the plaintiff nothing (this last assumption makes the example easier to follow).
5. If the plaintiff is indifferent between a trial and a settlement, the plaintiff will choose to settle.

The discrete nature of the example means that the defendant will offer $1,000, $2,000, $3,000, $4,000, $5,000, or $6,000 to the plaintiff. Any offer in-between will only increase the cost to the defendant without increasing the likelihood of an agreement. For example, if the defendant offers $3,000 or $3,999, then the plaintiff will accept the offer if the die was a 1, 2, or 3, and the plaintiff will reject the offer if the die was a 4, 5, or 6. So the defendant will want to offer the lower amount.

Suppose first that the defendant offers $3,000. Half the time the plaintiff accepts the offer (when the die has rolled 1, 2, or 3) and the defendant pays $3,000. The rest of the time, the plaintiff rejects the offer and the case goes to court. One-sixth of the time the defendant pays $4,000 + $900 court fees, one-sixth of the time the defendant pays a total of $5,900, and one-sixth of the time the defendant pays a total of $6,900. So the expected cost is $(1/2)(\$3,000) + (1/6)(\$4,900) + (1/6)(\$5,900) + (1/6)(\$6,900) = \$4,450$.

Suppose instead that the defendant only offers $2,000. Then one-third of the time (when the die lands 1 or 2) the plaintiff will accept the offer. So one-third of the time the defendant is better off by offering $2,000 instead of $3,000 because the settlement

---

[9] When the uninformed party makes the offer, this is known as screening; when the informed party makes the offer, this is known as signaling. In neither situation will all cases go to trial.

amount is $1,000 less. If the die lands on 3, the plaintiff will reject the offer and the defendant will end up paying $3,000 plus $900 in court costs. So one-sixth of the time the defendant is worse off by $900 by offering $2,000 instead of $3,000. The rest of the time when the die rolls 4, 5, or 6, the outcome is the same when the defendant offers $2,000 as when the defendant offers $3,000. By offering $2,000, the defendant's expected cost is reduced by $183 because $[1/3]\$1,000 - [1/6]\$900 = \$333.33 - \$150 = \$183.33$. So net the defendant is better off by being a hard bargainer and offering less than the expected outcome.

If all cases went to trial, then the expected trial outcome would be $3,500. Nevertheless, the defendant is better off by offering $2,000 than $3,000. If the plaintiff's actual observation were $3,000, there would not be a settlement even though the expectation differential were negative ($3,000–$3,500) and the diagram would show an overlap. Thus, even when the cost of a trial is greater the expectation differential and the expectation differential is itself negative, a case may not be settled.

Of course, other things being equal, the larger the expectation differential, the more likely the case will go to trial. In the present example, the case will be settled if the plaintiff has observed a 1 or 2 (and the expectation differential is therefore $1,000 – $3,500 = –$2,500 or $2,000 – $3,500 = –$1,500); and the case will go to trial if the plaintiff has observed 3 through 6 (and the expectation differential ranges from – $500 to + $2,500).

In a completely specified model where both sides have incomplete information and both sides make offers, both sides not only take into account that their information about the eventual trial outcome is partial but also they take into account that the other side is driving a hard bargain, as well.

C. THE SELECTION OF CASES FOR TRIAL

As we have shown in the previous section, the greater the expectation differential (plaintiff minus defendant expectation), the more likely there will be a trial. In this section, we will consider the source of large expectation differentials.

Suppose that there was an automobile accident and that the defendant was 100% at fault. Suppose further that one of the plaintiff's fingers was burned so that it took six months to heal. It is hard to determine what a jury would award in the case, but it seems likely that the award would be in the $1,000 to $10,000 range. Even if both litigants were optimistic about the trial, it seems unlikely that the expectation differential would be greater than $9,000 (where the plaintiff expected to receive $10,000 and the defendant expected to pay $1000).

Next consider the situation, where the plaintiff suffered severe burns over 90% of his body. It would be much harder to determine the jury award in this case. It might be $1 million or $10 million. If both sides were optimistic, then the differential could be as high as $9 million. And even if both sides accounted for the possibility that the other side has private information about the outcome of a trial, the expectation differential could be in the millions of dollars.

Thus, when the stakes are small, the difference in subjective expectation is likely to be small, as well. Because trials are costly, the extra surplus gained from being a hard bargainer in a small-stakes game is likely to be swamped by the cost of a trial when the litigants fail to settle. Why go to trial when the difference of opinion is at most $9,000 and the cost of a trial is $20,000? With larger stakes and larger differentials, the relative cost of a trial goes down, and therefore the demand for trials increases. Consequently, cases involving low expected awards are much more likely to be settled than cases involving high expected awards.

Cases that are tried differ from cases that are settled. In comparison to trials, settlements will have a smaller proportion of cases where the harm to the plaintiff is severe; the average settlement will involve smaller payouts to the plaintiff than the average trial. Note well that the reason is not that it is worthwhile to take larger award cases to trial, but rather larger award cases are more likely to involve larger differences in opinion over the outcome of the trial; and when both sides are mutually optimistic, this means that a trial is more likely. Of course, the litigants are as likely to be jointly pessimistic as they are to be jointly optimistic, but, when they are jointly pessimistic, a settlement is likely whether the case involved a burnt finger or burns over ninety percent of the body.

The large jury awards reported in newspapers exaggerate the average jury award because newspapers like to report and subscribers like to read sensational stories. It seems that nearly everyone knows about the woman who successfully sued McDonald's over burns to her thighs when the coffee cup held between her legs spilled as her car was being driven – the jury awarded her nearly $3 million.[10] Few would know about this case if the jury awarded $300. Trials too exaggerate the awards because cases with small-expected damages are unlikely to generate big positive expectation differentials and therefore are likely to be settled instead of going to trial. So even if we were to look at all product liability trials, for example, this set would greatly exaggerate the average cost of a product liability case, as the small cases are more likely to be settled.

D. CONCLUDING REMARKS

Very few civil disputes end in trial. Even if we restrict our attention to those cases that were filed in court, fewer than 5% ever get to trial.[11] The rest are settled one way or another, including the possibility that the plaintiff withdraws from litigation without any formal agreement with the defendant. These numbers can be seen as substantiating Coase's conjecture that people will tend to negotiate Pareto-improving trades. A trial is a negative-sum game; hence, there is room for a Pareto-improving settlement if the participants do not prefer risk and their subjective expectations are not overly optimistic.

A higher percentage of criminal cases go to trial. One reason is that the cost of a criminal trial often falls on a third party – the taxpayers who pay for the public defender. The percentage of murder cases reaching trial is greater than the percentage of cases involving theft. This is predicted by our analysis in the previous section – there is greater room for disagreement about the outcome when the expected award or punishment is large, which characterizes murder cases. In murder cases, the outcome might be zero

---

[10] Although a lot fewer people know that the judge reduced the amount of the punitive damages that the jury awarded the plaintiff from $2,700,000 to $480,000. See the *Wall Street Journal*, September 15, 1994.

[11] Fewer than 2% of all civil cases in federal courts are tried. See Judicial Business of the United States Courts 2003 http://www.uscourts.gov/judbus2003/contents.html Table C-4 Cases Terminated, by Nature of Suit and Action Taken.

ASHCROFT LIMITS PLEA BARGAINING

Attorney General John Ashcroft sent a memo on October 1, 2003, to all federal prosecutors saying they "must charge and pursue the most serious, readily provable offenses that are supported by the facts." He said the consistency demanded of federal judges in sentencing must be matched by a consistency in charging decisions and plea bargaining by prosecutors nationwide. Some defense lawyers and former federal prosecutors say that the attorney general's memo limits the discretion of line prosecutors to make independent decisions on charging, pursuing plea bargains, and acquiescing in downward departures under the guidelines.

BARRY BONDS'S HOME RUN #73 BASEBALL

Recall the trial outcome from this case. The litigants had to split the proceeds from the record-setting baseball, 50-50. The ball fetched only $450,000, far less than the $3 million for Mark McGuire's record-breaking seventieth home run. Hayashi had offered a 50-50 split, but Popov rejected the offer. Popov's lawyers charged Popov $473,500, which is more than twice as much as Popov received from his share of the baseball. Popov did not want to pay and his lawyers sued him. The lawyers for Hayashi reduced their fees so that Hayashi actually came out ahead by a significant amount. http://espn.go.com/mlb/news/2003/0709/1578432.html.

BEYOND A REASONABLE DOUBT OR PREPONDERANCE OF THE EVIDENCE

In criminal cases, the verdict is against the defendant only if the evidence is beyond a reasonable doubt (meaning that there is a very low probability that the defendant did not commit the crime). In civil cases, the verdict is against the defendant if the preponderance of the evidence is in favor of the plaintiff (which means that the chance of error could be nearly 50%). Why is there this difference between criminal and civil cases? In criminal cases, society wants to avoid punishing the wrong party. Hence, it chooses beyond a reasonable doubt. But in civil cases there are two sides. If the defendant is not liable, then the plaintiff is; if the plaintiff is not liable, then the defendant is. If society chose beyond a reasonable doubt in civil cases, then "innocent" defendants are protected at the expense of "innocent" plaintiffs. The only way to minimize the probability of making the wrong party liable is to use the rule preponderance of the evidence.

punishment or the death penalty. Therefore, there is room for considerable disagreement about the outcome of the trial. For shoplifting, the differential in expectations is unlikely to be large and in any event the differential is unlikely to be as large as the cost of the trial. So cases involving shoplifting have a lower percentage ending in trial than cases involving murder.

Settlements take place because they are Pareto superior to trials; both sides expect to be better off by settling. When murder defendants face the risk of the death penalty, they may settle for life-imprisonment instead. When the death penalty is not an option, then defendants will be less likely to settle for life imprisonment.

SUGGESTIONS FOR FURTHER READING

Much of this chapter is based on Friedman and Wittman (forthcoming). They modeled the case where each litigant takes into account the strategies and incomplete information by the other litigant. Earlier literature assumed that one side was perfectly informed and concentrated on screening by the uninformed litigant or signaling by the informed litigant. See Daughety (2000) for an extensive survey. The above assume that only one take-it-or-leave-it offer is made. This is not as problematic as it first seems because a series of offers and counteroffers may be uninformative, until the last offer. Rubinstein (1982) considered the possibility of an infinite series of offers and counteroffers when the amount of surplus to be shared between the bargainers declines after every offer. In his model, the person making the first offer offers just enough to encourage the other side to accept. For subsequent developments, see Ausubel et al. (2002).

Landes (1973) was the first to show that cases that went to trial differed from the cases that were settled. In particular, he showed that defendants not out on bail, were more likely to settle, because even if they did win, the defendants were facing jail time while awaiting trial. Priest and Klein (1985) emphasized the sample selectivity of trials. Wittman (1985) provided an alternative version. None of these papers considered strategic bargaining within the context of two-sided incomplete information.

Bargaining theory can be applied to a wide variety of areas. For example, bargaining within marriage depends on the outside option – how well each person will do when divorced (finding a new partner, being employed, etc.) See Chiappori et al. (2002), who find that the ratio of the wife's consumption to the husband's consumption depends on the ratio of men to women in the society and how favorable divorce laws are to women. For a general discussion of bargaining within marriage, see Lundberg and Pollak (1996).

REVIEW QUESTIONS

1. Why do litigants settle? (2) What determines the range of possible settlements (assuming that they have the same expectations)? Use a diagram to illustrate. (10)
2. Explain why a plaintiff might refuse the defendant's offer even if she did not expect to do better by going to trial? (4)
3. Why might cases that go to trial systematically differ from cases that are settled? (10)

REFERENCES

Ausubel, Lawrence M., Peter Cramton, and Raymond J. Denekere. (2002). Bargaining with Incomplete Information. In Robert J. Aumann and Sergiu Hart (eds.), *Handbook of Game Theory*. *Vol. 3.* Amsterdam: North Holland.

Chiappori, Pierre-Andre, Bernard Fortin, and Guy Lacroix. (2002). Marriage Market, Divorce Legislation and Household Labor Supply. 110 *Journal of Political Economy* 37.

Daughety, Andrew. (2000). Settlement. In Boudewijn Bouckaert and Gerrit De Geest (eds.), *Encyclopedia of Law and Economics*. Cheltenham, UK: Edgar Elgar.

Friedman, Daniel, and Donald Wittman. (Forthcoming). Litigation with Symmetric Bargaining and Two-Sided Incomplete Information. *Journal of Law, Economics and Organization.*

Landes, William. (1971). An Economic Analysis of the Courts. 14 *Journal of Law & Economics* 61.

Lundberg, Shelly, and Robert A. Pollak. (1996). Bargaining and Distribution in Marriage. 10 *Journal of Economic Perspectives* 139.

Priest, George, and Benjamin Klein. (1984). The Selection of Disputes for Litigation. 13 *Journal of Legal Studies* 1.

Rubinstein, Ariel. 1982). Perfect Equilibrium in a Bargaining Model. 50 *Econometrica* 97.

Wittman, Donald. (1988). Dispute Resolution and the Selection of Cases for Trial: A Study of the Generation of Biased and Unbiased Data. 17 *Journal of Legal Studies* 313.

Index of Authors

Akerlof, G., 267
Alchian, A., 339
Arrow, K., 267
Ausubel, L., 315, 377
Ayres, I., 162, 204

Bainbridge, S., 328
Baird, D., 139, 292
Barzel, Y., 188
Bebchuk, L., 100, 292, 321
Becker, G., 161–162, 363
Benston, G., 301
Bentham, J., 161–162
Bernstein, L., 215
Bhandari, J., 292
Blackstone, W., 181
Blume, L., 127
Borenstein, S., 227
Boyd, J., 237
Brinig, M., 227
Brown, J., 150
Buchanan, J., 127

Calabresi, G., 100
Carlton, D., 315
Chiappori, P., 99
Coase, R., 34, 339
Cohen, R., 218–219
Cohen, L., 227
Courant, P., 227
Cox, G., 346, 348
Cramton, P., 377
Craswell, R., 204
Crawford, R., 339

Daughety, A., 377
Davies, P., 321
Demsetz, H., 100
Denekere, R., 377
Dick, A., 339
Dnes, A., 227
Donohue, J., 161–162
Dreikurs, R., 358, 362, 363
Dubner, S., 162

Easterbrook, F., 321
Eggertsson, G., 97

Ellickson, R., 47, 101, 188, 311
Epple, D., 252
Epstein, R., 87, 118, 127, 178, 179, 237

Fiorentini, G., 339
Fischel, D., 315, 321, 328
Fischel, W., 127
Fortin, B., 99
Fried, J., 292, 321
Friedman, D., 377

Geistfeld, M., 252
Gertner, R., 139, 204
Gianluca, F., 339
Gibbons, R., 339
Goldberg, V., 204
Gordon, W., 111
Green, M., 315
Grofman, B., 355

Hadfield, G., 339
Hannsman, H., 274, 311, 321, 339
Hart, O., 339
Hatzis, A., 227
Hertig, G., 321
Hewins, R., 215
Hoffman, E., 47
Holmstrom, B., 339
Hopt, K., 321
Hoshi, T., 301
Hylton, K., 150

Ingerman, D., 237

Jackson, T., 292
Jenson, M., 321
Joskow, P., 339
Joyce, T., 162

Kanda, H., 292, 321
Kantor, S., 344
Kaplow, L., 100
Kashyap, A., 301
Kaufmen, G., 301
Klein, B., 237, 339, 377
Knetch, J. L., 47
Kraakman, R., 321

Krier, J., 100

Lacroix, G., 99
Landes, E., 227
Landes, W., 111, 150, 177, 179, 244, 274, 377
Laycock, D., 355
Leffler, K., 237
Levitt, S., 161–162
Levmore, S., 100, 118, 179, 227, 292
Lott, J., 161–162
Lueck, D., 100, 188
Lundberg, S., 99, 363

Malamed, A., 100
Manne, H., 315
Marshall, W., 348
Mattiacci, G., 118
McCubbins, M., 346, 348
Meckling, W., 321
Medema, S. G., 40
Meighan, K., 227
Mellody, P., 358, 364
Meyerson, R., 47
Micelli, T., 100, 173
Milgrom, P., 339
Miller, A., 358, 364
Miller, J., 358, 364

Nader, R., 315

O'Hara, S., 355

Pearson, J., 215
Peltzman, S., 339
Picker, R., 139
Plott, C., 47
Polinsky, M., 161–162, 215
Pollak, R., 99, 363
Posner, R., 111, 150, 161–162, 177, 179, 204, 215, 244, 355
Pottier, S., 339
Priest, G., 252, 267, 377

Ratcliff, J., 179
Raviv, A., 252
Ribstein, L., 355

Roberts, J., 339
Rock, E., 321
Rodden, J., 355
Roe, M., 288
Rogerson, W., 237
Romano, R., 321
Rowthorn, R., 227
Rubin, P.H., 252, 339
Rubinfeld, D., 127
Rubinstein, A., 377

Saitherwaite, M. A., 47
Sanchez, N., 47
Santilli, M., 274
Schwab, S., 100
Schwartz, A., 204
Scotchmer, S., 111, 188
Seligman, J., 315
Shavell, S., 100, 161–162, 204, 215
Sheplse, K., 348
Simpson, A., 161–162
Sirmans, C., 173
Solz, V., 358, 362, 363
Sommer, D., 339
Spitzer, M., 47

Tollison, R., 73
Turnbull, B., 173

Viscusi, W., 252

Wagner, R. E., 73
Weingast, B., 348
Weinrib, E., 179
Weiss, L., 292
White, L., 301
White, M., 52, 100, 150
Wildasin, D., 355
Willig, R., 28
Winter, R., 321
Wittman, D., 52, 87, 100, 118, 148, 150, 173, 227, 348, 355, 363, 368, 377
Woodward, S., 311

Zeiler, K., 47
Zerbe, R., 40
Zheng, M., 150

Index

accounting firms, 306, 307, 315
acts of god, 141–147
adverse selection, 239–245, 257–268
  banking crises and, 295–296, 299
  defined, 261–262
  insurance and, 257, 261, 280
  market unravelings, 262–263, 266
  medical malpractice and, 243
  moral hazard and, 262
  seller's property disclosures, 266
  takings clause and, 267
  See also specific subjects
advertising, 9–10
  celebrity names used in, 103, 107, 110
  rationality and, 9
agency problems, 313–321
  asymmetric information and, 316
  class-action suits, 319
  consumer-owned grocery stores, 319–320
  corporate charters and, 315–317, 318
  corporations and, 314–315
  government regulations and, 317
  in legislatures, 342
  market for corporate control, 320
  market for managers, 314
  mergers and, 313, 319
  partnerships and, 315
  poison pills, 318
  proxy fights, 313, 314, 318
  race to the top, 315, 320
  state incorporation laws, 315, 316–317, 320
  stock exchanges, choice of, 315
  tender offers, 313, 314, 317, 318
aggregate behavior, 8, 26
AIDS, 103–106
  disease transmission laws, 106
  patents and, 106
  testing incentives, 103, 106
airlines, 64, 73
articles of incorporation, 201. *See also* corporate law
artist royalties, 269–275
  authors and, 272
  moral hazard and, 272

privity of contract and, 274
  right to prevent alterations, 272, 274
  risk and, 270–271
  transaction costs and, 272
asymmetric information, 239
  agency problems and, 316
  consumer insurance and, 242
  exculpatory clauses and, 240
  exploding cola bottles, 240
  low probability events, 244
  more informed party held liable, 242
  stock options and, 311
  See also adverse selection; malpractice
authoritarian regimes, 342, 346–348
automobile accidents, 133, 146, 173, 194
  exploding gas tanks, 251
  See also automobile insurance
automobile insurance, 277
  collusion, 278, 279–280
  Proposition, 274, 280–281
  risk pools, 278
  urban-rural cost-shifting, 278–279
  young males, 279, 280–281
  zip codes, 277, 279, 280
automobile warranties, 247, 249
avoidable consequences doctrine
  avoidance costs, 33, 37
  breach of contract and, 198
  nuisance laws and, 167–172
  See also mitigation of damages; last clear chance

banking crises, 295–301
  American savings and loan crisis, 296–299
  capital requirements, 297–298, 299
  fraud and, 295, 299
  Japanese banks, 300
  monitoring failure and, 295, 296
  moral hazard and, 297, 299
  portfolio diversification, 295, 298
  regulatory system and, 296–297
bankruptcy, 283
  banking crises and, 295, 298
  bankruptcy insurance, 262–263, 297

bankruptcy (*cont.*)
   chapter 11, 284, 288
   chapter 13, 290
   chapter 7, 284, 288, 290–292
   claimant conflicts, 283, 284, 286, 295–301
   Coase theorem and, 285–286
   corporate, 283, 284
   creditor priority, 283, 286, 291–292
   ESOPs and, 311
   homestead exemption, 290
   moral hazard and, 292
   personal bankruptcy, 289–290
   personal debt contracts, 283, 289
   repossessions, 283, 289–290
   secured debt, 284–285, 286–287
   stockholders, 284–285
   student loans, 292
   unity of interest, 283, 288
   unsecured debt, 284–285
Bankruptcy Act of 2005, 289–290
bargaining. *See* negotiation costs; settlement-trial decisions
Barry Bonds' baseball, 59–66
behavioral law and economics, 12
beneficial use doctrine, 186
Bentham, J., 13–14
blackmail, 103–107, 110
Bonds, B., 59–66, 226, 376–377
booby trap, 160–163
boundaries, 172, 357–364
breach of contract, 193
   accident law and, 199
   avoidable consequences doctrine, 198
   bad music performances, 202
   bargaining power and, 196
   consequential damages and, 199–200
   contract interpretation, 194
   contributory negligence and, 199
   crime and, 337
   damages, determination of, 207, 209
   determining breach, 193, 195
   industry standards, 211
   cannibalism, 204
   liquidated damages, 197, 200, 211
   marginal cost liability rule and, 171–172
   mausoleum change-of-use, 202
   mitigation of damages, 168, 197–199
   opportunism and, 337
   punitive damages, 207, 210, 211
   relational contracts and, 193, 200
   remedies for, 193, 196
   specific performance, 196, 197, 209, 210
   stock prices and, 209–210
   World Trade Center, 194, 201
   See also default rules; divorce; contract law

cannibalism, 161, 162, 204
capital punishment, 154, 157. *See* also crime
cardinal scale, 11, 15–16, 17–18

child rearing, 357–364
class-action suits, 96, 98, 319–321
   agency problems and, 319
   crime and, 157–158
Clean Air Act of 1970, 65
cloud seeding, 73
Coase theorem
   diagrammatic exposition of, 52
   examples for, 36, 39
   legislatures and, 341–348
   liability and, 62–63
   Pigovian theory and, 49, 51
   pollution example, 53–54
   statement of, 34, 42
   symmetry and, 53–54
   transaction costs, 39
Coca-Cola, 108, 109. *See* exploding cola bottles
coffee cup, 375
collateral source rule, 150
coming to the nuisance, 167–173, 175–179, 181–188
committee structure
   legislatures, 341–348
common pool problem, 96, 341–342, 344–348. *See also* communal rights
communal rights, 76, 91–97, 187
   defined, 96
   excludability, 96–97
   information, 103–112
   in knowledge, 103
   liability rules and, 100
   over-fishing, 97
   property rights and, 96, 100, 103, 109, 186, 187
   transaction costs and, 96–97, 100
comparative negligence, 141–145
   contributory negligence and, 141, 146, 147, 150
   engagement-ring returns, 223
   fairness and, 144, 146
   jury outcomes and, 141, 147
   rapid convergence to equilibrium, 150
comparative statics, 69, 70
compensation principle, 21, 22, 23. *See also* Kaldor-Hicks compensation
competition, 213, 262, 313–321, 337, 343, 349–355
conflicting state laws, 349–355
congress. *See also* legislatures
constitutional law. *See* takings; federalism
   free trade and, 349–355
   patents and, 103–106
   welfare and, 320
consumers-and-producers cause damage, 247
   lawnmowers, 247–252. *See* lawnmowers
   trunk internal release mechanisms, 251
   See also automobile warranties
contingency fees, 273–275
contract enforcability, 207
   contract clarity and, 207, 212
   crime and, 207, 214

industry practices and, 213
negative externalities and, 214
unconscionability, 213
unsophisticated buyers and, 213
Walker Thomas Furniture, 207, 212
See also handshake contracts
contract law
complete contingent contracts, 194
personal debt contracts, 283, 289
relational contracts, 200–205
role of, 193, 194
See also breach of contract; default rules; mitigation
of damages
contracts of adhesion, 250
cooperatives, 307
consumer, 320
producer, 306
worker, 305–306, 308–311
corporate form, 306, 319
corporate law
market for corporate control, 320
market for managers, 314
mergers and, 313, 319
partnerships and, 315
poison pills, 318
proxy fights, 313, 314, 318
race to the top, 315, 320
state incorporation laws, 315, 316–317,
320
stock exchanges, choice of, 315
tender offers, 313, 314, 317, 318
See also agency problems; insider trading
cost-benefit analysis, 21–27, 50, 66
Clean Air Act and, 65
comparative statics and, 69, 70, 71
life-death decisions and, 250–252
Pareto improvement and, 21, 22
power line example, 62.
See also specific costs
cost minimization, 131–139
damage prevention and, 131, 132
decreasing marginal productivity and,
133–134
Cournot-Nash equilibria, 131, 134, 138. *See also*
equilibrium
court injunctions, 96
crime, 153–163
abortion laws and, 162
blackmail, 103, 106, 110
cannibalism case, 161, 162, 204
capital punishment and, 154
celebrity shoplifting case, 160
class action suits, 157–158
concealed handguns, 162
demand elasticity and, 154, 156, 161
detection probability, 153, 154–155,
158
deterrence, 153, 158
drug legalization and, 160–161
imprisonment as prevention, 153, 159
imprisonment as rehabilitation, 159
imprisonment costs, 154, 156

incentives and, 153, 154
intent, 153, 159
judgment proof status, 157–158
cannibalism case, 161
opportunism and, 331, 336
opportunity costs and, 154, 159–160
organized, 331, 336
punishment level, 153, 154–155, 158
punishment, marginal effects of, 156
punishment optimization, 153, 154
rape, 93, 95–96
rationality and, 154
risk preferences and, 155, 158–159
theft, 93
three-strike law, 159
tort system and, 153, 154, 157, 159
trespass booby-trap case, 160
witness incentives, 118
witnesses, murdering of, 156

debt vs. equity, 305–311
default rules, 193, 236
courts writing of, 202–203
defined, 194
legislatures and, 202–203
permanent vegetative state, 203
See also exculpatory clauses
defendants, 369
Del Webb, 167–173, 186, 334, 354
demand, downward sloping, 21
democracy, 342, 348. *See also* majority rule
deposit insurance, 295
adverse selection and, 296
moral hazard and, 296
reforms, 295, 299
See banking crises
descriptive-prescriptive theories, 14, 18
dictators. *See* authoritarian regimes
distribution, 13–18, 121–127, 342
just theories of, 18
Pareto optimality and, 18
reasons for ignoring, 18
redistribution and, 26, 27, 28,
354–355
welfare and, 354–355
divorce
alimony, 217, 222
educational loans, 221–222
no-fault, 217, 222
property division, 217, 220
state laws and, 218, 353
See also spousal support; marriage
dominant-strategy equilibrium, 135–136
drunk driving, 59–61
duty to disclose, 103–104

eagle feathers, 126
economic markets, 113–118
carrot v. stick approaches, 118
economics
analytic framework using, 1, 2
defined, 2

efficiency, 250
  definition of, 19
  exculpatory clauses, 248–249
  See also Pareto optimality
elections, 343, 345. *See also* democracy; majority rule
electoral competition, 341–348
embryos, 224, 225–227
employee stock ownership plans (ESOPs), 307,
    311
  bankruptcy and, 311
eminent domain, 36, 94, 95
enforcement costs, 33, 37
engagement rings, 217–224, 227
entitlements, 91–102
  body organs, 92
  Coase theorem and, 92
  defined, 92
  efficiency and, 123
  involuntary transfers of, 94
  mineral rights, 92
  protection of, 91
  split ownership, 92
  transferability of, 99
  See also property rights; liability rules; communal
    rights
Environmental Protection Agency (EPA), 65
equilibrium, 29, 134, 135, 136, 353. *See also*
    Cournot-Nash equilibrium
ethical issues, economics and, 2
exculpatory clauses, 231, 232, 240, 245
  adverse selection and, 242
  asymmetric information and, 240
  defined, 232
  efficient contracts and, 248–249
  exploding cola bottles and, 241
  symmetric information and, 231, 234
  See also default rules
exploding cola bottles, 231
  automobile accidents compared, 236
  cheaper insurer rationale, 236–237
  Coase theorem and, 233, 236
  consumer behavior, minimal effect of, 242
  exculpatory clauses, 241
  lawnmowers compared, 248
  optimal safety levels, 233–234
exploitation theories, 247, 250
  tie-in arrangements, 250
explosions, 251
externalities, 93, 113–115, 116–117, 121–125
  administrative costs and, 118
  moral, 241
  negative, 113, 114, 117, 118
  pecuniary, 138
  positive, 113, 116, 117, 118
  See also pollution; specific topics
Exxon Valdez, 338, 339

fair market value, 36
fairness, 12
families, 217–218, 357–364
  assortative matching, 226
  boundaries, 357, 358

child-rearing, 357, 359
  Coase and, 225, 359
  contests of will, 361–362
  economic analysis of, 217–218
  indifference principle, 357, 360, 361
  internal organization of, 357
  joint responsibility, 357, 358, 362
  naming of offspring, 226
  price system and, 360–361
  punishments, 361
  sibling fights, 357, 362
  surrogate motherhood, 224–225
  transaction costs and, 357, 359
  See also divorce; marriage
farmland, 308
federalism, 343, 349–355
  assigning costs among states, 349, 352
  common-pool problem, 353
  conflicting state laws, 349, 352
  divorce laws and, 353
  factor mobility and, 354
  free trade and, 349, 351
  redistribution and, 354
  state-local governmental competition, 349, 353
  See also governmental centralization
fencing in/fencing out, 41–44, 343
fiduciary duties, 314
first arrival, rights-allocations and, 175–179,
    181–188
  area-character determined by first use, 181, 184
  area-character determined by second use, 181, 184,
    186
  area-character predetermined, 181, 183
  coming to the nuisance doctrine, 181, 182
  indemnification, 181, 186
  nonconforming land use, 185–186
  relocation compensation, 184–185
  salvage operations and, 187
  traffic and, 75–80
  transaction costs and, 182
first theorem of welfare economics, 361
franchising, 331–338, 339, 351
  adverse selection and, 335
  bank cards, 335
  collective ownership in, 335
  fast-foods and, 334–335
  grocery stores and, 335–336
  job shirking and, 334–335
  monitoring costs, 335
free rider problem, 36, 46, 69–70, 285, 314
free trade, 349–355

game theory
  game of chicken, 136
  Cournot-Nash equilibrium, 135–136
  dominant-strategy equilibrium, 135–136
  duopolies, 136
  game matrices, 134–136
  Pareto-optimality and, 135–136
  Prisoner's Dilemma, 135–136
  zero-sum games, 135
germaneness rule, 343

good samaritan rule, 175–179
    Anglo-American rule, 175, 176, 177
    Continental rule, 175, 176
    compensation for, 121–127
    economic reasoning and, 175, 176
    mitigation of damages doctrine and, 178
    multiple tortfeasors argument, 177
    non-economic arguments for, 176
    rescue costs, high, 175, 178
    rescuee liability, 176–177, 178
    rescuer liability, 176, 178
Gorman preferences, 26
government regulation, 73, 100
    carrot v. stick approaches, 118, 125
    entitlements and, 98, 100
    liability rules and, 100
    of input, 91–100
    smoking and, 69
    substituting for civil law, 125
    traffic and, 75–80
    transaction costs and, 98, 100
governmental centralization
    coordination and, 350
    monopoly power and, 350
    role of central government, 349, 351
    gross domestic product (GDP), 24–25

handshake contracts, 207
    industry practices and, 207, 209
    Pennzoil v. Texaco, 208
haunted house, 111
hawks and power lines, 59–63
health maintenance organizations (HMOs), 264–265, 266
    adverse selection and, 265–266
hedonic pricing, 27
historical landmarks, 124
holder in due course, 291–293
homeowners' associations, 346–348
human capital markets, 221
Hutterites, 308

indifference principle, 357–364
information, 8, 231–238
    communal rights, 103
    consumer differences, 239, 241, 243
    gathering-disseminating incentives, 104
    more informed party held liable, 241
    neither side informed, 239, 240
    property rights, 103
    seller's duty to disclose, 103, 104, 111
    See also asymmetric information; patents;
        trademarks; intellectual property
insider trading, 323
    arguments against, 324
    benefits from, 323–328
    Coase theorem and, 326
    corporate charters and, 323, 325
    information reduces volatility, 323, 326
    market answer to, 323, 324
    short sales, 323, 325
    state laws and, 323, 324–325

insurance
    administrative costs, 257, 263
    adverse selection and. See adverse selection
    amusement parks and, 264
    automobiles. See automobile insurance
    comparative advantage in risk-spreading, 258, 259
    defined, 258
    earthquakes, 278
    health maintenance organizations. See health
        maintenance organizations
    high transaction costs and, 264, 266–267
    investor insurance, 269, 271
    life insurance, 331, 337
    monitoring costs, 262
    moral hazard. See moral hazard
    non-pecuniary damages and, 257, 264
    opportunism and, 331, 337
    pain and suffering suits, 264, 266
    precaution as substitute for, 235
    re-insurers, 260
    risk pools, 262, 263
    risk-spreading and, 257–268
    sports stars, 266
    tort system and, 264
    utility optimization and, 257, 263
intellectual property, 103–108, 112
    patents, 103–106, 187–188
    trademarks, 103–107

judgment proof, 98, 100, 123–124, 125–126, 156,
    157–158, 338–339
    crime and, 155–156
jury outcomes, 141–150

Kaldor-Hicks compensation, 21, 22, 23, 28

last clear chance, 167–173
    doctrine of, 169–170
    good samaritan rule and, 178
latent defect, 104, 111, 266
lawnmowers, 248–249
    court cases, 251–252
    efficient contracts, 247, 248
    exploding bottles compared, 248
    moral hazard and, 249
legal fee structures, 273
legal systems
    efficient outcomes, 14
    objectives of, 14
legislatures, 341–348
    agency costs and, 341, 343
    coalitions and Pareto optimality, 342
    Coase and, 341, 343
    committee structures, 341–348
    common-pool problem, 341, 342, 344
    default rules and, 202–203
    elections, as competitions, 341, 343
    germaneness rule, 343
    logrolling, 345
    parliamentary procedures, 80
    political parties, 345
    pork-barrel politics, 342

legislatures (*cont.*)
    range-fencing votes, 344
    transaction costs, 346–348
liability rules, 91, 94
    benefit-restitution v. harm, 113–117,
        119
    communal rights and, 100
    compensation is approximate, 95–96
    court imposed mandatory rules and, 240
    defined, 94
    efficiency explanations for, 250
    eminent domain and, 95
    government regulation and, 100
    imperfect estimation of relative values, 100
    incentives and, 232
    marginal cost rules, 168. *See* marginal cost liability
        rules
    more informed party held liable, 241
    property rights and, 94–96, 100, 155
    sequential inputs and, 168
    transaction costs and, 100, 155
    See also exploding cola bottles; lawnmowers; *specific*
        liability types
Lloyds of London, 309
logrolling, 345
long-run entry and exit, 113, 115
    negligence rules and, 147
lunch break, 202

Mafia. *See* crime
majority rule, 14, 75, 78, 79–80, 84
    irrationality of, 347
malpractice, 239–243, 244, 245. *See* medical
    malpractice
marginal cost liability rules
    accident law and, 171–172
    applications of, 167, 168
    bankruptcy and, 173
    breach of contract and, 171–172
    compensation and, 170–171
    contract law and, 171–172
    long v. short-run incentives, 173
    Pigovian taxes and, 170–171
    transaction costs and, 49, 51, 169
    See also specific rules
market solutions, 71
marriage, 217
    divorce. *See* divorce
    engagement rings. *See* engagement rings
    hands-off attitude of law, 217, 218
    polygamy, 224
    pre-nuptial contracts, 217, 222, 226
    wedding gifts, 225
    See also family law
McDonald's case, 107, 109, 334, 375
measurement scales, 11, 15–16, 17–18
medical malpractice
    adverse selection and, 243
    asymmetric information and, 244
    blood transfusions, 242
    court costs, 243
    defensive medicine, 243
    identifying negligent doctors, 239, 243

incentive effects, 243
    insurance premiums, 243
    liability as promoting information, 243
    patient self-insuring, 242–243
    patients fully informed, 239, 242
    Romero herniated disk case, 244
    strict liability and, 244
    See also negligence
mergers, 313–321
mitigation of damages, 167–173
    contract law and, 167, 168
    fallow land and, 173
    good samaritan rule and, 178
monitoring costs, 33, 37
monopoly holdout problem, 36, 94, 285–286, 333
monopoly theories, 247, 250
moral hazard, 257–268
    adverse selection and, 262
    banking and, 278, 299
    contingency fees and, 273
    insurance and, 257, 260
    takings clause and, 267
    See also opportunism
    murder. *See* crime; cannibalism
mutuals, 306, 331–339. *See also* cooperatives

naked call options, 300
natural law, 18
Navajo Generating Station, 332
NCN. *See* negligence with contributory
        negligence
negligence
    contributory negligence and, 144
    economic definition, 142
    strict liability and, 141, 146
    See also medical malpractice
negligence rules, 141–151
    acts of God and, 141, 147
    courts and, 236
    efficient outcomes and, 143
    jury outcomes and, 141, 147
    nuisance cases, 147
    owners of wild animals, 146–147, 149
    sequential inputs and, 173
    ultra-hazardous activities and, 147
    zoning regulations and, 147
    See also comparative negligence; simple negligence
negligence with contributory negligence (NCN), 141,
        143–144
    comparative negligence and, 146, 150
    courts and, 236
    definition of, 143
    efficient equilibrium and, 144
    fairness and, 144, 146
    jury outcomes and, 141, 147
    rate of convergence to equilibrium, 150
negotiation costs, 33, 35, 109–110
nonconforming land use, 185
nonpecuniary damages, 257–268
nuclear power plants, 136, 137, 147

opportunism, 331–339
    agency costs and, 332

bilateral monopolies, 337
breach of contract and, 337
exploding cola bottles and, 332–333
franchising. *See* franchising
hold-up problem, 333
job shirking and, 334
judgment proof, 338–339
life insurance companies and, 331, 337
long-term contracts and, 333, 336
monitoring costs, 336–337
moral hazard and, 332
organizational response to, 331
organizational veil, 338–339
organized crime and, 331, 336
quasi-bilateral monopolies and, 332
reputation and, 332–333
residual rights to control and, 333
solutions for, 331, 332
specific investment and, 332–333
vertical integration and, 333–334, 336, 338
ordinal scale, 11, 15–16
organizational governance, 305–311
collectivized farms, 308–309
consumer-owned, 306
corporate forms, 306
cost of governance, 305, 306
ESOPs and, 307, 311
Hutterites, 308–309
investor-owned, 306–307
Kibbutz example, 308
Lloyds of London, 309–310
partnerships, 306, 307
private property and, 305, 308
producer co-ops, 306, 307–308
stockholder limited liability, 305, 309
transaction costs and, 309
unity of interest, 305, 306, 309–310
worker-cooperatives, 306–307
See also franchise; legislatures
organizational veil, 338–339
organized crime, 331–339

Pareto improvement, 16, 17
cost-benefit analysis and, 22
transaction costs and, 41, 44
Pareto optimality, 13, 16
advantageous characteristics of, 17–18
criterion for, 22
defined, 16–17
distributional judgments and, 18
improvement. *See* Pareto improvement
preference orderings and, 17–18
utilitarianism versus, 13
See also efficiency
Pareto, Vilfredo, 16
partnerships, 306, 307, 313–321. *See also* cooperatives
patents, 103, 105, 111
government research subsidization and, 105
governmental product purchases and, 105–106
incentives for innovation and, 105
intellectual property, 103–106
life of, 105
races to patent, 188

transaction costs and, 105
pecuniary externalities, 138–139
personal debt contracts, 283–293
Pigovian theory, 49
Coase and, 51
pollution and, 50–51
symmetry and, 53
taxes, 49–50, 52, 98
transaction costs and, 49, 52
plea bargaining, 367–377. *See* settlement-trial
decisions
pollution, 50–51, 53–54, 114, 115, 116, 133. *See* externalities
polygamy, 224–226, 227
pork-barrel politics, 342
power lines, 59, 61
preferences, 7, 10
collective, 14
prices and, 11
rationality and, 11
See also utility functions; Pareto optimality
prenuptial contracts, 217–226, 227
pretrial discovery, 372–373
price systems, 7, 11, 77, 159
costs of instituting, 76
indifference principle and, 360–361
negotiation costs, 77
preferences and, 11
rules of thumb and, 76, 77
Prisoners' Dilemma, 135, 350
privity of contract, 92, 274
producer-owned cooperatives, 306, 307
property rights, 91, 92
body parts, 92, 93, 99
communal rights and, 82, 83, 96, 100, 103, 109, 186, 187
contingent in space and time, 185
cost-benefit analysis of, 94
defined, 92–93
efficiency, 93
enforcements costs, 93
excludability, 92–93
fair use copyright doctrine, 93
in knowledge, 103
liability rules and, 94–96, 100, 155
private property, 305, 308
transaction costs and, 100, 155
voluntary exchange, 93–94
See also entitlements; crime
prosecutors, 368–369. *See* settlement-trial
decisions
proxy fight, 314
public access, 125
public goods, 76
punitive damages, 207–215
hotel bedbugs, 214
probability of being caught and, 214

quasi-linear utility, 21, 25
downward-sloping demand and, 21, 27
spending and, 38

race to the bottom, 320–321

race to the top, 315
rancher/farmer example, 41, 42. *See also* fencing
 in/fencing out
rationality, 7, 8
 advertising and, 9
 defined, 8
 preferences and, 11
 profit maximization and, 9
 selfishness and, 9
redistribution, 354. *See also* distribution; welfare
redistribution welfare, 354–355
regulation, 100. *See* government regulation
relational contracts, 193, 200
reputation, 236, 237, 261, 273, 331–339, 361
restitution, 118
rights allocations. *See* first arrival; rules of thumb;
 entitlements
royalties. *See* artist royalties
rules of thumb, 75, 78, 79
 beginnings of games, 81, 82
 cost-benefit analysis and, 76–77
 demand for close games, 83–84
 four-way stop signs, 75, 77
 first-come first-served, 78, 79–80
 during games, 81, 82, 83
 handedness, 79, 86
 majority rule and, 75, 78, 79–80, 84
 objective sports, 83
 offensive-defensive sports, 83
 organizational modes and, 84
 price systems and, 76, 77
 property v. communal rights, 82, 83
 random assignment and, 79
 rights allocations and, 75
 rule complexity and, 75, 85
 skill levels and, 75–84
 transaction costs and, 76, 77
 unorganized play, 75, 84

Sarbanes-Oxley Act of 2002, 327
savings and loan crisis, 296. *See also* banking crises
scales, cardinal/ordinal, 11, 15–16, 17–18
selfishness, 12
settlement-trial decisions, 367
 beyond a reasonable doubt criteria, 376
 court costs, 371
 criminal cases, 367, 368, 375
 criminal v. civil cases, 376
 defendant utility functions, 369–370
 defendant's risk preferences, 370
 different expectations, 371
 each side considers that other has different
  information, 367, 371
 plea bargaining, 367, 368, 376
 pre-trial information exchanges, 372–373
 preponderance of the evidence criteria, 376
 prosecutor utility functions, 368–369
 selection of cases for trial, 367, 374
shipwreck, 187–188
sibling fighting, 357–364
simple negligence
 formal exposition of, 141, 142
 intuitive exposition of, 141, 142

precaution and, 142
 product liability cases, 143
smoking regulations, 69
specific investment, 331–333, 339
spousal support, 217, 219
 moral hazard and, 220
 specialization in household production, 217,
  219
state of domicile, 353
stockholder limited liability, 305, 309
strict liability, 131–137
 comparative advantage in insuring, 231, 235
 contributory negligence with, 143
 courts and, 236
 disadvantage of, 247, 249
 exculpatory clauses and, 231, 234, 247, 249
 exploding cola bottles and, 234
 negligence and, 141, 146
 producers-consumers equally good insurers, 231,
  234
 ultra-hazardous activities and, 147
surrogate motherhood, 224, 225
symmetry, 53

takeovers, 318, 355. *See also* corporate law
takings clause, 121, 125, 126, 267–268
 adverse selection and, 267
 city zoning regulations, 123–124, 125–126
 compensation for regulation, 121
 endangered species, 126
 historical landmarks and, 124–125
 incentives and, 123
 inefficient regulation and, 125–126
 moral hazard and, 267
 negative externalities and, 122
 positive externalities and, 124
 public access to coastal land and, 125
 transaction costs and, 123–124
tender offers, 313–314, 317–319, 321
Terri Schiavo, 203
Tiebout hypothesis, 355
tort system
 criminal justice system and, 153, 157
 insurance and, 264
 non-pecuniary damages and, 264
trade secrets, 108. *See also* intellectual
  property
trademarks, 103, 107, 108–109
transaction costs
 children and, 357–364
 Coase theorem and, 39
 high, 40, 41, 45, 49, 52, 69
 law and, 40
 legislatures and, 346–348
 non-market, 35
 Pareto improvement and, 41, 44
 Pigovian taxes and, 49, 52
 zero costs, 49, 51, 52
trial, 368, 375. *See* settlement-trial decisions
Truth in Lending Act, 291

unions, labor, 35
unity of interest, 283–293, 305, 306–310, 311, 342

contracts, 283, 288
  creating, 310, 311
  maintaining, 304, 309
unlawful conversion of property, 99
utilitarianism, 14
utility, 13
  functions, 7, 10, 114
  interpersonal comparisons of, 15–16
  maximization methods for, 13–14
  quasi-linear. *See* quasi-linear utility
  tradeoff frontier, 24

vertical integration, 333, 336, 337, 338
Visual Artists Rights Act of 1990, 272, 274

Wal-Mart, 138, 201, 202
water rights, 99, 186
wealth maximization, 21, 24, 28, 39
  GDP and, 24–25
wealth, spending and, 38
Webb, Del, 167–173, 186, 334, 354
welfare, redistribution and, 320,
  354–355
welfare economics, first theorem of, 361
wild animals, 146, 147, 149
worker cooperatives, 306, 308, 310–311
World Trade Center, 194, 201–205

zoning, 123, 126, 147, 346

Case Index

Chase v. Washington Water Power, 61, 63
Cornucopia Gold Mines v. Locken, 66

D'Amore v. Ritz Carlton, 149
Daniell v. Ford Motor Company, 251
Davies v. Mann, 170
Davis v. Davis, 225
Dean Milk Company v. City of Madison, Wisconsin et al., 351
Dexter v. Hall, 93

Edwards v. Sims, 101
Erie R.R. v. Tompkins, 353
Escola v. Coca Cola Bottling Co., 236–237

Fontainebleau Hotel v. Forty-Five Twenty-Five, Inc., 66

Gau v. Ley, 183
Goodwin v. Aggassiz, 324
Grimshaw v. Ford Motor Company, 251
Guille v. Swan, 151

Hadacheck v. Sebastian, 123
Hadley v. Baxendale, 199
Hale v. Bimico Trading Inc., 352
Harria v. Poland, 281
Helling v. Carey, 238
Henningsen v. Bloomsfield Motors, 213
Henningsen v. Bloomsfield Motors Inc., 274

In Spur Industries v. Del E. Webb Development, 186

John W. Carson v. Here's Johnny Portable Toilets, 109
Johnson v. Calvert, 225

Kaiser Aetna v. United States, 125
Katko v. Briney, 160, 162
King-Seeley Thermos Co. v. Aladdin Industries, 109
Kinney v. United Healthcare Services, 213
Kluger v. Romain, 213
KPH Consolidation, Inc. v. Romero, 244

Leebov v. United Fidelity and Guaranty Co., 117, 119

Mahler v. City of New Orleans, 124
Mahlstadt v. City of Indianola, 184
Marcotte v. Kohler Co., 252
Mathias v. Accor Economy Lodging, 214
Miller v. D.F. Zee's Inc., 338

Miller v. Schoene, 122, 127
Miltenberg & Samton v. Mallor, 214
Moore v. Regents of the University of California, 99
Moseley v. Victoria Secret Catalog, 109

Neill v. Shamburg, 104

Obde v. Schlemeyer, 104
O'Mara v. Council of the City of Newark, 185
Oreste Lodi v. Oreste Lodi, 218–219

Parkersburg Rig and Reel Co. v. Freed Oil and Gas Co., 169
Penn Central Transport v. New York City, 124
Pennzoil v. Texaco, 359, 377

Queen v. Dudley and Stephens, 161

re Baby M, 225
re Bonds Baseball, 59, 63
re Cox, 292
re Marriage of Bonds, 226
re Marriage of Sappington, 220
Riggs v. Palmer, 64
Rylands v. Fletcher, 119

Schwarzenegger v. Fred Martin Motor Co., 110
SEC v. Texas Sulphur Co., 324
Shapiro v. Thompson, 320
Sheppard v. Speir, 226
Southwest Weather Research v. Rounsaville, 73
Spur Industries v. Del E. Webb Development Corporation, 172
Stambovsky v. Ackley, 111
State Farm Mutual Ins. Co. v. Campbell, 214

Tahoe Sierra Preservation Council v. Tahoe Regional Planning, 126
Topping v. Oshawa Street Railway, 171
Towne v. Eisner, 201
Tsakiroglou v. Noblee Thorl A.C., 195

United States Finance Co. v. Jones, 291
United States v. Carroll Towing Co., 142
United States v. O'Hagan, 328
United Verde Extension Mining v. Ralston, 172

Veazey v. Doremus, 353

Williams v. Walker-Thomas Furniture Co., 212